The
City
of
Musical
Memory

Music/Culture

A series from Wesleyan University Press
Edited by George Lipsitz,
Susan McClary, and Robert Walser

My Music by Susan D. Crafts, Daniel Cavicchi, Charles Keil, and the Music in Daily Life Project

Running with the Devil: Power, Gender, and Madness in Heavy Metal Music by Robert Walser

Subcultural Sounds: Micromusics of the West by Mark Slobin

Upside Your Head! Rhythm and Blues on Central Avenue by Johnny Otis

Dissonant Identities: The Rock 'n' Roll Scene in Austin, Texas by Barry Shank

Black Noise: Rap Music and Black Culture in Contemporary America by Tricia Rose

Club Cultures: Music, Media, and Subcultural Capital by Sarah Thornton

Music, Society, Education by Christopher Small

Listening to Salsa: Gender, Latin Popular Music, and Puerto Rican Cultures by Frances Aparicio

Any Sound You Can Imagine: Making Music/Consuming Technology by Paul Théberge

Voices in Bali: Energies and Perceptions in Vocal Music and Dance Theater by Edward Herbst

Popular Music in Theory by Keith Negus

A Thousand Honey Creeks Later: My Life in Music from Basie to Motown — and Beyond by Preston Love

Musicking: The Meanings of Performing and Listening by Christopher Small

Music of the Common Tongue: Survival and Celebration in African American Music by Christopher Small

Singing Archaeology: Philip Glass's Akhnaten by John Richardson

Metal, Rock, and Jazz: Perception and the Phenomenology of Musical Experience by Harris M. Berger

Music and Cinema edited by James Buhler, Caryl Flinn, and David Neumeyer

"You Better Work!": Underground Dance Music in New York City by Kai Fikentscher

Singing Our Way to Victory: French Cultural Politics and Music During the Great War by Regina M. Sweeney

The Book of Music and Nature: An Anthology of Sounds, Words, Thoughts edited by David Rothenberg and Marta Ulvaeus

Recollecting from the Past: Musical Practice and Spirit Possession on the East Coast of Madagascar by Ron Emoff

Banda: Mexican Musical Life across Borders by Helena Simonett

Global Noise: Rap and Hip-Hop outside the USA edited by Tony Mitchell

The 'Hood Comes First: Race, Space, and Place in Rap and Hip-Hop by Murray Forman

Manufacturing the Muse: Estey Organs and Consumer Culture in Victorian America by Dennis Waring

Bright Balkan Morning: Romani Lives and the Power of Music in Greek Macedonia by Dick Blau, Charles and Angeliki Keil, and Steven Feld

The
City
of
Musical
Memory

Lise A. Waxer

Salsa,
Record Grooves,
and Popular Culture
in Cali, Colombia

Wesleyan University Press
Middletown, Connecticut

Published by Wesleyan University Press
Middletown, CT 06459

ISBN 0-8195-6441-9 cloth
ISBN 0-8195-6442-7 paper
Printed in the United States of America
Design and composition by Chris Crochetière,
B. Williams & Associates

5   4   3   2   1

Library of Congress Cataloging-in-Publication Data
Waxer, Lise.
    The city of musical memory : Salsa, record grooves, and popular culture
in Cali, Colombia / by Lise A. Waxer.
        p. cm. — (Music/culture)
    Includes bibliographical references, discography, and index.
    ISBN 0-8195-6441-9 (cloth : alk. paper)
    — ISBN 0-8195-6442-7 (pbk. : alk. paper)
    1. Salsa (Music)—Social aspects—Colombia—Cali.
    2. Salsa (Music)—History and criticism.
    3. Salsa (Dance)—History and criticism.
    4. Cali (Colombia)—Social life and customs.
    I. Title.   II. Series.

ML3918.S26 W38 2002
781.64—dc21   2002066162

For Medardo Arias Satizábal,
el poeta de las noches caleñas

Contents

Illustrations

Tables

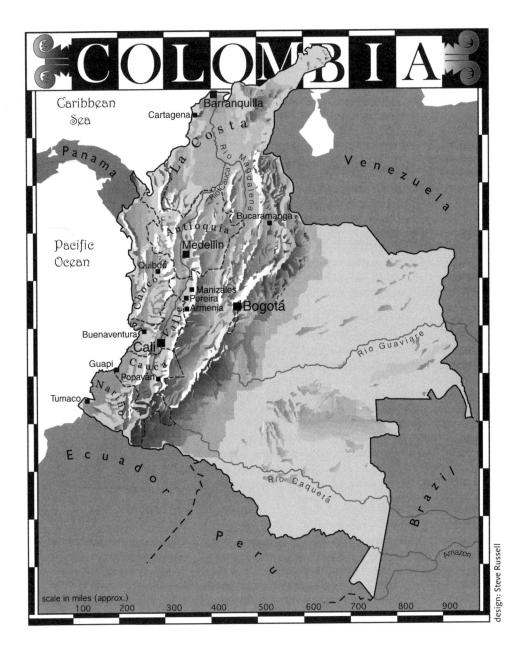

COLOMBIA

Caribbean
Sea

Cartagena

Barranquilla

La Costa

Rio Magdalena

Rio Cauca

Panama

Venezuela

Pacific
Ocean

Quibdó

Antioquia

Medellín

Bucaramanga

Choco

Manizales
Pereira
Armenia

Bogotá

Buenaventura

Valle

Rio Guaviare

Cali

Guapi

Cauca

Popayán

Tumaco

Nariño

Ecuador

Rio Caquetá

Brazil

Peru

Amazon

scale in miles (approx.)

100   200   300   400   500   600   700   800   900

design: Steve Russell

Preface

My husband, to whom this book is dedicated, likes to recount an anecdote about the Brazilian crooner Miltinho, who gave a concert in Cali in 1983. The singer was much loved by local audiences for his three albums of *boleros* (love ballads) in Spanish, produced in the 1960s. Long retired from music and with faded, patchy memories of the boleros and scores of other tunes he recorded in his lifetime, Miltinho valiantly tried to remember the lyrics to his old hits as he sang before his expectant Caleño (Cali-based) fans. Each time he began a song, however, memory failed him, and he could not complete the tune. To his surprise, the audience—who had memorized his songs by heart from the recordings—took up where he left off and finished each song in chorus from the rafters. The old man, stunned and overwhelmed by the loving tribute of his fans, wept openly onstage.

I love this story, because it—along with many others that unfold on the pages of this book—embodies the powerful ties between musical memory and recordings in Cali. While conducting field research in this Colombian city, I often heard it said that Cali was "the city of musical memory," and nearly everything I encountered in my study of local popular culture drew me back to this point. More familiar is Cali's vociferous claim to be "the world capital of *salsa*." Colombians are also familiar with Cali's slogan as "heaven's outpost"—a pleasure hub of fantasy and *alegría* (happiness). The first saying, however, is the most potent. To anyone fascinated by sound recordings and their capacity to generate links to new, imagined spaces— past or present—the Caleño obsession with records offers a particularly potent vein for ethnomusicological study. For instance, many Caleños assert that they are "Caribbean" despite their geographic distance from its sparkling blue waters. This cultural identification has emerged by virtue of their having embraced salsa and its Cuban and Puerto Rican roots, and Caleños proudly acknowledge the role that recordings have played in first introducing and then maintaining these sounds in local popular culture. This is an imagined space built from technological links. Having myself tumbled into an Alice's Wonderland of sonically induced imaginary land-scapes when I discovered Benny Goodman's 1938 Carnegie Hall recording at the public library when I was twelve—with ensuing metamorphoses via exposure to records of different musical styles ever since—I could easily relate to such a claim. These are worlds Walter Benjamin scarcely dreamed of when describing the work of art in the age of mechanical reproduction (1936). Far from being alienated, Caleños have formed a rich and vivid musical culture based on recordings and the memories pulled out of their vinyl grooves.

In the following chapters, I explore the theoretical ramifications of the music-memory link and its conjuncture through sound recordings, unfolding my study through an ethnographic analysis of this process in one Latin American city. I was initially drawn to Cali because of stories I had heard about its being the supposed "world capital of salsa." During pilot field-work conducted in Caracas in 1992, musicians urged me to visit Cali, especially since the Venezuelan scene had diminished greatly since the mid-1980s. "Cali is the place to be!" they exclaimed—a salsa paradise with dozens of bars and nightclubs specializing in salsa, all-salsa radio stations, and many local bands. Later, I decided to relocate my research to Cali, using Caracas as a point of comparison for my Colombian research.

I conducted fieldwork for this book from November 1994 through June 1996, with follow-up trips in January 1997, December 2000–January 2001, and September 2001. During this time I resided and worked primarily in Cali, but I also made regular trips to towns near the city and out to the Pacific coast port of Buenaventura. I traveled to the Atlantic Coast region on various occasions and had the chance to observe Barranquilla's Carnival and Cartagena's Festival de Música del Caribe. I also made regular visits to the capital city of Bogotá and traveled to Medellín, Quibdó, Pasto, and other towns throughout Colombia in order to round out my sense of the country and its diverse geographic, cultural, and musical landscapes. Field trips to Cuba and Ecuador provided important perspectives for considering the projection and reception of salsa in other Latin American cities, under highly diverse historical conditions. The visits to Cuba, in particular, were important for my work in Cali, since Colombians have a strong sense of Cuba as the motherland of salsa music. Colombians who had been able to save money and travel to Cuba often spoke to me with pride about their trips and about the musical wonders they had seen on these pilgrimages.

My research in Cali and other parts of Colombia included intensive documentation of musical venues and salsa performances, as well as interviews with musicians, aficionados, collectors, radio disc jockeys, record producers, dancers, club owners and journalists. I myself needed to learn much about salsa history and its Cuban and Puerto Rican roots, which I compiled through investigation of books, newspapers, magazines, television archives, and conversations with writers and record collectors. I archived local newspaper and magazine articles and collected books written by Colombian authors on salsa and other local popular genres. Thanks to some street vendors who sold salsa records in downtown Cali, I was able to accumulate a large collection of secondhand LPs of Colombian salsa, which I listened to and studied in order to determine components of local musical style.

Although I eventually began participating in the local musical scene as an active musician, my first—and what became predominant—avenue for understanding the mechanisms of Cali's salsa tradition was to participate in the weekend *rumba* (partying) that is the hallmark of local popular culture. Social dancing, usually spiked with generous amounts of *aguardiente* (anise-flavored cane liquor) or rum, is a tremendously important part of Caleño cultural life. Not being much of a drinker or partyer before I arrived in Colombia, I often found the weekend rumba to be exhausting and would complain to my amused friends that the good life was wearing me thin. What those sessions did provide, however, was a view of the immense passion with which Caleños have adopted salsa as their own: head thrown back, arms spread wide, singing loudly and earnestly (if not always in tune) along with the song playing at the moment.

Halfway through my sojourn in Cali, I began to perform as pianist with an all-woman Latin jazz ensemble called Magenta. (The name was chosen by the band's cofounder Luz Estella Esquivel to characterize the group's self-identity as integrally female and feminine, but stronger and deeper than the usual feminine color association of rosy pink.) The six-member combo was formed by musicians from various all-woman salsa bands in Cali who were interested in Latin jazz and wanted a break from the diet of commercially oriented salsa tunes they had been playing. Having heard that I could play a bit of jazz piano and hold a salsa piano *montuno* (groove), I was invited to join them. My musical debut in Cali surprised many of my research informants, who, despite my explaining that I was an ethnomusicologist conducting fieldwork on salsa, usually pegged me somewhere between journalist and hippie. My participation in Magenta Latin Jazz served considerably to establish my acceptance among local musicians and also provided an invaluable tool for understanding the resources and restraints that shape musicians' lives in this city.

During the course of my research, I came to know people from a wide range of socioeconomic sectors in Colombia. Since salsa was first adopted in Cali by working-class people and is still largely identified with these populist roots, much of my work was with aficionados, fans, and musicians from this sector. My friendships and closest working relationships tended to be with university-educated people from working- and middle-class backgrounds—people with dispositions and values very much like my own. I also spoke with many people from the upper middle class, including both fans and detractors of salsa, which gave me an idea of the complex social and economic discourses cross-cutting popular musical tastes within Cali and in Colombia generally. My core network of friends, however, comprised musicians, aficionados, and record collectors. Ranging in age from our early twenties to our late thirties, most of us were unmarried and only partially employed (most salsa musicians in Cali do not have steady work). So, unhampered by family and work obligations, we spent much time hanging out and listening to music.

For most of my stay in Cali, I shared a flat with Sabina Borja, a Caleña woman my age. Our place soon acquired a reputation as a meeting place and hangout, as friends would drop by at all hours to chat, drink beer or rum, and sample the latest acquisitions of my record collection. For a brief time, the Latin jazz group I played with would meet for rehearsals at our place, and these, too, became a pretext for friends to drop by and hang out, our music serving as a backdrop for the impromptu socializing. Thankfully, the neighbors tolerated our bohemian gatherings and never once complained about the noise, although the music and animated conversation often reached intrusively loud levels. Had I lived in a more affluent neighborhood, this would not have been possible, since these barrios, like their North American and European counterparts, are characterized by a respectful observance of social distance, which includes keeping one's music at a discreet and unobtrusive level (cf. Pacini Hernández 1995: xxi). Having grown up in a reserved Toronto neighborhood, I witnessed these transformations of our living space with bemusement and wonder (is this really my house?), letting people take charge of putting on the music, prepare drinks, cook, and roam about the flat as they wished. What these gatherings afforded me was a firsthand experience of informal social life in Cali and the role that salsa plays in this context. Over time, as Sabina and I became friends with our neighbors, some of them would come up and join our parties, and this, too, gave me a sense of how everyday life in working- and middle-class Cali both frames and is framed against a lively panorama of musical sound.

During my time in Colombia, I had some of the most intense and exhilarating experiences of my life. I did not grow up with salsa or Cuban music; I became interested in these sounds only in my mid-twenties, when I began studying Latin popular music in Toronto as an aspect of ethnic identity and cross-cultural integration (Waxer 1991). Over the years, however, I have become intensely interested in and involved with the study of salsa and Cuban music, finding this music to somehow embody the diverse and dynamic circumstances of my own life. As a young Canadian woman of mixed Chinese and Jewish ethnic heritage, I have had intense personal experiences of the ways in which diverse cultural flows can shape individual subjectivity. In salsa's rich and variegated diffusion through the Americas, I have found a metaphorical expression for my own complex background. I believe it was no mistake that I ended up in Cali, a city where, like myself, people have not been among the original creators of a musical style but have nonetheless found meaning in its rhythms, embracing it as their own.

∿∿

Just as salsa music cannot be performed by one person alone, neither can its study be completed by one sole scholar. It is with sincere gratitude that I thank the many, many individuals who collaborated on various stages of this project. The first tip of the hat goes to my mentor and former doctoral advisor at the University of Illinois, Thomas Turino, who has guided and given feedback on this project since its initial conception as a doctoral thesis. My thanks also to Bruno Nettl, Charles Capwell, Alejandro Lugo, and Norman Whitten, who served on my doctoral defense committees and whose helpful comments on earlier drafts of this material served greatly for its transformation into a book. Special mention also goes to Lawrence Grossberg, whose teachings have strongly influenced my own thinking on popular culture. I would also like to thank Peter Wade, whose trenchant observations during my fieldwork and over the ensuing years have proved enormously helpful in my understanding of Afro-Colombian music and culture within the national context. His book *Music, Race, and Nation: Música Tropical in Colombia* (2000) has stood as an inspiration and counterpoint to my own work here.

Deborah Pacini Hernández merits special credit as the fairy godmother of this project. Not only did she help with many practical suggestions before I left for the field, but she also provided me with several key contacts in Colombia. Finally, she gave useful feedback on portions of the material and facilitated the links that led to publication of this book with Wesleyan University Press. Thank you for guidance, inspiration and friendship, Debbie. I would also like to thank Gage Averill for providing me with my initial contacts in Cali, which made it possible for me to have commenced this project in the first place. Carlos Ramos and Marta Zambrano provided useful comments and insight when I returned from the field. Dario Euraque and my other colleagues at Trinity College have been of great assistance in helping me refine my notions of race, ethnicity, and diaspora. Wilson Valentín's use of the concept of surrogation (2002) has been very useful for my work here. Especial thanks to Douglas Johnson for moral support and light. Paul Austerlitz made several invaluable recommendations on earlier versions of this manuscript, and Su Zheng and Frances Aparicio also provided helpful feedback on portions of the work here.

Heliana and Gustavo de Roux were my first hosts in Cali and became my adoptive guardians and mentors while I was in the field. As scholars themselves, their comments, observations, and guidance proved invaluable for my research. Shortly after I began my fieldwork, Jaime Henao and Gary Domínguez became my first key collaborators. Jaime introduced me to several important musicians in Cali and also outlined many musical concepts for me. Gary, the owner of the Taberna Latina, was my main link to the salsotecas and tabernas, in addition to providing key contacts in Cuba; his club became an important place where I met many music lovers. I am indebted to both Jaime and Gary, for without their enormous assistance I could never have realized this project. My deep gratitude also goes to Pablo Solano, who recorded several rare recordings for me to study and whose rooftop listening room is a place to which I always return on my visits to Cali.

This book is woven out of innumerable conversations and interviews with people in Cali and elsewhere in Colombia, not all of whose voices I have been able to include in the account here. Among them are Stellita Domínguez, Kike Escobar, Lalo Borja, Andrés Loiza, Toño Romero, Luisa and Jairo, Baltazar Mejía, Fanny and Jorge Martínez, Jaime and Rochy Camargo, Alejandro and Ruby Ulloa, Henry Manyoma, Rafael Quintero, Richard Yory, Art Owen, Ozman Arias, Gonzalo, Cesar Machado, Lisímaco Paz, Pepe Valderruten, Edgar Hernan Arce, Amparo "Arrebato" Ramos, Evelio Carabalí, Andrés Luedo, Miguel Angel Saldarriaga, Phanor Castillo in Puerto Tejada, Guillermo Rosero, Luis Adalberto Santiago, Fernando Taisechi, Timothy Pratt, Osvaldo González, Diego Pombo, Richard Sandoval, Isidoro Corkidi, Pablo del Valle, Orlando Montenegro, Fabio Arias, Memo Vejerano, Jaime at Zaperoco, Doña Marina de Borja, David Kent, Benjamin Possu, Jorge Mario Restrepo, and Alvaro Bejerano. These people showed great warmth and interest in my project, and it is thanks to their collaboration that I soon felt at home in Cali's scene. A special tribute goes to Doña Stella Domínguez and Beto Borja, who are no longer with us in body but whose generous laughter and spirit live on.

My conversations with the musicians Luis Carlos Ochoa, Alexis Lozano, Cesar Monge, Wilson and Hermes Manyoma, Enrique "Peregoyo" Urbano, Julian Angulo, "Piper Pimienta" Díaz, Alexis Murillo, Cheo Angulo, Hugo Candelario González, Richie Valdés, Ali "Tarry" Garcés, Felix Shakaito, Santiago Meíja, Alvaro Granobles, John Granda, Hector Aguirre, Nelson González, Gonzalo Palacios, Jon Biafará, Elpidio Caicedo, Jon Granda, Henry, Jorge, Daniel Alfonso, Edgar del Castillo, Fredy Colorado, Jorge Herrera, José Fernando Zuñiga, Carlos Vivas, and others helped to clarify many aspects of the live scene. I am grateful for their willingness to let me sit in on rehearsals and plague them with endless questions. Among the members of all-woman bands, María del Carmen, Francia Elena Barrera, Olga Lucía Rivas, Lizana Mayel, Ana Milena González, Paula Zuleta, Cristina Padilla, and Doris Ojeda offered helpful comments and inspiration. Dorancé Lorza, Chucho Ramírez, and José Aguirre provided valuable information about musical production and arranging. Jairo Varela generously allowed me to observe several recording sessions at Niche Studios, and I had the opportunity to collaborate with him on translating "Solo tú sabes" for his album *Prueba de fuego* (1997). My conversations with the Puerto Rican musicians Edwin Morales and Ricky Rodríguez of Orquesta Mulenze gave me additional important perspectives on international styles.

Jairo Sánchez generously gave me access to the video archives at Imagenes TV. Emilio Larrota cheerfully allowed me to observe recording sessions at Paranova; Carlos Mondragon was helpful at RCN. In Barranquilla, Gilberto and Mireya Marrenco proved to be solid allies; thanks also to Edwin Madera at La Troja. I am grateful to Antonio Escobar for allowing me to participate in the 1995 Festival de Música del Caribe; conversations with Daisanne McLane provided further insight into that event. I would also like to thank Luis Felipe Jaramillo at Discosfuentes in Medellín and Cesar Pagáno in Bogotá, who were generous with both their time and their knowledge.

My trips to Cuba were made especially enjoyable by the friendship and generous assistance of Adriana Orejuela and the Terry family. Conversations with Leonardo Acosta and Helio Orovio provided important information that consolidated my understanding of Cuban music and helped me to better study Cali's scene. I would also like to give special acknowledgement to Cristóbal Díaz Ayalá, whom I met in Cartagena; he provided materials and important information related to my earlier work on the mambo and Cuban music during the 1940s and 1950s and continues to be a great inspiration and mentor for all of us working in this field.

My special gratitude goes to the following for their solidarity, their time, their insights, and their friendship in the field: Sabina Borja (my unfailing comrade-in-arms), my roommates and fellow doctoral researchers Kiran Ascher and Pablo Leal, the *mosqueteros* Elcio Viedmann and Kuky Preciado, and Daniel Chavarría and Dennis Pérez. Thanks also to Patricia Galvez; Larry Joseph; Umberto Valverde; Victor Caicedo and family; the Varela family and Catalina Malaver in Bogotá; María Ofelia Arboleda in Medellín; Sugey Moreno in Quibdó; and Cristina and Ramiro Velázquez in Barranquilla. Thanks also to the percussionist Memo Acevedo, my first teacher when I was a fledgling salsiologist in Toronto, who got me started on the long road to Cali and his native Colombia. My gratitude also to Gerardo Rosales, *hermano* and teacher in Caracas. An especial *abrazo* to my sisters in Magenta Latin Jazz—Amy Schrift, Luz Estella Esquivel, Dora Tenorio, Sarli Delgado, Alexandra Albán, and Ana Yancy Hoyos. Performing with them was one of the most rewarding experiences of my entire research.

Financial support for this work was provided by generous grants and fellowships from the Social Sciences and Humanities Research Council of Canada, the Wenner-Gren Foundation for Anthropological Research, the American Association of University Women, the Nellie M. Signor Fund, and the University of Illinois at Urbana-Champaign, all of which I gratefully acknowledge. I would also like to thank Trinity College in Hartford for institutional support through various phases of this book, and the junior leave that facilitated part of its writing. To the Wenner-Gren Foundation I owe an additional debt of gratitude for the Richard Carley Hunt postdoctoral fellowship that supported completion of this manuscript for publication. Some of the material appearing in this book was published in earlier versions as articles in *Latin American Music Review* (Colombian salsa; see chapters 4 and 5), *Ethnomusicology* (all-woman bands; see chapter 5), *Popular Music* (the *viejoteca* revival; see chapter 2), the anthology *Sound Identities* (arrival and impact of recordings in Cali; see chapters 2 and 3), and *Situating Salsa* (overall history; see introduction and chapters 1–4). I thank the editors of these publications for permission to incorporate revised and expanded renditions of that material here.

Suzanna Tamminen at Wesleyan University Press has been as wonderful and supportive an editor as one could possibly wish for; I am grateful for her encouragement and feedback. Thanks also to George Lipsitz for his enthusiastic response to the project and his support as series editor. I am also grateful to Thomas Radko at Wesleyan University Press and to Chris Crochetière and Barbara Norton at B. Williams and Associates for their input and support during the publication stage. Pablo Delano assisted with the preparation of some of the photographic illustrations in this volume. I am indebted to Fabio Larrahondo and Jaime González of the newspaper *El Occidente* in Cali for archival photographs. William Cooley prepared most of the musical notations that appear here, and Steven Russell designed the maps; my thanks to both for their terrific collaboration. All translations from written sources and interviews are my own, as are tables and charts.

Finally, with great pleasure I thank my entire family for their unconditional love through my many years of researching salsa music. Not only did they give me freedom and encouragement to explore this path and travel to Colombia, but they also provided moral support, calls, letters and care packages whenever the going got tough. I am also indebted to the Arias-Satizábal family for their love and support through this project. An especial vote of gratitude and love goes to my husband and research collaborator, Medardo Arias Satizábal. He provided important contacts during the final stages of fieldwork and follow-up and offered several observations and perspectives of his own. His magnificent support and understanding during these months of writing have been without equal. *Gracias, amor lindo.*

Introduction

This book is about a Latin American city and its people. More specifically, it is about how those people found themselves—like residents of many Latin American cities—dealing with rapid urbanization and change in the twentieth century, and the ways in which they responded to these transitions in popular cultural practice. The city in question is Cali, the bustling center of southwest Colombia and now the second largest city in the country after the capital, Bogotá. As any Colombian will tell you, popular culture in Cali is based on the localization of salsa music, a widespread Spanish Caribbean dance style developed in the 1960s by Puerto Ricans in New York City, based upon the Afro-Cuban and (to a lesser extent) Puerto Rican roots known in Colombia as *música antillana* (an-tee-YA-nah). Since the late 1960s, salsa's centrality in local culture has been particularly visible in the week-long bout of collective merrymaking known as the Feria de la Caña de Azucar, or Sugarcane Carnival, held between Christmas and New Year's Eve. Highlighted by live performances by international and local salsa bands, salsa dances, bullfights, neighborhood festivities, and huge gatherings by local salsa record collectors, the Feria is Cali's largest event of the year. Unlike salsa's adoption in other Latin American cities, however, such as Panama City, Caracas, or Guayaquil, the embrace of salsa in Cali has been so strong that by the late 1970s, Caleños (inhabitants of Cali) began asserting that their city was the "world capital of salsa." This is a bold claim, given salsa's primary performance and production nexus in New York City and Puerto Rico. I am less interested in proving or disqualifying Cali as the world salsa capital, however, than in exploring how this claim arose in the first place.

Among various factors that he cites as reasons for salsa's adoption in Cali, Alejandro Ulloa points to Cali's rapid urbanization, accompanied by heavy migration into the city from other regions (1992: 195).[1] While he observes that urbanization and internal migration created a heterogeneous population in Cali's working classes, he does not draw out the implications of this diversity. On the one hand, it served to create a climate wherein social and cultural difference was positively received. On the other, it also established a new cultural reality in which no single group predominated over any other—hence, no single regional musical tradition was capable of representing this complex new urban environment. Salsa and música antillana, hence, were adopted as representative styles of the increasingly heterogeneous and cosmopolitan context of the city.[2] Notably, the image of fun and tropical revelry tied to these styles stands in stark contrast to the abrupt upheavals that characterized Cali's rapid urbanization after the 1950s and the specter of violence and civil war that engulfed the nation during this period.

Cali's self-image as the world capital of salsa challenges core-and-periphery models of cultural diffusion. Most salsa fans, including those in Cali, have never ceased to recognize salsa's roots in Cuba, nor the role of New York and Puerto Rico in continuing to lead the world salsa scene. The move by Caleños to claim center stage on the world salsa scene is, on the surface, a clear instance of the periphery demanding to become the core. On a deeper level, however, the "world salsa capital" claim points less to Cali's centrality in world salsa than to the central position of salsa in local popular life. Salsa became a resource for forging a sense of location and identity on the world map during a period when Cali was virtually invisible in national political and cultural arenas. The practices shaping salsa's localization and resignification in Cali hence enabled Caleños to bypass national channels of cultural identity (without eschewing them entirely) and allowed Caleños to voice their own participation in transnational cultural and economic flows beyond regional and national confines. A central concern of this study is the way in which salsa and its Cuban and Puerto Rican predecessors served as a vehicle for Caleños to formulate an alternative cosmopolitan identity as they became increasingly tied to world markets, while being excluded from national and elite spheres of cosmopolitan culture.

The contradiction that lies in Cali's claim to be the world salsa capital while still recognizing Cuba, New York, and Puerto Rico as the artistic wellspring for this music leads us in two directions. In the first instance, it points us to the transnational network of transport and communications through which salsa was circulated throughout the Caribbean and into several Central and South American sites. By the time Cali's media began proclaiming the "world salsa capital" banner in the late 1970s, salsa's transnational diffusion was so broad that tastes and reception could not be governed directly from New York or Puerto Rico—if they ever were to begin with. Salsa now embraces a wider geographic and cultural context than its Cuban and Puerto Rican predecessors did. The localization and resignification of salsa in Cali offers important cultural perspectives for recent scholarship on globalization and our understanding of local-global cultural links at several levels: barrio, city, region, nation, transnational circuits, and larger global networks. The transnational circulation of música antillana and salsa and their localization in Cali forms one important trajectory of this book.

In the second instance, the contradiction behind Cali's "world salsa capital" bid leads us to the issue of modernity in Latin America. While cultural contradictions have been the subject of postmodern studies since the late 1980s, Latin Americanists have recently observed that such incongruities are not signs of postmodernism but rather are characteristic of Latin America's particular engagement with modernity. In a region that was excluded from the Industrial Revolution and largely underdeveloped before 1950, rapid urbanization and technological development during the twentieth century have produced several rifts and contradictory tendencies (García Canclini 1989; Rowe and Schelling 1991). Cali's recent history provides a clear illustration of the disjunctures accompanying Latin American modernity. During the twentieth century, Caleños were abruptly inserted into an escalating series of world economic markets (coffee, sugar, and cocaine, respectively), which contributed directly to waves of urban expansion and created spaces for new, hitherto unimagined cultural links to occur. Cali's self-image as the world salsa capital flows directly from this complex process, which forms the second trajectory of my study.

As its title suggests, this book is concerned with the nexus of music and memory as a particular affective site for understanding Latin American modernity. Particularly, I am interested in the bridges created between mass-media forms of music (e.g., records, radio, and film), cultural practice, and popular memory, and how these serve as affective links in the formation of subjective experience and popular identity in Cali. When I arrived in Cali to commence fieldwork in late 1994, I was immediately struck by the way so many of the popular practices surrounding salsa's localization had to do with records of salsa and its Cuban and Puerto Rican antecedents. Indeed, sound recordings have acquired the status of fetishes in Caleño popular culture. Dancing, collecting, listening to, and talking about salsa records are activities common to salsa consumption around the world; what is different about Cali is that these practices have often superseded an emphasis on live music making. Cali's case displaces the prevalent academic notion that live music is more "real" or "authentic" than its recorded versions, since in this city salsa recordings were until recently much more important than musicians themselves. Salsa records were the focal point of popular culture during the 1960s and 1970s, when a unique local style of dancing to salsa emerged. These same records provided the basis for the rise of *salsotecas* and *tabernas* (specialty bars for listening to records) in the 1980s, and later, in the 1990s, for the *viejoteca* ("oldie club") revival of the early dance scene. Even when local live salsa boomed after 1980, recordings continued to exert a strong influence on performance practices.

Owing to the importance of recorded music in local popular culture, many Caleños see themselves as guardians of salsa tradition, which is documented and stored in the grooves of acetate and vinyl record discs. Indeed, at the same time as people began regaling me with claims about Cali as the world salsa capital, a smaller group—mainly salsa DJs and record collectors—also began telling me about Cali's status as "the city of musical memory." The phrase "city of musical memory" was coined by one of Cali's most prominent DJs and collectors, Gary Domínguez, who has spearheaded many events that have further reinforced Cali's embrace of salsa. As another collector and disc jockey explained to me, records have served as a "vinyl museum" for the preservation and maintenance of Caleño popular culture and identity.[3]

What does it mean for Caleños to identify their city as a site of musical memory? How did this semantic link emerge? What are the practices and rituals entailed in constructing popular memory as "musical"? Through the combined trajectories of sound, physical movement (e.g., dancing to old records), record collecting, and shared listening, local subjectivities and cultural experience have been virtually re-membered—in other words, recreated, put back together, and reaffirmed. But what memories? How does the Caleño affinity for music associated with *alegría* (happiness), frivolity, and good times contrast with Colombia's history of violence? Why is this particular form of recreation (and re-creation) particularly significant?

In the following chapters I attempt to answer these questions by tracing the social history of salsa in Cali and the unique practices through which Caleños made salsa an emblem of local popular culture. Key to the multiple theoretical perspectives framing this work is an emphasis on the everyday musical practices and subjective spaces through which Caleños have experienced and understood large-scale forces of modernization, urban development, and global capital flow. Using interviews, field observations, oral histories, archival resources, and musical analysis, I have tried to ground some of the current academic debates about power struggles over race and ethnicity, class hierarchy, gender roles, and generational difference. This book is also intended, however, as a case study in the localization of salsa. It traces the specific and sometimes fascinating practices through which salsa—a style with roots in the Caribbean—has come to hold great meaning for a particular South American city. My study hence unfolds through two interrelated stories. One is about the history of salsa and its Cuban and Puerto Rican roots, specifically as they were localized in Caleño popular culture. The other is about the ways this localized transnational style served to anchor larger economic, political, and cultural processes that affected Caleños at several levels. Together, these two strands coalesce to reveal how dancing, listening to, collecting records of, and performing salsa have been central for the development of a contemporary urban, cosmopolitan culture in Cali.

Salsa's Rise and Transnational Spread

Salsa music developed in New York City's Latino barrios during the 1960s and 1970s. Based largely on Cuban forms popular in previous decades, such as *son, guaracha, danzón, mambo,* and *bolero,* salsa also incorporated elements of Puerto Rican *bomba* and *plena* and influences from North American jazz and rock. Salsa's Cuban and Puerto Rican antecedents—referred to in Colombia as música antillana (music of the Spanish Antilles)—were themselves a fusion of African and European elements. I discuss these further in chapter 1 (see also Alén 1984; Echevarría Alvardo 1984; Dufrasne-González 1994). Most people agree that salsa's primary musical foundation is Cuban; in particular, salsa generally follows the same two-part structure and rhythmic base of Cuban son. Yet, several Puerto Rican musicians on the island and in New York City made important contributions to this tradition, including Rafael Hernández, Noro Morales, Daniel Santos, Pedro Flores, Rafael Cortijo, Tito Puente, and Eddie Palmieri and it would be inaccurate to define this style as exclusively Cuban (Glasser 1995). The stylistic innovations accompanying salsa's development in the 1960s and 1970s moved this tradition significantly beyond its Cuban roots. In Cali, people include both Cubans and Puerto Ricans when they refer to música antillana. In the Caleño context, hence, this makes it impossible to define música antillana solely as Cuban or even Cuban based—despite the fact that the influence of Cuban musical elements clearly outweighs Puerto Rican contribu-tions overall. In this volume, I use the term "Cuban and Puerto Rican music" in conjunction with "música antillana," with the caveats outlined above. In chapter 1 I explore elements of style and structure in música antillana in greater detail.

There is considerable debate over the origins of the term "salsa." The word literally means "sauce," invoking culinary references to the spicy mixture found in to most Latin American and Caribbean cuisine. Cuban son musicians in the first half of this century frequently used to say, "Toca con salsa!" (roughly, "hit it!" or "swing it") when the excitement and energy of the music began to rise. This metaphor was first used in a commercial setting by Ignacio Piñeiro in his famous 1933 composition "Échale salsita." It is probable that a Venezuelan radio DJ, Phidias Danilo Escalona, was among the first to use the term "salsa" to denote Latin and Cuban dance music in the early 1960s (Rondón 1980: 33), although the New York publisher Izzy Sanabria claims to have coined the name at the end of the decade (Roberts 1979: 187).

During the early and mid-1960s two early prototypes of salsa emerged. One was the *pachanga,* a fast version of the Cuban guaracha that was usually performed on the flute-and-violin *charanga* ensemble. The other was *bugalú* or boogaloo, a fusion of Cuban son with African American soul that became an important crossover genre for New York blacks and Latinos (Flores 2000). Both of these genres had a huge impact in Cali, for reasons I analyze in chapter 2. But as experimental elaborations on earlier música antillana, pachanga, and bugalú also laid important groundwork for the dynamic, experimental edge now associated with the classic New York and Puerto Rican sound of the late 1960s and 1970s, known as *salsa dura* ("hard" or "heavy" salsa), *salsa brava* ("strong" or "wild" salsa), or *salsa gorda* ("fat" salsa). As I describe in the next chapter, several salsa dura artists returned to a more conservative approach that cleaved to Cuban and Puerto Rican models from the 1940s and 1950s, but in the dynamism between innovative and conservative schools, salsa music flowered. Importantly, by the early 1970s, "salsa" had become the standard term of reference throughout Latin America, owing in large part to its use by Fania Records as a commercial label under which to market this music.

Salsa's development and international spread have given rise to much debate about its genesis and legitimacy as a musical category. Cuban specialists and musicians, in particular, have long contested the use of the term, claiming that salsa is nothing more than Cuban music, or a Puerto Rico adaptation thereof (Roberts 1979: 188; Manuel 1994). Some Puerto Rican musicians also support this argument—most notably Tito Puente, who often said, "The only salsa I know comes from a bottle. What I play is Cuban music" (Santana 1992: 17; Loza 1999: 40–41). Marisol Berríos-Miranda and other critics demonstrate, however, that significant stylistic *and* ideological characteristics differentiate salsa from its Cuban predecessors (see Waxer

2002). Even a casual listening to 1960s and 1970s salsa dura (e.g., Eddie Palmieri) and Cuban son bands from the 1940s and 1950s (e.g., Arsenio Rodríguez) provides strong evidence for distinguishing between the two. While the rhythms and forms are the same, the stylistic treatment is quite different. Salsa uses more percussion and larger horn sections than do its Cuban antecedents.[4] The arrangements are more aggressive, and the social and cultural milieu to which the lyrics refer is not Cuban. Although some might argue that such differences hardly suffice to categorize salsa and its Cuban roots as different styles, we should keep in mind that similar kinds of distinctions separate such closely related sounds as rhythm and blues, rock and roll, funk, and hip-hop — styles usually recognized as distinct without the vociferous debate that the salsa–Cuban music split engenders.

The New York community in which salsa developed was strongly Puerto Rican, and during the 1960s and 1970s salsa became a potent emblem of working-class Puerto Rican cultural identity both for islanders and for those living in the United States (Duany 1984; Padilla 1990). The use of the ten-stringed Puerto Rican *cuatro,* an icon of cultural identity, by Willie Colón and the Fania All-Stars during the early 1970s underscored salsa's Puerto Rican affiliations and marked a further difference between salsa and its Cuban roots.[5] The music's own interracial heritage was mirrored by the strong interethnic participation that marked the New York scene, with Jewish and African American musicians performing in several bands. The Jewish pianist Larry Harlow even became an important bandleader and producer in the New York scene.

During this same period, salsa music also spread to other parts of Latin America, especially Venezuela, Panama, and Colombia — countries with close geographic and economic ties to the Caribbean.[6] Significantly, salsa's lyrics reflected the experiences of the Latino and Latin American black and mixed-race working class, and — in distinction to its Cuban antecedents — the songs mirrored the violence and discontent of the inner city. Salsa and its predecessors were initially reviled by the Latin American and Caribbean upper classes for being the music of the dark-skinned working classes — often in grossly racist terms such as *música de monos* (music of apes). When salsa's exuberant beat and social message caught on with Latin American leftist intellectuals from the middle and upper-middle classes in the early 1970s, however, salsa music began to shed its lower-class associations to establish a devoted following not only across national boundaries, but also across social ones. Ironically, it was *salsa romántica* (romantic salsa), a smoother, less aggressive style developed in the late 1980s, that truly succeeded in breaking class barriers in Latin America. Avoiding the political messages of early salsa dura that had alienated conservative middle- and upper-class audiences, salsa romántica captured a larger market; thus, it was when commercial salsa stopped promoting messages about Latino unity that salsa actually became more widespread in Latin America. By the end of the 1980s salsa was firmly entrenched as a transnational musical genre, with followers throughout the Americas and in Europe, Africa, and Japan.

Currently, there are five principal "schools" or transnational styles of salsa performance: New York, Puerto Rican, Venezuelan, Colombian, and Cuban, with the development of *timba* or "Cuban salsa" in the early 1990s.[7] Some observers might add Miami to this list, although the common pool of arrangers and studio musicians used in New York, Miami, and even Puerto Rico has made much contemporary salsa produced in these places sound very similar (Washburne 1999). Cross-cutting these transnational schools is another stylistic matrix that correlates to salsa's historical development. Negus (1999: 138–39) characterizes these as: (1) the "old school" (salsa dura), which follows the classic 1960s–70s sound; (2) salsa romántica, a continuation of 1980s *salsa erótica* (sensual salsa); (3) "soulful salsa," incorporating Top Forty pop, rhythm 'n' blues, and soul harmonies and arrangements (e.g., Luis Enrique and Victor Manuel); and (4) "dance club salsa," which fuses salsa romántica with elements of hop-hop, R & B, and Cuban timba (e.g., Marc Antony and La India). In each of the five transnational schools of salsa, there are bands that follow one or another of these four stylistic matrices, hence combining a regionally or nationally defined way of playing salsa with these broader categories.

Salsa research to date has focused primarily on salsa's Cuban roots and its development in New York and Puerto Rico (Blum 1978; Roberts 1979; Rondón 1980; Arias Satizábal 1981; Singer 1982, 1983; Duany 1984; Alén 1984; Padilla 1989, 1990; Gerard 1989; Arteaga 1990; Boggs 1992; Santana 1992; Manuel 1991, 1994, 1995; Quintero Rivera 1998; Washburne 1999). Colombian writers, mainly journalists and sociologists, have also produced a notable body of work on salsa and música antillana, mostly detailing the impact of Cuban and Puerto Rican artists in Colombia (e.g., Valverde 1981; Arias Satizábal 1981; Arteaga 1990; Jaramillo 1992; Betancur Alvarez 1993). A definitive history of Colombian salsa remains to be written, although journalists in Cali and Bogotá have contributed important commentaries about Colombian artists and fans to local newspapers and magazines.[8] While my own work in this book and other publications attempts to redress the gap, I do not focus on Colombian salsa from a complete national perspective, and I omit discussion of artists and developments in other parts of the country.

Alejandro Ulloa's detailed sociological study *La salsa en Cali* (1992) stands as the only extant book-length exploration of salsa's impact in urban Colombia written by an insider of Cali's salsa scene. Indeed, the work can be seen as a product of the self-image as the world salsa capital that was being widely circulated in Cali by the late 1980s. Although Ulloa's frequent shifts between sociological analysis and nostalgic rhapsodizing make the book difficult to follow for readers unfamiliar with his inside references, the work is invaluable and has served as a basic reference for my own research in Cali. Ulloa conducted his study on salsa in Cali during the mid-1980s, when Cali was emerging on the international scene as an important salsa center. My research, coming at the close of this epoch, serves as an extension of the themes planted in Ulloa's research, updating his discussion of musical venues, local bands, and radio stations. I also address issues that he does not deal with, such as the stylistic components of Colombian salsa, the artistic and commercial processes that shape the lives of contemporary Caleño musicians, and salsa's impact in the region around Cali. Sections of Valverde and Quintero's recent work on Cali's all-woman bands, *Abran paso* (1995), also deal with local salsa history and serve as an additional reference for my work.

This book represents an attempt to go beyond the New York-Cuba-Puerto Rico focus of current salsa scholarship, particularly that published in English, by focusing on a South American case. My study follows recent scholarship on Latin American and Caribbean music (e.g., Guilbault 1993; Pacini Hernández 1995; Glasser 1995; Averill 1997; Austerlitz 1997) that systematically examines the links between popular music, race, class, the music industry, transnational flows, and local and national identity. Ulloa 1992, for example, despite recognizing social differences of class, race, and gender in Cali, does not always clarify where or how or even why these lines are drawn, nor does he analyze the fluidity of these categories with regard to key developments in Cali's scene. I attempt to highlight such processes by exploring how salsa's local adoption intersects with shifting lines of class, racial and ethnic identity, gender, and age. I am also influenced by recent research in Latin American and Latino/Latina studies about dancing and listening bodies as sites for the internalization and enactment of social difference (e.g., Savigliano 1995; Fraser Delgado and Muñoz 1997). In the following sections, I outline the key theoretical concerns that shape my study.

Recordings and Popular Memory

The centrality of recorded music for Caleños challenges the privileging, in most scholarly work, of live performance as more "real" or "authentic" than its mediated versions.[9] Indeed, for many decades "playing music" in Cali literally meant putting on a record, as a source of music for other social and expressive activities. The term *disco* (literally, a record disc) still exists as a local synonym for "song," even when it is a live rendition of a song—as in "Vamos a tocar ese disco" (Let's perform that song). Despite the presence of a few local ensembles before 1980 and the flowering of live salsa bands after this point, recordings still constitute a central source of musical sound in Cali's scene. (In chapter 1 I discuss early musical activity in Cali and also describe regional genres in the rest of Colombia.) At the same time that local *orquestas,* or salsa bands, began to flower, so did salsotecas and tabernas, small specialty bars where people went to listen to records of classic salsa and música antillana; I discuss these at length in chapter 2. When the live scene collapsed in 1996 (owing in part to the fall of the Cali cocaine cartel), the early record-centered dance scene was revived, in the viejoteca phenomenon that I analyze in chapter 2. The rise of the viejotecas, which was paralleled by a resurgence of activity by salsoteca owners and record collectors, represents a surprising recuperation and reaffirmation of Cali's record-centered popular culture.

Although recordings and other media have contributed to new musical hybrids and identities around the globe (Lipsitz 1994; Taylor 1997), recent research suggests that the appropriation of such technology to local musical practice and creativity is an area in need of more attention than it has conventionally received. Studies of Japanese karaoke (Keil 1984; Mitsui and Hosokawa 1998) and cassette cultures in India (Manuel 1993) demonstrate that the appropriation of media technology to local musical practice and creativity calls for a more thorough analysis of this complex development. The predominance until recently of records over local musicians in Cali is an unusual social phenomenon that requires a different perspective. Jeremy Wallach suggests that records should be treated as actual music and not just a document (in the way notation is), since recordings generate a "sonic presence" that provides a basis for musical sound and meaning just as live performance does (1997). Although the experiences created through recorded music are often different from those of live music (for one, face-to-face interaction between performers and audiences is absent), they can be equally powerful.

Recordings, as sound vehicles, serve as powerful tools for fostering new, hitherto unimagined sources of memory. Through their capacity to reproduce past moments, recordings also become potent triggers for memory in the present. George Lipsitz observes that "[i]nstead of relating to a past through a shared sense of place or ancestry, consumers of electronic mass media can experience a common heritage with people they have never seen, they can acquire memories of a past to which they have no geographic or biological connection" (1990: 5). This schizophonic (Schaeffer 1977) displacement of time and space has particularly strong ramifications for considering the consumption of recorded music in Cali. In his study of the links between phonographs and popular memory in the United States from 1890 to 1945, William Howland Kenney (1999) analyzes the role of recorded music in generating constructions of group identity, mediating social and cultural differences in multiethnic and multiclass environments. In a lengthy and detailed analysis, Kenney traces the complex processes through which recordings influenced, but also reflected, the sensibilities of various U.S. listeners during the first four and half decades of phonograph technology. Key among these processes was the success of recordings in creating new audiences for certain types of music by breaking through barriers of socioeconomic class, ethnicity, or geographical distance that had previously prevented such links. This process also occurred in Cali, where the entry of recordings of música antillana, and later salsa, established a fervent local audience for a musical style created thousands of miles away.

Notably, the "stopped-clock" technology of recordings virtually captures musical performances and freezes those moments for perpetuity, serving (much as photographs and films do) as the basis for constructing a selective memory of the past. This memory, though legitimated by an appearance of reality, derives meaning and emotional impact from its usefulness in the present. Kenney, for instance, observes that for people in the United States, phonograph music served as a basis for the construction of a romanticized, tranquil past between 1890 and 1945, a time of turbulent social changes. Certain songs and genres "helped to generate collective aural memories through which various groups of Americans were able to locate and identify themselves" in the tumult of new influences inundating the cultural landscape (1999: xvii). Similarly, for three generations of Caleños, recordings have provided a cultural terrain that has helped people to maintain and situate themselves during continued struggles over urban spaces.

Joseph Roach's theory of surrogation as a vital element in the process of memory (1996) suggests further ways to understand how music and memory are linked through sound recordings. According to Roach, memory is a process that operates through selective remembering and forgetting, in which certain objects, images, or personae are substituted for some imagined original located in the past. In this process, cultural performances of all kinds become vehicles for the embodiment and enactment of memory. Roach uses the term "effigy" to explain how objects and images become surrogates in this act of substitution: "The effigy is a contrivance that enables the processes regulating performance—kinesthetic imagination, vortices of behavior, and displaced transmission—to produce memory through surrogation. . . . [I]t fills by means of surrogation a vacancy created by the absence of an original." Although effigies usually refer to a sculpted or pictured likeness, an effigy can also be an indirect likeness that consists of "a set of actions that hold open a place in memory" (1996: 36). Roach uses his theory to analyze circum-Atlantic urban performances such as theater and Carnival, particularly as they historically informed each other to produce the New Orleans Mardi Gras. His theory, however, also offers a potent model for understanding the impact sound recordings had in Cali—particularly the way performative practices such as dance and public listening shaped Cali's position as a city of musical memory. Recordings became surrogate effigies of Cali's cultural roots, used in the imaginative construction of origin myths in local popular life. (See Wade 2000 for a comparative account of origin myths about Colombian popular forms.) The circulation of salsa and música antillana recordings as rare, cosmopolitan commodities in Cali further complicates this process, as the meaning of effigy becomes elided with that of a fetish—another characteristic that Roach identifies in circum-Atlantic performance (1996: 41). As I discuss in chapter 3, the positioning of salsa and música antillana recordings as cultural fetishes in Cali is particularly prominent in the activities of record collectors and salsoteca DJs and audiences, but this fetishization is deeply interwoven with other spaces in local popular culture. In particular, the similarity of Cali's annual Feria to other circum-Atlantic Carnivals points to the vivid way in which the fetishization of recordings in Caleño life maps onto citywide public enactments of surrogation and creative memory. During the Feria, discussed in chapter 6, Caleños literally re-member themselves in a week of kinesthetic merrymaking that directly and indirectly evokes the record-centered practices that consolidated música antillana and salsa as local cultural emblems in the first place.

My use of the term "popular" follows that established in British and North American cultural studies. I understand popular music as a set of genres and styles that are produced and largely consumed in urban environments, disseminated through the mass media, marketed as a commodity, and often subject to a great deal of ideological negotiation over issues of authenticity, control, and representation (Middleton 1990). This usage contrasts strongly with common Latin American usage of the term, where "popular" is understood in primarily in oppositional, populist terms—that is, "of the people"—without consideration of the ways in which popular culture often also plays into dominant capitalist structures and modes of production. This latter view has framed Latin American musicology throughout the twentieth century (e.g., Abadía Morales 1973; Aretz 1991; Ramón y Rivera 1977), leading to essentialist categories of *folklor* (indigenous, Afro-American, and rural mestizo forms), art music, and "popular" styles that are grassroots, semiurban, and largely uncontaminated by mass media. Only recently have Latin American scholars begun turning their attention to the tensions and contradictions that arise in urban popular musical practices and to the ways in which politics, money, race, and gender articulate with these sounds (see Torres 1998; Ochoa 2001[10]).

In their engaging volume *Music Grooves* (1994), Charles Keil and Steven Feld explore the complex relationship between physical, participatory grooves and their commodification in the vinyl furrows of record discs. Cali's case embodies the theoretical links mapped out by Keil and Feld in a particularly vivid fashion that I am not sure even they could have imagined when they coauthored this book. The strong role of recordings in Caleño popular life cannot be read merely as an instance of cultural massification through media technologies—an argument often raised in debates about cultural imperialism or global homogenization. Expressive record-centered practices (dancing, collecting, listening, and talking) have provided the basis for collective social activities, reaffirming community bonds and values that could be called upon in times of need. The fetishization of recordings in local popular culture—probably the most striking feature of salsa's localization—is far too complicated to explain by a simple equation of cultural homogenization. The actual uses that Caleños have made of mass media technology over the past three generations indicate a highly original and creative approach in which transnational sounds and objects are adapted to local expressive practices.

These developments, while in many ways unique to Cali, are also markers of contemporary dynamics in Latin American culture and urban experience. Rowe and Schelling observe that the massive migration and urban development in Latin America have blurred the boundary between rural and urban cultures and moved cities to the fore of regional and national cultures.

> Almost all cultures in Latin America are now mediated to some extent by the city, both in the sense of its massification of social phenomenon and of the communication technologies which it makes available. To see the city as a corrupting and contaminating force, in opposition to a pure and authentic culture rooted in the rural areas, is to indulge in

nostalgia. On the other hand, the city is the place of entry of trans-national culture, of TV programmes, comic-strip heroes and advertise-ments, whose references are to a different environment, that of the advanced capitalist countries. Is it possible, given the configuration sketched out here, to continue using the term "popular culture" as des-ignating a distinctive area? The answer given in actual usage is yes: the term popular culture, according to common usage in Latin America, evokes the possibility of alternatives to currently dominant cultural patterns. (1991: 97)

The rise of a salsa-centered popular culture and record-centered cultural practices in Cali is part and parcel of that city's urbanization, a means Caleños found for "negotiating the transitions" (Rowe and Schelling 1991: 98) from a small provincial town to a major urban center. Record-centered cultural practices became the modality through which Caleños first experienced and made sense of the city's rapid urbanization, and they continued to serve to rekindle and reaffirm Caleños' subjective experiences through successive waves of urban development. These experiences, in turn, became the basis for the development of popular culture and identity in Cali, upheld by its majority working-class, mixed-race population while alternately repudiated, contested, or embraced by members of the middle and upper classes.

Cosmopolitan Culture and Globalization

Perhaps the most significant factor in the adoption of música antillana and, later, salsa in Cali, over and above regional or national musical styles, was the symbolic significance this music had as a transnational and hence cos-mopolitan style at a time when the city itself was becoming increasingly tied to world markets. A central theme of this book concerns the formation of an imagined bond between Cali and the Caribbean (including Hispanic Caribbean migrants in New York City). Despite Cali's location hundreds of miles away from the Caribbean—let alone New York—Caleños claim unity with Cubans, Puerto Ricans, and New York Latinos by virtue of having adopted salsa and its Afro-Caribbean roots as their own, over local and na-tional musical styles. The consequences of this sensibility are profound and point to a cultural identity that is simultaneously local and global.

The term "cosmopolitan" denotes being "of the world" (from the Greek *kosmo* [world] and *polites* [citizen]) and is usually associated with those from elite social ranks, who have more resources for travel, education, and accu-mulation of goods from different parts of the planet. This common usage, however, often ignores people from less privileged ranks who are also tied to cosmopolitan flows. As Cali's case clearly indicates, people can have cosmopolitan values, tastes, and lifestyles no matter what their socioeconomic rank. In contrast with its usual connotations, by "cosmopolitan" I specifically mean the ways in which increased transportation and communications links, colonialism, mass media, and other channels have helped to spread practices and values around the globe, so that actual or symbolic ties to a specific point of origin are weakened or complicated by cultural formations in multiple sites (Turino 2001: 8–10). The term is more useful than the Eurocentric notion of "Westernization" in understanding issues of globalization and modernity, since it does not grant Europe or (white) North America an a priori position as the source of all modern or transnational processes. Throughout this book I will trace the role of salsa and its Cuban and Puerto Rican predecessors in forging the emergence of cosmopolitan identity in Caleño popular culture.

In analyzing the social history of salsa in Cali, I understand globalization to deal primarily with large-scale economic and political shifts at the international level and related flows via which cultural images, ideas, and products circulate in an increasingly deterritorialized fashion. I invoke the term "cosmopolitanism," on the other hand, to describe the ways in which people at the local level (home, neighborhood, and city) began to react to and internalize the effects of these changes through their belief systems, values, outlooks, tastes, cultural choices, and expressive practices. Unlike those who see cosmopolitanism to be an "inauthentic," voyeuristic, shallow pose that allows people only superficial participation in the local realities of others (Friedman 1995: 78), I maintain that—at least in Cali's case—cosmopolitanism provides a dynamic resource for negotiating and authenticating new cultural and social processes that cannot easily be contained within localist, regionalist, or nationalist models. For Caleños, cosmopolitanism has been part of the forging of an authentic sense of self and group amid the escalating ruptures and struggles that shaped Cali's transformation into a major urban center. Indeed, the neologism "cosmopolitics" aptly characterizes Caleños' agency and deliberate use of transnational sounds, images, and styles to formulate a response to local and national realities through connections to the world beyond.

This process is not the opposite of nationalism (a common misunderstanding) but is produced dialectically within the context of the nation. As the essays in Pheng Cheah and Bruce Robbins's volume *Cosmopolitics: Thinking and Feeling beyond the Nation* (1998) show, the active formation of transnational sensibilities and allegiances as a way of working out difference from national processes and cultural norms is a defining characteristic of the mid-to late twentieth century. This is especially so in the Americas, where nationalist independence struggles and the rise of republican nation-states occurred much earlier than in Africa or Asia. Indeed, the emergence of cosmopolitan dynamics during the second half of the twentieth century, as a renegotiation of nationalism in various parts of the world, parallels what Fredric Jameson has called "late capitalism" (1991). Borrowing from Jameson's concept, perhaps we can think of contemporary cosmopolitics as a sort of "late nationalism." In Cali, local culture before the twentieth century had been dominated by norms emanating from the economically and politically powerful interior of the country, despite the fact that Cali had an otherwise insular and distant relationship from the rest of Colombia. As the city's economic ties to world markets began to emerge between 1940 and 1990 through the growing coffee, sugar, and, later, illegal cocaine markets, salsa and its Cuban and Puerto Rican roots provided a way for Caleños to articulate their continuing sense of difference from the rest of the nation, while it was simultaneously becoming caught up in transnational economic flows. The rhythms of salsa and its antecedents became the soundtrack for a city in flux, where Caleños developed a cosmopolitan identity that did not ignore nationalist trends but dialectically emerged from opposition to them.

The terms "cosmopolitanism" and "globalization" have increasingly been linked in much recent scholarship (Hannerz 1990; Held 2000). Indeed, salsa's rapid spread through Latin America during the 1970s, followed by its adoption in Europe, Japan, and Senegal during the 1980s and 1990s, necessitates including this genre in discussions about globalization. Salsa in Africa, a recent trend related to the earlier popularization of Afro-Cuban music in West and Central Africa—particularly Congo (Zaïre)—during the 1930s through the 1960s (see Stewart 2000), must be considered a new branch of salsa's international flowering. Salsa's multiple sites of production and reception around the globe flow directly into its status as a significant popular style.[11] Mayra Santos Febre observes that salsa's potency hinges on a cultural enterprise that "is larger than national and broader than ethnic. . . . [T]his [can] be understood as multinational." The very fluidity with which salsa has been enjoined to oppositional, counterestablishment ideologies (from the black and mixed-race working-class margins), at the same time that it plays into dominant modes of production and consumption, has further facilitated its transnational spread (1997: 179). While salsa's international diffusion is not the same kind of globalization spawned by McDonald's, MTV, Microsoft, and Michael Jackson, the distinction between "transnational" (cutting across national boundaries) and "global (truly worldwide) is not always clear in salsa's case. Although salsa's spread to different countries within Latin America might best be classified as transnational, its adoption in Europe, Japan, and Africa certainly approaches global proportions. Furthermore, the increasing presence of the Big Five record companies—EMI/Virgin, Warner/WEA, Universal/Polygram, and especially Sony and BMG—in the salsa industry during the 1990s clearly ties salsa to globalizing forces in the music business, even when these companies' products are not necessarily promoted with the same emphasis in different world markets. The dozens of salsa-related Web sites that have emerged on the Internet also speak to increasing globalization in this medium.[12]

My specific concern with studying globalization processes has to do with the global within the local—that is, the way in which the trend toward globalization is manifested and understood as part of Cali's emerging local reality. Much recent discourse tends to pit the local against the global, as if the two concepts were polar opposites constantly in tension with each other. Scholars such as the sociologist Roland Robertson caution us against this type of thinking, observing that globalization is intimately and simultaneously bound up with local processes and experiences. Robertson uses the neologism "glocalization" to describe this relationship.[13] According to him, it is precisely in the localization of internationally diffused images, ideas, and forms that globalization actually occurs (1995: 31). Whether we can qualify salsa's glocalization as being a transnational or a truly global phenomenon does not concern me here. Even a superficial familiarity with salsa activity in different transnational sites reveals two important processes. The process of "cultural homogenization" by dominant countries and/or multinational organizations feared by globalization's critics (Barber 1992) is not operative in the case of salsa. This is primarily because salsa and its roots emerged from racial and socioeconomic opposition to the dominant colonial and neocolonial order (Quintero Rivera 1998). Furthermore, salsa's transnational diffusion initially occurred beyond direct corporate control, and even now its production and distribution occupy a marginal position in the agendas of major record companies (Negus 1999: 140–45). Although salsa certainly retains strong indexical links to the Caribbean, the very fact that it has undergone diverse resignification in sites as far-flung as Cali, Tokyo, and Dakar points to a significant process that has direct links to what social scientists identify as globalization. Salsa's glocalization in several world cities has primarily followed routes of dissemination and adoption between members of the so-called Third World, with relatively little manipulation by the corporate music industry.

Some scholars define globalization as the last of three stages of global transformation, beginning in the 1500s, shifting during the 1800s, and accelerating sharply in the post–World War II period beginning in 1945 (see Mignolo 1998; Wallerstein 1974). This timeline roughly accords with key points in Colombia's own history: colonization, independence, and increased economic participation in world markets from the 1940s on (coupled with the onset of extreme political violence and civil war after 1948 resulting from unequal distribution of resources). Música antillana's appearance in Cali in fact corresponds almost exactly to the 1945 date, since it was around this time that Cuban and Puerto Rican sounds began moving out of Cali's red-light district to become a centerpiece of popular life in working-class neighborhoods.

The adoption and resignification of salsa in Cali offers us a particularly clear illustration of the ways in which localization of a transnational or global style anchors local experience and understanding of large-scale global flows, such as the urban explosion that accompanied the country's economic entry into the world coffee, sugar, and cocaine markets.

It has also led to a transformation of salsa's significance, sound, and cultural formation. While some of my colleagues might argue with me on this point, salsa no longer points to just New York, Cuba, and Puerto Rico. Although Caleños certainly embraced some of the values articulated in salsa and its Caribbean roots, other meanings that they ascribed to this style were not necessarily present for the original producers and consumers of this music. They now, however, have become part of the symbolic and expressive apparatus that Caleño fans, dancers, and musicians have transmitted not only to other parts of Colombia, but back to New York, Cuba, Puerto Rico, and the world beyond.

Subjectivity and Popular Identity in Cali

There is a striking paradox in Cali's adoption of salsa: at the same time Caleños have become cosmopolitan, they have remained extremely localist, participating only secondarily in regional and national cultures, and using their participation in transnational salsa and música antillana to underscore their sense of local difference from the national. What does this suggest for our understanding of Caleño subjectivity, in relation to concentric spheres of popular culture? Within the Colombian context, Caleños form a very particular sort of subject, born out of the historical conditions that have positioned Cali both within and against the national grain. As I discuss in greater detail in chapter 1, the insular hacienda economy established in southwest Colombia during colonial times fostered weak economic and political ties between Cali and other regions. This contrasted with the Atlantic Coast region—oriented outward to Caribbean commerce and culture—and the wealthy, politically powerful interior regions of Antioquia and the capital of Bogotá, which had ties to Spain. By the twentieth century, Cali's economic insularity had been radically transformed by shifts in Colombian export markets in coffee and sugar, but this change was not accompanied by a marked entry into national cultural and political life. Rather, Caleños continued to define and extend their insularity by adopting a musical style that stood outside of national genres and hence served to reposition Caleño difference from the national arena. The influence of salsa and its Afro-Caribbean roots served as the basis for the formation of an alternative cosmopolitical identity that expressed the local sense of disparity from the rest of the nation, without forcing them to sacrifice engagement with larger transnational processes.

My concern with social identities, spaces, and experiences in Caleño popular culture has not always provided clear answers to the question of how subjectivity is constructed in Cali. Where do we draw the line between context-specific subjective experiences, tied to certain moments, places, and people, and the larger "popular identity" to which these experiences accrue?[14] Identity politics, mooring on the "interrelated problems of self-recognition and recognition by others," have formed a crucial body of scholarship in recent social science. Identity, in turn, constitutes a crucial basis for the formation of subjectivity, which emerges not only from context-specific experience, but also from the way people are constituted as political and economic subjects within particular regimes of power (Calhoun 1995: 213). Subjectivity and identity are not always clearly distinguished in contemporary ethnography, although philosophical work on human beings as historically constituted subjects has been developing since the early-nineteenth-century writings of Hegel. It is beyond the scope of this work to outline the theoretical debates on subjectivity and identity (see Foucault 1978–88; Habermas 1987; Derrida 1967, 1978; Bourdieu 1990). The issue is rooted in the age-old philosophical debate between universalism and particularism, but the complex conditions of the late twentieth century—including mass-media communication, diaspora, migration, economic globalization, fracturing of group identities, and greater choice of personal identities—make it difficult to pin these terms down.

Caleño subjectivity encompasses a definitive sense of self that operates on three interrelated levels. On one level, it incorporates Colombian (and in some instances, larger Latin American) norms about personhood in relation to immediate social groups (family, friends, neighbors, and co-workers) and in indirect relation to the state. These norms are complicated and elaborated through ideas and discourses about race, class, gender, and age. On a second level, I see Caleño subjectivity as an assertion of difference from other Colombian regions and from national cultural, economic, and political currents that are controlled by political and economic elites in the country's center. This is the subjectivity that led to the embrace of salsa and música antillana, which in turn flowed into the construction of the popular image of Cali's citizens as fun-loving, dance-crazy, music-loving, party-oriented merrymakers. On this level, Caleño subjectivity flows directly into what I consider to be popular identity—that is, the codes and images shaping recognition of self and community from within and by others. On a third level, however, subjectivity can also be understood as the sense of self that frames individual, context-specific experience. Here it becomes tied to the subjectively experienced spaces of local popular life: family parties, nightclubs, the annual Feria, listening to records at home, going to salsotecas, dancing, and so forth. Some of the spaces that shaped local subjective experience are historical—for instance, the teen *agüelulo* dances of the 1960s and the adult *griles* of the 1970s. Interestingly, as I discuss in chapters 2 and 3, memories of these spaces prevailed long after they themselves had disappeared, serving as the basis for new contexts in which to revive and maintain a historicized subjectivity associated with these early venues and their role in shaping Caleño popular culture. In the following chapters, my analysis moves fluidly between the three levels outlined here in order to demonstrate how different forms of Caleño subjectivity have influenced and shaped local cultural practice and identity.

Race, Ethnicity, and Class in Cali

A challenging issue that emerges in the study of salsa's rise in Colombia concerns its adoption by a working-class population that is also of predominantly Afro-Colombian heritage, that is, black and *mulato*. (Owing to the difference between Colombian and U.S. racial politics, I have chosen to use the Spanish spelling for the category of *mulato* [mixed black and white heritage] rather than the English "mulatto," since these terms are not easily interchangeable in terms of their social meanings and the race-class background they denote.) Although Cali's population is ethnically quite diverse, its geographical proximity to the Pacific Coast region (populated predominantly by Afro-Colombians) and its own colonial legacy of hacienda slavery has made it the city with Colombia's largest urban black population (Wade 2000: viii). In the national context, Cali is strongly identified as black and mulato or mestizo, in contrast to the white and mestizo identification of the country's interior. Indeed, Cali's racial identity in the national eye is quite similar to that described by Peter Wade for the Atlantic Coast region (2000).

How, then, do we position salsa's rise in Cali? Angel Quintero Rivera notes that a fundamental underpinning of salsa's significance in Puerto Rico and the Caribbean has to do with an empowerment of subaltern populations. Salsa revindicates black and mixed-race culture and music by freely drawing upon several Afro-Caribbean traditions in defiance of dominant Eurocentric cultural canons (1998). In the counter-plantations made up of freed blacks and maroons, rural Indians and mestizos, and outcast Andalusian (Arab Spanish) peasants, the cultural dynamics that fed into salsa's roots emerged beyond the jurisdiction of the state (Rowe and Schelling 1991: 101). What does it mean, however, for black, mulato, and mestizo proletariats in Cali to have embraced these Caribbean sounds as their own? There is no tight fit between race and class position that could have predetermined the adoption of salsa by Cali's dark-skinned working classes. Yet, an understanding of the complicated nexus of race, ethnicity, and class is absolutely crucial for analyzing this cultural process.

Colombia is a complex nation, marked as much by the diversity of its cultural and ethnic groups as by the sharp contrasts of its geographic regions. The country can be seen as a microcosm of South America's so-called triethnic heritage,[15] and the mixing of indigenous, African, and European peoples and cultures is invoked and manipulated in many ways to support competing versions of national and regional histories (Wade 2000). Colombian national identity, nonetheless, has been blanketed under the incorporative ideology of *mestizaje* (cultural or racial mixing), which reinforces concepts of social and cultural equality it the same time it obscures the ways in which indigenous and black peoples have been systematically marginalized. Political and economic elites in Colombia's mountainous interior have promoted white and mestizo images of national culture while ignoring or downplaying the contributions of other groups. In Colombia people claim not to "see" race; although phenotypical features are recognized, they are not correlated directly to socioeconomic standing and poverty. The rub is, as Winthrop Wright points out for neighboring Venezuela, to a great extent people are poor *because* they are black or indigenous (1990). Ultimately, racial categories denote ethnicity, not immutable biological classifications. As such, however, they are complex identity markers, shot through with elements (themselves socially determined) related to biological phenotype and socioeconomic status. Difference is acknowledged as a legacy of Colombia's triethnic heritage, but it is reconfigured as part of a colorful mosaic—difference is not supposed to really be different. Rather than being merely invisible, however, indigenous people and especially Afro-Colombians have long suffered from negative images that have served as points of reference for elite superiority (Wade 2000: 32). According to Peter Wade, mestizaje does not mean a literal blending of races into indistinction, for such homogenization would dismantle the very social hierarchies that lighter-skinned elites have a vested interest in maintaining. Rather, cultural difference is constantly present in concepts of mestizaje and is invoked in various ways to support competing discourses of cultural heterogeneity or unity depending on the agendas at stake (Wade 2000: 210–12).

As in other Latin American and Caribbean nations (see Whitten 1981; Whitten and Torres 1998), distinctions of socioeconomic class in Colombia are often also distinctions of ethnic difference, tied up with biological concepts of race that have been inherited from colonial times. Despite prevailing ideologies about a colorblind "racial democracy," the legacy of slavery and genocide that shaped Colombia's colonial history has resulted in a tight weave between race and class in defining structural positions in Colombian society, which determine access to economic and political power and resources (Wade 1993). Unlike the one-drop system of ethnic identification that prevails in the United States, "black" and "white" are not essentialized as polar opposites in Latin America. Rather, they are conceived of as a continuum where the makeup of one's ancestry (i.e., the percentage of black or indigenous blood that one has) is combined with aspects of social style, wealth, and other class markers in determining one's position up or down the social ladder.[16] The fact that in many Latin American countries people with "Indian" or "black" physical characteristics consider themselves to be upper-middle class and hence "white" points to some of the problems in conceptualizing race in contemporary Latin America.

In Colombia the marginalization of blacks has been particularly strong.[17] Wade asserts that in Colombia, racism—as a "set of ideas about the inferiority of blackness"—and fluid racial categories are "woven into specific sets of unequal social relations." At the core of racist dynamics lie discursive formations that associate blackness with backwardness and impoverishment. Wade analyzes in detail the ways in which these notions of inferiority are manifested and internalized in different local and regional contexts. Notably, those few Afro-Colombians who have successfully climbed the social ladder have had to "whiten" themselves, leaving behind cultural markers of their blackness (such as speech patterns, cuisine, style of dress, choice of marriage partners, and musical tastes) in order to do so (1993: 342).[18]

Enslaved Africans first arrived in Colombia with the fortification of

Cartagena de las Indias in 1533. They were brought to work in agricultural settlements on the Atlantic coast and to mine for gold in the country's Pacific Coast region.[19] Slave labor also supported the haciendas of the southwest Cauca Valley (around Cali), which provided food for mining activity in the Pacific and also for the colonial administrative center of Popayán. After Brazil, Colombia has one of the largest black populations in South America (Wade 1998: 312). Population figures for people of African descent in Colombia vary widely, depending on which sources you consult. The 1995 census officially designates 21 percent of the population as of African origin,[20] but this does not include mestizos, who may also recognize a black relative or ancestor even if they do not identify as mulato. The substantial presence and contribution of black peoples to the country's economic and cultural history, however, has been little recognized. Despite their significant numbers, Afro-Colombians were not officially acknowledged as a distinct ethnic group until the 1991 constitution, and only then as a result of intense lobbying by Afro-Colombian organizations. Indigenous communities, on the other hand, who officially constitute about 2 percent of the nation's population, have consistently received more political and cultural recognition during the twentieth century.

Such discrimination has had direct consequences for black communities. Owing to Afro-Colombian concepts of communal land ownership, most of the Pacific coastal lands and rivers populated and worked on by Afro-Colombians for centuries were not registered under individual names and were hence officially categorized as *baldíos* (vacant properties) until the ratification of black land rights in 1993. This made Afro-Colombian territories open for development and resource extraction without any due consideration for the area's actual residents (Arocha 1992). Underscoring the lack of political rights, the Pacific has been among the nation's most economically underdeveloped regions, and migrants from the Pacific coast to urban centers such as Cali, Medellín, and Bogotá tend to live in the poorest and most underserviced neighborhoods (Wade 1993).[21]

Economic and political marginalization of Afro-Colombians has paralleled their invisibility and disparagement in academic and popular discourses. In 1965 a colleague told the anthropologist Nina S. de Friedemann (one of Colombia's leading scholars on black culture) that studying Afro-Colombians was not a legitimate endeavor, on the grounds that they were an insignificant cultural group in the national context (1984: 509). Despite increased interest since the 1980s in exploring and reconstructing Afro-Colombian history and culture,[22] research on Afro-Colombian communities and cultural practices remains secondary to the study of indigenous groups. Images of blacks in Colombian popular discourse have been even more disheartening. For generations black people have been characterized as backward, lazy, infantile, stupid, and sexually promiscuous. Racist jokes and media images still abound in Colombia—until 1997 racist "humor" was a mainstay on a nationally televised Saturday evening variety show.[23] While many Colombians like to believe that they do not live in a racist country, for Afro-Colombians the experience of racial discrimination is real.

Given their historical experience of marginalization from the nation's cultural, political, and economic arenas, it is perhaps not surprising that black and mulato Caleños would have adopted a style that signified opposition to a similar system of discrimination in the Caribbean. There is a strong degree of racial essentialism among dark-skinned Colombian salsa fans, who often explained to me that they loved this music because it was "born in their skin" or "in their blood." I heard such claims not only in Cali, but from Afro-Colombians of different socioeconomic classes in the rural black towns of the Cauca Valley, in Buenaventura, in Quibdó, and in Cartagena and Barranquilla, on the Atlantic coast. While these ideological assertions flow more from socially constructed notions of racial identity than from any "natural" correlation between ethnicity and musical preferences, there are strong historical precedents for the successful entry of música antillana into Cali's black and mixed-race culture.

Elsewhere I have explored the role that transnational popular styles of the African diaspora have played in establishing contemporary, self-affirming identities for people of African descent in Colombia (Waxer 1997). Following Paul Gilroy (1993), we can link this process to the Black Atlantic—a transnational space born out of the terrors of the slave trade, in which black people's double consciousness about being simultaneously self and other has given rise to a particularly cosmopolitan approach to expressive culture. If the contributions of black people have been crucial for the rise of modernity, as Gilroy and other scholars maintain, it is hardly surprising that people of African descent have asserted their own modes of participating in the contemporary world: after all, this world was virtually constructed on their backs. In the case of Colombia, however, the necessity to index cosmopolitan identity has been made all the more urgent by the historical placement, in national discourse, of black people on the margins of time and space.

Gender and Generation in Cali

When I arrived in the field in the mid-1990s, I discovered several local all-woman salsa bands active on the scene. Founded between 1989 and 1995, these bands, known as *orquestas femeninas,* mark an unprecedented and unique development in international salsa. The women in these bands were overwhelmingly young, in their teens or early twenties. My curiosity about these all-woman bands led me to larger questions about gender in Caleño society and generational shifts in gender patterns and social roles among men and women. What opportunities did these young salseras have that their mothers, aunts, and grandmothers did not? How did this relate to changing gender roles for women and men in Colombia and Latin America generally? Is this reflected in other areas of salsa's local consumption in Cali?

Between the 1970s and the 1990s, economic shifts for women in Colombia and Latin America in general resulted in a transformation of gender roles for Caleño men and women. These changes were particularly notable along generational lines: younger Caleños were raised in an environment of increasingly open economic and social opportunities for women to participate in domains that had been previously restricted to men. I explore the ways this played out in local salsa consumption and musical performance in the following chapters, but it is worth establishing a larger context for understanding these developments here.

In her book *Listening to Salsa* (1998), Frances Aparicio analyzes at length the ways in which salsa music has been produced as "a man's world." This construction relates to general codes of patriarchy and male dominance in Latin American cultures, which have traditionally operated to keep women from assuming public roles as performers. Few Latina musicians have received attention in the history of salsa and its Cuban and Puerto Rican roots. Women instrumentalists are even further obscured, and so only vocalists such as Celia Cruz, La Lupe, and La India have become famous (172–73). Although Latina singers and instrumentalists have gained increasing international prominence since the mid-1980s, their careers have still largely fallen under male control. Men control the music industry and own the nightclubs. Most Latina artists and all-woman bands have male managers, who exert an enormous influence on their public image. The fact that many women perform songs that are written by men also subverts the notion that women's voices are finally being heard in Latin music. Salsa tunes tend to reinforce patriarchal standards in Latin American society, exalting macho definitions of maleness in lyrics that center around male bravado and sexual conquest. In the rituals of salsa dancing, men enact their relative superiority over women through ballroom dance styles in which the man leads the woman.[24] In Latin America, men can also exert control over "their women" (wives, girlfriends, and sisters) off the dance floor through social codes that regulate how and with whom women can interact. Where, then, do we begin to understand a phenomenon such as Cali's all-woman bands?

In Cali people often cite the adage that Caleña women are the prettiest in all Colombia. Those who hail from other cities (particularly on the Atlantic coast) are wont to contest this, but the saying did become the basis for one the first Colombian salsa hits, "Las caleñas son como las flores" (Caleña Women Are Like Flowers), recorded by the Caleño salsa pioneer Piper Pimienta in 1975 and quickly adopted as a local anthem. Cali's all-woman salsa bands mirror important shifts for women in Colombian society as a whole during the late twentieth century (see Velásquez Toro 1995). The image of Caleña women as beautiful flowers stems from a traditional patriarchal attitude in which women are objects of aesthetic and sensuous contemplation. Using new economic and social opportunities open to them, however, young Caleña musicians appropriated this objectifying gaze to their own benefit, gaining access to the male-dominated sphere of salsa performance. Cali's orquestas femeninas, hence, upheld the image of Caleña women as delicate flowers but simultaneously transcended that stereotype by carving out a space for the women as respected professional musicians (see Waxer 2001a).

While my initial concern with gender issues has been rooted in my own response, as a woman, to the sexual stereotypes reproduced in salsa, in this book I am concerned with the gender dynamics that shape musical production and consumption practices in Caleño popular culture as a whole. Throughout Latin America and the Caribbean, salsa is enjoyed and consumed by both men and women. Frances Aparicio observes that salsa can be used both to reaffirm standard constructions of gender and as a point of contestation in struggles over traditional roles and identities (1998). In a groundbreaking study of gender and Latin popular music, she looks not only at how images of women have been constructed in Latin popular music, but also at how women musicians have responded to and negotiated gender portrayals through songs of their own. Importantly, Aparicio not only examines the ways in which processes of musical production bear a decidedly gendered stamp, but also looks at how salsa audiences filter their consumption practices and interpretations of salsa songs through their own understanding of gender roles and identities.

The rise of Cali's orquestas femeninas raises two questions central to scholarship about gender and music. One issue concerns the processes through which gender has become a significant category of social difference for salsa performance in Cali. In other words, why are current local salsa orquestas divided into male and female categories, and what do these distinctions mean? How have recent international shifts in the definition of male and female musical roles affected local musical identities? Historically, Cali's orquestas femeninas mark an important break with the predominance of male performers in Latin popular music. That Caleña women choose to become salsa musicians, bandleaders, and even composers illustrates their courage in challenging and reappropriating social conventions while struggling with men's continued economic control over their sound and commercial image.

The second question concerns whether there is anything essentially "female" or "male" about the style of salsa performed by all-female and all-male bands, or in the styles of salsa listened to and purchased by Caleño men and women. Although these distinctions are easy to determine in societies where specialization of musical roles and repertoire is clearly assigned to the sexes,[25] no such division exists in Cali. Musical sound and behavior do not convey inherently "male" or "female" properties. As Susan McClary (1991) and Marcia Citron (1993) have argued, the attribution of "male" or "female" characteristics to musical composition and performance is historically constructed. The categorization of music along gender lines grows out of (and feeds back into) the larger system of power relations prevalent at a given moment, and the ways in which differences between men and women are defined so as to maintain a particular social order.

In addition to examining how issues of race, ethnicity, and class have framed the Caleño adoption of salsa, we must also look at how gender roles and age differences have also shaped meanings and practices in local popular culture. The process through which salsa has been localized and resignified opens a wide window onto larger social dynamics in rapidly urbanizing Latin American cities. Although Cali's case cannot necessarily be applied to the rest of Colombia, let alone other countries, the rise of all-woman salsa bands among the second generation of Caleño salsa fans, along with other developments in the local scene, points to a particularly clear instance of the difference that gender and generation, along with race and class, can make.

The City of Musical Memory

During the twentieth century, Cali grew from a minor town into Colombia's second largest and second most powerful city. Several ruptures and struggles framed the city's rise. As an elaborate archive of personal memoirs entitled *Recuerdos de mi barrio* (Memories of My Barrio) testifies, Cali's sudden growth encompassed the mushrooming of new neighborhoods, the remodeling of the city center and the concomitant destruction of historical buildings, and—most vividly—the struggles of new citizens to find work, build homes, and win battles over running water, electricity, sewage, and paving for their streets (*Recuerdos* 1986).[26] These are among the transitions that accompanied Cali's transformation into a modern urban center. The rise of Cali's recent urban culture—based on a new musical style adopted from abroad—points to a process of creative self-production among Caleño citizens as they strove to anchor their experiences of these tumultuous changes (Harvey 2000: 159).

The organization of this book, which documents and analyzes key stages in the emergence of salsa culture in Cali, is roughly chronological. I focus on the rise of Cali's self-image as a world salsa capital and the ways in which this development is interwoven with deeper notions about Cali as the city of musical memory. My study traces three important spheres that encompassed Caleño popular culture by the early 1990s, each with a particular performative tradition, each with its own particular roots and routes back through Cali's recent history, and each with a particular way of enacting the process of surrogation (Roach 1996) in local popular memory. I then draw these chapters together by exploring how these three spheres, or "scenes" (Straw 1991), come together in the most visible and exciting public event in Caleño life—the annual Feria.

Chapter 1 sets the general stage for my narrative. In it I outline Cali's history in regional and national contexts, discuss the links between music and region in Colombia, and trace the general rise of música antillana in three overlapping spheres: the transnational (Latin America), the national (Colombia), and the local (Cali). The relationship of música antillana to the rise of Colombian *música tropical*—"tropical music" from Colombia's own Caribbean coast—during the 1940s and 1950s is analyzed with regard to Cali's relationship to national culture. Here I try to consolidate the complex historical reasons for Cali's adoption of salsa and música antillana over and above regional and national musical styles.

In chapter 2 I focus on the rise of Cali's record-centered dance scene as the first instance in which sound recordings were literally incorporated into local popular culture. I explore the routes via which recordings first entered Cali and how they acquired the cosmopolitan associations that entrenched their centrality in local expressive practices. The flowering of salsa dance culture in the 1960s and 1970s gave birth to a distinctly Caleño style of dancing to salsa—unique in Latin America and famous throughout Colombia. The revival of this scene in the viejotecas that mushroomed after the fall of the Cali cartel in 1996 points to a highly significant process of reactivating record-centered dance in local popular culture and memory.

The emergence of salsotecas and tabernas in the 1980s as public spaces for listening to records of salsa and música antillana points to another trajectory of local popular life that branched out from the record-centered dance scene. In chapter 3 I look at the development of the salsoteca scene in record collecting, a significant practice in local popular culture, and the rise of the *melómano,* or music aficionado, in Caleño life. In this sphere Caleño identity has become strongly tied to discourses about preservation, history, authenticity, and purity, in which record collections and salsotecas are constructed as vinyl museums for the active maintenance of Cali's musical roots.

The third sphere of popular culture, and perhaps the one that succeeded best in placing Cali on the international salsa map, was the rise of a bustling live music scene in the 1980s and early 1990s—the subject of chapters 4 and 5. In a mere decade, dozens of local salsa bands were formed, with a frenzy that mirrored the invention of salsa dance steps a generation earlier. Internationally famous Caleño orquestas such as Grupo Niche and Guayacán emerged during this period, and lavish marathon salsa concerts became a key attraction of the annual Feria. While the rise of a live scene might suggest that real musicians had finally come to replace sound recordings in local popular culture, Cali's live scene was indelibly marked by the centrality of recordings in other spheres, in ways that complicate the relationship between live and mediated musical expression.

In chapter 6 I explore the ways in which dancing, listening, and live music coalesce as performative practices during Cali's annual Feria. This annual celebration, heightened by its calendrical proximity to two other important celebrations, Christmas and New Year's, is a vivid reaffirmation of Caleño popular culture. As in other carnival celebrations, the tensions, paradoxes, and contradictions of daily life are revealed and embraced in a transgressive revelry (Stallybrass and White 1986) centered around salsa music. If "Cali Is Feria," as a local salsa song put it, Cali's Feria is salsa, in a vociferous, joyous and kinetic commemoration of salsa and música antillana that lies at the heart of local popular life.

As interrelated spheres, dancing, listening, musical performance, and the Feria are deeply embedded in Caleño subjectivity. In the following chapters I look at the ways in which public space, cultural topographies, kinetic movements, and other activities have framed these scenes, embedding physical and bodily locations for popular memory. The strands of this social history are taken up in the epilogue, where the themes of transnational culture, cosmopolitan identity, and urban life in Latin America are drawn together.

1
"In Those Days, Holy Music Rained Down"

Origins and Influence of Música Antillana *in Cali and Colombia*

One evening my husband and research collaborator Medardo Arias Satizábal took me to visit the artisan Hernán González. A colorful person much loved by his neighbors, González is renowned for the carnival masks he makes in his home in the older working-class barrio of Loma de la Cruz. He is also a veteran of Cali's popular music scene during the 1940s and 1950s and maintains his passion for that era by collecting videos of old movie musicals. González was a youth when Cuban (and to a lesser extent, Puerto Rican) styles were spreading throughout Latin America and the Caribbean, gaining enormous popularity in urban centers in Puerto Rico, Mexico, Venezuela, and Panama, and in the Latino community in New York City. These sounds also spread to Colombia, where they took hold in the Atlantic coast ports of Cartagena and Barranquilla, and in Cali.

González led us back to the dining area behind the grocery store that he also runs out of his house, where he turned on the television set and videocassette player to show us some choice excerpts from his collection. As we watched famous stars croon and mambo their way across the screen, he regaled us with anecdotes about Cali's scene in those days—famous dancers who knew all the Cuban styles; the bars, cabarets, and brothels where you could hear the latest recordings of this music; the movie houses where you went to learn the dances from new musicals; and the ballrooms where local bands performed música antillana. Flashing us his mischievous and charismatic smile, González said, "En esos días llovió música sagrada sobre Cali" (In those days, holy music rained down on Cali).[1]

González's remark is hardly the raving of a lone music fan. His attitude is typical of working-class Caleños of his generation, who embraced Cuban and Puerto Rican sounds during the 1940s and 1950s. While the music they love is hardly "sacred" or "holy" in the literal sense (especially given its initial rise in the city's red-light district), it certainly is revered as both the root of contemporary local tradition and the glorious musical emblem of a bygone era. González's recollection of his youth as a time when "holy music rained down on Cali" points to a widespread Caleño origin myth in which the arrival of música antillana is constructed as a virtual genesis of the modern city. Indeed, his remark invokes the Old Testament book of Genesis, in which holy rain figures not only during the Creation, but also during the biblical flood that washed away the old and renewed the Earth again (Genesis 2:7 and 7:12).

Origin myths are a vital part of cultural beliefs, whether in the context of nations, ethnic groups, or subcultural scenes. They are intricately tied to discourses about authenticity and purity, anchoring subjectivity and social identities through a number of codes, representations, and practices.[2] In this chapter I explore the roots of Cali's contemporary origin myths by looking at the city's history in regional and national contexts, linking this to the development of música antillana and its influence in Colombia and Cali from the 1920s through the 1950s. I situate the emergence of música antillana as a widespread cosmopolitan dance music in Latin America, analyzing the political economy that led to the predominance of Cuban genres in música antillana but also made space for Puerto Rican elements and artists to be included. The transition from música antillana to salsa is explored through the influence of two pivotal groups that, not surprisingly, had a great impact in Cali—the Sonora Matancera and Cortijo y su Combo. I also explore the role played by música antillana in the formation of Colombian música tropical ("tropical" dance music based on Atlantic coast genres) and look at the ways in which both música antillana and música tropical competed for attention in Caleño musical life in the middle of the twentieth century—later replaced by the origin myth about música antillana's predominance. This chapter contextualizes how struggles over local, national, and cosmopolitan identities in Cali set the stage for many cultural practices that I analyze in the rest of this book.

Cali in the Regional and National Context

Cali is located in southwest Colombia, two hours' drive inland from the Pacific coast, in a broad valley between the western and central ranges of the Andes Mountains. The old part of the city lies on the banks of the Río Cali, a western tributary of the Río Cauca. As the main artery and primary waterway of the Colombian southwest, the Cauca River flows thousands of kilometers to the north, coverging with the Magdalena River to empty into the Caribbean Sea. Urban expansion in the middle of the twentieth century filled in the pasture and swampland between Cali's historic downtown and the docks (now demolished) on the Cauca, and Cali now extends from the western mountain foothills eastward to the banks of the Cauca. The construction of luxury condominium towers and sprawling shopping centers during the economic boom of the 1980s and early 1990s has further expanded Cali's urban landscape, yet the city retains the lush tropical climate and pleasant, tree-lined ambience that have been its hallmark for generations. Average year-round temperatures hover around 78° F (25° C), and every afternoon the midday heat is dispersed by a refreshing breeze that blows in from the Pacific coast over the mountains that line the city's western reaches. Indeed, the celebrated congeniality of Caleños is often attributed to the tempering effects of the tropical sun and the delicious afternoon breeze.

Founded in 1536 by the Spanish explorer Sebastián de Belalcázar, Cali was established as a secondary administrative center during the colonial era, linked to the governor's seat in Popayán, 150 kilometers to the south. Through the sixteenth century, warrior bands from the various Carib-speaking tribes that lived in the Cauca Valley[3] made repeated attempts to oust the encroaching Spaniards but were finally quelled through military force. The names of tribes and *caciques,* or native chiefs, remain as geographic place-names throughout the area (e.g., Jamundí, Calima, and Petecuy); indeed, the name "Cali" is thought to be a derivation of the name either of the Lilí or the Calima people. During colonial times, the principal economic activity in Colombia's southwest was based on gold extraction from the mines and rivers of the western cordillera and Pacific lowlands, sustained by the labor of African slaves brought into the country through Cartagena.[4] To feed this indentured work force, large haciendas were established in the Cauca Valley around Cali, where the fertile soil proved ideal for cultivating a variety of fruits, grains, and vegetables, as well as livestock. Also maintained through slave labor, the haciendas differed from the plantations set up in the Caribbean in that agricultural activities on the former were based on mixed-crop farming for an internal market, rather than on monoculture or cash-crop farming for an export market. The colonial gold mines and haciendas paid tribute to the regional administrative seat of Popayán, not the viceroyal capital of Santafé de Bogotá. As a result, economic and political ties to the interior were relatively weak.

The dual hacienda-mine system peaked in the second half of the eighteenth century and began to wane after independence from Spain in 1810, weakened by the declining gold market and also the increase of *cimarronaje* as rebel slaves fled to freedom. Through the middle of the nineteenth century, many *cimarrones* (escaped slaves) organized land invasions of hacienda properties in the Cauca Valley. Such invasions continued after the abolition of slavery in 1852 and formed the basis of the Afro-Colombian *minifundio* (small-plot) peasantry that prevailed in the region surrounding Cali from the late 1800s until the middle of the twentieth century.

Still a small provincial town in the early years of this century, Cali began to grow after the construction of a railway line linking the interior to the Pacific coastal port of Buenaventura in 1915–17.[5] Completed shortly after the construction of the Panama Canal in 1914, this railway enabled transport of all products from Colombia's southwest interior to the port and greatly opened Colombian foreign trade, which until then had been conducted mainly through Cartagena and Barranquilla on Colombia's Atlantic coast. For the *zona cafetera* (coffee-growing region) north of Cali, the railway provided easier access to international trade arteries than the previous route north through the arduous waterways of the Magdalena up to Barranquilla. Coffee exports through Buenaventura increased fivefold from 1916 to 1926, and with the construction of further railway links in the interior, by 1944 nearly 60 percent of all Colombian coffee was exported through Buenaventura. As the midway point for coffee transported by steamboat down the Cauca River and loaded onto trains bound for the port, Cali became the business headquarters and central clearing house for major coffee exporters (Posada-Carbó 1996: 160–61).

Although coffee served as the basis for Cali's initial urban expansion in the first part of the twentieth century, it was sugar—the favored sweetener for this caffeinated brew—that consolidated Cali's agroindustrial boom and second wave of urbanization from the 1950s through the 1970s. The fertile lands and sunny climate of the Cauca Valley provide one the most ideal zones on earth for cultivating sugarcane. Friends informed me, as we drove through countryside checkered by dazzling emerald-green canefields, that new crops are sown and harvested throughout the year.[6] After the Cuban Revolution in 1959 and the subsequent U.S. blockade of Cuban sugar, the United States turned to Colombia and other Latin American countries to satisfy its sweet tooth. Already the hub of Colombia's national sugar industry, Cali quickly expanded with the influx of laborers required to work in the expansion of sugarcane cultivation, harvesting, and processing. Migration from surrounding regions—caused in part by the bloody strife of La Violencia[7]—further contributed to Cali's rapid urbanization in the 1950s and 1960s. Finally, the establishment of a regional hydroelectric authority in 1954 enabled the construction of dams and power plants along the region's principal waterways, consolidating a nearby energy source for industrial and urban development. In addition to the sugar industry, others such as paper and cardboard products and cement were established; the traditional agricultural base of mixed crop and livestock framing also continued, for local and regional consumption. During this time Cali's population more than doubled, expanding to nearly a million by 1973.[8] On the crest of this industrial and economic wave, in 1971 Cali hosted the Pan-American Games, a key moment for international recognition of the city. The Pan-American Games stimulated urban development along the city's southern flank, resulting in the growth of new neighborhoods that nearly doubled the geographical span of the city in the 1970s. In addition to the long-standing Caleño passion for swimming, track, basketball, and especially soccer, the Pan-American Games also helped to consolidate sports and physical recreation as an important basis of local cultural identity alongside salsa music (Gómez 1986: 284).

Another white powdery substance—cocaine—is said to have been the basis for Cali's third wave of urbanization during the 1980s and early 1990s, as the Cali cartel grew in power and began to pump inordinate sums of money into the local economy. Real estate projects (condominiums, townhouses, and shopping malls) mushroomed, new businesses opened, and the local market was flooded with luxury consumer items. The city's population nearly doubled as migrants poured in from other regions of the country seeking jobs and better economic opportunities. By 1985 Cali's inhabitants numbered 1.4 million; by 1994 there were 1.8 million.[9] Unofficial sources estimate Cali's current population at over two million. In the early 1990s Cali surpassed Medellín to become the second largest city in Colombia; the economic influence it wielded was subordinate only to that of Bogotá. Most important for musicians, however, the cartel bosses reputedly patronized salsa bands and encouraged the formation of new groups. There was a constant demand for live music in the many new nightclubs that were appearing on the scene and at lavish parties held at private mansions and country estates. (In chapters 3, 4, and 5 I discuss the effects of this "third wave" of urbanization on Cali's salsero culture.)

Of key importance in understanding Cali's contemporary salsa scene is the role of the annual December Feria, or fair, in providing a focal point for Caleños to affirm their assertion as the world salsa capital. Held from 25 December to 30 December, the Feria is to Cali what Carnival is to Barranquilla, Rio de Janeiro, and Port of Spain. Although conducted in more modest circumstances than these carnival celebrations (for one, the extravagant parades central to those events have never been realized at the Feria, and processionals with costumes and floats are a minor feature of the festivities),

Cali's Feria is certainly carnivalesque. City residents and tourists alike have spoken to me in glowing terms of the five days of nonstop *rumba* (merry-making) that mark this time, when people indulge in a spree of drinking, dancing, concertgoing, and club-hopping. Unlike in other parts of Colombia (and Latin America, for that matter), *fiestas patronales,* or patron saint days, are not widely observed in Cali. Rather, the Feria has become the city's representative celebration and parallels the emergence of contemporary popular identity after Cali began to expand in the middle of the twentieth century. (In chapter 6 I examine the position of the Feria in local popular culture, focusing on its critical role in shaping the city's salsero identity.)

Salsa music has influenced not only Caleño subjectivity, but also the image of Cali that is widely held in the rest of Colombia. Caleños are renowned for their inclination to partake of a *rumba,* that is, a party or festive gathering (not to be confused with the specific Afro-Cuban musical tradition of the same name). Since at least the 1960s, Cali has promoted itself with catchphrases such as *la ciudad pachanguera* (the "partying" city), *la ciudad alegre* (the happy city), and *el sucursal del cielo* (heaven's outpost). These slogans illustrate the inclination for revelry and the all-important rumba that have become essential to Caleño social life—elements shaped through decades of listening and dancing to salsa and música antillana.

Music and Region in Colombia

In his study of salsa in Cali, Alejandro Ulloa cites the lack of a local musical tradition as one of the principal factors contributing to salsa's adoption and popularity in this city (1992: 194–95). The notion that Cali did not have a musical tradition prior to salsa and música antillana is common among Caleños; I heard several other observers cite this same reason. It is another version of the origin myth introduced at the beginning of this chapter. In a country whose geographic and cultural diversity is paralleled by the wealth of its musical styles, however, this statement is highly peculiar. What stake would Caleños have in claiming that they had no local tradition prior to that established by the adoption of música antillana and salsa? Clearly, the concept emerges from local origin myths that position the flowering of contemporary popular culture and identity with the arrival of música antillana. Caleño musical life certainly predates this moment, although in ways that did not anchor a distinctive Caleño identity. In order to clarify the significance of Ulloa's claim, however, we must first understand the nexus between music and regional identity in Colombia.

Colombian regional identities are strongly articulated by musical style and other cultural practices, in ways that are closely tied to struggles over economic and political control of the nation. In Colombia, *cachacos* (people from the interior, particularly in or near the capital city of Bogotá) and *paisas* (people from the Antioquia region) have long been identified as the two groups that have held the political and economic reins of the nation. Accordingly, through the nineteenth and early twentieth centuries, the representative national style was long identified with *música andina,* or music of the Colombian Andes, which features such lyric genres as *bambuco* and *pasillo,* played by string trios of *tiple, bandola,* and guitar (see Abadía Morales 1973). Associated with the mountainous interior regions of the country (the provinces of Antioquia, Cundinamarca, Boyacá, Santander, Caldas, Tolima, and Huila), this tradition is distinct from the music usually thought of in North America and Europe as "Andean," that is, the highland traditions of Ecuador, Peru, and Bolivia. Música andina is also played in the northeastern part of Valle province, only an hour's drive from Cali. The promotion of Colombian música andina over other regional styles during the nineteenth century and early decades of the twentieth century was closely tied to the economic and political power historically held by the interior. Indeed, the term *música colombiana* (Colombian music) was commonly understood through the late nineteenth century and early twentieth centuries to refer to bambucos and pasillos (Wade 2000: 51–52). In terms of regional cultural stereotypes, the rather serious, refined and introspective air associated with música andina is also that associated with the character of people from the interior.

During the 1930s and 1940s, music from Colombia's Atlantic or Caribbean coast began to replace música andina in the national eye. In Colombia, this region is usually referred to as La Costa (the coast), despite the fact that Colombia has another coast on the Pacific (usually referred to as *el litoral pacífico* [the Pacific littoral]).[10] Costeño (Atlantic coastal) traditions combine African, European, and indigenous influences, typified in the flute-and-drum ensembles that perform *cumbia, porro, gaita, fandango, mapalé, chandé, bullerengue,* and other genres (see Jaramillo 1992; Camargo 1994). As La Costa began to play an increasingly critical role in national political life, urbanized versions of porro, cumbia, and gaita formed the basis for the dance-band adaptations of Costeño rhythms that swept into national circles as música tropical during the 1940s (Wade 2000). Since the 1970s, *vallenato,* an accordion-based style related to cumbia and música tropical, has become the most popular Costeño genre, replacing the big-band sound of música tropical as a national style. As Peter Wade discusses at length in his book *Music, Race, and Nation,* the sensual, playful, and carefree associations of música tropical are closely tied to national images of Costeño identity.

Colombia's other coast, the Pacific, is populated by a predominantly Afro-Colombian population, with two distinct traditions: the *chirimía* bands in the northwest Chocó province and the marimba-based *currulao* tradition that prevails along the southwest littoral of Valle, Cauca, and Nariño provinces and into Esmeraldas, the northwest corner of Ecuador. The Chocoano chirimía tradition is similar to Costeño town bands that adapted European wind-band instrumentation to black musical aesthetics and stylistic practices. Featuring clarinets, trumpets, euphonium, and European percussion, they differ from the fife-and-drum ensembles used in the indigenous and mestizo processionals that range from Mexico down through the Andes and are also found in southern Colombia. In the southwest Pacific Coast region, the currulao represents a more direct connection with African diasporic roots, employing marimba, single-headed drums, and shakers modeled on West and Central African instruments and a dense polyrhythmic texture in 12/8 meter similar to those of many sub-Saharan African styles. Like that of the Atlantic Costeño people, the music and culture of Afro-Colombians from the Pacific is also seen as sensuous and playful.

Other musical traditions frame Colombian regional diversity. The grassy plains of the southeast, which are geographically and culturally linked to the Venezuelan grasslands, form the heartland of the courtship dance known as *joropo,* which is associated with the cowboy culture of the region. Performed on harp, bandola, cuatro, and maracas, joropo is a dynamic, polyrhythmic mestizo style that fuses Andalusian, African, and indigenous elements. In rural and semiurban areas of Antioquia province, the guitar-based *carrilera* is associated with the urbanizing peasant or worker class, where economic suffering is configured into mournful songs of romantic loss in a manner similar to the one Deborah Pacini Hernández describes for *bachata* in the Dominican Republic (1995). Throughout Colombia, a number of indigenous traditions are also practiced within small native communities located along the Atlantic and Pacific coasts and in the Sierra Nevada, the highlands of Cauca and Nariño provinces, and the southeast Amazon region. In the highland region bordering Ecuador, mestizo and indigenous peoples perform a style of Andean music distinct from Colombian música andina and similar to Ecuadorian and Peruvian genres. Another Afro-Colombian tradition relevant to this study is the body of religious songs specific to the rural towns and settlements of the Cauca Valley that flank Cali's southern limits. This repertoire, adapted from Catholic songs and hymns, is performed by small brass-and-wind bands and played during the Fiesta del Niño Dios in January, and also for funeral rituals.[11]

Urban popular styles also coalesce around regional and even local identities in Colombia, although, as Wade notes, the intensified pull between processes of hybridity and homogeneity make it impossible to correlate these to specific social groups in any absolute terms (2000: 23–25). Several urban sounds in Colombia have transnational origins, reflecting the ways that Colombian cities have been entry points for international influences. In general terms, vallenato, salsa, and rock are the most widespread urban styles in Colombia. Vallenato, a Costeño style, has been predominant mainly on the Atlantic coast, but in the early 1980s it followed música tropical's footsteps into the interior, becoming prominent in Bogotá and Medellín. Only in the late 1990s did vallenato finally puncture salsa's foothold in Cali to gain audiences there. Salsa's spread in Colombia has been concentrated primarily along the Atlantic and Pacific coasts. Apart from Cali—a city with close economic ties to the Pacific coast—salsa's most significant urban nuclei have been Barranquilla, Cartagena, and Buenaventura, all coastal port towns through which Cuban and Puerto Rican sounds first entered the country. Contemporary *rock en español*—Spanish or Latin American rock—first flowered in Bogotá and Medellín, the cities with the strongest economic and cultural ties to the international rock scene. Reflecting recent trends throughout Latin America and the Caribbean, however, rock en español has swept the country, its youthful audience defined more along lines of age than of region. Indeed, the Barranquilla native Shakira (an MTV darling) and Bogotá's Andrea Echevarría (of Los Aterciopelados) have become icons of current Colombian youth culture and its most visible symbols abroad (see Cepeda 2001).

Also important, although less widespread, has been the localization of Argentine tango in Medellín and Manizales, where it functions similarly to salsa and música antillana in Cali as an emblem of cosmopolitan identity. Likewise, among Afro-Colombian inhabitants of Cartagena and Barranquilla the adoption of *soukous*, Afro-pop, *mbqanga*, soca, zouk, and other African and Afro-Caribbean genres into the style known locally as *champeta* or *terapia* has become an emblem of black cosmopolitanism on Colombia's Atlantic coast since the 1980s. Significantly, champeta emerged after Afro-Costeño forms were appropriated (as música tropical) into national mestizo culture, providing a new vehicle for expressing a distinct Afro-Colombian subjectivity and experience (Pacini Hernández 1993; Waxer 1997).

Other transnational styles have entered Colombian urban life, reflecting popular currents in other parts of Latin America. *Balada,* or Spanish romantic pop music, was popularized primarily as a result of control by Latin American music industries (Manuel 1991). Balada's influence in Colombia peaked during the late 1960s and early 1970s, when the *nueva ola,* or new wave, of romantic crooners such as Julio Iglesias, Leo Dan, Sandro, and Rafael washed up on Colombian shores. Dominican *merengue,* which swept several Latin American and Caribbean countries during the 1980s, made inroads into Colombia, but only in the Atlantic coast cities of Barranquilla and (to a lesser extent) Cartagena. When I arrived in Cali in 1994, merengue still faced a virtual blockade on local airwaves and in clubs that was not broken until later in the decade. Interestingly, the Dominican bachata, which has become very important for U.S. Latino audiences (especially in the northeast), was still unknown in Colombia by the year 2000, pointing to uneven processes of distribution and marketing within the Latin American music industry.

To return to the question I pose at the outset of this section: what stake have Caleños had in maintaining that no local tradition existed before the adoption of música antillana and salsa? Certainly, the diversity of musical styles that compete for attention on the national cultural landscape offers one explanation. Given that regional difference in Colombia is strongly marked by musical and cultural distinctions, the shaping of Caleño identity has been stimulated by the need to develop a distinct musical emblem for the city. Why, however, were local genres not remembered or performed? Many of the musical styles played in Cali during the early years of this century were dominated by national tastes adopted from the interior of the country. Although Cali has been marked by economic and political isolation from the Colombian interior since colonial times, local cultural tastes tended to follow national norms. This can be attributed in part to control of the city by elites who felt a need to maintain the appearance of being "cultivated" along national standards, even if other ties to the interior were weak. Through the 1940s and 1950s, however, burgeoning industrial and urban expansion fostered the rise of a new middle and upper-middle class with less allegiance to national standards and cultural images from the interior. This growth was reinforced by new social and cultural forces that entered the city and further ruptured allegiances to earlier musical practices. Certain key influences affected Cali's musical landscape through the mid-twentieth century, and a number of factors led to the displacement of earlier local genres by a transnational one—música antillana.

Música Antillana: The Rise of a Cosmopolitan Latin American Dance Music

In Colombia, Cuban and Puerto Rican genres from the 1920s–50s are usually referred to as música antillana—music from the Spanish Caribbean islands. I have also heard the term *música caribeña* (Caribbean music) used, but this is less frequent, perhaps because Colombia already has a rich vein of traditions from its own Caribbean coast. Indeed, música antillana and música caribeña are terms that are commonly used throughout Latin America, but their meanings have different nuances from country to country. In Puerto Rico, for example, these terms refer generally to any Caribbean popular dance style, especially those from Hispanic Caribbean nations, regardless of epoch.[12] This can include old Cuban son and guaracha from the 1930s, Puerto Rican bomba and plena, contemporary salsa, and commercial Dominican merengue. While theoretically connected to musical genres from throughout the Caribbean, however, in Colombia "música antillana" usually refers to the Cuban and Puerto Rican popular musical styles diffused to the rest of Latin America from the 1920s through the 1950s. This probably relates to the fact that Cuban and Puerto Rican artists were better known in Colombia than were music and musicians from the Dominican Republic or other Caribbean nations. Indeed, the isolationist policies of the Dominican dictator Rafael Trujillo curbed the widespread dissemination of merengue, the principal genre of that island, and it was only after the large wave of Dominican migration to New York in the 1970s and 1980s that merengue began to enjoy the same level of international popularity that Cuban music had attained during the first half of the century (Austerlitz 1997: 73–74). The predominance of Cuban and Puerto Rican artists on the international Latin market during the 1940s and 1950s appears to have reinforced the association in Colombia of música antillana with Cuban and Puerto Rican sounds from the epoch. Following Colombian usage, I shall refer to Cuban and Puerto Rican popular music of the 1920s through the 1950s as "música antillana" and use the term "Cuban music" when referring specifically to Cuba alone.

Style and Structure in Música Antillana

Música antillana is defined by a number of basic elements and stylistic procedures emerging from its mixed African and European roots.[13] Although there are also vestiges of indigenous musical influence in the presence of maracas and *güiro* (a notched, scraped gourd), the indigenous populations of Cuba and Puerto Rico (the Siboney and Taino Indians) were wiped out during the first century of colonial encounter. Cuban and Puerto Rican popular genres are characterized by simple European harmonic progressions and melodic lines, string and wind instruments, the use of the Spanish language, and certain harmonic and melodic patterns typical of Iberian music. Many of their musical elements, however, point to a strong sub-Saharan African influence. These include a variety of drums and other percussion instruments; interlocking polyrhythmic, timbral, melodic, and harmonic ostinati; a percussive approach to playing; call-and-response vocals, and a preference for dense or buzzy timbres. Harmonic progressions in música antillana songs are very basic, for example, ||: I–V–V–I :|| or ||: I–IV–V–I :|| or ||: I–VI–II–V :||. These repeated harmonic patterns, voiced in the bass and piano or guitar, underscore the other interlocking rhythmic and timbral patterns.

In Colombia, the term "música antillana" also indexes the commercial sound of cosmopolitan urban culture through the use of instrumentation that came to predominate in urban ensembles in the Americas during the first half of the twentieth century. Perhaps one of the most prominent features of música antillana ensembles of the 1940s and 1950s is not only their use of Afro-Caribbean percussion (usually Cuban), but the increasing prominence of dance-orchestra instrumentation, modeled on North American popular dance bands. These groups usually featured full trumpet, trombone, and saxophone sections (with four or five musicians in each section), plus piano, bass, and drum set or other percussion. In Latin America, Cuban instruments such as the conga drum, bongo, and maracas were often used in place of the drum set typically employed in North American bands. These bands were sometimes referred to in Latin America as *jazzband*, even though they did not really perform jazz, but more often this format was simply known as an *orquesta*. Such groups typically performed for the middle and upper-middle classes in the elegant ballrooms of private social clubs, but they also played for the general urban populace in radio theaters, nightclubs, and hotel salons. In other words, not all Cuban and Puerto Rican genres or styles are recognized as música antillana—for example, *rumba guaguancó* played in the traditional percussion-and-vocals format would not be called música antillana but Cuban music. (A commercial dance-band tune labeled a "guaguancó," however, would be recognized as música antillana.) The orquesta or jazzband format became a significant marker of cosmopolitan identity during the first half of this century, and was widely adopted in cities throughout Latin America and the Caribbean.[14] Even the small Cuban *conjunto* (combo), which originally featured only string

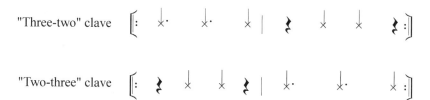

"Three-two" clave

"Two-three" clave

Figure 1.1   Clave pattern

and light percussion instruments, expanded in the late 1930s, adding horns, piano and heavier percussion, partly as a result of this influence.

Cuban genres—whether performed by Cuban or Puerto Rican artists— are characterized by a number of specific elements not necessarily present in Puerto Rican forms. The most important element is the *clave* pattern, a rhythmic time line around which all other rhythmic figures are organized. This pattern is a two-bar figure that can be played with a three-two or two-three emphasis depending on where one starts in the cycle (Figure 1.1). It is often played by two wooden sticks struck together, called *claves,* but even when not played, musicians are aware of the pattern. All the syllabic accents of the lyrics and also the melodic accents and breaks of horn lines and percussion parts must coordinate with the clave, whether it is felt as a two-three or a three-two pattern. The structure of a musical phrase and its main accents determine whether a melody is in three-two or two-three clave. The clave is derived from West African patterns (Mauleón 1993) and is present in different variations in other Afro-Cuban genres (e.g., rumba and sacred *batá* drumming) and is also embedded in the time line used in Puerto Rican bomba (Dufrasne-González 1994). The clave pattern is not used in the Puerto Rican plena.

Another distinctive trait of Cuban popular styles is the *habanera* bass line, a 3 + 3 + 2 pattern, which was also modified to become the *bajo anticipado* (anticipated bass line) essential to Cuban and Cuban-derived styles (Figure 1.2; see Manuel 1985 for discussion of its roots in Afro-Cuban drumming). This pattern is distinct from the basic pattern typical of Puerto Rican plena and Dominican merengue, where the bass line falls on strong downbeats and does not have the syncopation of the anticipated bass line in Cuban music.

Since the 1920s the most important genre of Cuban popular music has been the son, which developed from rural nineteenth-century forms in the eastern part of the island and was consolidated in Cuba's major cities through the first two decades of the twentieth century. Son is divided into a two-part structure consisting of lyric verses sung by the lead vocalist, and

Figure 1.2   Habanera and anticipated bass patterns

then a call-and-response *montuno* section sung between the leader and *coro* (chorus). This two-part structure has continued into the salsa tradition, and most salsa tunes are written in verse-montuno form. Traditionally, the lead vocalist improvises the calls, or *pregones,* a convention that continued in salsa through the 1960s and 1970s. (Vocalists of the current commercial *salsa romántica* [romantic salsa ballad] style have lost this art and tend to sing precomposed lines.) The montuno section also serves as a basis for improvised instrumental soloing over the basic groove set by the rhythm section (the principal of improvisation over an established polyrhythmic base is another African musical trait). This two-part structure is also present in other Cuban forms, such as rumba guaguancó, and is also characteristic of Puerto Rican plenas.

In the 1920s and 1930s son was performed by a small six- or seven-piece conjunto, also referred to simply as a *sexteto* or *septeto.* Instrumentation in these groups consisted of guitar, *tres* (a Cuban guitar tuned in three double courses), bongo (a pair of small single-headed drums), claves, maracas, and contrabass, with an optional trumpet. This is the typical ensemble that emerged in the eastern part of Cuba, Oriente, and that still prevails in Santiago de Cuba. (The 1999 film *Buena Vista Social Club* features this format.) During the 1930s a simplified version of son called "rhumba" was adapted for cosmopolitan dance bands (e.g., Xavier Cugat) and became a huge dance craze among North American and European audiences.[15] In Havana, however, innovators such as Arsenio Rodríguez (referred to by fans and scholars as "Arsenio") began experimenting with the son format during the late 1930s and early 1940s, expanding the ensemble with the addition of a conga (a cylindrical single-headed drum of Afro-Cuban tradition, usually referred to as *tumbadora* in Cuba), piano, and up to three more trumpets. The catchy piano vamp, adapted after the tres parts of earlier son and referred to as a *guajeo* or montuno, became another characteristic element of Cuban music, as did the basic conga pattern, known as *tumbao* (Figure 1.3).[16] In ad-

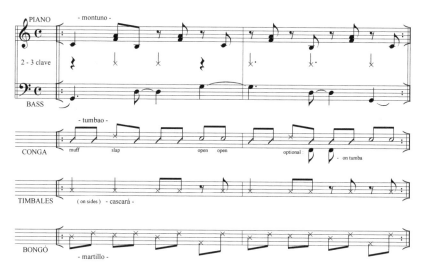

Figure 1.3 Basic rhythmic patterns in Cuban *son* and salsa

dition to an enlarged conjunto format, the montuno section was expanded to include dynamic horn "shout" choruses between call-and-response sections. Arsenio adopted the slower tempo, denser polyrhythmic texture, and improvisational percussive approach of Afro-Cuban rumba, a contemporary percussion-and-vocals tradition of the black Cuban working classes in and around Havana. These slower sones were also referred to as *son montuno,* perhaps owing to the fact that the verse part was frequently omitted, starting right at the montuno.[17] Arsenio's innovations on the Cuban son were adapted in Puerto Rico and became the basis for the ensemble Cortijo y su Combo, which performed original and traditional bombas and plenas in this format. Later, the heavier percussive sound and rhythmic drive of Arsenio's style became the model for several New York salsa bands in the late 1960s and 1970s.

A lighter and faster-paced variant of son called *guaracha* (derived from the nineteenth-century topical song form of the same name) was also very popular, especially for their picaresque lyrics, which often related typical anecdotes of daily life. The guaracha numbers of the Sonora Matancera were particular favorites. It is probable that the popularity of guaracha in Colombia is related to its light rhythmic touch, similar to that of música tropical—especially in the quarter note–two eighths rhythmic pattern played by the maracas.

Parallel to son's rise in the lower classes, the flute-and-violin charanga ensembles performed a genre known as *danzón,* developed from the colonial Spanish *contradanza* for the middle and upper class. Despite the danzón's Europeanized melodic and harmonic structure, however, principles of repeated interlocking rhythmic, melodic, and timbral patterns also prevailed, especially in the habanera bass line and the *cinquillo* pattern [♩ ♫♫ ♩] performed on two mounted tom-toms known as *timbales*. By the late 1930s the charangas had become popular among the working classes and had also absorbed elements of son. Most important was the addition of an improvisatory montunolike section—called the *mambo*—to the end of the danzón structure. By 1943 a conga was added to the charanga ensemble to create extra rhythmic drive in this section. The mambo section was subsequently separated and adapted to big-band formats in New York, where it flowered into a highly popular genre of its own. The mambo big bands were the first to consolidate the combination of congas, timbal, and bongo that is now standard for all salsa bands. The Cuban musician Dámaso Pérez Prado also established a mambo big band in 1947, which helped to popularize the mambo from his base in Mexico City. The charangas, meanwhile, continued in popularity, developing the *chachachá* rhythm in the early 1950s. (See Waxer 1994 for a detailed history of these developments.)

In Puerto Rico the two most important genres to be incorporated into música antillana have been bomba and plena. Bomba is a traditional Afro-Puerto Rican dance style similar to the Afro-Cuban rumba. Performed on drums made from rum barrels, bomba is associated with colonial slave plantation culture. Like Cuban rumba, it features heightened interaction between drummers and dancers and is categorized into subgenres according to tempo, meter, and polyrhythmic patterns (see Dufrasne-González 1994). Adaptations of bomba by groups such as Cortijo y su Combo and later salsa bands highlighted the basic patterns of the common 4/4 *bomba sicá* rhythm (Figure 1.4).

Plena, on the other hand, emerged at the turn of the last century among Afro-Puerto Rican migrant laborers living in the city of Ponce. It is less rhythmically complex than bomba and is performed on frame hand drums known as *panderetas*. Its characteristic pattern is notated in Figure 1.5.

Figure 1.4   Basic *bomba* rhythm

Figure 1.5   Basic *plena* rhythm

Plena's principal attraction lies in its topical lyrics, which, as with the Trinidadian calypso, Jamaican mento, and other Caribbean genres, have earned it the sobriquet "the singing newspaper." Although still widely performed in its traditional instrumentation, plena underwent several transformations during the first half of the twentieth century, when it was adapted to cosmopolitan dance band formats (see Glasser 1995 for details).

The Cuban Predominance in Música Antillana

The predominance of Cuban artists and styles in música antillana is related to the strong political and economic ties between Cuba and the United States in the first half of this century. This led to the diffusion of Cuban sounds over and above other Latin American styles—including the Argentine tango, internationally popular during the first two decades of the century (Savigliano 1995), though it never had the long-lasting commercial impact of Cuban styles. Cuba's strategic position in the Caribbean made it a prime center of economic activity under Spanish colonialism, which it continued to enjoy under a reign of virtual economic domination by U.S. business interests from the time of the Spanish-American War in 1898 until the Cuban Revolution in 1959.

The development of improved transportation and communications links between Cuba and the United States facilitated travel, especially between Havana and New York. Buoyed by American dollars and unhampered by Prohibition, Cuba became a tropical playground for Americans from the 1920s through the 1950s.[18] The popularization of the Cuban son during the 1930s, introduced to U.S. audiences in the watered-down form known as rhumba, usurped tango's position as the most popular Latin American dance in North America and Europe (Roberts 1979). The popularity of Cuban rhumba in North America during the 1930s, followed by the widespread mambo dance craze of the late 1940s and 1950s, served to reinforce North America's affinity for the island.

Havana became the "Paris of the Caribbean," an exotic and cosmopolitan city scarcely ninety miles from Miami. This glittering image spread to other Latin American centers, especially through films, reinforcing the growing popularity of Cuban music throughout Mexico, South America and the Caribbean.

In the meantime, U.S. recording companies such as RCA Victor and Columbia began recording an unprecedented number of Cuban artists and groups, first bringing musicians to their studios in New York and later setting up recording facilities in Havana. Between 1925 and 1928 alone, hundreds of son, guaracha,and bolero compositions were recorded by such important groups as the Sexteto Boloña, the Sexteto Habanero, the Sexteto and Septeto Nacional, the Trio Matamoros, and María Teresa Vera. The number of artists and recordings increased throughout the 1930s, 1940s, and 1950, and recordings were distributed not only throughout the Americas, but also in Europe and even Africa.[19] Although these companies also recorded a number of other Latin American musical styles, many of these recordings received limited production and distribution runs, confined to specific "ethnic" series. Cuban artists, however, were placed both in specialized series and in the general mainstream catalog (Spottswood 1990). Recordings of Cuban music also entered the cities of Guayaquil, Ecuador, and Lima, Peru, on South America's Pacific coast—brought by sailors traveling through the Panama Canal who docked regularly at these major ports. Local radio stations throughout Latin America featured these records, and in countries or regions situated on the Caribbean, Cuban radio could be picked up via shortwave radio sets. Since live-to-air musical broadcasts were a mainstay of Cuban radio programming, the nightly performances of groups such as the Sonora Matancera, Arcaño y sus Maravillas, the Orquesta Aragón, and Benny Moré were heard simultaneously by listeners not only in Havana , but also those in points as far-flung as San Juan, Veracruz, Panama City, Caracas, and Barranquilla.

Concert tours and movie appearances strengthened the popularity of Cuban artists. Groups such as the Trio Matamoros visited several Latin American countries in tours that lasted months. Musical films in the 1940s and 1950s—most of them made in Mexico City—further increased the presence of Cuban musicians in Latin America. Stars such as Daniel Santos gained tremendous international popularity not only through live appearances but also through movie musicals such as *El angel caído* (1948). In the circular loop characteristic of twentieth-century mass popular culture, Cuban musicians were popularized through record promotion, but their records sold well because of concert and (in some cases) movie appearances, which increased their popularity, which sold more records, which brought them back for more concerts, and so forth.

Cuban music had a particularly strong impact in Puerto Rico (see Manuel 1994). This musical interchange has its roots in the close historical ties between Cuba and Puerto Rico. These links, both political and cultural, emerge from the fact that they were the last remaining Latin American colonies of the Spanish Empire and remained virtual or (in the case of Puerto Rico) literal colonies of the United States through the first half of the twentieth century. The islands constituted "the Caribbean" for the United States, and because of this they provided more economic and political gains than the neighboring Dominican Republic, which—despite a similar colonial history—failed to establish a solid export-oriented exchange economy (Martínez Fernández 1994: 58). According to Martínez Fernández, despite the potential profits that investment in the Dominican Republic promised in the last century, internal "political instability, the threat of Haitian aggression, and the zealous interference of European merchants and consuls blocked such economic endeavors," essentially cutting the country off from the Atlantic-Caribbean commercial system (1994: 94–95). Cuba and Puerto Rico were thus in a much better position for their musical expressions to be diffused to the rest of the hemisphere, and of the two, Cuba was the stronger, because of its geographic proximity to the United States and its larger economic base. (Some observers say that Puerto Rico's current affluence resulted from the shift in U.S. tourist–oriented development after the 1959 revolution terminated such investment in Cuba.[20])

United States record producers clearly felt that they had a more profitable commodity with Cuban popular music than with other styles. The fact that Cuban songs are in Spanish made Hispanic Latin America an obvious target for promotion of Cuban recordings, but it is probable that Cuba's economic subordination and proximity to the United States contributed to the predilection of New York record companies for Cuban artists. The economic ties between and geographic proximity of these two countries certainly stimulated migration from Cuba to New York, and many Cuban musicians headed north in search of work and opportunities. New York's economic strength and position as a principal international communications and entertainment center in turn launched this Cuban presence into the world.

Hollywood's images also influenced the international glamour tied to Cuban sounds. For instance, the movies of Fred Astaire and Ginger Rogers (great favorites in Cali) frequently featured Cuban music, usually in the simplified rhumba form. For U.S. audiences, Cuba was seen as exotic, but not too exotic, and hence became an ideal, unthreatening other for North American projections and fantasies. While Mexicans were stereotypically portrayed as rural, sombrero-wearing bumpkins, Argentines were conventionally typecast as smoldering Latin lovers. Brazilians were presented as hot-blooded but frivolous, embodied in the image of Carmen Miranda and her ridiculous fruit-bowl headdresses. Cubans, however, were exuberant and festive, sexy but also charming, fun but not mawkish—in other words, enticing but safe. Compare the domesticated exoticism of Desi Arnaz, for example, who romped through the nation's living rooms every week as Ricky Ricardo, Lucy's cute Cuban hubby, with the dark and slightly menacing sensuality of the Argentine tango dancer epitomized by Rudolph Valentino (Pérez Firmat 1994: 61–63). These images influenced Latin American consumption patterns. Although música antillana was promoted and controlled through a highly impersonal industry, the key link to its popularity was its level of face-to-face enjoyment. Certainly, dancing to Cuban music was perceived as fun, and for many, the rhythms of rumba, conga, and mambo were more compelling than, say, the melancholy, marchlike compass of the tango. The joy and release generated in the intimate, vital physicality of dance and motion has contributed most directly to Cuban music's widespread adoption, reinforcing the commercial channels through which it attained prominence. It is this affective power, ultimately, that transcended geographic and cultural boundaries to literally move thousands.

Puerto Rican artists also performed Cuban music and creatively reworked Cuban elements to create new Puerto Rican expressions that became internationally popular (Manuel 1994). By the 1950s, Puerto Rico's most popular dance band—Cortijo y su Combo—performed Puerto Rican bomba and plena on Cuban percussion instruments instead of Puerto Rican drums. While the Cuban influence in música antillana is often overstated, Puerto Ricans not only adopted Cuban elements but also transformed them into musical vehicles that expressed a distinct Puerto Rican sensibility. As Ruth Glasser notes, "Puerto Ricans on the island and the mainland did not adopt Cuban music wholesale to the detriment of their own traditions but incorporated it into an ever-evolving repertoire of available cultural materials" (1995: 6). The hegemony of Cuban styles and artists in música antillana history is based on the predominance of Cuban instruments, rhythms, genres, and artists who were recorded, filmed, and distributed far more widely than were their Puerto Rican counterparts. I am not entirely comfortable, however, with the Cuba-centered discourse of many Latin music specialists. I think the Colombian term "música antillana" is actually more useful in this regard, since it does open a conceptual space for thinking about the historical ties that linked Cuba and Puerto Rico and led to the emergence of a transnational sound that by the 1950s could no longer be contained solely by the label "Cuban music."

From Música Antillana to Salsa:
The Sonora Matancera and Cortijo y su Combo

Two of the most important groups to play a role in the transition from música antillana to salsa were Cuba's Sonora Matancera and Puerto Rico's Cortijo y su Combo. Although the style established by the Cuban innovator Arsenio Rodríguez and continued by the conjunto of Felix Chappotín and Miguelito Cuní[21] was also important for several New York musicians and collectors, many productions made by Fania Records in the 1970s were modeled directly on the sound of the Sonora Matancera. In fact, one of salsa's biggest stars from this period—Celia Cruz—was a key vocalist with the Matancera in the 1950s and recorded nearly identical versions of her former hits for Fania with a band directed by Johnny Pacheco. Pacheco also produced several albums in this vein with other musicians. The salsa historian Cesar Miguel Rondón criticized this trend, accusing Pacheco of strangling salsa's innovative potential by "Matancerizing" the industry and imposing a commercial formula based on the old 1950s sound (1980: 90). Indeed, a retrospective of classic 1960s and 1970s New York salsa can be envisioned as a beast with three heads: one in the experimental vein led by Eddie Palmieri and Willie Colón; a second, "heavy" one in the Arsenio-Chappotín vein, led by Larry Harlow and Ray Barretto; and a third in the lighter Matancera style, led by Johnny Pacheco and Celia Cruz, that at times appeared to overpower the others. Of course, these schools are interrelated, and to an outsider the differences between these artists may not be clear—after all, "it's all salsa." To aficionados, however, their stylistic nuances are marked.

Puerto Rico, in turn, had its own schools, growing out of the combined influence of Cortijo and also the Sonora Matancera. The most famous group, El Gran Combo de Puerto Rico, was founded in 1962 by members of Cortijo's original combo after Rafael Cortijo and his lead vocalist, Ismael Rivera, were incarcerated for drug possession. El Gran Combo carried Cortijo's legacy into the 1960s and 1970s, even after Cortijo and Rivera formed salsa bands of their own. Puerto Rico's other principal band, the Sonora Ponceña, was founded during the 1950s. Originally modeled on Cuba's Sonora Matancera, the Ponceña underwent several transitions and by the mid-1970s emerged with a style that retained the bright trumpets of its Cuban model but was fused with the heavy sound of the Arsenio school and the dynamic delivery of the Cortijo school. Marisol Berríos-Miranda notes that Rafael Cortijo and Ismael Rivera also had a significant influence on Venezuelan salsa musicians (1999).

In order to understand the impact of the above groups on Caleño audiences, it is worth examining the stylistic elements that characterized the Sonora Matancera and Cortijo y su Combo—the two most-loved música antillana ensembles in Cali. The Sonora Matancera featured a modified version of the Havana conjunto format established by the pioneer Arsenio Rodríguez, with only two trumpets in place of the three or four featured by Rodriguez and his successor Chappotín. When Caleño música antillana fans discuss the local popularity of the Matancera, they often refer precisely to these trumpets, which had a very bright timbre and piercing projection. In addition, the Matancera's sound was characterized by the crisp detonation of the maracas, the distinct nasal quality of the coros (backup vocals), and the fluid, driving montunos of pianist Lino Frias. The principal draw of the Sonora Matanacera for its international audiences, however, was in its gallery of vocalists, which included some of the most legendary singers of música antillana: Daniel Santos, Bienvenido Granda, Celia Cruz, Nelson Pinedo (an expatriate Colombian from Barranquilla), Leo Marini, Miguelito Valdes, and Alberto Beltrán, among others (see Ramírez Bedoya 1996; Valverde 1997). These artists left a musical legacy that was popular not only in Cuba, but also served to define the Cuban sound for many listeners outside of Cuba.[22] These songs expressed scenes of daily life and relationships, and although they reflected primarily a Cuban or Caribbean context, Caleño audiences identified greatly with the lyrics.

Among the singers who established the Matancera's international fame, the two who have had the most profound impact in Cali have been Daniel Santos and Celia Cruz. Santos, born in San Juan, Puerto Rico, rose to fame in the 1940s as a kind of Latin Frank Sinatra, fronting groups such as that of Pedro Flores in Puerto Rico and the Sonora Matancera in Cuba. His scandalous drinking sprees, drug use, love affairs, and marriages added to his celebrity. After leaving the Sonora in 1953, Daniel Santos continued performing as a solo artist. He toured Colombia frequently during the 1950s and 1960s and in Cali often performed with Tito Cortes's Los Cali Boys, a local Cuban-style conjunto renamed La Sonora Cali after their first concert together in 1953. Santos always stayed in Cali's Zona de Tolerancia (redlight district) during these visits, and stories of his marijuana habit and crazy exploits became legendary. Rumor has it that he even had an official license to smoke cannabis (Ulloa 1992: 371.) His songs also reflected this figure of the romantic *camaján,* the barrio hustler—a smooth talker, ladies' man, good dresser and skilled dancer. Eventually, in the 1980s, he married a young Caleña decades his junior and bought a farm close to Cali. No doubt the local contact with such a bohemian and famous character as Santos reinforced his tremendous local popularity, already established through the witticism of his songs and the deep, mellow voice in which he sang them. [Santos] was one of the first commercially popular Caribbean singers to become famous for his mastery of the Cuban musical convention of *sonerismo,* or skilled vocal improvisation, for which other Puerto Rican singers such as Ismael Rivera and later salsa vocalists became famous.

Celia Cruz is the best-known female *música antillana* artist, and her fame continued through her transition from son to salsa. A native of Havana, she rose to stardom in the 1950s with the Sonora Matancera[23] before leaving Cuba for New York in 1961. Under the aegis of Johnny Pacheco, she began recording with Fania records in the late 1960s, helping to popularize a brand of salsa based essentially on the old Matancera sound. Cruz's majestic voice and extraordinary vitality onstage have marked her as the grand dame of Latin music, and in the salsa world she holds a position similar to that of opera divas such as Maria Callas or great jazz vocalists such as Ella Fitzgerald. In Cali, Cruz is best known as *la reina rumba*—the queen of the party. While it is de rigueur for most Latina musicians to acknowledge Cruz as a point of inspiration for their careers, in Cali she has acquired a special position, making her influence even more significant for local woman musicians (see Waxer 2001a). Her recordings and tours with the Sonora Matancera during the 1950s made Cruz a local favorite, and by the time she appeared in Cali with the Fania All-Stars in 1980 she was already a legendary figure. Umberto Valverde's 1981 biographical tribute to her, *Celia Cruz: reina rumba* (1981), based on interviews conducted with her during that 1980 tour, is particularly significant given her prominence among local fans.[24] Cruz's regular concert appearances in the city since 1980 have consolidated her presence as a key performer for Cali's salsa fans. In 1994 the Caleña all-woman salsa band D'Caché recorded an album also titled *Reina rumba,* whose title cut is dedicated to Celia Cruz.

Cortijo y su Combo, led by the percussionist Rafael Cortijo during the 1950s, is considered by aficionados throughout Latin America to be the most important and most popular Puerto Rican ensemble of its time. Like the Sonora Matancera, the group was also based on the small Cuban conjunto format but featured two trumpets and two saxophones, bridging the gap between groups with the larger dance-band instrumentation and the smaller conjuntos. This trumpet-saxophone combination was copied by many Colombian ensembles of the time. While Cortijo's group performed Cuban genres such as guaracha, son, and bolero, his fame stems principally from his adaptation of Afro-Puerto Rican bombas and plenas to the conjunto format. Cortijo's predecessor, Cesar Concepción, had attempted to fashion a cosmopolitan sound for these traditional genres in the 1940s, writing bombas and plenas for large dance orquestas, but in the process he lost much of the dynamism and vitality of the traditional style (Pagano 1993: 18). The ten members of Cortijo's combo, however, performed in a lively and spontaneous manner, animating their live shows and television appearances with energetic dance routines. According to the famed salsa composer and musicologist Tite Curet Alonso, Cortijo's band revolutionized Latin popular music by using dance choreography as a way to fill up the visual space left on the stage by the absence of a full dance orchestra.[25] These lively dance routines were continued by El Gran Combo and became a standard for 1970s salsa bands throughout Latin America.[26]

Of particular importance to Cortijo's unique sound was his lead vocalist, Ismael Rivera. Rivera, known as Maelo, had a distinct vocal timbre (both growly and nasal) that caught on widely with listeners. Gifted with an extraordinary talent for improvising pregones, Rivera truly merited the title granted him by Cuba's own Benny Moré: *el sonero mayor* (the greatest sonero).[27] After Cortijo's original group disbanded in 1962 (many of the members left to form El Gran Combo), Rivera continued as leader of his own group, Los Cachimbos. By the early 1970s he had become one of the premier salsa vocalists of the time, and he continued performing until his death in 1987. Rivera's impressive abilities as a sonero, in turn, stem from the Puerto Rican tradition of improvising *décimas,* lyric verses with a fixed ten-line poetic structure. In this tradition, emphasis is placed not only on improvising a pleasing combination of words and rhymes, but at the same time telling a good story. In montuno sections Rivera was able to spin out dozens of pregones on the spot, all thematically related and able to keep listeners engaged. Daniel Santos, already famous by the time Rivera emerged in the early 1950s, is another Puerto Rican vocalist with tremendous gifts as a sonero.

The ability to improvise verses characterized the great Cuban soneros of the 1940s and 1950s—Benny Moré, Miguelito Cuní, Miguelito Valdes, Orlando "Cascarita" Guerra, Celia Cruz, and the New York–based Machito were all talented vocalists in this regard. Since 1960, however, surprisingly few Cuban singers have emerged who match this old school.[28] In Puerto Rico, however, Maelo's example spawned a whole succession of talented soneros who became legendary salsa vocalists during the 1960s and 1970s: Hector Lavoe, Cheo Feliciano, Pete "El Conde" Rodríguez, Marvin Santiago, and Cano Estremera. Although the art of improvised soneros has diminished greatly with the current generation of romantic salsa singers, who sing precomposed lines, Puerto Rican vocalists such as Gilberto Santarosa maintain the sonero tradition. Despite the extensive literature on salsa, few commentators have pointed to this quality as a specific contribution of Puerto Rican artists to the development of salsa.[29] No other country has produced the quantity and quality of salsa soneros that Puerto Rico has—even recognized salsa vocalists such as Venezuela's Oscar D'León and Panama's Rubén Blades do not have the improvisational skills displayed by Puerto Rico's premier salsa singers. Although scholars have recognized the great ability of Puerto Rican vocalists, usually this comment passes without further analysis.

Música Antillana and Música Tropical in Colombia

Música antillana first reached Colombian shores in the early 1920s, through Cuban radio broadcasts from Havana. Live programs on Radio Progreso, CMQ, and La Cadena Azul—the principal Cuban stations—could be picked up by shortwave radio sets on the Atlantic coast of Colombia and as far inland as Medellín. One shortwave radio hound told me that during the 1950s he had received signals from Havana stations as far as Cali.[30] Tuning in to Cuban radio seems to have been a fairly regular practice among musicians and aficionados in Colombia's Atlantic coast, at least through the early 1940s, when national stations began to flower and local airspace began filling up, blocking radio airwaves from Cuba (Múnera 1992).[31] According to Adolfo González, "The musical programming of these stations was so influential that, for many of the best Costeño musicians, tuning in was a pressing daily task that provided inspiration and prime material for their work. From this moment, the Cuban contribution was predominant and absolutely necessary to produce the most lively popular music in the country" (1989: 41).

The advent of música antillana in Colombia was prefaced by the development of national and transnational transport and commerce since the second half of the nineteenth century. Increased contact and trade with the Caribbean region through the late 1800s, as well as with the United States, opened the doors for outside cultural influences. Urbanization and industrial expansion through the first half of the twentieth century grew hand in hand with channels of transportation, communication, and musical diffusion. In the first part of this century, a steady transnational flow of people, musicians, sounds, and ideas began linking Colombian cities to other urban centers in Latin America and the United States. With the evolution of mass media between the two world wars, the flow of musical styles through the Americas spread even more rapidly, via recordings, radio, film, and concert tours. The popular dance music of this time reflected and also contributed to this process. Cuban and North American styles were particularly influential and were listened and danced to in Colombia's urban centers. Regional Colombian traditions were also fused with cosmopolitan musical practices and styles for city audiences.

Through radio broadcasts, musicians and fans were introduced to the sounds of Cuban son, played by groups such as the Trio Matamoros and conjuntos such as the Sexteto Habanero and Septeto Nacional. The sounds of danzón were also popularized, played by such charanga ensembles as that of Antonio Romeu and, later, the famed *radiofónica* of Antonio Arcaño. In these early decades of radio, from the 1920s through the 1950s, bands performed live-to-air in radio theater studios (see López 1981). Hence, those perched by their shortwave radio sets in Colombia actually heard the music as it was being performed in Havana.

Records have comprised the most important avenue of diffusion for música antillana in Colombia. The first 78 rpm records arrived with sailors docking in Barranquilla, Colombia's principal port on the Caribbean. Indeed, Barranquilleros, when challenging Cali's claim to be the Colombian stronghold of this musical tradition, often point to the fact that música antillana arrived first in their city. Exact dates of the first Cuban recordings in Colombia are uncertain, but González notes that local newspaper advertisements for Cuban music appear by September 1927 (1989: 41). Radio stations in Barranquilla purchased recordings of Cuban music for local airplay, a practice that continued through the 1950s.[32] Recordings of música antillana soon found their way into other urban centres in Colombia, brought through the main ports of Barranquilla and Buenaventura (on the Pacific) by sailors or by special dealers traveling directly from New York, then the capital of the recording industry. In the late 1940s the Colombian record mogul Antonio Fuentes purchased national distribution rights for recordings made by several Cuban artists. The 1950 catalog of his company, DiscosFuentes, lists such groups as the Sonora Matancera, Orquesta Riverside, Hermanos Castro, and Miguelito Valdés (Betancur 1993: 288). Most records of música antillana, however, arrived in Colombia via sailors in Barranquilla, Cartagena, and Buenaventura. The difficulty of obtaining recordings heightened their value as consumer items and contributed to the cachet this music had already acquired as an index of cosmopolitan cultural identity. Owing to Cali's geographical distance from the Caribbean, many of the Cuban bands touring Colombia did not include Cali on their itinerary; thus, recordings became all the more important as a source of this music.

González notes that radio and record diffusion intensified the process of contact, hitherto intermittent, between Cuban and Colombian musicians and audiences. Such contacts had been established in the nineteenth century by individuals who traveled from Cuba to Colombia and vice versa. Trade between Cuba and Colombia's Atlantic coast—centered around tobacco, coffee, and livestock—was established in the second half of the 1800s (Posada-Carbó 1996). Cuban and also Dominican migrants settled in various towns along the coast, some near Mompox and some further east, near Valledupar. Among these settlers were Cuban musicians including the great accordionist Hernando Rivero—better known as Nendito El Cubano—who left his native Manzanillo in 1878 shortly before Cuba's war for independence.[33] Colombian musicians who went to Cuba in the 1880s and 1890s to help fight for Cuban independence brought Cuban musical styles back home with them and also introduced Colombian genres, such as the bambuco, to Cubans (Betancur 1993). The extent of Colombo-Cuban contact was perhaps best symbolized by the construction in 1889 at Puerto Colombia of a huge dock, designed by the famous Cuban engineer and *independentista* Francisco Javier Cisneros. This public work, some thirty kilometers east of Barranquilla, was built to facilitate transport connections, since Barranquilla's location in the sandy Magdalena River delta prevented larger ships from landing there.

During the 1940s and 1950s Cuban, Puerto Rican, and Mexican performers appeared in widely distributed movie musicals. For many viewers, films starring Miguelito Valdés, Daniel Santos, and Bobby Capó were the first and perhaps only opportunity to see these famous vocalists. Famous scenes from *Acapulqueña* (1947), where Valdés performs his signature "Mr. Babalú" number,[34] and Daniel Santos's rendition of the guaracha "Tíbiri Tabará" in *El angel caido* (1948) are still occasionally featured on large videoscreens in Cali's tabernas. Another important musician was the "mambo king," Pérez Prado, who popularized this sound not only through his recordings, but in films such as *Al son de mambo* and *Qué rico el mambo,* which played in movie theaters throughout the country (Betancur 1993: 288). Such musicians not only played and sang in this films—they also danced, providing images of corporal expression to go along with the music. Dynamic screen dancers such as Tin Tán, Resortes, Antonietta Pons, and Tongolele, however, really fired the imagination of local dancers, especially those in Cali. These dancers, Mexican artists who had adopted and refined Cuban styles, were key in disseminating the popular dances of música antillana.

In conjunction with growing channels of mass mediation for the diffusion of música antillana to Colombian shores, improved transportation links facilitated regular concert tours by Cuban and Puerto Rican artists, reinforcing the presence of música antillana for Colombian audiences. Visits by Cuban musicians had already been established before the turn of the century but increased greatly after the 1930s. Fabio Betancur scrupulously documents the concert appearances by these leading artists; his description serves as the basis for my discussion here (1993: 201–299). Owing to their location on the Caribbean, Cartagena and Barranquilla became principal destinations for touring artists; no doubt geographic conditions and ease of travel made it more feasible for entrepreneurs in these cities to contract Cuban and Puerto Rican artists than for those farther away in Cali. Although Cuba's acclaimed Trio Matamoros visited Cali during their 1933 tour, it was not a regular stop on many of the concert tours of música antillana performers until the 1950s and 1960s. Artists did frequently travel to Bogotá and Medellín, however, since they were important economic and political centers with enough resources to support concert tour appearances. Social clubs in these cities often contracted major Cuban orquestas such as the Sonora Matancera or Benny Moré for carnival balls and other fiestas. During these visits Cuban and Puerto Rican musicians also made appearances in local concert halls and radio theaters that were open to the general public. Cesar Machado recalls that during the December Ferias of the late 1950s and early 1960s, radio stations in Cali competed for the opportunity to broadcast live-to-air performances of the most famous visiting artists, backed by radio house bands.[35]

In keeping with the cosmopolitan aspirations of urban Colombian audiences, Colombian dance orquestas — like their counterparts in other Latin American cities — performed a variety of international popular musical genres. These included North American fox-trot and charleston, Argentine tango, Spanish *pasodoble,* and Cuban genres such as son (rhumba),[36] guaracha, bolero, and by the late 1940s and early 1950s, mambo and chachachá. More significantly, however, they adapted national styles to dance band arrangements, performing genres such as bambuco, *pasillo,* cumbia, *porro* and *gaita.* By the 1940s, cosmopolitan adaptations of Atlantic coast folkloric styles such as cumbia, porro, and gaita coalesced into a style known in Colombia as música tropical. Colombia's most prominent dance orquestas of this period — led by Lucho Bermúdez and Pacho Galán, respectively — were leaders of the música tropical style. Both hailed from Colombia's Atlantic coast, but owing to their national fame, they worked at hotels and salons in Medellín and Bogotá and also made regular appearances on national television into the 1960s.

In musical terms, música tropical is distinguished from música antillana

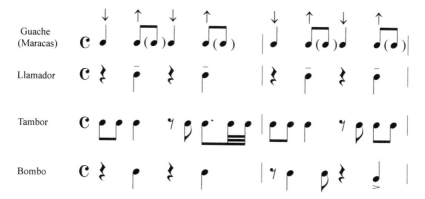

Figure 1.6   *Cumbia* and *porro* rhythmic patterns used for *música tropical*

by a simpler rhythmic treatment and a more florid melodic style. Rather than the syncopated habanera bass or anticipated bass pattern of música antillana, música tropical uses a basic tonic-dominant pattern that falls on beats one and three of each measure. The rhythmic patterns of traditional cumbia ensembles such as the *conjunto de gaita* are often transferred to Cuban percussion in música tropical dance bands (Figure 1.6). The *llamador* drum, which traditionally played the basic accents on beats two and four, is replaced by Cuban conga drums, and the contrasting *bombo* (bass drum) pattern is played by the larger conga drum (*tumba*). The improvised rhythmic fills traditionally played by the *tambor* may be omitted altogether or played on bongo or even North American drum set. Accents on beats two and four are also played on large *guaches* (maracas)—the one Costeño percussion instrument typically retained in música tropical ensembles. During the horn choruses, a ride cymbal is struck for additional emphasis. Melodic phrases in música tropical, unlike those in música antillana, emphasize downbeats more than offbeats. Melodic style in música tropical leans toward a wider melodic range than that of música antillana and extensive triadic arpeggiation. Horn lines are shorter than those used in música antillana and are often based on repeated melodic cells (Figure 1.7). Although call-and-response refrains are common in música tropical, as in many genres originating in the Caribbean region, these sections do not have the rhythmic improvisation and interplay characteristic of the montuno section in Cuban-based styles. Rather, the emphasis is on catchy melodies, saucy lyrics, and a basic dance beat.

According to Peter Wade, the adoption of música tropical in the Colombian interior emerged from a number of complex changes in the national

Figure 1.7   Typical melodic cells in *música tropical*

cultural landscape. A "home-grown" version of música antillana, música tropical developed as part of a process of incorporating regional and cultural differences, based on race and class, during a time when Colombian political leaders were searching for new symbols of national identity (2000). Indeed, the national rise of música tropical marks a shift in domestic politics from cloistered regionalism toward some sense of national identity that incorporated all regional cultures and differences within Colombian borders. Wade analyzes this in terms of a "transformist hegemony" whereby potentially disruptive elements from a minority cultural group (black and mulato Costeños) were absorbed and neutralized, in contrast to earlier periods when they were scorned and rejected by the Colombian elite. During the 1940s música tropical was seen by audiences in Bogotá and Medellín as something new, exotic, and somewhat foreign. It became quickly accepted by young cosmopolitan elites and soon swept the country by storm. In Buenaventura, on Colombia's Pacific coast, musicians experimented with similar adaptations of traditional currulao to the dance orquesta format in the 1950s and 1960s, but these orquestas did not have the same resources or entrepreneurial drive as Costeño bands such as Bermúdez's, and their endeavors remained localized (Waxer 2001b).[37] Ironically, música tropical succeeded in uniting people on the nation's urban dance floors at the same time that the grisly civil war known as La Violencia (1948–58) was tearing the countryside apart. According to Wade, the adoption of a happy, tropical musical style served in part to offset the overpowering images of this violence (2000: 229).

Not all Colombians, however, appreciated the charms of música antillana and música tropical. Older and more conservative sectors were scandalized by the frenetic rhythms that were sweeping the nation's ballrooms. In a sermon delivered in 1952, the bishop of Antioquia diocese (one of the most powerful in the country) condemned the mambo and música tropical as "a mortal sin and scandalous dance" that upright Catholics should avoid (Betancur 1993: 289).[38] One also wonders whether the proscription against this music had less to do with Christian morality than with racially tinged anxieties that Colombian tastes would be dangerously touched by the tar brush, which would threaten the social power of the white ruling elite. The interdiction against the "scandalous dances" of música antillana and música tropical also points to an upper-class prejudice against lower-class styles. Through most of the twentieth century, the Catholic church was a bastion of conservative political and economic values in Colombia, closely aligned with the country's powerful oligarchies. The negative pronouncements against the mambo and other new sounds in the 1950s is a somewhat predictable example of establishment reaction to popular forces that threatened to subvert the social control of the dominating classes. Such denunciations tended to fall on deaf ears, however. For both the upper echelons who consumed música antillana as part of a cosmopolitan musical smorgasbord and those in the lower classes who were adopting and resignifying these sounds as part of local popular tradition, música antillana had become an important musical stream in Colombia.

Toward the late 1960s a simplified variant of música tropical emerged, known in Colombia as *raspa* or *chucu-chucu*. Marketed widely by the national record industry, this style abridged the música tropical orquesta, using electric bass and keyboards, drum kit, and only two or three horns, usually trumpets or saxophones. The rhythmic swing and complexity of Costeño rhythms was reduced to a basic pattern of a quarter note and two eighth notes, played on *guacharaca* (scraper) or woodblock, and arrangements were characterized by gimmicky electric organ sounds and formulaic melodies and harmonies. Groups such as Gustavo Quintero y Los Graduados modeled their haircuts, uniforms, and album covers on the stock 1960s international pop image established by the Beatles. Raspa bands became popular mainly among middle-class audiences in Bogotá and Medellín (Wade 2000: 144–86). Other Colombians consider raspa to be a degradation of música tropical, a banal musical product (Ulloa 1992: 403). Ironically, however, recordings by Colombian raspa bands such as the Sonora Dinamita became very popular in Mexico, Central America, and the Andean region, establishing the basis for a simplified style of cumbia that has become extremely important in those countries. It is this style that is most commonly identified outside Colombia as cumbia—the more rhythmically complex styles of Afro-Colombian folkloric cumbia and even 1940s música tropical are relatively unknown beyond Colombian borders. In chapter 6 I discuss the tension between raspa and salsa fans in Cali during the late 1960s and early 1970s, especially as it coalesced symbolically around the appearance of Los Graduados opposite the New York salsa stars Richie Ray and Bobby Cruz at the 1969 Feria.

Música Antillana and Música Tropical in Cali

During the late nineteenth century and the first three decades of the twentieth century, musical life in Cali centered around brass and wind bands that performed for religious fiestas and also gave Sunday afternoon concerts in the Plaza Caicedo, Cali's urban and commercial center (Figure 1.8). Such ensembles were common throughout Colombian cities and towns during this period (Wade 2000: 48) and did not establish a particularly Caleño musical identity. Some of the more prominent groups of the early twentieth century were the Banda de Garrón de Puerco, the Banda de los Porrongos, and the military band of the Pichincha Battalion, located downtown at the time. According to Alejandro Ulloa, these bands performed an eclectic mix of styles that included Colombian música andina (bambucos, pasillos, guabinas, and torbellinos), Spanish pasodobles, North American fox-trots, Cuban contradanzas, and European light classics. Both rich and poor attended town band performances, although during the Sunday concerts in Plaza Caicedo they sat in different areas of the park. Notably, as Ulloa observes, these performances constituted the first form of collective public listening to music in Cali (Ulloa 1992: 341).

Other Caleño musical contexts in the early twentieth century included choral and instrumental performances of religious music; small ensembles that performed during interludes at local cinemas; touring *zarzuela* (operetta) productions; and evening soirées among the elites, where European classical chamber music and Colombian música andina, played by small string ensembles (*tiple, bandola,* and guitar) were heard (Ulloa 1992: 341). These coexisted with the pan–Latin American tradition of *serenatas,* or street serenades performed by small groups of guitarists and other instruments. According to Ulloa, beyond public town band concerts, the majority of live musical contexts were restricted to Cali's upper classes. The burgeoning working class had its own zones for musical entertainment, primarily the bars and cafes that sprung up around the central marketplace, the loading docks by the Cauca River, and in the Zona de Tolerancia downtown. It is here that música antillana first entered Cali.

Surprisingly, regional musical traditions rooted in the areas surrounding Cali made few advances into the small city. The string-based música andina tradition based in the northern districts of Valle province was limited

Figure 1.8   Plaza Caicedo (c. 1925). Photo by Alberto Lenis

mainly to private gatherings in people's homes. The marimba-based currulao tradition of Colombia's southwest Pacific Coast region lay on the other
side of the western Andean cordillera that divided Cali from the sea. Although some observers speculate that the nineteenth-century author Jorge
Isaacs refers indirectly to currulao in his famous novel *María* (1867),[39] there
is little concrete historical evidence that currulao was actively practiced in
the Cauca Valley before migrants from the Pacific littoral brought currulao
to Cali in the late 1960s. (Indeed, it was not until in the late 1990s
that Caleño audiences became widely receptive to currulao; see Waxer
2001b). Finally, the tradition of religious songs performed in Puerto Tejada,
Santander de Quilichao, Villarica, Quinamayo, and other small Afro-
Colombian farming towns directly south of Cali seems to have been restricted to this area—probably for reasons of race and class—and had no
effect on urban musical life.

Música antillana was introduced to Cali in the 1930s by record vendors
and cabaret owners who first heard the strains of Cuban and Puerto Rican
music on visits to the nearby port of Buenaventura. The rhythms of música
antillana, brought inland to Cali's Zona de Tolerancia, became a mainstay of
the quarter's bars and brothels in the 1930s through the 1950s. Recordings
were the central vehicles in this musical culture and formed the basis for the
development of Cali's vibrant salsa dance scene in the 1960s and 1970s.

For most Caleño fans, the Sonora Matancera and Cortijo are synony-mous with the golden era of música antillana. The popularity of the Sonora Matancera and Cortijo in Cali may be partially accounted for by both com-mercial and aesthetic factors. In the case of the Sonora Matancera, the repertoire performed by the Matancera included several guarachas, sprightly upbeat numbers with a prominent rhythmic pattern ♩ ♫ ♪ ♫ similar to the porros and gaitas of música tropical and other Colombian genres. It is probable that the light, clean sound of the Sonora Matancera— closer to Colombian popular styles than the heavy, driving son montunos of Arsenio, for instance—also contributed to their predominance for Caleño fans. In addition, Cuban racial dynamics during the 1940s and 1950s directly affected performance venues and access to record production and distribution. At this time, Arsenio and Chappotín's conjuntos were ear-marked as "black" and the Sonora Matancera's as "white" or "mulato" (see D. García 1999). Although these racial distinctions did not in fact play out in terms of actual audience make-up—Cubans of diverse backgrounds en-joyed and listened to both bands—they did affect which clubs each band performed at and the record deals they obtained.

According to Pepe Valderruten, a Caleño expert on the Sonora Matan-cera, the ticket to the Matancera's popularity throughout Latin America lay in their contract with Sidney Siegal, the wealthy New York owner of Seeco Records, who signed the Matancera from 1950 to 1966 (Ramírez Bedoya 1996: 75) and promoted the group internationally.[40] Caleño aficionados cherished their 78 rpm recordings of the Matancera, locally dubbed *sonora-zos*. The records of Arsenio and the Chappotín-Cuni group were certainly enjoyed in Cali but paled in comparison to the local impact of the Sonora Matancera. I speculate that the greater popularity of the Sonora Matancera among Caleños stemmed not only from the sound of the group, but also from commercial factors related to the greater availability and promotion of their records. The Sonora Matancera's fame in Cali was reinforced by live concert tours during the 1950s and again in 1976 and 1985, along with Daniel Santos's frequent visits to the city through the 1950s and 1960s.

By the 1960s the sound of the Sonora Matancera had become so indeli-bly stamped on local (and even national) musical tastes that several Caleño ensembles modeled on this group had emerged, including La Sonora Cali (with Tito Cortés) and Los Hermanos Ospino. Even local salsa pioneers such as Julian Angulo and Piper Pimienta were strongly influenced by the Sonora Matancera's sound, as were later Caleño salsa bands such as Grupo Niche. The enthusiastic reception of the New York salsa stars Richie Ray and Bobby Cruz—whose 1968 appearance at the Cali Feria marked the first visit by an international salsa band—was also predicated on the sharp, clean lines of Ray's sound, modeled in the tradition of the Sonora Matancera.

The reasons for the success of Cortijo's group in Cali are less clear. I am able to account for this only by looking to the black Caribbean sailors who touched on Colombian shores and introduced Cortijo's records into Barranquilla, Cartagena, Buenaventura, and Cali during the 1950s. It is probable that many of these sailors were Puerto Rican and hence brought many recordings of Cortijo y su Combo, the most popular band among Afro–Puerto Ricans during the 1950s. Once introduced into Buenaventura and Cali, Cortijo's records no doubt caught on not only because of the catchy rhythms of bomba and plena, but also because of the band's infectious drive, the accessible, simple arrangements they performed, and—above all—Maelo's inimitable growly vocals.

During the 1940s and 1950s Cali had a small but active number of musical ensembles that performed at the larger cabarets, hotels, and radio stations, and—for the lucky ones—in the exclusive Club Colombia and the middle-class Club San Fernando (Ramírez Bedoya 1996: 367). These groups were divided into orquestas that performed música tropical and other international styles, including música antillana. Among them were the orquestas of Edmundo Arias, Efraín Orozco, Julio García, and Sebastián Solarí. By the 1950s, however, smaller groups modeled on the Sonora Matancera had also been established, using the conjunto format of two trumpets, piano, bass, conga, bongó and small percussion. Some groups, following the model of Cortijo y su Combo, also added two saxophones to their instrumentation. In Cali the most prominent groups included Los Cali Boys (later renamed La Sonora Cali and then Sonora Juventud) and the Hermanos Ospino. The local música tropical bandleader Edmundo Arias formed his own conjunto, the Sonora Antillana, to specialize in Cuban-style dance music. During this time, similar ensembles also appeared on Colombia's Atlantic coast (such as the Sonora Silver, formed by Lucho Bermúdez) and in Mexico and Venezuela (such as the Sonora Mexicana, the Sonora Veracruz, the Sonora Marinera, and the Sonora Caracas; Betancur 1993: 264).

Los Cali Boys of Tito Cortés and the Hermanos Ospino are generally remembered as being the most prominent Caleño bands of the 1950s. Cortés, a native of Tumaco, had a mellow and expressive tenor similar to that of the Sonora Matancera star Daniel Santos. Although celebrated for his renditions of the currulao "Mi Buenaventura" and the *vals* (waltz) "Alma

Tumaqueña" (a tribute to his home town of Tumaco), he was an established singer in the música antillana style right up until his death in 1996. With the dynamic inflection and rhythmic accents characteristic of good soneros, many of his tunes contained the witty and picaresque lyrics that made música antillana so popular with Caleño listeners. His song "El Gago" (The Stutterer), recorded in 1954, is a good example of this, demonstrating Cortés's ability to deliver a rapid string of tongue-twisting vocables with great rhythmic precision. According to the local record collector Pablo Solano, this tune was a favorite among Caleño audiences.[41] The Ospino brothers, who hailed originally from Barranquilla, were noted for the piercing, concise attack of their trumpets, so admired in the Sonora Matancera, and for their Cortijo-inspired instrumentation of three trumpets and three saxophones. Interestingly, some of the children and grandchildren of Tito Cortés and the Hermanos Ospino became prominent salsa musicians during the flowering of Cali's live scene in the 1980s and 1990s, carrying on the family tradition in the way that musical kin in Cuba and Puerto Rico do.

∿∿

During the 1950s, as Cali began to change from a sleepy provincial town into a dynamic urban hub, música tropical and música antillana competed for attention on the local music scene. While música tropical served in part to signal socioeconomic distinction—it was certainly the preferred style of the middle and upper classes, who scorned música antillana as a lowly and indecent working-class genre—Cali's large working-class population enjoyed and consumed both styles. Through the 1960s and 1970s, however, as Cali's identification with salsa grew stronger, música tropical waned in local cultural life. As raspa, the simplified variant of música tropical, gained popularity in the Colombian interior during the late 1960s and 1970s, Caleños turned their back on national tastes and asserted their allegiance to música antillana and salsa.

Notably, if we take Hernán González's recollections to be any sign of popular memory during the mid-1990s, the "holy music" that rained down during the creation of local popular culture is selectively remembered as being música antillana. While evidence shows that música tropical actually shared center stage with música antillana during the 1950s, it is usually remembered as a secondary style. My conversations about music with people at family or neighborhood dances and local nightclubs almost always highlighted the names of Cuban and Puerto Rican artists. When I asked, "What about música tropical?" people would usually respond, "Oh yes, we also listened to that, Lucho Bermúdez and so on, that was also important"—but these comments clearly followed my solicitation, as if memories of what actually happened needed jogging. My presence as a salsa researcher probably influenced people's tendency to foreground música antillana with me, but this discourse is also present in local journalism and public events, where I did not influence the privileging of música antillana and salsa.

Música antillana and salsa are central to processes of Caleño popular identity and memory because of the ways in which they were tied to experiences of the city's sudden growth, prompting the need to find a distinct cultural identity that mirrored social changes in this new urban environment. Although Caleño musical life during the nineteenth and early twentieth centuries certainly followed trends elsewhere in the country, Cali's rapid urbanization during the second half of the twentieth century created ruptures that broke previous cultural patterns and created spaces for new forms and tastes to emerge. During this same period, discourses about music and culture among Colombia's elites saw radical shifts in national musical identity, as the Costeño sound of música tropical replaced the bambucos and pasillos of música andina. It is little wonder, then, that Caleños, caught in the same moment of questioning, began to seek their own musical self-image. As a result, música antillana served to create a Caleño identification with the Caribbean—not Colombia's Caribbean, but a larger, imagined space that helped define the Caleño sense of difference from the nation. Cali's history of weak ties to the interior widened this rift.

Música tropical, although enjoyed and consumed by most Caleños, could not really serve to represent Cali because it was already emblematic of another region of the country. Life on Colombia's Atlantic coast, shaped by cattle ranching, banana plantations, and an arid, dusty environment, is quite distinct from that in the sugarcane fields and lush, verdant tropics of the Cauca Valley, which further heightened cultural differences between the two regions. Yet, the national adoption of an *alegre* (happy) tropical musical identity during the 1940s and 1950s as an antidote to the climate of extreme violence, mistrust, and bloody civil war must also have resonated in Cali; certainly the parallels arc too striking to ignore. As I discuss in chapter 2, the city's ranks swelled almost daily with displaced refugees from La Violencia. Hence, Caleños embraced their own brand of tropicality in música antillana. Ironically, however, the two groups that Caleños most loved—the Sonora Matancera and Cortijo y su Combo—were more popular than other Cuban and Puerto Rican conjuntos precisely because of their similarity to Costeño music, indicating local acceptance and internationalization of national musical aesthetics. The paradoxical nature of this process defies any linear explanation of Caleño popular culture. In his study of música tropical, Peter Wade presents a strong case for understanding modern Colombian popular culture as a complex and ambivalent process that constantly slips between homogeneity and difference, making it impossible to conceive of direct correlations between musical style, taste, and social position (2000: 25). It is not surprising to see this same tendency at work in Cali, although to different ends than in other parts of the country. While historical processes led to the incorporation of Atlantic coast música tropical into the national sphere, these same processes catalyzed a swing in the opposite direction for Caleños, toward the cosmopolitical adoption and re-signification of a transnational style: música antillana. It is this sound that became incorporated into the city's self-image, through the central practices of dancing and listening to records.

2
Memory and Movement in the Record-Centered Dance Scene

One of the most telling indicators of how important recordings are in Cali's musical culture was the unprecedented revival in 1995 of the old, record-centered dance scene. Looking for ways to increase flagging profits, local discotheques began holding Sunday afternoon dances called *viejotecas,* or "old-theques," borrowing the name from an activity initiated in a local senior citizens' club two years earlier. Initially restricted to people aged forty years and over, clubs soon abandoned the age barrier, and Caleños began flocking to the viejotecas en masse to dance to recordings of the old Cuban mambos, boleros, guarachas, and other genres that had been popular during the 1940 and 1950s. Pachanga and bugalú, two early forms of New York salsa that were enormously popular during the 1960s, were also added to the mix. By the end of 1995 nearly every nightclub in town featured viejoteca progams at least once a week, and several new establishments opened that featured viejoteca dance music all week long. Radio stations, long dominated by the music industry's promotion of new salsa, began to broadcast viejoteca shows hosted by famous local salsa radio announcers from the 1960s and 1970s. Even live viejoteca concerts were organized, bringing together aging New York salsa pioneers such as Joey Quijano and Joe Cuba to perform the old pachanga and bugalú hits they had popularized over thirty years earlier.

Much like the "golden oldies" revival in North America, the viejoteca phenomenon has tremendous implications for our understanding of the role that mediated music can play in the formation of local subjectivity, social identities, and popular memory. Indeed, Caleños even speak of their popular classics in much the same as North Americans do. Just as someone might refer to an old rock and roll hit as a "chestnut," Caleños will talk about favorite salsa and música antillana numbers as *panelas,* referring to the cake of compressed raw sugar used to sweeten many Colombian dishes and beverages. In both contexts, food terms redolent with sweet nostalgia are used to evoke images of an idealized past. Unlike the North American context, however, where popular records from the 1950s, 1960s, and 1970s are now used mainly for listening to (e.g., on radio shows and in rere-leases), Cali's viejotecas revived the actual dance scene that was centered around old recordings. In this process, Caleño subjectivity has been quite literally re-membered. Kinetic memories, stored in the body and main-tained through years of repeated (if somewhat less lively) dancing, sud-denly acquired new significance in the context of abrupt changes in Caleño social life in the mid-1990s.

The viejoteca phenomenon in Cali could hardly have been predicted in advance; like many unexpected subcultural booms, it seems to have emerged from nowhere to catch the city by storm. Yet, once established, the viejotecas seemed to be entirely natural, an organic return to the roots of lo-cal popular culture. Dancing to records of música antillana and salsa has long been a favorite practice in Cali. Through the 1960s and 1970s, instead of taking up instruments and imitating the sounds they heard on records, Caleños poured their creative energies into dancing, using recordings as the primary source for musical sound. Owing to the significance of records as cultural objects whose local meaning and value extended far beyond the catchy rhythms in their grooves, not until the 1980s did Caleños actually witness the development of a significant live performance scene. In hind-sight, the success of the viejotecas hinged on a good entrepreneurial read-ing of the desire held by many Caleño citizens to reconstruct their city as the place they recalled it to be. The viejotecas became a highly symbolic per-formance space that memorialized the history through which música anti-llana and salsa became emblems of local identity. In order to understand this phenomenon, we must trace the historical conditions under which records of this music first entered the city.

"Lo Que Trajo El Barco" (What the Ship Brought)

As both a product and a vehicle of mass media, recordings have played a pivotal role in the development of contemporary Caleño subjectivities, offering "new resources and new disciplines for the construction of imag-ined selves and imagined worlds" (Appadurai 1996: 3).[1] From the 1940s through the 1970s, "playing music" in Cali more often than not was literally a matter of sliding a nickel in the jukebox or spinning records on the old home gramophone. Unlike music scenes in other parts of urban Latin America, where records have served mainly as an adjunct to or tool for musical creation and live performance, in Cali recordings have constituted the focal point of musical activity, even though live music also began to flourish there in the early 1980s. Sound recordings have had such an influential presence in local popular culture that the Caleño vernacular word for "song" is *disco* (literally, record disc). It took me a while to become accustomed to such local usage, especially since the word is used as a synonym for *canción* or *tema*—that is, a single tune, not a whole album. "Vamos a bailar este disco" or "Tócame ese disco," for instance, means "Let's dance to this song" or "Perform that song for me." I have not heard this usage in other parts of Latin America, but its prevalence in Cali indicates the strong impact that recorded music has had on local cultural meanings. The impact of media technology on local musical concepts can be seen in another 1940s–50s term. The collector Pablo Solano recalls that during his childhood in Dagua, a town forty miles northwest of Cali, jukeboxes were jokingly referred to as "pianos," indicating the plasticity with which people humorously conceived of playback machines as musical instruments.[2]

Where did this process begin? Recordings of música antillana first entered Colombia's southwest region in the 1930s, through Buenaventura. As Cali's only immediate connection to routes of international transport and communications, Buenaventura was an important and active port, the first South American stop for ships passing through the Panama Canal before moving on to Guayaquíl, Lima, and down around the cape to Buenos Aires. Until Cali's international airport was built in 1970, maritime transport was the principal mode of travel for both commerce and leisure. Not only did cargo ships dock in the port, but also luxury ocean liners such as those of the Graceline fleet, which ran regular South American cruises from San Francisco before it folded in the early 1970s. For the upper classes of Cali and the surrounding regions, trips to Europe or North America for study or pleasure were the norm, and the only route was out through Buenaventura and the Panama Canal. These passenger ships provided live music, usually a Cuban-style dance orquesta that performed the standard cosmopolitan fare of fox-trots and Cuban rhumbas. Similar bands performed for tourists at the luxurious Hotel d'Estación, which was located next to the docks across from the train station that brought passengers to and from Cali.

From the 1930s through the early 1970s Buenaventura was a lively, cosmopolitan port, much more so than its current neglected condition would suggest.[3] The loading and unloading of cargo, the hustle of informal markets in the street, the arrival of glamorous cruisers and rich foreigners, the babble of tongues from around the world, the strains of dance music from the hotel, the sartorial elegance of sailors and ship captains, the innuendo of their cologne—all these combined to create a kaleidoscopic ambience, set against the lush tropical rainforest surrounding the port. It seems only natural that the Cuban-based sounds of música antillana, with their wide diffusion and cosmopolitan associations, should have entered Buenaventura.

Despite the presence of Cuban-style jazzbands in the port, however, it is through recordings, not live music, that these sounds reached the majority of the populace. For one, it is likely that these bands performed watered-down versions of Cuban music, and in any case, the wealthy hotel and ship patrons who were the main public for these orquestas did not have substantial contact with the lower classes. Radio broadcasts from Cuban stations cannot be factored in as an influence either—although important for the diffusion of Cuban music to Colombia's Atlantic Coast in the 1920s and 1930s, Buenaventura and Cali were too far from Cuba to receive a clear broadcast signal. In any case, it is probable that most people would not have had easy access to costly shortwave radio sets.

The sailors who docked in the port became pivotal actors in the dissemination of música antillana and salsa recordings, particularly the Caribbean and black American sailors who worked on ships en route from New York, Cuba, and Puerto Rico. Referred to locally as *chombos,* these sailors were admired for their worldly ways, their manner of dress,[4] and their style of dancing. Not only did they bring their musical tastes and dance moves with them, they also brought recordings of these sounds. Medardo Arias, a mestizo native of the port, recalls:

> I can remember back to when I was about nine or ten years old, I saw troops of sailors arrive in the streets of the port, from Jamaica, from Puerto Rico. Almost all of them from the Graceline Company, which was the passenger line at the time that docked in Buenaventura. And back then, those sailors, who some referred to as *chombos,* instigated one of the most important musical phenomena of that time. Not only for their particular manner of dressing, but also for a style of dancing that wasn't known among us at the time. It was a very Caribbean way of dancing, with some steps that totally revolutionized the concept we had of dancing. And so the people learned from them too, not only how to dance, but also about the music that was arriving by sea.[5]

According to Cesar Machado, a working-class white Caleño, sailors began bringing 78 rpm records to hawk from port to port in the late 1930s, and this informal traffic increased through the 1950s.[6] Machado says that sailors also carried other items to sell, but records were their most valuable commodity. Local residents of the port would often buy entire boxes of records from chombos and then sell them in the street to individual buyers. He himself purchased his first 78 rpm recording in 1953 from one such vendor for the price of two Colombian pesos, a significant purchase for him at the time, since he was still a teenager and did not have much money. Most working-class Caleños who traveled to the port during this period usually went for reasons of commerce. Machado, for instance, frequently accompanied a friend who sold trousers in the port.

Obviously, the fact that sailors merely showed up with flat acetate discs for sale does not explain why they became such a hot commodity. The key factor leading to popularization of these records lies in the bars and cabarets of Buenaventura's red-light district, La Pilota. This was the area frequented by the chombos, who went there to drink, dance, hang out, or find a woman for the night. According to Arias, La Pilota was the largest red-light district in all South America, and sailors saved up their money to spend in the bars and brothels there.[7] Most of the prostitutes working in La Pilota were not the local Afro-Colombian women, but white and mestiza women from the interior, as well as Venezuelan and French women. There was even a geisha house with prostitutes brought from Japan. By the 1940s most of these bars had jukeboxes—called *traganiqueles* ("nickel-swallowers") and later *rockolas* (rock-and-roll machines)—and because many of the sailors docking in the port favored música antillana, this is the music that was played. Popular spots that featured such music include El Bar de Prospero, a canteen opened by Prospero Lozano in 1962 and one of the first places to specialize in salsa. The Monterrey cabaret was another spot and featured live music and floor shows in addition to the latest recorded sounds; Piper Pimienta, one of Cali's pioneer salsa musicians, fronted the Monterey's house band during the early 1960s.

Since La Pilota was the center of port nightlife and entertainment, música antillana and salsa quickly caught on among the locals. Although it is important not to essentialize racial identity when analyzing the transnational spread of música antillana, the fact that Buenaventura's population was (and remains) predominantly Afro-Colombian must be taken into account when considering why this music became so popular. The chombos who listened to música antillana and brought these recordings were also black or mulato, and the lyrics of countless songs are filled with references to a black racial or ethnic identity: *eh, negro* (hey, black man), *mulata linda* (pretty mulata), *el tambor/ritmo africano* (the African drum/rhythm), and so forth. Although distinct in specific instrumentation and musical form, the basic stylistic features of Afro-Cuban and Afro–Puerto Rican music are similar to those of the local Afro-Colombian currulao tradition, as both derive from musical elements found throughout sub-Saharan African music. These include interlocking polyrhythms, call-and-response vocals, improvisation over rhythmic and melodic ostinati, percussion, and a preference for dense or buzzy timbres and textures. Since their musical habitus was already oriented to a similar musical aesthetic, it was not much of a stretch for *porteños* (natives of the port) to adopt música antillana and, later, salsa. Based on people's anecdotes and my own trips (accompanied) to the port's current red-light district, I assume that this happened first among porteño men, who hung out in La Pilota not so much for the prostitutes as for the drinks, music and ambience. Young boys, attracted by the music, lights, and bustle of these clubs, also took to música antillana and salsa. Too young to be allowed into the bars, they hung around on the streets outside, peeking in and imitating the dance moves of the sailors they admired. Some of these youngsters, such as Orlando Watussi, later became important figures in Cali's record-centered dance scene. Local musicians, too, took up música antillana, and by the late 1960s various local bands in Buenaventura were performing in this style and adapting the traditional currulao to this cosmopolitan sound.[8]

The cosmopolitan associations of música antillana no doubt reinforced its local popularity. If we consider cosmopolitanism in its literal sense—being "of the world"—then the term must be applied not only to those from the elite socioeconomic ranks with whom it is usually associated, but also to sailors. The two groups shared the position of moving between different cultural spheres and locations. By the very nature of their work, sailors have been central to processes of commodification, commerce, and the movement of international capital that has shaped contemporary globalization and cosmopolitan technologies. Since they have little economic power or status in relation to those who own shipping companies or use them to transport goods and services, however, perhaps it is most appropriate to think of sailors as "working-class cosmopolitans," a proletarian sector laboring within the transport operations of international capitalist expansion. Indeed, as Paul Gilroy observes in *The Black Atlantic,* sailors have been key to the process of modernity and globalization ever since Columbus's maiden voyage to the New World in 1492 and the subsequent centuries of colonization, resource extraction, and slavery that joined Europe, Africa, and the Americas: "Ships were the living means by which the points within [the] Atlantic World were joined. They were mobile elements that stood for the shifting spaces in between the fixed places that they connected. Accordingly they need to be thought of as *cultural and political units* rather than abstract embodiments of the triangular trade" (1993: 16–17; emphasis mine). Connected to multiple localities and distinguished through particular codes of dress, physical bearing, talk, musical taste and manner of dancing—themselves adapted and resignified from other cosmopolitan styles—sailors transmitted this alternative working-class cosmopolitanism to urban black Colombians. While economic growth and technological developments were tying working-class people in Cali to international markets and cultural flows, they were blocked for reasons of socioeconomic status, color, and lack of resources from accessing the elite spheres of cosmopolitan culture. Música antillana and salsa, adopted from sailors, hence became accessible signifiers for being "in the world." As such, they became central expressions of urban working-class identity, a sensibility that was simultaneously local but also connected to the larger world.

Through the 1950s and 1960s, the image of the record-toting sailor, welcomed with open arms for the latest musical sounds he brought with him, became a typical one in Buenaventura. Ivan Forbes recalls:

> With the creation of the Grand Colombian Merchant Fleet, many natives of the region had the opportunity to travel, and these people brought back the latest musical hits. If we think about the epoch around 1955 or the 1960s, maybe it's a fellow Buenaventuran, a black man with his hair straightened, with a really nice shirt, blue jeans, loafers, maybe a cap, and he's chewing gum. He carries one bag with foodstuff for his house on one side, and in another bag on the other side, there's records, twenty-five or thirty records. And this guy starts the long stroll from the docks to his house, "long" because on every corner they stop him to ask, "What did you bring me? Show me those records." "No, that's Cortijo, this is Daniel Santos, and this one, that's Celia Cruz." Finally, he arrives home, and the party starts.[9]

Arias told me similar stories about homecoming for sailors. He himself had an uncle who worked in the Colombian Merchant Fleet, and the family always looked forward to the times when this uncle came back to the port, since he brought the latest salsa releases from New York City as well as posters of salsa concerts and related events. Because many of the sailors working for the Colombian Merchant Fleet were from Buenaventura, it is not surprising that they should have brought their newly adopted musical preferences back to the port, serving as culture brokers in the local adoption of música antillana and salsa. This influence then spread to Cali.

By the late 1950s and lasting through the 1960s, enterprising record dealers in Cali had established a solid trade with sailors, traveling regularly to

Buenaventura to purchase records. These dealers often placed special orders with sailors to bring bulk shipments of particular recordings that they would then sell to salsa dance clubs and individual collectors in Cali. Lisímaco Paz, a mestizo Caleño who became involved in this trade during the mid-1960s, says this was the only way to obtain recordings of música antillana and salsa.[10] Those Caleños who were wealthy enough to travel to New York, where most of these recordings were produced and sold, still looked down on this music, considering it low class and *un relajo* (scandalous), in Paz's words. Owing to Buenaventura's distance from Cali, there were relatively few record dealers who made routine trips to the coast—only some fifteen to twenty individuals, according to Paz. (Although Buenaventura is now less than a three-hour drive from Cali by the new highway, back then the trip involved a twelve-hour journey by railway.) One usually placed orders with sailors based on the samples they carried or on local demand back in Cali, especially if a record was already a hit among local salsa fans. Paz says that the size of these orders varied, depending on whether it was a varied selection of albums or several copies of one particular recording (e.g., a hundred or more copies of an especially popular album). When the sailors with whom orders had been placed passed through the Panama Canal on their way back from New York, they contacted the record dealers in Cali to notify them they would be arriving in Buenaventura in two or three days. The dealers would then travel out to the port to receive their musical cargo.

According to Paz, most of these dealers also offered DJ rental services for private functions (providing records, sound equipment, and DJing), thus creating a market for their records. With the advent of salsa on local radio airwaves in 1965, producers further stimulated the demand for the latest New York sounds by supplying radio programmers with the latest records. Indeed, Paz himself became a radio producer in 1969, providing exclusive hits for the show *Ritmo, sabor, y salsa,* which was enormously popular through the 1970s.

As Cali's record-centered dance scene blossomed through the 1960s and the craze for pachanga and bugalú seized the city's working classes, competition developed among record dealers and DJs to obtain the most recent and exclusive recordings from New York. In order to preserve their exclusivity, DJs began erasing the record labels so that the name of the artist and song could not be read, hence preventing competitors from ordering the album. Pacini Hernández observes a similar practice among DJs in the *picó* (large sound system, from the English "pickup") phenomenon of Cartagena and Barranquilla during the 1980s, when sailors were the only means of obtaining recordings of Afro-pop, Zairean soukous, and Caribbean soca

(1993). By the mid-1990s these genres had been adopted locally in the hybrid style referred to as *champeta* or *terapia*. The parallel with Cali's early scene is striking. Given that the picós started in the late 1960s with salsa dura, it is likely that in those days Cartagena and Barranquilla DJs also erased the labels of their most exclusive salsa recordings, just as their Caleño counterparts did. In both cases, it is clear that the difficulty of obtaining recordings enhanced their desirability as commodities, since the amount of time, effort, and money invested in acquiring them was converted into symbolic capital and social prestige, which the DJs used to generate more economic capital.

With the advent of Fania Records in the late 1960s and its aggressive push into South American markets during the 1970s, salsa recordings became easily available as domestic distribution networks replaced the earlier trade through Buenaventura. The symbolic value attached to recordings persists, however, especially among collectors and aficionados. As indices of cosmopolitan connections and also markers of prestige, salsa recordings emerged as highly significant objects in local popular life during the 1960s, which explains in part why they have continued to be so important. Their use as a principal source of music for the creation of a vibrant dance scene— much in the same way recordings were used for break-dancing during the rise of hip-hop in the late 1970s (see Rose 1994)—helps us to fully understand why recordings have been so crucial to local popular culture.

The Zona de Tolerancia: Developing Local Dance Culture

Cali's dance scene began downtown in the clubs and cabarets of the Zona de Tolerancia during the 1940s (see Appendix 1). This official "tolerance zone" for prostitution was legislated by the city in 1910.[11] Cuban son, guaracha, and mambo predominated in these bars, especially the recordings of the Sonora Matancera, Daniel Santos, Celia Cruz, and Pérez Prado. Cortijo's recordings of Puerto Rican bomba and plena were also very popular. In addition, Mexican boleros and Argentine tangos were enjoyed, as was Colombian música tropical. Cesar Machado, who grew up near the Zona, notes that as many bars featured recorded tango music as featured música antillana, but the cabarets with Cuban sounds were flashier and more exciting. Most people in the tango joints tended just to listen, while música antillana was the favored music for "hot" dancing.[12]

In these clubs and cabarets, the jukeboxes provided a wide selection of Cuban sones, guarachas, mambos, chachas, and boleros, obtained via the record trade through Buenaventura. Cesar Machado recalls that many cabarets were rather dark and visibility was low, so in order to attract customers some establishments had lighted window cases in which a nubile young woman danced to the music emerging from within. Signs announced the talents of these dancing girls, who usually bore exotic nicknames such as "Suzy" or "Mimi," whether they were actually foreigners or not. As in the port, white French prostitutes were more highly prized than darker-skinned local women, despite the supposed "erotic powers" of the latter; Savigliano notes a similar situation in turn-of-the-century brothels in Buenos Aires (1995: 246). One of the biggest draws in the cabarets, however, was the drum set mounted on a small platform over the jukebox. In a curious prefiguring of the pounding drum machines that popularized North American disco music around the globe in the 1970s, a drummer was hired to play along with the records, adding more rhythm and drive to the music. Both Cesar Machado and Medardo Arias confirm that this custom originated in the cantinas and cabarets in Buenaventura, perhaps another influence of the chombos.[13] Lisímaco Paz notes that the drumming increased the lively mood of the music, inciting people to dance harder and drink more, so club owners encouraged this practice.[14] Machado remembers that a certain Carlos Paniagua, a wild character who has since renounced his former ways to become a devout Christian, was one of the most famous *bateristas* (drummers) of the Zona. The practice of accompanying a jukebox with live drumming was particular to the Zona and died out after it was shut down in 1965. Not having heard of a live drummer performing along with jukeboxes anywhere else in Latin America, or in the world for that matter, I consider this practice unique to Cali and Buenaventura, one that exemplifies the creative use of media technology in local expressive culture.

In the Zona de Tolerancia, listening and dancing to música antillana were connected to the explicit atmosphere of sex, drink, and prostitution. One is reminded of the brothels of New Orleans at the turn of the century, or their Argentine counterparts in Buenos Aires, where places of prostitution and bodily pleasure were also incredibly rich sites of musical creativity, giving rise to new sounds, rhythms, and styles of dance. While the ambience in Cali's Zona de Tolerancia did not foster the development of original musical expressions, as happened in the case of jazz or tango, it was pivotal in the adoption of música antillana dancing as a principal creative activity among locals. From personal accounts related to me by veterans of the Zona, as well as those presented by Ulloa (1992: 353–66), it seems that the Zona was a hub of intense subcultural activity, a point of congregation for hustlers, prostitutes, marijuana smokers, transvestites, and other marginal types. One could obtain anything in the Zona: there were restaurants, an all-night pharmacy, even a taxi fleet where you could get a ride home. Just as in the Buenos Aires slums where a dialect called *lunfardo* was spoken among the *compadritos* (ruffians) and *milonguitas* ("broads") who created the tango (see Savigliano 1995), in Cali's Zona de Tolerancia a special street argot called *refajo* was spoken among this crowd.[15]

No doubt the moral charge against the Zona served to heighten the tensions between taboo and pleasure that highlighted the emergence of música antillana in Caleño popular life. Race and class discrimination compounded the issue. The Zona lay in a lower-class area whose residents were predominantly black, mulatto, and mestizo, as were many of the patrons at the bars and cabarets of the Zona. Old-timers told me that the best dancers were usually mulato and black—echoing still-prevalent racial stereotypes about the "natural rhythm" of blacks, but also suggesting that being a good dancer was a valued pursuit among local blacks and mulatos. Musical style emerged as a key element in mapping out race and class distinctions in Cali. Although Colombian música tropical had become widely adopted as the urban national style by the 1950s, música antillana was seen by Cali's white elites as low-class *música de negros* (black people's music). Men from the upper classes were able to participate in this scene without blemishing their social reputation, but upper-class women, constrained by codes of decency and moral propriety, were not permitted the same access. Cesar Machado, who reached his late teens during the early 1950s, recalls the simultaneous reviling of and attraction to Cuban-based sounds within Cali's upper classes. Unfortunately, I do not have data on how upper-class women viewed música antillana, but from informal conversations I had with various people, it is probable that at least some women experienced the conflicting pressures of subscribing to upper-class morality and wanting to join the party. No doubt they resented their men's liberty to participate in a scene that was off limits to them.

Machado: Porro was "decent music," if we can say that, and the other type was uncultured music, popular music, that of the people. But this was hypocritical, no? Because the gentlemen who danced to this music with their wives in the social clubs, as soon as they could, they flew to Juanchito [an all-night party spot] and the red-light district, to dance with the girls, to dance their mambo, spin on the floor, do all the pirouettes that the working-class people did. Understand? It was a matter of appearances. Because this music was very good, no question, but what happens is that it had been given a particular social status, since certain people assigned a certain category to this music. And especially the women who couldn't, the wives of these gentlemen, of the elite classes, they couldn't go to the Zona de Tolerancia like their husbands did, so they hated this music! Not for the music but because they couldn't go.

Waxer: So, really, a man from this sector never went with his wife?

Machado: No, no, never, ever. It was a crime, no, it was a crime, it was looked down on and everything. So, this was—the elite ladies liked this music of course, but what happens is that they couldn't go dancing to it, so it made them angry, they became jealous, and besides, they realized that their husbands were stealing away. Of course they realized their husbands went there, to the Zona de Tolerancia where the girls danced so deliciously. Meanwhile they had to dance decently, even though their blood boiled inside! [*laughs*]

Waxer: Sure. And there was no space for this class of woman, not even a radio show broadcasting the Sonora Matancera or something?

Machado: Oh, no no no, the radio stations did play that music. Some of it, anyway. For example, when we were working at Radio Pacífico, when we operators put that music on, the director used to say, "Ah! You're putting on black people's music, we're playing pots-and-pans music, we're broadcasting vulgar music." So then we had to put on boleros, you see, *guabina* [a genre of música andina], because there was prejudice.

Marta Savigliano notes a similar case for upper-class men who liked to go to tango bars in Buenos Aires at the turn of the century. She traces the facility with which such men could cross class boundaries to the economic power they held, which allowed them to retain moral and social superiority even when "slumming it" (1995: 137–38).

Among working-class men, however, such proscriptions carried no weight, and many were those who flocked to the Zona for its exciting ambience. The figure of the male *pachuco* was of key importance in the Zona during the 1940s and 1950s. Also referred to as a *camaján* (from a popular Cuban son of the time), the pachuco was a ruffian and a hustler, corresponding to the zoot-suited figure that had emerged as a sort of antihero in Latin America and the United States during this period. Dressed in baggy pants, oversized jacket, and shiny two-toned shoes, with a long watch chain draped from one pocket and hair slicked into a pompadour, the pachuco was modeled on images derived from Mexican, Cuban, and Hollywood films. In particular, the Caleño pachuco was an excellent dancer, strongly influenced by Mexican film stars such as Tin Tán and Alberto Martínez (known as "Resortes") and also the Cuban sonero Benny Moré.

Film provided resources for more than just dress styles. While acetate recordings provided a key source of music, their celluloid counterparts played a critical role in providing images and models for dancing. In Buenaventura the chombos frequenting the bars and cabarets of La Pilota had a marked influence on local dancers, and it is probable that this style was subsequently transmitted to Cali. However, musical films from Mexico and Hollywood had as much impact, if not more, on Caleño dancers. Cuban, Mexican, and Hollywood musicals transmitted visual models of how to dance son, tango, guaracha, mambo, fox-trot, and other genres. In these films, Caleños learned the basic steps of the Cuban son and guaracha,[17] as well as the elaborate twists, turns, and shakes of mambo, the Latin dance craze then sweeping Mexico and North America. Evelio Carabalí notes the impact of Resortes on local male dancers, who imitated his moves and assigned imaginative names to them: *las tijeretas* ("scissors," i.e., splits), *la caída de la hoja* (the falling of the leaf), *el salto de la pulga* (the flea jump), *la caída del muerto* (the dead man's fall), and *la ruleta* (the roulette wheel).[18] In addition, following the elegant moves seen in the films of Ginger Rogers and Fred Astaire, dancers learned ballroom styles such as fox-trot and charleston.

Pablo Solano, a working-class record collector who grew up with música antillana, told me that Hollywood's lavish musicals made a particularly big impression on Caleños.[19] Such films, in conjunction with Mexican movies, served as resources for creating new, cosmopolitan identities, expressed through popular dance. Returning to the movie houses as many times as was necessary to memorize a style, Caleño dancers copied the steps, turns, jumps, kicks, and arm movements of the genres depicted on film, synthesizing them into a rich and nuanced repertoire for corporal expression. While the convoluted footwork and acrobatic gestures of Mexican stars such as Tin Tán and Resortes were absorbed by the pachuco mambo dancers, Fred Astaire's sophisticated elegance was favored by others. Indeed, even a generation later, dancers such as Evelio Carabalí drew upon these old ballroom styles to dance salsa (see Figure 2.1). Says Carabalí:

> I learned with him—Fred Astaire, Jack Carlin, I saw all those films. I was fascinated by how he danced with his partner, how he led her. *That's* my style of dancing. They showed me how to dance nicely. Because I watched all those cheap show-offs from around here, but they would dance really wildly, very open! Everything was filigree and splits

Figure 2.1 Evelio Carabalí and Esmeralda (early 1970s). Courtesy of *El Occidente.*

and falling down and stuff, I didn't like that. Since to begin with, I didn't like getting my pants dirty, so [*laughs*] — I have never thrown myself on the floor, not once. And that's how dancing was. So, while they threw themselves on the floor, I danced with my lady. And I made her look nice, I made the dance look nice, of course, with a caress. . . . I make dancing seem like something very passionate, very appealing, and I convey that. . . . I dance salsa with the cadence of Fred Astaire.[20]

The best dancers congregated in the Zona, asserting their physical prowess and creative skill on the dance floors of its cabarets and nightclubs. Ulloa mentions three distinct groups or "generations" of famous local dancers, corresponding to the decades of the 1940s, 1950s, and 1960s (1992: 360–65).[21] All of these came from Cali's working-class sectors and were experts at dancing not only Cuban mambo and guaracha, but also tango, *fox* (fox-trot), and charleston. The 1960s dancers would add pachanga and bugalú to the menu, as well as the twist. Demonstrating one's grasp of these dance styles, and the differences between them, was of utmost importance (Ulloa 1992: 361).

In the 1940s and 1950s most of the famous dancers were men, although the women who frequented these bars to offer sexual services were also skilled dancers, providing able partners for local dance "stars."[22] During the 1960s, however, women unrelated to the sex trade emerged as famous dancers in their own right. Amparo "Arrebato," a young mestiza woman who lived in San Nicolás, recalls sneaking out of the house to attend these clubs while still a teenager:

> When I was young, I went to dance alot at Picapiedra ["Flintstones"].
> . . . It was a place for women who went after, well, after men. I went
> there because I really liked the music at Picapiedra, but there was a
> girl there who they called "The Lioness." And so she told the men
> who went there, "Please don't touch her because she's not like us, she
> only came here to dance." So, I was a young girl and I went with my
> brother to Picapiedra, but only for the music. Since it was two blocks
> from our house, I sneaked away from my mother for a little, but only
> to dance.[23]

Although most of the young women with an affinity for dance did not go to the Zona, not wanting to risk being mistaken for a prostitute, Ulloa notes the increased presence of women in popular dance during the 1960s (1992: 388–89). I discuss this development further below, describing how dance parties and the teen *agüelulos* provided new social outlets for young women at this time.

Located downtown, the Zona initially comprised a small area of three city blocks. By 1945 this had expanded to nearly twenty-five blocks, bounded by Calle 15, Carrera 9, Calle 19, and Carrera 12. The Zona de Tolerancia comprised a part of the Sucre barrio and bordered the neighborhoods of Obrero and San Nicolás. Living close to the clubs where música antillana was always heard, it is not surprising that residents in these barrios were among the first to develop a strong affinity for these sounds. Indeed, these neighborhoods are traditional strongholds for música antillana and salsa in Cali, with the strongest concentration of fans of the Sonora Matancera in the 1950s and, later, of the pachanga and bugalú emanating from New York in the early and mid-1960s. After the Zona was officially closed by the city in 1965, the area continued to be a focal point for salsa and prostitution, especially in bars and clubs along Calle 15. Although the center of the salsa dance scene relocated a few miles eastward along Carrera 8 (see Appendix 1), some of the city's best spots for listening and dancing to salsa remained in this area.[24]

The Neighborhood Scene

Parallel to the rise of música antillana in Cali's Zona de Tolerancia during the 1940s and 1950s was its adoption within the working-class barrios surrounding the Zona: Obrero, Sucre, and San Nicolás. Local neighborhood men were probably the key culture brokers in this process. Free to move between the cabarets of the Zona and the more quotidian sphere of the barrio street, they brought the new sounds of música antillana into their homes. Although records and Victrolas were an expensive investment many working-class people could not afford, there was always at least one person on the street (or within a few blocks) who had equipment. Neighbors, especially men but also women and curious children, would often congregate in or around this person's house to listen to music. These informal gatherings were linked to other modes of socializing, such as drinking, discussing sports and politics, catching up on barrio gossip, and so on.

In Cali's working-class barrios, a close link between popular music and sport evolved, in particular between a passion for music of the Sonora Matancera and a passion for *fútbol* (soccer). In Colombia, as in many other South American countries, soccer is a national pastime, especially among the working-class majority. In Cali local interest in soccer began in the early decades of this century, brought by English and German expatriates who had settled in the city's wealthier neighborhoods. The sport was appropriated by the working class, which by the late 1920s had formed amateur soccer teams of its own. By the 1940s soccer had become the principal working-class sport, and barrio teams such as América (founded in Barrio Obrero) went professional and started competing in the national leagues. Both players and fans, meanwhile, developed a strong interest in the new Cuban-based sounds that were entering the city through the Zona. Indeed, many soccer players were also pachucos (Ulloa 1992: 381). If dance styles observed during the 1990s viejoteca phenomenon are any indicator of the times, soccerlike dance moves were even incorporated into local dance steps.[25]

As emblems of working-class cultural identity, soccer and dancing to música antillana became intertwined, providing the key spaces of socialization in which Caleños have formed a disposition toward friendliness, gregariousness, and physical expression (Ulloa 1992: 379). These cultural practices grew out of and reinforced the local inclination to congregate outdoors that was facilitated by Cali's warm, sunny climate and the city's many parks and plazas (a legacy, as in other Latin American countries, of colonial Spanish town planning).

By the 1950s and continuing through the 1960s, a typical weekend leisure activity involved getting together to discuss soccer and listen to records. Victor Caicedo, an Afro-Colombian salsero, recalls that in his native Barrio Obrero, *sonorazos* (78 rpm recordings by the Sonora Matancera) and other música antillana records provided over 60 percent of the music, the rest being a varied mix of música tropical, tangos, and other genres. Since his father owned one of the few Victrolas in the immediate vicinity, the family home served as a meeting place for these weekend rituals—and they were indeed rituals, with an established progression through stages of drinking, heated discussion, putting on recordings, and continuing the conversation with background music. I quote at length from one of our conversations.

Caicedo: I remember that, on that little set, it was a gramophone that my
  dad had there in Barrio Obrero, every Saturday and Sunday was spent
  by that gramophone, drinking there on the walkway and listening to
  music. Why? Because there was a room, of course it was very small,
  the first friends arrived with a flask of *aguardiente* ["fire water," i.e.,
  cane liquor] or half a dozen beers, and started to talk about soccer.
  That is, the subject was soccer, they started talking about soccer.
Waxer: It's said that there's a very close link between salsa and soccer in
  Cali.
Caicedo: Yes, in Cali that goes without saying, they're joined, they run
  parallel to each other. Yes? So the first and main topic was soccer. After
  that, talking about soccer, they drank their beer, their aguardiente, and
  when their spirits rose, when they got into a good mood, right, they
  started to listen to music. Especially the music of the Sonora Matancera, that was—
Waxer: Oh, okay. So, first soccer, talking without music, and after—?
Caicedo: And afterward, talking about soccer with music, because they
  didn't—that is, the whole menu was soccer and music. Otherwise, one
  without the other, it doesn't work. Never! Not that I know, it never
  worked. . . . Here there's always been a strong rivalry between
  América, the fans of América, and the fans of Deportivo Cali [two
  local soccer teams], right? So, the arguments started between friends,
  arguments about which of the two was better. And these arguments
  would get more and more heated, and so to calm down a little, this
  manner of, the tension created by the arguments over soccer, then
  "No! Let's put on some music!" First thing they put on was a sonorazo, right? And they continued talking about soccer, but now much

calmer. That was like the incentive, like the, how do I tell you? Like something to reduce the tension.

Caicedo explained that after this stage, sometime during the afternoon perhaps, people would tire of arguing about soccer and become more interested in listening and dancing to the music. By this point the women of the household (wives, daughters, and sisters) would have completed household tasks and would join the men, and often more neighbors would have dropped by.

> Around the aguardiente flask and the beer, they would start listening to music. But like good Caleños, with the blood, the vein for dancing, sitting around a flask and then the drink gets someone going, so he starts to dance alone, still sitting. Then with the second flask, forget it, he pulled the neighbor out to dance, his wife, his daughter, no? And finally the whole neighborhood would gather and in that moment, hard feelings were forgotten.[26]

Informal conversations with other people confirmed Caicedo's anecdote about typical weekend gatherings in the barrios. Of particular significance is the way in which the boundaries between domestic and public spheres (the house and the street) in these working-class neighborhoods became blurred within the context of friendly social activity, reinforcing a sense of social collectivity and community that could be called upon in times of need. An important point in the weekly cycle of work and leisure among Cali's working classes, these informal gatherings were not merely a routine way to pass time. Rather, they became cultural rituals in which recordings of música antillana were intertwined with other important elements of local cultural practice—dance, drink, sport, and conversation—to establish and strengthen social ties.

Social collectivity was reinforced through other barrio activities in which dance and música antillana figured strongly. The Caleño tradition of "house parties" or *champús bailables* began during the 1930s. Similar to North American "Sunday socials," these dances were usually held on Sunday afternoons, lasting from about 2:00 P.M. until 8:00 or 9:00 P.M. They took place not only in barrios such as Obrero, San Nicolás, and Sucre, but also in other nearby working-class neighborhoods such as El Hoyo or San Antonio. Often chaperoned by the matriarch of the host family, these dances provided a "decent" and socially acceptable environment in which teenagers and young adults could socialize with members of the opposite sex. Although the men (fathers and older brothers) attending these dances often carried hidden flasks of aguardiente with them, alcohol was not served at these dances, but rather *champús*—a local beverage made from corn, pieces of pineapple and *lulo* (a native fruit), and bitter orange leaves—from whence these events took their name. These dances were also called *empanadas bailables,* since meat pastries or empanadas were also often served, but the latter designation seems to have prevailed only when champús was not provided. Indeed, from the 1930 through the 1950s, afternoon dances called empanadas bailables were common in all Colombian cities, albeit with different kinds of music depending on the region (Wade 2000: 200). Ulloa tells us that in the first half of the 1930s some of these Caleño parties featured Colombian música andina played by a typical string trio, in addition to recordings of tangos and other genres played on an old Victrola. Through the later 1930s and into the 1940s, Cuban genres such as son, conga, guaracha, bolero, and mambo replaced these styles, as well as Colombian música tropical, Spanish pasodoble, and North American fox-trot. Although the center for this dance music was the Zona, it was also learned and danced in people's homes, especially at these dance parties.[27] Ulloa affirms that many of the great dancers of the Zona first learned and honed their steps at such gatherings (1992: 348–51).

Through the 1940s, 1950s, and 1960s, as Cali's working-class neighborhoods expanded and new ones were consolidated, the champús bailables were gradually replaced by a similar type of dance party called *baile de cuota.* At these a small cover fee was charged and cold snacks served; alcohol was acceptable, but people were expected to bring their own liquor. While a version of the champús bailables continued in the form of the teen agüelulos, the bailes de cuota tended to attract a slightly older crowd, mainly young adults in their twenties and thirties. Occasionally a baile de cuota would feature live local bands in addition to recordings (Ulloa 1992: 350), but the gramophone and, later, hired DJ services remained the norm. Guaracha, mambo, chachachá, Colombian música tropical (porro), and other international genres (tango, fox-trot, and pasodoble) were the main fare through the 1950s; pachanga and bugalú were added to the mix in the 1960s. Música antillana predominated, forming nearly two-thirds of all the styles usually played. The bailes de cuota and festivales disappeared in the 1970s as people shifted their interest to the growing circuit of *griles* (nightclubs). Local neighborhood dances continued instead through the *verbenas,* or street parties, held during the December Feria.

Struggles to Secure the City

During my conversations with Caleños residents in the mid-1990s, many people recalled the 1950s and 1960s with great nostalgia, claiming that it was a time of innocence and "clean fun," in contrast to the violent ambience established after the rise of the Cali cocaine cartel during the 1980s. A closer recollection of this era, however, points to the mid-twentieth century as a time of substantial upheaval, when Caleños were caught up in struggles to establish a foothold in the city. Several migrants to Cali came as refugees fleeing La Violencia. Spurred by bipartisan tensions between the Conservative and Liberal parties in the Colombian interior during the 1940s, La Violencia erupted when the Liberal leader Jorge Eliécer Gaitán was assassinated prior to general elections in 1948. The bloody *Bogotazo* (torching of Bogotá) that resulted from his assassination torched off ten years of violent reprisals, rampant massacres, torture, and atrocities by both Liberal and Conservative factions. Although Cali also witnessed initial outbursts of violence following the Bogotazo, it remained relatively peaceful during the rest of this period, becoming a haven for displaced peasants and townspeople fleeing the Colombian interior. The town of Puerto Tejada, however, only twenty miles southeast of Cali, was the scene of one of the grislier chapters in La Violencia's history: upon receiving news of Gaitán's murder, Liberal partisans allegedly decapitated Conservative sympathizers and played soccer with their heads in the town plaza (Taussig 1980: 82). La Violencia officially ended in 1958, when a power-sharing accord between the Liberal and Conservative parties was struck. Isolated waves of violence continued through the 1960s, however, establishing the basis for a return of uncontrolled violence between guerilla and paramilitary forces in the 1990s.[28]

An archive of personal memoirs of barrio life, *Recuerdos de mi barrio* (1986), attests to the battles of Cali's new residents. Compiled as part of celebrations to commemorate the 450th anniversary of Cali's founding, nearly two hundred people contributed memoirs to this project. One resident recalls how Barrio Alfonso López was formed as part of a collective land invasion in 1958:

> The images that could be seen daily in the streets of Cali were very telling. The migrants came basically from the regions where the partisan Violence had made its mark in previous years. The Sultana of Valle province [a nickname for Cali] was converted into a magnet for thousands of households; entire families walked the streets in search of a place to settle down. But the limitations became ever stricter, to the

point that you saw signs that emphatically stated: "Room for rent to a single person or couple without children," even though they knew *you can't live alone,* everybody had their wife, two or more children, and as additions to this household there was usually a cat, a dog, or a parakeet. (*Recuerdos* 1986, memoir no. 22)

With available housing so scarce, groups of displaced migrants waited for night and (with or without the clandestine collaboration of military officers) moved onto an unsettled lot—usually marshland or scrub pitted with swamps and muddy terrain that needed draining. The story of the founding of Barrio Alfonso López is mirrored in the history of virtually every working-class Caleño barrio established after 1945—even up through the 1980s and into the twenty-first century. Requests to city authorities for running water, electricity, and paved roads were often ignored or interminably delayed, spurring people to set up illegal taps on water and power lines. Worse, the municipal government sometimes sent police troops to oust migrants from their camps, a practice that continues to this day in the outlying shantytowns of Aguablanca district.[29] According to Ulloa, working-class barrios founded in the 1940s and 1950s took almost twenty years to establish themselves with complete services, utilities, and transportation (1992: 323). During my fieldwork I lived in an area near two early 1990s land invasions and witnessed their similarly slow march toward integration with the rest of the city.

Music and dance became an arena for negotiating the effects of this daily struggle. In addition to providing a safe outlet to let off steam and temporarily forget one's troubles, they also formed an important avenue for reaffirming the community bonds needed in other contexts for group survival and development. Thomas Turino describes a similar process of community bonds forged through music and dance among highland migrants in Lima, Peru (1993). As in the case of Cali, the links created among Limeños served as the basis for communal work projects such as building houses or adding rooms to one's residence. In contrast to the Limeño case, however, where migrants tended to form regional associations based on common home districts, in Cali migrants from diverse regions came together. Local *juntas de acción communal* (communal action boards) were formed to address immediate physical and social needs. Reflecting the heterogeneity of their new communities, the juntas helped establish the openness, democratic receptivity, and generosity that characterizes working-class Caleño neighborhood life to this day (Sinisterra de Carvajal 1986: 88; Ulloa 1992: 382).

A special form of neighborhood dance party emerged in Cali's newly established barrios during the 1950s and 1960s to raise funds for community projects such as building a local school or church or paving streets and sidewalks. These would be organized within each barrio, sometimes on a street-by-street basis, or by the local junta communal. Such dances, called *festivales,* were held in small neighborhood *casetas* (dance halls) or *kioscos* (pavilions), usually on Saturday nights rather than the Sunday afternoon of the bailes de cuota. Alejandro Ulloa, a working-class Caleño of mestizo background writing about the social history of his native Barrio San Carlos (founded in 1963), observes: "For many years, the festivales have been (along with soccer games) the main pastime of the locals, and the most effective medium for integrating neighbors and acquainting young folks. But beyond that, the festivales were the best and perhaps only form of raising funds for the common good" (1986: 46). Both economically and socially, the fundraising festivales helped to build community spirit and integration. Ulloa might have overstated the efficacy of such gatherings as "the most effective medium for integrating neighbors and acquainting young folks," since other sorts of neighborhood dance parties also provided opportunities for neighbors to socialize. In terms of collective organization at the grassroots level, however, the festivales were the most direct way to instill neighborhood solidarity.

The attempts of Cali's new residents to transform their squatter's camps into legitimate neighborhoods fostered an extraordinary degree of communal solidarity and grassroots activism that continues to characterize Caleño subjectivity and social relationships (Escobar Navia 1986: 73). Linked to this, social dance became a modus vivendi in itself, entrenched as a key expressive practice that affirmed patterns of socialization and neighborhood interaction. I was told that people in Cali will get together to dance under any pretext—as I found out one night when accompanying a local orquesta to a *bingo bailable,* a dance where bingo games alternated with sets of live and recorded salsa music. Beyond private family parties, street and neighborhood festivities have comprised a crucial space in which dancing to música antillana and salsa—as a "technique of the body" (Mauss 1973)—has inscribed a particular mode of embodied urban practice on Caleño life. In a country devastated by civil war and violence, the Caleño penchant for dancing was not merely an escapist, frivolous pastime. Rather, dance served as a critical expressive avenue through which to consolidate human and financial resources for community projects, sustained by the vision of a new society untainted by the ravages of war. *Alegría* (happiness) and dance music became part of local subjectivity, a vehicle for community bonds and an antidote to daily struggles. During the 1960s and into the 1970s, the emphasis on alegría and dancing was reinforced by the rise of teen agüelulos and the commercial sphere of nightclubs.

Nightclubs and Agüelulos

During the 1960s the range of cultural practices and semiotic nuances tied to sound recordings music expanded. As new neighborhoods expanded toward the east and south of the city, griles that specialized in música antillana began to open up along the main road connecting the docks on the Cauca River to the railway station in town. These nightclubs included Séptimo Cielo (Seventh Heaven), Nuevo Mundo (New World), and La Costeñita—local spots whose legacy was revived by viejotecas of the same name during the late 1990s. The site of dancing to recorded music shifted from neighborhood house parties to these clubs, where the music included recordings of Cuban son, guaracha, bolero, and mambo, as well as the newer rhythms of pachanga and bugalú that began to emanate from New York City.

At the same time, teenagers—barred from the griles because of their youth—established their own space, called agüelulos. Alcohol was not served at these events, which were usually held on Sunday afternoons from 2:00 P.M. to 8:00 or 9:00 P.M. The name *agüelulo* derives from *agua 'e lulo*, or *lulo* fruit juice (made from an acidic fruit native to the region), but soda pop tended to be the main beverage provided at these dances, not juice. The agüelulos were held in private family houses but also spread to larger spaces such as griles, which would open their doors for these afternoon events. In both cases a small entrance fee was charged. Attracting teenagers from throughout the city, the dances moved from barrio to barrio every weekend, and news of upcoming agüelulos was usually spread by word of mouth. The youngsters who frequented agüelulos were called *agüeluleros,* or, since Coca-Cola® was the main refreshment, *cokacolos.*[30]

In both the agüelulos and the griles, dancers developed high standards of athletic prowess and stamina, inventing complex and virtuosic new dance moves. Local *salsómanos* (salsa fans) developed a lexicon of colorful phrases to describe good dancing:[31] *castigar la baldosa* (punish the floor tiles), *azotar baldosas* (whip the floor tiles), *sacarle brillo al piso* (polish the floor), *meneando el esqueleto* (shaking your bones), *mover la angarilla* (move the saddlebag, i.e., hips), *machacando pasito* (grinding up a step), and *brillar chapas* or *sacarle brillo a la hebilla* (polish the belt buckles).[32] Although now dated and in disuse, such phrases typify the frenzied spirit that characterized local salsa dancing during the 1970s. I occasionally heard middle-aged

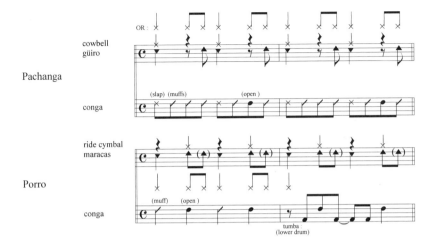

Figure 2.2   Comparison of *pachanga* and *música tropical* patterns

dancers use these lines from their youth (sometimes to lament that they could not "punish the tiles" as they used to).

During this era pachanga and bugalú caught on with particular force in Cali. Both genres bear certain stylistic elements similar to those featured in Colombian música tropical, still prominent in Cali in the early 1960s. Rhythmically, pachanga uses the anticipated bass and piano montunos of música antillana, but the conga plays a specific rhythmic pattern called *caballo* (horse) instead of the standard tumbao. Over this the cowbell plays a rhythm consisting of an accented quarter note and two eighths, doubled heterophonically by the güiro in a dotted quarter–eighth note pattern, both of which contribute further to the sprightly, "trotting" feel of pachanga. This pattern is similar to that used in música tropical (Figure 2.2), which no doubt contributed to its popularity among local audiences. Bugalú, on the other hand, emphasizes accents and catchy hand-claps on beats two and four—once again, elements found in música tropical. Bugalú's slower "backbeat" feel is also comparable to some Colombian porros, especially those popularized by Lucho Bermúdez.

Although the New York vogue for pachanga had waned by the second half of the 1960s, in Cali its popularity continued, and it is still enjoyed by many dancers to this day. The Cuban musicologist Helio Orovio notes that Caleños have developed a passion for pachanga unmatched in any other part of the world.[33] During the early 1960s, while fans in other Colombian cities such as Barranquilla continued to prefer Cuban son, Caleños embraced pachanga en masse.[34] Some non-Colombian observers have com-

Figure 2.3 Caleño salsa
dancer (1996). Photo by
Lise Waxer.

mented to me that Caleño bands sound like they play salsa with a cumbia
feel, but I would say that they sound at least as much like bands playing
salsa with a pachanga feel—on top of the beat, with sprightly tempos and a
clipped rhythmic attack. During the 1960s and 1970s Caleños developed a
unique style of dancing characterized by a rapid "double-time" shuffle on
the tips of the toes (Figure 2.3). In Colombia, this idiosyncratic local style
is still known as *el paso Caleño* (the Cali step). It is distinct from the way
salsa is danced in the rest of Latin America (and in other parts of Colombia,
for that matter), where the basic short-short-long step developed from
Cuban son is the norm (see note 17 of this chapter). High kicks and rapid
footwork also became a hallmark of Caleño salsa dancing.

The Caleño style was a hybrid of elements from Cuban guaracha and mambo, along with North American popular dances such as the jitterbug, twist, and charleston. The hyperkinetic shimmy of the film star Tongolele, whose performances of ballroom rhumba, conga, and mambo graced many Mexican movie musicals, was also influential. A unique fusion of these forms was introduced into Buenaventura by the chombos and spread to Cali by the influential dancer Orlando Watussi (Hernández Vidal 1992: 37).[35] An Afro-Colombian native of Buenaventura, Watussi learned how to dance música antillana and salsa by watching the chombos in the port as a young boy and often performed for sailors in the bars of La Pilota, who, fascinated, threw him coins and chewing gum.[36] He moved to Cali around 1972 and landed a job performing at local nightclubs, making a huge impression on Caleño dancers. In the tradition of African diaspora male solo dancing, Watussi was a virtuoso, combining rapid speed with elements of jitterbug and Afro-Cuban *rumba columbia*. According to Medardo Arias, Watussi even did the rapid backward moonwalk typical of later New York break-dancing, which was appropriated by Michael Jackson. It is possible that Watussi learned this step from Puerto Rican sailors adept in the traditional dance of Afro–Puerto Rican bomba, where sliding, jerky motions are common. Bomba has certainly been recognized as an important choreographic source for 1970s break-dancing (Flores 2000).

Fast dance tempos became key for Caleño dancers. The upbeat pachanga was ideal for this, but other rhythms were felt to be too slow—especially bugalú, a fusion of son with rhythm and blues that was all the rage in the mid-1960s. In a creative use of media technology, Caleño youth began playing their 33 rpm bugalú recordings at 45 rpm.[37] Hence, a widely loved bugalú number such as Pete Rodriguez's "Micaela," recorded in 1966, would be transformed from its original M.M. $\quarternote$ = 65 tempo to M.M. $\quarternote$ = 85—still not quite as fast as most pachanga tunes, but fast enough to satisfy local dancers. Other popular bugalú tunes such as Eddie Palmieri's "Palo de Mango," however, would be accelerated from the original tempo of M.M. $\quarternote$ = 160 to M.M. $\quarternote$ = 220, well within the rapid pace preferred by salsómanos.

The teen agüelulos were central to the development of this rapid dance style, since teenagers—more than anyone else—had the requisite physical energy and stamina. In *¡Que viva la música!*, a celebrated novel about teenage life in Cali during this time, the author, Andrés Caicedo, described the ethos of dancing salsa at this accelerated tempo: "The 33 rpm recording at 45 rpm is almost as if one were flayed while dancing, with that need to say it all, so that there's time to repeat it sixteen times more and see who can stand us, who can dance with us" (1977: 138). The agüelulos became an important site for youth subculture, where youngsters vied for prestige on the dance floor (Arteaga 1990: 109). They parallel the emergence of similar dance spaces for teenaged youth in other Latin American cities where salsa was flourishing during the 1960s and 1970s, at a time when cosmopolitan notions about a distinct "youth culture" were beginning to emerge internationally (Hall and Whannel 1964). In Caracas, Venezuela, for example, teenagers flocked regularly to afternoon matinées, often held in the tenement apartments of the city's working-class barrios.[38] In Barranquilla, on Colombia's Atlantic coast, young people gathered to dance salsa at outdoor street parties, where music was provided by the large picó sound systems. Cali's agüelulos were focused very much on competition through dance, probably more than the Caracas scene (although I do not have clear information) and certainly more than Barranquilla's. José Arteaga notes that in Barranquilla prestige was accorded primarily to the picó owners and DJs (1990: 114) in terms of who had the most exclusive recordings, the fanciest rig (e.g., lights and decoration; see Pacini Hernández 1993), and the loudest speakers. Although Caleño DJs also competed among themselves for ownership of the rarest or most recent records, in the agüelulos attention was definitely focused on dancers: who had the most innovative steps, the most athletic moves, the most intricate figures, and so forth. The creative energy poured into dance largely replaced an interest in live performance, which one might expect to find in a burgeoning salsa scene.

Other elements reinforced the emphasis on physical ability and stamina in the agüelulos. Unlike at the griles or neighborhood dances, music was played nonstop, without breaks between the songs, and there were no tables or chairs for resting or hanging out. The main objective of the agüelulero was to dance:

> Imagine a person drinking only Coca-Cola® and dancing, from two or three in the afternoon until eight at night. That was the idiosyncracy of the agüelulo.[39]
>
> We couldn't go to the griles because we were underage . . . so they didn't let us in. So the alternative, within the musical scene, was to go to the agüelulos, which were between two and six in the afternoon, eight at night maximum. There we heard the rhythms, and that meant throwing out a few dance steps. And another characteristic was that you went there to sweat. Because it was—the rhythm there didn't stop, it was continuous. It was straight through, pure dance, and you'd come out all sweaty, but sweaty, sweaty, sweaty.[40]

The emphasis on physical exertion corresponded with a propensity for athletic recreation in Caleño life. Outdoor sports such as soccer, swimming, basketball, and track and field have been as central to popular lifestyles as dancing, and it is not surprising that since the 1940s many of Cali's best dancers have also been athletes. Amparo "Arrebato" Ramos, the famous local dancer who as a teenager used to sneak into clubs in the Zona de Tolerancia, was a national track and field champion. In 1971 Cali hosted the Pan-American Games, a landmark occasion that not only confirmed Cali's international importance, but also consolidated the athletic orientation of the city. Indeed, another common activity among Caleño youth during this time, either in groups of friends or with family, was to go bathing or swimming in nearby rivers or outdoor pools on the weekend. Kiosks and pavilions for dancing to salsa were usually located close by, so swimming and dancing salsa became inextricably linked as a recreational activity for young locals. This was the case not only for Caleños, but also for those growing up in nearby towns; the Palmira native José Fernando Zuñiga told me that he learned how to dance salsa as an adolescent during these weekend excursions.[41]

For young Caleña women, the agüelulos became an important space for asserting their independence from patriarchal conventions that "nice girls" stay at home and do not cause trouble. Henry Manyoma, an Afro-Colombian musicologist from Barrio Trébol (and also the brother of the famous salsa vocalist Wilson "Saoco" Manyoma; see chapter 4), recalls: "At that time in Cali, I'm talking about the 1960s, most girls weren't allowed to go to those parties, because, well—overall, the girls had to sneak out to go to those dances. It wasn't like us guys, we went and there was no problem. But for the girls it was, so they went secretly, they snuck out. Back then, parents had more control over their daughters, and didn't let them go."[42] Dance was as much of a passion for young teenage women as for young men, however, since Caleño youth at that time were socialized from an early age into the joys of dancing. Since the 1930s champús bailables and other neighborhood dance events had been key arenas in which young people interacted. Beneath the eye of family and community elders, girls and boys gained their first experiences of extended physical contact and sociable interchange. Through the steps and turns of couple dancing, Caleño youth learned a certain physical comportment toward members of the opposite sex. In his history of salsa in Cali, Alejandro Ulloa writes:

> This early interaction, seen in the fact that one learns how to dance before knowing how to read or write, has repercussions for future social relations, in terms of behavior and in the conception of the role of women with regard to her self-representation and that which men im-

pose on her. . . . Perhaps this has an impact on the family structure and an influence on the "Cali-ness" of the Caleña woman, who besides being beautiful is liberated, independent, enterprising, and decisive. From a certain position these traits can be wrongfully confused with immorality. In my viewpoint, this attitude, more intuited than actually defined, was constructed through collective participation in parties and dance, at different levels. . . . *The body was educated for dance and for a hedonistic attitude that conceives of the body as an object of pleasure more than as an instrument of labor.* (1992: 389; emphasis mine)

In this way, the body and its presentation through repeated, expressive movement became central elements to inscribing social identities and interactions (Mauss 1973). Ulloa goes on to note that the presence of chaperoning matriarchs in the champús bailables and family parties served to legitimate this socialization of Caleño bodies, consolidating social dancing as an urban cultural practice in which women have been active participants.[43]

Although the tradition of neighborhood dances instilled a certain disposition toward movement and pleasure in young Caleños, patriarchal codes about a young woman's "honor" aimed to regulate the contexts in which she could express this. The agüelulos hence represented a threat to family propriety, being a new context in which youngsters could dance beyond the watchful gaze of their parents. Indeed, personal accounts and semiautobiographical writings of the time clearly indicate that the agüelulos were a prime site for attracting and "scoring" with members of the opposite sex, underlining the erotics of dance as part of urban social identity. As a rebellion against patriarchal dictates, the surreptitious fleeing of teenage girls to dance in the agüelulos marked a site of contestation over social convention and gender roles.

By the late 1960s the practice of speeding up records had been adopted by DJs in the griles and eventually became entrenched as a unique feature of Cali's dance scene. Indeed, when the New York superstars Richie Ray and Bobby Cruz performed in Cali at the 1968 December Feria, they met with requests to speed up the tempo of their bugalú numbers in compliance with local practice.

The Puerto Rican musician[s], whose band has enlivened New York's best nightclubs, seemed very surprised by the singular way in which Caleños dance bugalú. At first, Richie Ray played one of these rhythms like he normally does, but he was immediately advised that in Colombia and especially Cali, people prefer to increase the speed of their record players so that the tempo is faster. Thereupon he accelerated the music, putting in motion the giant Caseta Panaméricana, which was fit to burst last night and the night before.[44]

Keeping with tradition, some current local salsa bands perform "golden oldies" such as "Micaela" at the accelerated 45 rpm speed, and not the original 33 rpm tempo. Indeed, one night I heard the all-woman salsa band Canela perform this tune at a concert, and the combined effect of the fast tempo and higher-pitched women's voices created an uncanny reproduction of 45 rpm playback, establishing a kind of Baudrillardean, hyperreal feedback in the cycle between live and mediated music.

By the early 1970s Caleños could go salsa dancing every night of the week. The scene became somewhat of a "mobile party" in which different griles were the "in spot" on successive nights of the week. Depending on which variation of the circuit one ascribed to, Mondays were for going to Honka Monka, Estambul, or Aguacate; Tuesdays, La Manzana or Marcia; Wednesdays, Mauna Loa or Escalinata; Thursdays, Schira and, later, the Village Game; Fridays, Séptimo Cielo; Saturdays, an open night, all clubs were full; and Sunday afternoons and evenings, Séptimo Cielo, El Grill Río Cali, or El Escondite.[45] Sometimes a local live band might appear at one of this places, usually performing cover versions of the current New York and Puerto Rican hits. Furthermore, when griles in the city were obliged to close their doors at 2:00 A.M., revelers could continue to dance until dawn in Juanchito, an Afro-Colombian settlement on the city's outskirts that was not subject to municipal ordinances and became an all-night salsa party spot for Caleños. Although it was the rare salsómano or salsómana who could endure going out to dance every single night of the week, most Caleños remember these as the glory days of Cali's dance scene.

Salsa Ballets and Dance Competitions

Through the late 1960s and into the 1970s, dance competitions were a regular feature at many griles, spurring dancers to further refine their moves and invent new steps. The winners of such events usually received little more than a free bottle of aguardiente; although some also received cash prizes,[46] dancers competed mainly for enjoyment and social prestige (Ulloa 1992: 411). Salsa floor shows also emerged in the early 1970s, with such groups as the Ballet de la Salsa performing choreographed salsa dance routines (Figures 2.4–2.7). Organized in 1971 by Alfonso Prieto and José Pardo Llada, the Ballet de la Salsa was a troupe of six men and four women, including such famed local dancers as Amparo "Arrebato," Telembí King, and

Jimmy "Boogaloo."[47] The effort to formalize local salsa dance styles for public shows paved the way for other groups. These include Evelio Carabalí's Ballet Folclor Urbano, founded in the 1970s and still active,[48] and the Cali Rumba school (1985–88). More recent salsa exhibition projects include Liliana Salinas's Ballet de Azucar and Andrés Leudo's school. During the late 1980s salsa was even fused with the elite forms of classical ballet and modern dance to produce the Barrio Ballet, a troupe connected to Incolballet, the city dance company.

To my knowledge, the Ballet de la Salsa was the first enterprise of its kind on the international salsa scene, appearing long before choreographed salsa shows began to be performed in New York and Puerto Rico. Not only the dance routines but the very costumes troupe members wore pointed to a creative refashioning of cosmopolitan symbols. From old Hollywood films dancers borrowed Roaring Twenties flapper dresses, beads, candy-striped jackets, straw boaters, and canes—clothing I have never encountered in salsa scenes elsewhere. No doubt these garments and accessories were meant to reinforce salsa's glamorous image. Notably, if one is to judge from photographs of salsa show dancing the era, most of the men were black, while the women were either mestiza or light-skinned mulatas. I am not able to fully account for this—indeed, during the 1980s and 1990s salsa exhibition dancers in Cali came from all racial backgrounds, while the top teachers and most skilled dancers, men and women, tended to be dark-skinned Afro-Colombians, so there is no consistent pattern here. What is certain, however, is that even in the mid-1990s, the stereotype that Afro-Colombians were the best dancers—prevalent during the heyday of the Zona de Tolerancia—persisted among Caleños. I frequently heard stereotypical comments (especially from light-skinned, middle-class Caleños) about the "rhythmic power" of black salsa dancers.

The local sphere of competitive salsa dancing reached its peak with the staging of the Campeonato Mundial de la Salsa (World Salsa Dance Championship) in 1974 and 1975. One of the judges in the first year was the legendary Cuban vocalist Rolando LaSerie, whose presence was seen as consecrating the event. The second year built on the success of the first and featured live salsa by the rising Colombian band Fruko y sus Tesos. With a grand prize of a 100,000 Colombian pesos (equivalent to roughly us$15,000 back then), these were major competitions indeed. Although nearly all the contestants were actually from Cali and there was not a single international participant, these "world" dance competitions served as public spectacles that not only reinforced salsa's prominence in local popular life, but also emphasized the cosmopolitan sensibility linked to salsa and música

Figure 2.4   Ballet de la Salsa (early 1970s). Courtesy of *El Occidente*.

Figure 2.5   Ballet de la Salsa (early 1970s). Courtesy of *El Occidente*.

Figure 2.6 Ballet de la Salsa (early 1970s). Courtesy of *El Occidente*.

Figure 2.7 Ballet de la Salsa (early 1970s). Courtesy of *El Occidente*.

antillana. Dancing to salsa, in other words, became the expressive mode through which Caleños conceived of and projected their own position in the world at large. In his weekly column the expatriate Cuban journalist José Pardo Llada, a cofounder of the contest, wrote: "In Cali salsa is not a passing fad, but rather a manner, a form, a style of interpreting dance by the people of this city. And only in Cali do they dance this way. Not even the Costeños, with their singular sense of rhythm, dance salsa 'the Caleño way.' Salsa is, definitively, the musical emblem of a city and a province, Cali and El Valle."[49] That Caleños were proclaiming their city the world capital of salsa by the late 1970s stems less from whether Cali was actually a bonafide salsa capital than from the conviction that Caleños believed they were more passionate about salsa than anyone else on the planet. The emotional investment Caleños had in defining themselves as world-class salsa fans hence constituted for them a move to stake their position on the international popular cultural map.

Salsa Radio

During the second half of the 1960s and the 1970s, salsa programs began to appear on local radio airwaves, reinforcing the dance-oriented euphoria generated by the griles and agüelulos. According to Lisímaco Paz, Radio Reloj was the first local station to put salsa on the air locally, playing individual pachanga and bugalú numbers.[50] The first show dedicated to salsa, however, was *Festival en el aire,* launched in 1965 on La Voz del Valle. In 1969 the enormously popular *Ritmo, salsa, y sabor* began its nineteen-year run on Radio El Sol. This show was produced by Paz, who supplied material for the program from his contacts with sailors in Buenaventura. These early programs were key in diffusing the new salsa sound to local audiences, since recordings were still very difficult to obtain. Salsa radio permeated the local soundscape, played not only in people's homes but also in shops and on public buses.

Through the early and mid-1970s, several more salsa programs appeared. Radio announcers such as Edgar Hernan Arce and El Diablo Cajiao became media personalities who helped boost the excitement surrounding salsa in local popular life. Both these men were working-class Caleños of mestizo background. As Ulloa describes, a distinct dialect developed that was associated with salsa announcers, whose colorful and animated speech peppered their programs and heightened the *rumbero* (party) ambience of the local scene (1992: 483–97). Typical phrases that announcers would interject over the music included "Más salsa que pescao" (More salsa [or sauce] than fish) and "Salsaludando" ("Salsalutations"). Arce recalls that he and other announcers had great fun coining new phrases.[51] Since announcers tended move around between different stations, their argot became a common vernacular for local salsa broadcasting. Notably, Cali's radio announcers were the ones who first started promoting the slogan of "world salsa capital," which print media had picked up on the late 1970s.[52]

The peak years for salsa radio in Cali during the record-centered dance scene were 1975–76. By this time some of the local stations had gone to an all-salsa format and were broadcasting salsa twenty-four hours a day. These included Radio El Sol and La Voz del Valle, stations that had pioneered local salsa programming in the 1960s. The national radio chain Caracol also launched a local all-salsa station called Radio Tigre in 1973 and decided to schedule the station's debut during Holy Week. Prior to this time, Holy Week had been a time of solemn observance in Cali, when only religious music was played on the radio and people put aside the rumba. The non-stop broadcasting of salsa dura by Radio Tigre caused a huge scandal and earned the station tremendous publicity. The fact that one of the station's key announcers was nicknamed El Diablo Cajiao (The Devil Cajiao) further scandalized the church. Hernan Arce was involved in the launch and explained the commercial strategy behind this move.

> It involved a big push for publicity. We laid a trap for Father Alfonso Hurtado Galvis, who is the one who rules in Cali during Holy Week. We wanted to do something that would make a big impact and that would affect city life. And that's how we programmed only salsa, on Holy Thursday, Good Friday, and Holy Saturday. Father Hurtado Galvis, who was broadcasting his mass, realized this because some people called to tell him that there was a radio station playing party music, and so he began to denounce us, how this was a lack of respect, that the Ministry of Communications should be called to suspend us. And so many people who were listening to him, they began to look for Radio Tigre and stayed listening to it because only salsa music was played, without commercials or announcements. Effectively, Father Hurtado fell into the trap, and without realizing it he gave us a lot of publicity, just as we had foreseen. (Quoted in Ulloa 1992: 472)

Radio Tigre's audacious stunt dramatized the fervent atmosphere that Cali's record-centered dance scene had begun to generate by the first half of the 1970s. Notably, the incident reveals continued tensions between elite and working-class sectors of Caleño society over música antillana and salsa, and the ways in which control over public space, airwaves, and musical tastes was considered important for the constitution of local subjectivity. The Catholic Church, whose hold on Colombian society and politics had steadily waned since the nineteenth century, clearly wanted to retain power over what they felt was the last area upon which they could exert authority— Holy Week. Knowing this, however, local salseros devised a tactic to assist their expansion into city radio waves, by encroaching on the Catholic Church's dominance of Holy Week and turning church denunciations into free publicity.

In contrast to a similar scenario twenty years earlier, when the archbishop of Antioquia denounced the mambo and música tropical in the 1950s, local working-class salseros did not merely ignore elitist indictments against their culture but actually subverted them to their own ends. Interestingly, neither *El País* nor *El Occidente,* the two local daily newspapers, reported a single line about this incident, indicating that the church still had some degree of control over local media.[53]

Radio Tigre, one of Cali's first all-salsa radio stations, mirrored the boom in all-salsa programming that dominated local soundscapes during the early 1970s. By the end of the decade the excitement had declined, and radio stations reverted to mixed-format programming. It was not until the late 1980s, at the apex of Cali's live scene, that Caleños had all-salsa radio stations again.

The Decline of the Dance Scene

A number of factors led to the decline of the local record-centered dance scene in the 1980s. The teen agüelulos had ended in the early 1970s, owing to the logistical complications and gang violence associated with the increasingly large gatherings (I was told that the last agüelulo drew nearly two thousand people).[54] The nightclub scene also shifted toward a wealthier clientele, as money poured into the city with the rise of the Cali cocaine cartel. This period coincided with a new era of rapid urbanization in Cali, since the influx of wealth also spurred the construction of luxury condominiums, shopping centers, and residential villages.

The tendency toward material display and high spending in the new salsa nightclubs led to economic inflation throughout the local scene. By the early 1990s clubs were charging as much as 40,000 pesos (US$50) for a bottle of local rum or aguardiente (which cost only $2–3 in the store); imported whiskey could easily run over $100 a bottle. The city also became much more violent: cocaine mafiosos began to attend nightclubs armed with pistols and submachine guns, and people risked getting shot in gangland-style shoot-outs. The sharp rise in muggings and hold-ups further discouraged individuals from going out to dance.[55] Given the combination of high nightclub prices and urban violence, most Caleños simply chose to stay at home.

As a result, local popular culture developed two distinct branches. One was the flourishing of the live salsa scene in the 1980s, associated with the rise of the cocaine cartel. Importantly, the style of salsa associated with the live scene was not 1960s and 1970s salsa dura, but rather salsa romántica. Following international commercial trends, local radio stations and luxury nightclubs also played salsa romántica instead of the classic sounds. People continued to dance in these venues, but the creative fervor of the earlier scene diminished considerably. Salsa dance contests and floor shows disappeared altogether. By the time I arrived in Cali in 1994, it was very difficult to see good salsa dancing in such clubs—indeed, I did not witness the famous Caleño style of dancing until the resurgence of the viejotecas in 1996.

Die-hard fans of classic 1960s–70s salsa, on the other hand, established spaces of their own in the salsotecas and tabernas, discussed in the next chapter. Through the 1980s and 1990s, the salsotecas and luxury nightclubs emerged as parallel salsa zones in Cali. With few exceptions, their physical location and the style of music they played mapped onto the socioeconomic stratification of Cali's neighborhoods (see Appendices 1 and 2). Luxury nightclubs featuring salsa romántica prevailed along the Avenida Roosevelt, Avenida Sexta, and Calle Quinta near Imbanaco (Carrera 39)— all major roads in middle- and upper-middle-class neighborhoods. The salsotecas and tabernas, on the other hand, which featured classic salsa dura and Cuban music, were concentrated along or near Calle 44 (dubbed *la calle de las salsotecas* [the salsoteca street]), a three-mile-long artery running through the heart of several working-class barrios.

This dual salsa culture is unique in Latin America. By the early 1990s luxury nightclubs and salsa romántica had largely replaced earlier establishments in major salsa cities such as New York, San Juan, Miami, and Caracas. While Cali was not immune to this trend, local aficionados of 1960s and 1970s salsa maintained public spaces in which to gather and collectively reaffirm their love of this style. The very recordings that were the focus of Cali's earlier dance scene were easily transferred to the new spaces of the salsotecas and tabernas, which maintained an active role for recorded music in local popular culture.

The Viejoteca Revival

The first viejotecas appeared in 1993, during the height of the live scene. They were created initially as a recreational activity for senior citizens and were gradually adopted by a few venues in Cali's working-class neighborhoods as a special sort of dance not only for senior citizens, but for anyone over forty. The key draws of the viejotecas were cheap liquor prices (a flask of aguardiente cost only one or two dollars above grocery store prices, a chance to be among people of one's own generation (and not feel overrun by youth), and, most important, the opportunity to dance all afternoon long to the music one had grown up with.

The turning point for the viejoteca phenomenon came in July–August 1995, shortly after the leaders of the Cali cocaine cartel were captured and many of those associated with their illicit trade left town or went underground. (Gilberto Rodríguez Orejuela, the supposed leader of the cartel, was arrested on 9 June 1995). For luxury nightclubs, this meant a significant loss of clientele. Looking for new ways to salvage plummeting business, they adopted the viejoteca idea, with unprecedented success. A huge and long-neglected market had been tapped, one that had felt alienated by modern salsa, high prices, and the threat of violence that pervaded the nightclub scene by the early 1990s. Viejotecas mushroomed throughout the city. Many places abandoned the age restriction, and teenagers and young adults who had grown up listening to their parents play this music at home also attended en masse. Some older customers told me they resented the presence of younger folk, seeing the viejotecas as their special territory,[56] but most seemed to enjoy the convivial family atmosphere that emerged in these places—recuperating the feel of the 1940s and 1950s neighborhood dance scene.

Notably, the viejoteca scene witnessed a revival of the unique local dance style associated with the agüelulos and salsa nightclubs of the 1960s and 1970s. While the dance style of this earlier scene did not die completely during the 1980s—it was maintained in small bars and casetas in Juanchito—by the mid-1980s most Caleños had adopted the standard short-short-long step of international salsa dancing.[57] With the emergence of the viejotecas, many older dancers unpacked their old dance shoes, ruffled satin shirts, fringed dresses, and other garb associated with the golden era of local salsa dancing. Professional troupes such as Evelio Carabalí's Ballet Folclor de Urbano presented tightly choreographed routines in the viejotecas. Some dancers made a junket, going around to viejotecas on weekends and performing impromptu numbers for clubgoers in return for a few pesos or a round of drinks. I remember one fellow, outfitted in a ruffled shirt and baggy pants, who performed an outrageously funny act with a life-size rag doll attached to his shoes; he never failed to bring down the house.

Many people with whom I spoke talked about the viejotecas as a return to the "good old days," when Cali was pure festivity and dance. My subsequent return trips to Cali in 1997 and 2000 confirmed that the viejotecas were still going strong. They had even spread to other Colombian cities, including Medellín and Cartagena.[58] It is clear that the viejoteca revival represents a symbolic victory over the perceived evils wrought by the Cali cocaine cartel on the local salsa scene. The economic bonanza associated with the cartel certainly fostered an extraordinary and rapid growth of the local scene, providing resources for the presentation of international salsa bands, the rise of local orquestas, and the promotion of salsa in local media. This expansion, however, caused a significant rupture with the older dance scene, displacing a large sector of salsa fans who did not identify with the new style of salsa being promoted.

How in the Devil Do We Situate the Viejotecas?

Among most Caleños animosity toward the cocaine cartel and its domination over city life ran deep, but public criticism of this intrusion could not be openly voiced without incurring certain reprisal. A tale that began to circulate widely in the early 1990s about the appearance of the devil in a salsa nightclub reveals these prevalent but necessarily muted sentiments. Tales of Faustian encounters with the devil are found throughout Latin America and the Caribbean, as Michael Taussig (1980), José Limón (1994), and others have discussed. The Cali devil story concerns a diabolically good salsa dancer (what else?) who seduces local women with his charms. I know four versions of the Cali devil story, but, given the Colombian penchant for spinning a yarn, I am sure that more exist. Notably, all of the variants are located in Juanchito, the Caleños' preferred after-hours party spot.

I will not recount all the versions I know of this tale, in which the devilish dancer's racial identity is portrayed variously as black or white. In the rendition that concerns me here, a handsome, well-dressed white man pulls up at Agapito (the most popular salsa nightclub in Juanchito) in a brand-new red Jeep. Red Jeeps are a status symbol that by the early 1990s were associated with the upwardly mobile ranks of cocaine mafiosos in the city. It is not enough that he pulls up in a flashy car, however—he also commits the blatant sacrilege of pulling up to this club to dance salsa during Holy Week, a time of solemn religious observance in this very Catholic country. His expensive clothes and elegantly pomaded hair catch the eye of other nonbelievers who have also gone to dance, and people crowd around his charismatic and seductive figure before realizing that he is the devil in disguise. While this fellow is dancing with an attractive young woman, he begins to levitate, before disappearing in a billowing, sulfuric cloud of smoke. This sighting supposedly occurred in 1991 or 1992 and was reported in all the newspapers the next day.

This story resonates with a similar tale shared among black campesinos of the rural area south of Cali, who have encapsulated their losing battle with the powerful sugarcane industry as an encounter with the "green devil" (Taussig 1980). The Cali devil narrative parallels this. It is clearly a metaphor for the encroachment of the cocaine mafiosos on the local scene — an allegory about their unholy traffic and its conspicuous intrusion into the lives of "decent folk." The identity of Juanchito as a poor Afro-Colombian settlement further underscores this similarity. Most of Juanchito's actual inhabitants do not own the nightclubs built there and profit only indirectly from this trade (the main subsistence activity of the village is dredging sand from the Cauca River for sale to contractors in Cali's construction industry). As in the case of the black peasants, the devil is cast as a white male whose evil stems from wealth (white, in this case, also indexes the color of cocaine powder). The presumably working-class female dancer and onlookers of both sexes are inferred to be the innocent and guileless victims (perhaps of darker skin?) taken in by his power. According to various informants, this metaphor was clearly understood by Caleños, especially because of the red Jeep, associated with the mafiosos. In this version of the Juanchito devil legend, there is also an implicit pairing of racial and gender terms, where blackness and femaleness — represented in the figure of a women dancer from the working-class barrios — are constructed as categories of weakness and vulnerability in a way that mirrored the actual relationship between the cocaine barons and the citizens of Cali.

Viejotecas and Collective Memory

Recent scholarship in psychology suggests that the emotional intensity of a memory resides less in its meaning at the time an event took place than in its significance at the time of its recall (Singer and Salovey 1993: 51–52). Understanding the mechanics of collective memory therefore involves looking at the ways recollected moments are selectively chosen and sustained by a group in the present as a tool for maintaining a cohesive social identity during times of flux and upheaval. The reenactment of those moments — in Cali's case, through dancing to classic salsa records — is recreational not only as a leisure pastime, but also as a constant reconstitution of the social body. Cali has undergone successive waves of rapid urbanization and instability since the middle of the twentieth century. Working-class Caleños, however, have chosen to remember the 1960s and 1970s not as a time of struggle and precarious existence at the city's margins, but as a time of innocent fun, when new friendships and community bonds were forged through dancing together to records. The semantic and affective ties linking memory, dance, and recordings have cemented a collective identity that continued to anchor the city's working classes through the new and unsettling changes wrought by the cocaine economy during the 1980s and 1990s.

A 1995 poster advertising the viejoteca at a nightclub called Changó invokes these links.[59] Framing the central image of two dancers, nostalgic images of Hollywood and Mexican movie stars are interspersed with those of phonographs, palm trees, and famed singers and instrumentalists of the 1940s and 1950s. At the top of the poster appears a poetic manifesto of viejoteca philosophy:

Disfrutar recordando	Enjoy yourself remembering
tiempos de ayer	the times of yesterday
al compás de música aprendida	to the beat of music learned
a fuerza de bailarla.	by the power of dancing to it.
Revivir la emoción de aquellos	Relive the emotion of those
momentos inolvidables	unforgettable moments
y sentir que somos los mismos.	and feel that we are the same.

In this epigraph, memory, music, dance, and emotion are tightly linked. Music is literally incorporated into one's body and feelings "by the power of dancing to it," and listening to and moving to these rhythms in turn unlocks powerful and pleasurable memories. The final line, "sentir que somos los mismos," is particularly evocative and points to the mythic image of a kinder, gentler Cali before the advent of the drug cartel.

The viejoteca revival can be seen as a grassroots response to the upheavals caused by the Cali cartel. Significantly, in contrast to the tendency of cultural revivals to be romanticized, middle-class appropriations of working-class expressions (Livingston 1999), the viejotecas are primarily working-class venues, established by and for the populace, who developed the record-centered dance culture in the first place. The economic boom associated with the cartel not only changed the local salsa scene, it also galvanized a huge wave of migration from other, non-salsero regions of Colombia. This development, in conjunction with other commercial styles that were being promoted by the national media and record industry, opened the city to new cultural flows, further threatening to displace the established image of Cali as a salsa capital. The viejotecas hence mark a seizing back of local popular culture at the moment the cartel's hold on the city was broken, before other factions that had entered as a result of the cartel's influence were able to dislodge salsa's primacy. In short, the viejoteca revival constitutes a symbolic victory dance for the forces of musical memory that created and continue to fashion Caleño popular culture.

3
Life in the Vinyl Museum

Salsotecas *and*
Record Collectors

During the 1980s a new space opened up for Caleño salsa fans. By this time the record-centered dance scene was in decline, displaced by the boom in live music and local media that was clearly oriented toward new commercial trends in international salsa, particularly salsa romántica. In response to these changes, small drinking spots sprang up in working-class neighborhoods, dedicated to keeping alive the older strains of salsa dura that had shaped the vibrant local dance scene of earlier years. These "vinyl museums," as one DJ called them, are the salsotecas and tabernas, and they emerged as public extensions of private record collections. The salsotecas feature classic salsa, while the tabernas also promote traditional Cuban son, Latin jazz, and contemporary Cuban songo and timba. Unlike the earlier scene, however, which was geared toward dancing to salsa dura records, the salsotecas and tabernas are oriented specifically toward listening—often because there is not enough room to dance.

When I arrived in Cali in 1994, the salsotecas and tabernas were still going strong. Of all the elements contributing to the Caleño self-image as the world salsa capital, these venues are surely unique. When I described Cali to non-Colombian friends and colleagues, it was the salsotecas that most often caught their attention. They certainly fascinated me. I was introduced to the salsotecas and tabernas soon after arriving in Cali, and these places remained my hangouts during my fieldwork. Being a record collector and aficionado myself, it was here that I felt most as if I were among kindred spirits. Hanging out among fellow melómanos—literally, people "crazy for sound" (*melos*)—I perceived the cultural differences engendered by my being a foreigner and an ethnomusicologist dissolve in a mutual enthusiasm for salsa dura and its Cuban and Puerto Rican roots.

I visited similar venues in Barranquilla, Cartagena, Bogotá, Medellín, and other Colombian cities, but Cali's salsoteca scene was by far the strongest. To my knowledge, such establishments do not exist outside Colombia. While collectors and fans often get together to share their records and listen to music in several other parts of Latin America and the Caribbean—indeed, in Puerto Rico there is a formal association of collectors that meets annually[1]—their gatherings are generally limited to private meetings in people's homes. Even in New York City and Puerto Rico, where a broad community of collectors and fans continues to preserve a passion for classic salsa and its Cuban and Puerto Rican roots, public spaces akin to Cali's salsotecas and tabernas simply do not exist. Why? What are the particular historical conditions that led to the emergence of salsotecas and tabernas in Cali and other parts of Colombia and not elsewhere? Furthermore, how did record collecting emerge as such a prominent cultural activity in Caleño popular life? In North America we often think of collecting as a middle-class practice and associate it with disposable income and leisure time. This is not borne out in Cali's case, where collecting records of salsa and música antillana transgresses class boundaries in very particular ways, forging class alliances in some instances while reinforcing class distinctions in others.

The salsotecas and tabernas gave birth in the 1980s to a new set of cosmopolitan cultural practices centered around salsa records. The aficionados and collectors, in a growing network that cut across class lines, became self-appointed guardians of the city's musical memory, and their cultural practices augmented the cosmopolitan ties of salsa and música antillana records established in earlier decades. Acquiring records and building intellectual knowledge about their contents became an important new focus in local popular culture, a refinement of the cultural capital used to garner prestige and to enhance one's social status. While dancing to records remained a mainstay at parties and nightclubs, the fervor and uniqueness of the earlier 1960s and 1970s record-centered dance scene declined substantially. In its stead, live music making finally emerged as an important focus for musical activity, with concerts and local media following international commercial trends in salsa. Within this context, the salsotecas and tabernas formed an important rearguard for the preservation of the sounds that first accompanied Cali's development into a major urban center. In this chapter I explore the history of record collecting in Cali and the rise of the salsoteca and taberna scene, examining the more recent shifts during the 1990s and the changing meanings for this sphere of local popular culture.

Alliances with Middle-Class Youth

The emergence of Cali's salsotecas and tabernas in the 1980s was prefaced by the expansion of salsa into other social sectors of the city during the late 1960s and early 1970s. A key factor in this growth was salsa's adoption by the local university crowd. In Cali, both the Universidad del Valle (Univalle, the departmental university), and the Universidad de Santiago de Cali (USACA) were prime points of contact between youths and intellectuals from the working and middle classes. Here friendships were forged not along class lines but around common interests and political ideologies. As in other parts of Latin America during the late 1960s and 1970s, Cali's universities were hotbeds of leftist intellectual discourse, with young protagonists forging alliances across class lines around the ideology of class struggle against elite domination.

In Cali salsa music became the center of ideological debates about class difference. Colombian música tropical was associated with the bourgeoisie, while salsa was clearly identified with the city's majority working-class sector. Although salsa was looked down upon by older conservative middle- and upper-class Caleños, many of their sons and daughters became attracted to its pulsing rhythms, especially young university students who rejected their class values and identified politically with the working classes. Most of these youths were what would be identified in Colombia as white or light-skinned mestizos, and their embrace of music associated with the darker-skinned working classes posed a significant challenge to dominant bourgeois values. The process was captured by Andrés Caicedo in what is considered the quintessential novel of the period, the semiautobiographical *¡Que viva la música!* (Long Live Music!), published shortly before the author committed suicide in 1977. The book narrates the story of a white middle-class teenager and her friends, who rebel against family mores by taking up salsa music, sex, drugs, and alcohol. (Rock music is also invoked as an influential international current on local youth culture but is secondary to the focus on salsa.) The parallel between Caicedo's heroine and the working-class teenage girls who escaped to the agüelulos without parental approval is striking, since both cases concern a contesting of patriarchal codes and parental authority.

The adoption of salsa among the university crowd in the late 1960s and early 1970s marked a significant development in salsa's impact on local popular identity. In addition to loosening the prejudices that had branded salsa a working-class expression, university intellectuals began ascribing additional meanings to salsa that enlarged its value as enjoyable social dance music. Salsa was tied to leftist ideologies that upheld working-class music and culture as a key element of validating "the people" and contesting the dominance of the bourgeois elites. Fernando Taisechi, a melómano and radio host who grew up in the middle-class neighborhood of San Fernando, explained to me that salsa is music about the barrio, filled with images common to every Latin American neighborhood—the corner store, the gossiping neighbors, the drunken bum, the kids playing in the street, and so forth.[2] While the cloistered streets of most upper-midde-class areas in Latin American belie Taisechi's claim that anyone can relate to salsa's stories, what is significant is his projection of an *imagined* sense of community, providing a base of communication for those who otherwise had little in common. I have heard similar comments from many other salsa aficionados, all echoing this romanticized discourse.

Such notions emerged gradually as young bohemian intellectuals picked up on new currents emanating from New York. During the late 1960s and early 1970s, many of Cali's young middle-class leftists listened only to música antillana and the salsa of Richie Ray and Bobby Cruz—local heroes after their 1968 appearance in Cali. During this time, the style being developed by New York artists such as Willie Colón, the Fania All-Stars, and the Lebrón Brothers was still confined to lower-class areas, particularly in the griles and casetas that attracted a predominantly black clientele. The leftist bohemian crowd, which included many students from the Univalle and USACA, congregated at El Bar de Wiliam (later renamed the Havana Club), a small hole-in-the-wall establishment that primarily featured the music of the Sonora Matancera and of Richie Ray and Bobby Cruz.[3] Middle- and upper-middle-class salsa fans began to expand outward from their meeting place at El Bar de Wiliam, however, to working-class establishments, where they were exposed to these newer salsa styles. Juanchito's position as an all-night party spot was key in this transitional process. Taisechi remembers: "At two in the morning these places kicked us out. . . . And we started to form a group of friends to go to Juanchito. . . . There we sat down to listen to music on the black people's turf, where black couples were partying. And there we learned another kind of salsa that wasn't what we heard in William's Bar or the Havana Club."[4] Dance halls in Juanchito featured the newer, more rugged sounds that were beginning to come out of New York City by 1970. This style was more aggressive than the traditional música antillana featured in El Bar de Wiliam, or the pachanga and bugalú still popular in the agüelulos and many griles. By the early 1970s most New York and Puerto Rican salsa orquestas had expanded from earlier Cuban ensembles, with a full arsenal of percussion instruments (conga, timbales, and bongo) and a horn section that included both trumpets and trombones (usually two or three of each). This format made for a louder and denser sound than the son conjuntos or the flute-and-violin charangas that performed pachanga in the early 1960s. With dynamic arrangements, driving percussion, and strident horns—particularly the rugged trombones introduced by Eddie Palmieri and Willie Colón—this new style seemed to echo the accelerated pace and tumultuous ambience of city life. The term "salsa dura" reflects this emerging aesthetic. Although the salsa performed by Richie Ray and Bobby Cruz at this time certainly incorporated some of the hard-driving percussion typical of salsa dura, their sound was essentially modeled after the Sonora Matancera and did not have the aggressive edge heard in other New York bands from this period.

In addition to these musical features, the thematic content of most salsa dura lyrics shifted. While picaresque situations and the joys of dance music prevailed in salsa tunes as they had in música antillana and pachanga, salsa dura also depicted the harsh realities of urban working-class existence, especially that of U.S. Latinos. Struggling for political recognition and access to resources, Latinos in the United States rallied around salsa as a vehicle for protest and ethnic solidarity during the early 1970s (Singer 1982; Padilla 1989). Salsa lyrics expressed an increasing discontent with the conditions confronting working-class Latinos and called out to Latin Americans of all social classes and national origins to join hands against U.S. political and economic domination. Back in Latin America, the influence of U.S. Latino ethnicity contributed, at least in leftist circles, to the emergence of an idealized pan-Latino identity. In this expanded context, resentment against underdevelopment and U.S. political and economic control throughout Latin America and the Caribbean (Frank 1967) helped to situate pan-Latino identity in global terms. Leftist intellectuals in Latin America embraced salsa not only because it was the music of the working class, but also because it represented an alternative to the hegemonic presence of U.S. rock and pop music in mainstream international media (see Duany 1984). During the 1970s salsa dura was seen as protest music, a danceable counterpart to *nueva canción* (new song). Songs by the Puerto Rican composer Tite Curet Alonso and the Panamanian star Rubén Blades detailed everyday scenes of the Latin American working-class barrio and spoke out against the dominant forces that oppressed all Latinos, regardless of nationality.

The message of struggle and pan-Latino solidarity was not lost on leftists in Cali, who saw salsa as a force uniting people across social boundaries. For Caleño intellectuals, a hopeful vision of and identification with "the people" was derived from salsa's lyrics and its working-class ties, augmenting its significance in their eyes. Salsa, unlike pachanga, was seen not merely as "party music," but rather as an expression of authentic grassroots identity and a rallying point for social mobilization.[5] Indeed, the leftist guerilla movement M-19 embraced salsa as an inspirational force during the 1970s. Guerilla leader Jaime Bateman coined the phrase *la social vacanería* ("societal grooviness") as a slogan for M-19's bohemian agenda in those early days—a life of joy, happiness, and good times for all. The impact of salsa music on M-19 guerrillas was so strong that clandestine meetings with invited salsa "experts" were organized, in order to discuss the ideological message and liberating potential of salsa as a tool for revolutionary struggle. Some salsa intellectuals, not only in Cali but also in Bogotá, were actively involved with M-19 before the movement shifted to a strategy of violent aggression, which led to the notorious and tragic bombing of the national Palace of Justice in 1985.[6]

While there is nothing about salsa that inherently unifies people from diverse backgrounds, its spread in Cali is closely tied to the social and political interests of people of different classes. Alberto Borja, another fan from the middle-class neighborhood of San Fernando, explained why he and his buddies became salsómanos: "I see it as a *social* evolution, it's not just a matter of music. Apart from being music that we also liked . . . it made groups of people who are linked through that medium, which is [salsa] music. And we're left with some incredible bonds, precisely because of that. Because we talked the same thing, you see? And we experienced the same thing."[7] Borja and the circle of friends he refers to (which includes Taisechi) were young men during the late 1960s and early 1970s, aware of and affected by international events and the climate of social upheaval and protest occurring throughout the Americas during this time. In North America young people were involved in civil rights struggles, anti–Vietnam War demonstrations, and the women's liberation movement. In Latin America the cause of leftist revolution was being taken up by students and intellectuals inspired by such figures as Che Guevara, Fidel Castro, and Salvador Allende. In Cali many young intellectuals of all classes were involved in leftist political activities, ranging from Marxist and Maoist study groups to covert acts of sabotage.[8] Salsa music became a banner for this group, associated with the deeper personal and political struggles they were undergoing.

Alongside political debates around salsa, through the 1970s and 1980s there was a flowering of salsa-inspired artistic work among young Caleño intellectuals and bohemians. Most of this was literary and comprised a profusion of short stories, poems, and novels in which salsa formed the soundtrack for everyday dramas and desires. Some of the more notable titles from this time include Umberto Valverde's *Bomba camará* (1972), a book of short stories titled after a Richie Ray tune; Valverde's semiautobiographical tribute, *Celia Cruz: reina rumba* (1981); and an important anthology of short stories by Caleño authors titled *Historias de amor, salsa, y dolor* (Stories of Love, Salsa, and Heartbreak; Cuervo 1989). In addition to this are countless poems by various authors. Through all of these works, local writers presented not only narratives about salsa's presence in daily life, but also salsa's very sounds and rhythms. Following the school of the 1920s Cuban poet Nicolás Guillén (author of *Songoro cosongo,* among others), devices such as repetition, onomatapoeic phrases, call and response, fragments of salsa lyrics, street jargon, and run-on sentences were deployed to convey the sensation and flow of salsa music itself. Salsa music was also the point of inspiration for paintings, film, and theater. One notable cinematic tribute to local salsa is *Tacones* (Heels; 1981), directed by Pascual Guerrero Jr. (the son of a famous local soccer player after whom the central stadium in Cali is named). Mounted as a comedic battle between salseros and disco fans, the film features local and international salsa musicians and many scenes of famous Caleño dancers. Finally, dance companies such as the Barrio Ballet fused classical ballet and salsa, constituting an important formalization of local salsa dancing.

The wellspring of salsa-inspired literary and artistic work among Caleño intellectuals transcended lines of socioeconomic class and race. Many literary authors, in particular, hailed from mixed racial backgrounds and grew up in working-class and lower-middle class neighborhoods that were strongholds of música antillana and salsa. Leftist ideologies heightened the intensity of a music that was already part of their personal identity and experience. For those from the upper classes, on the other hand, salsa became an emblem of cultural resistance and a vehicle for solidarity with the working class. According to Timothy Pratt, an expatriate white American poet and journalist living in Cali, the burgeoning of salsero art emerged organically from salsa's position at the heart of local popular culture. He explained to me that the refusal of the city's elites to accept and support this movement indicated their deeply entrenched classist and racist attitudes.[9] This position is also drawn along generational lines, since some younger members of the bourgeosie were indeed attracted to salsa. While members of the city's upper echelons may have denied salsa's legitimacy as a cultural expression, however, significant ties had already been formed between members of Cali's working and middle classes.

When the salsotecas and tabernas began to appear in the early 1980s, they drew many individuals from the bohemian, intellectual crowd. While the ideological, romanticized discourse about salsa was not adopted in its entirety by all who attended the salsotecas, it did intersect in significant ways with the practices of collecting and listening from which the salsotecas emerged. For leftists and non-political fans alike, the salsotecas opened an important space for upholding salsa as a "serious" music made not only for dancing, but also for intellectual appreciation and discussion.

Collecting Records

In addition to the expansion of salsa into leftist and bohemian circles in the 1960s and 1970s, Cali's salsotecas and tabernas have their origins among the working-class individuals who collected salsa records. As I noted in the previous chapter, this practice actually began during the 1940s and 1950s, but it was a solidly entrenched feature of barrio life by the 1960s. Recordings, as consumer items, have always represented a significant investment for the average Caleño. The cost of a new record during the 1950s, 1960s, and 1970s was roughly two or three times the cost of a pound of meat or a flask of aguardiente—approximately the same ratio that applies nowadays.[10] As an index of cosmopolitan tastes and as the primary source of music for barrio parties, records were already a valued commodity. Given the high cost of albums and playback equipment, however, records also acquired importance as a marker of social prestige and symbolic capital.[11]

Collecting recordings emerged as a practice of commodity festishism among Cali's working classes. During the 1960s and 1970s Caleños were caught up in a booming transnational economy (sugar) that not only wrought profound changes in the urban environment, but also accelerated the manner in which capital accumulation had become the dominant mode in local, regional, and national economies. As modestly paid laborers in the local sugar mills and other industries (construction, manufacturing, and retail of hardware, textiles, and household goods), working-class Caleños did not have the means to acquire many goods. Surplus earnings were usually invested in purchasing a modest house, so that a family might own and not merely rent their home. Owing to their symbolic links to sailors and cosmopolitan Latin American culture, salsa and música antillana records became fetishes—in the sense in which Joseph Roach uses the term—for evoking and "filling in" the desire to express a sense of worldliness and cosmopolitan identity (1996). Buying and collecting these valuable items hence became sources for boosting one's social status at the barrio level. Gary Domínguez, a record collector and taberna owner from a mixed-race, middle-class family observed:

Domínguez: It seems crazy but poor people buy more music than the rich.

Waxer: Still?

Domínguez: It's always been that way. Because for them it's more than a musical need, to have good music at home. That is, it's like food for the working and middle classes. You just buy a record, but for someone else it's a ritual. And it's a big effort, because while you have the cash to buy a compact disc you're never going to listen to, the other guy is sweating so he can buy a record album a week, imagine. So, the value that one can give to that record for the same economic, sentimental, and a whole bunch of other reasons—the very difficulty of buying an album, and having your idol on the jacket cover—well, just think about it.[12]

My informal conversations with collectors and aficionados from Cali's working-class barrios confirmed these remarks. For many of these people, investing in records has been a sign of financial resources, however limited. Luis Adalberto Sánchez, a working-class Caleño of mestizo background, noted that when he started buying records in the 1970s, these purchases represented his sweat and labor—his ability to earn an income that, while not large, always covered basic expenses and left a little extra for items such as music.[13] The affective impact and immediacy of music as a conduit for bodily pleasures of dance and listening no doubt contributed to working-class conceptions of recorded music as more "essential" than other luxury items such as automobiles or fine jewelry. In Cali, therefore, records became a key sign of distinction in this social sector (see Bourdieu 1984; Douglas and Isherwood 1979). Those who had playback equipment (a gramophone or, later, a stereo) and who invested in the latest records from New York and Cuba provided music for the street and became important people in their neighborhoods. As we saw in Victor Caicedo's anecdote about the Saturday afternoon sonorazo (Sonora Matancera) listening sessions recounted in chapter 2, their houses served as meeting places for neighbors to gather, drink, argue about soccer teams, and eventually, form impromptu dance parties.

During the 1960s and 1970s, the main center for buying records of música antillana and salsa was along Calle 15, a commercial artery in the former Zona de Tolerancia. As I mentioned in chapter 2, 78 rpm recordings and, later, LPs were brought from Buenaventura and sold by vendors from *carritos* (small stands) in the street. These vendors still exist, located on the corner of Calle 15 and Carrera 8; some have been there for nearly three decades, while others have become involved in the business more recently. Other casual vendors are a common sight in Cali's downtown, parked on virtually every corner or major pedestrian thoroughfare; they usually sell inexpensive "reprints" or even pirates of classic salsa albums, manufactured in Venezuela.[14] Most of my own collection of used and reprinted salsa albums came from these record vendors. The carritos also carry such stock, but their specialty is buying and selling *pasta americana,* the thicker and better quality "American vinyl" of the original 1960s and 1970s salsa editions. Depending on the condition of the album, one of these records might sell for anywhere from US$9 to $30, as opposed to $5 to $7 for the cheaper Venezuelan reprints. Not only do vintage albums index an older musical style (salsa dura) that is considered superior to current commercial salsa romántica, but, like comic books and other collectibles, they also represent a large financial investment. Because it is no longer possible to obtain such records from New York, imported salsa recordings have become even more exclusive, augmenting their value as symbolic and cultural capital.

Through the 1970s and 1980s working-class record collectors served as culture brokers of música antillana and salsa for the rest of the barrio, especially for the younger generation. My friend Elcio Viedman, an Afro-Colombian born in 1967, grew up across the street from Luis Adalberto Sánchez in Barrio Antanasio Girardot and explained that he and other neighborhood boys acquired most of their knowledge about salsa from him. His friend Edwin, a light-skinned mestizo from the same street, told me that as a youngster he regularly visited Adalberto, asking the older man if he could listen to and tape his records. This was how he built up his own collection of recordings, although most of them consist of dubbed cassette tapes. Friendships made at school widened the circle of youths from different neighborhoods, as young fans traded cassettes among themselves and expanded the arena of musical diffusion.[15]

The process of musical transmission from older barrio collectors down to the next generation served as an important counterpart to the dance scene. Not only did it help diffuse música antillana and salsa, it also entrenched these sounds as part of a local cultural tradition. In these circles, melómanos emerged organically at the barrio level: sitting and listening attentively to music, discussing aspects of style (e.g., instrumental solos, horn arrangements, and lyric content), and exchanging information on artists, recording dates, and other discographical information.

Alliances with middle-class youth helped to further diffuse this music, and the additional meanings ascribed to salsa among this set—such as its populist messages and revolutionary potential—were in turn accepted, to a certain degree, among working-class aficionados. One striking feature of this scene is the way in which commodity fetishism—as a practice of prestige and distinction—existed in tandem with contradictory Marxist ideals about working-class solidarity, egalitarianism, and the negation of individual material accumulation. Most significantly, however, the growing sphere of record collectors and melómanos formed a new cultural space in which the intellectual appreciation of music drew together members of Cali's working, middle, and upper-middle classes. While record collecting and intellectualizing music is usually (and too narrowly) identified as solely a middle-class pastime, Cali's case illustrates the need for us to engage in less static models of class distinction. In Cali salsa and música antillana certainly did not do away with class boundaries, but they did open up new spaces in which these differences could temporarily be bridged.

Record Collectors

As música antillana and salsa acquired fans across class lines during the 1970s and 1980s, a notable subculture of record collectors began to emerge. This subculture split into two categories that continue to define salsa record collectors in Cali today. The first group comprises people who collect in quantity and carefully guard their collections, often organizing and cataloging their collections according to genre and artist. Collectors in this category, interested as much in the accumulation of records as in listening, zealously build and maintain their collections. According to Gary Domínguez, a true collector would own at least a thousand records, and many Caleño collectors own five thousand to ten thousand records or more.[16] Domínguez further divides these "big numbers" collectors into two camps; those who collect primarily recordings of música antillana and maybe also pachanga and bugalú, and those who collect primarily salsa from the late 1960s on. He himself falls into the salsero group, but the family also owns several hundred música antillana recordings collected by his father, Edgar Mallarino, a local soccer star during the 1950s.[17]

In both Cali and Barranquilla, many big-numbers record collectors are from the middle and upper-middle classes, mainly because greater economic resources have permitted a larger investment of time and money in collecting. Others, however, such as Pablo Solano (discussed later) are from Cali's working class, so it is impossible to make generalizations along class lines. One characteristic that does unite collectors, however, is the tendency to treat their collections like "shrines" or "altars"—terms they themselves use. I visited the homes of many of these individuals and was surprised by the constant devotion with which these collectors maintain and organize their records. Records are usually all located in one area of the house, along a wall or in a specially reserved room, and are carefully ordered according to artist, genre, and even country. Within each section albums are usually arranged alphabetically, and different sections can be ordered either alphabetically or chronologically, in terms of stylistic development. Some record collectors even catalog their albums, numbering each acquisition and carefully noting any discographical information. Many big-numbers collectors also accumulate other memorabilia associated with salsa and música antillana—photographs, concert ticket stubs, autographs of famous artists, souvenir figurines, books on the subject, and even instruments. In North America I have seen similar items in the homes of jazz and blues record collectors.

Among the more colorful collections I encountered was that of Jaime Camargo, a white Cartagena native who lived in Cali for over twenty years. Camargo, who calls the study where he houses his collection *el templo de Babalú* (the temple of Babalú), was proud to show off his recordings, books, photographs, and other memorabilia, all diligently cataloged according to style period, geographic area, and artist or author (Figure 3.1). Camargo's "temple" was named after the Yoruba deity Babalú, saint of healing, whose importance in Afro-Cuban Santería was invoked in many popular Cuban songs of the 1940s and 1950s, especially those recorded by Miguelito Valdés (known as "Mr. Babalú")[18] and Celina y Reutilio. Like dozens of others collectors, Camargo has created his own private corner of the Cali scene, and his possessions are proof of the considerable investment that marks his participation in the cosmopolitan world of música antillana and salsa.[19] The festishistic aura through which record discs and memorabilia become converted from mere effigies of the past into its living, spiritual embodiment (Roach 1996) is clear enough. Much like Hernán González's recollection of música antillana as "holy rain," Jaime Camargo's "temple" becomes a space of worship and mystery, of direct communication with his musical gods and what they represent for him.

The second category of record collectors includes individuals who regularly purchase records but are more casual about their property, frequently lending albums, making them accessible to friends, and not worrying too much about maintaining the condition or order of their records. Such people include Luis Adalberto Sánchez, the man who passed salsa along to youths in his neighborhood. He currently does not own many albums but has endeared himself to friends and neighbors for having generously

Figure 3.1 Jaime Camargo's *templo de Babalú*. Photo by Lise Waxer.

shared his knowledge and collection. The spirit of this type of collector influenced the development of the salsotecas and tabernas.

Although a handful of Caleña women collect salsa records, all the big-numbers collectors are men. This correlates to the greater economic resources that men in Cali have had until recently as the principal family wage earners. Gilberto Marrenco, a middle-class collector from Barranquilla, also pointed out to me that in Colombia boys are socialized more than girls to collect things (such as insects or stamps), and this practice continues into adulthood.[20] Certainly, the glee with which people showed their rare recordings to me was reminiscent of that of a delighted child.

Though admired for the dedication and financial investment with which they have built their collections, big-numbers collectors have been perceived by some Caleño aficionados as inaccessible—that is, they keep the wealth of their collection to themselves. These collectors usually do not frequent salsotecas or even tabernas, preferring to stay at home and listen to their own recordings in the company of a few friends. Although the salsotecas and tabernas made *música de colección* (rare recordings) accessible to the general public, the majority of these establishments have not had the same resources or knowledge about music as private collectors. Among big-numbers collectors, much emphasis is placed on ownership and on the condition and exclusivity of one's holdings, whereas the salsoteca crowd is more interested in spreading their resources around. This split is further illustrated by the tendency of collectors to specialize in música antillana and early salsa—owing perhaps to the rarity and exclusivity of these discs—while salsotecas concentrate on salsa from the 1970s to the present. Styles of dress (formal *guayabera* shirts versus casual T-shirts) are further markers of the division between these two groups. Gary Domínguez observed, "I always divide them: the collectors from 1970 on back, and the salsotecas from 1970 onward. So just imagine, in the very form of the music, the manner of dressing, what the songs said, they're two generations separated by an immense abyss."[21] Since there are collectors in their thirties and early forties who are in the "old guard," Gary's reference to "two generations" of aficionados denotes not so much age groups as taste communities defined by their preference for different styles of salsa and música antillana.

The rift between record collectors and the salsotecas is complex because it crosses lines of socioeconomic class and educational background and is also bridged at several points by people who identify with and maintain loyalties to both camps. While affective factors no doubt influence the preference for one or another camp (e.g., pleasant memories of growing up with certain sounds or nostalgia for a former era), the split between collectors and salsotecas relates to larger social divisions. Salsotecas are seen as somewhat *populacho*—"common"—and associated with working-class salseros. Domínguez noted that record collectors often look down on salsoteca owners for their casual attitude and sometimes imprecise knowledge of artists, recording dates, and stylistic developments. Indeed, an attempt to organize a formal association of record collectors and salsoteca owners in 1996 called the Asociación de Melómanaos y Coleccionistas del Valle de Cauca resulted in a pronounced cleavage between these two camps, with the salsoteca owners feeling alienated from the decision-making process and withdrawing from the organization. Even though there are working-class record collectors, many of Cali's big-numbers collectors are middle- and even upper-class doctors and lawyers—people with more economic resources to become collectors. The influence of class-based elitism and commodity fetishism may have compounded this tendency. Wanting to distinguish themselves as superior fans and melómanos, record collectors use the capital of their collections to distance themselves from the salsero masses at the same time that they uphold a romantic, populist idealism by collecting records of what was once looked down on as working-class music (MacGuigan 1992).

Few individuals have successfully realized the dual projects of having large, specialized collections *and* a successful taberna from which to disseminate their holdings.[22] Many observers acknowledge the key role that record collectors have played in preserving the city's musical memory in all its diverse facets. Despite their importance, however, it was the salsotecas and tabernas that ultimately became more important in actively maintaining this musical memory among the general public.

Salsotecas and Tabernas

Located primarily in Cali's working-class neighborhoods, most salsotecas began as mom-and-pop operations in people's garages, when enterprising record collectors realized that the local weekend custom of having friends over to drink, hang out, and listen to music could be turned into a modest business to supplement household income. Although recordings had already acquired weight as cultural capital in previous decades, as a source of income-generating activity they now also represented economic capital. According to Domínguez, the salsotecas first emerged as a space for men who wanted to drink a few beers and listen to their favorite salsa recordings but did not have the time or money (for instance, in midweek) to take their wives or girlfriends dancing.[23] With the shift of the nightclub scene to luxury discotheques patronized by cartel bosses and their men, many working-class Caleños lost an important space for gathering together to enjoy salsa. According to Kuky Preciado, an Afro-Colombian salsero born in the mid-1960s who was raised in a working-class barrio, the salsotecas emerged as a new alternative for salsa fans too busy to sustain the week-long rumba but still interested in having spaces for their music.

Preciado: I think that the salsoteca became necessary, for sure. Because by then the heavy parties were already declining, right? They were like ending, the originators, those who held these parties maybe now were assuming other obligations, now there's no time to be staying up all night and putting on music, nor opening one's house like that. So things went along like this and tended to disappear, that is, the parties became less and less, right?
Waxer: The ones in people's houses. So that's when the salsotecas come up.
Preciado: The salsoteca emerges. And with it, the need that one has as an aficionado and dancer to go to a place where you can hear your own music.[24]

Kuky observed that despite the decline of the dance scene, the link between salsa music and socializing remained important for salsómanos, ex-

Figure 3.2   La Barola, with owner Miguel Angel Saldarriaga and wife.
Photo by Lise Waxer.

plaining that one did not enjoy the music as much cooped up at home listening to the stereo alone. As with the earlier record-centered dance scene,
the salsotecas also attracted bohemians and intellectuals. In short, the salsotecas and tabernas maintained the gregarious and participatory atmosphere of the earlier record-centered dance scene, providing places for salsa
fans of diverse backgrounds to come together and reaffirm social bonds
based on common musical interests.

Cali's first salsoteca, La Barola (Figure 3.2), was established in the barrio
of 20 de Julio in 1980. La Barola had actually been open for many years as a
bar where one could hear música antillana, pachanga, and tango (indeed,
the place was named after a famous tango bar in Buenos Aires). When the
new owner, Miguel Angel Saldarriaga, took over in the late 1970s, however,
he decided that this fare was passé and after 1980 began to specialize in pure
salsa.[25] The salsoteca was a hit and drew many melómanos from all over the
city. Several more salsotecas opened through the first half of the 1980s, and
by the end of the decade there were nearly fifty in Cali, the majority of
them located in the city's working-class barrios. The other centers for salsotecas and tabernas in the 1980s and early 1990s were Calle Quinta and
Avenida Sexta, the same areas where many luxury nightclubs also appeared.

Table 3.1   *Salsotecas* and *tabernas* in Cali, 1980–96

1. In the working-class neigh-
   borhoods of Cali's north and
   northeast:
   - La Barola*
   - Cachana*
   - La Clave
   - Los Latinos
   - Lebrón
   - La Selecta
   - El Ven-ven

2. The "Calle de las Salsotecas":
   - El Bronx
   - Caballo y Montuno
   - Caney
   - Caravana
   - Chaney
   - El Corso
   - La Duboney
   - Fuego en el 23
   - Guanacho
   - El Guateque
   - Impacto Afro-Latino
   - La Mulenze
   - La Ponceña*
   - Punto del Son
   - Soneros
   - Poporopo
   - Quinta Avenida
   - Rincón de Mallarino
   - Roena
   - Swing y Son
   - El Verdadero Son

3. On the city's western flank, along
   or close to Calle Quinta:
   - Bachatá
   - La Bodeguita del Medio
   - Congo Bongó
   - Gucaja (a *cevichería*)*
   - Nuestra Herencia
   - Olafo I
   - Olafo II
   - La Rumba
   - Sabor de Moño
   - El Sapo Cancionero
   - Taberna Latina*
   - Tin Tin Deo

4. In the middle-class north end,
   along Avenida Sexta:
   - El Chuzo de Rafa
   - Convergencia
   - Cafe Libro
   - Rincón Porteño
   - Ritmo Caliente
   - Tiempo Libre
   - Zaperoco

*Indicates one of the early salsotecas or
tabernas that opened in 1980–82.*

The main zone for salsotecas, however, was along Calle 44, a major artery running through the heart of several working-class salsero barrios. Extending along a three-mile strip from Barrio Salomia to 12 de Octubre, several salsotecas were established: La Ponceña, Punto del Son, Congo Bongó, El Bronx, La Mulenze, Caney, and many others. (See Appendix 1 for the geographic distribution of salsotecas and Table 3.1 for a complete list of salsotecas.) Although the majority of the patrons in salsotecas along this street were from the neighboring area, it became a key pastime for middle-class salsómanos to do a *recorrido,* or round, of several salsotecas along Calle 44. Prices for beer and liquor were inexpensive in these establishments (maybe only fifty cents or a dollar for a bottle of beer), which was another important draw.

The name "salsoteca" derives from words such as *biblioteca* (library) and *discoteca* (discotheque)—that is, a place specializing in salsa. Medardo Arias seems to have coined the word, which appeared as a newspaper headline in his award-winning series on salsa history published by *El Occidente* in 1981. Others, however, maintain that the word was simply "in the air" at the time, emerging gradually in local usage. Miguel Saldarriaga, owner of La Barola, said that he does not know where the word came from—it just seemed appropriate to call the bar a "salsoteca" after it began to concentrate solely on salsa.[26]

Luis Enrique "Kike" Escobar, an Afro-Colombian collector, DJ, and club owner born in the early 1960s, notes that the salsotecas have been an important alternative to the griles and commercial radio. This became especially pronounced after nightclubs and local media shifted from salsa dura to salsa romántica in the late 1980s. He cogently observes:

> Through the musical history of the city, the tabernas have taken on the role of being spaces where melómanos can have access to vintage and contemporary music and, furthermore, to the exclusives that still haven't gotten to the radio stations. . . . It seems to me that this is the notion of what a salsoteca or taberna in Cali does, which has allowed for music in Cali—let's say for twenty, twenty-five years—to survive independently of the destruction that radio has generated with its manipulation of commercial music. *Thus, we have to give the tabernas credit for maintaining our people and our cultural ideology of the Caribbean and Antilles, at least in these corners.* Because at least at the level of business and the goals of radio, this is being lost, but in those corners they will always go on, they are emerging as *vinyl museums* that maintain those jewels and those materials for posterity, and also, we can say, for the future of the city.[27] (Italics mine)

This preservation role of these "vinyl museums" is especially important for younger salseros who were born or grew up after this music was made, and who have limited access to older recordings.

The tabernas and salsotecas, however, have had a dual function. According to Kike Escobar, they exist not only to preserve the classic sounds of Cali's salsa scene, but also to keep this tradition evolving by providing exposure to new musical developments ignored by the commercial main-stream. In addition to maintaining classic recordings of salsa dura and música antillana, the salsotecas and tabernas also introduced melómanos to new salsa dura recordings—Puerto Rican artists such as Willie Rosario, Bobby Valentín, and Orquesta Mulenze, who have adopted contemporary salsa romántica aesthetics while maintaining the aggressive edge of salsa dura. Other sounds typically featured at the salsotecas include "superband" recordings by the Descarga Boricua and the Puerto Rican All-Stars, with virtuosic salsa dura arrangements performed by Puerto Rico's best salsa musicians. Such recordings, despite their danceability and immediate popularity among local melómanos, have never been aired on commercial radio. Kike Escobar observed that Caleño salsotecas have often created hits among local audiences without any support from radio or other sources. Examples of this include "La fuga," "La isla," and "Pánico organizado," by Dom Perignón; "Conversemos," by Camilo Azuquita; and "El camino equivocado," "Recuerdo recuerdo," and "Isla bonita," by Pedro Conga. According to Kike, these tunes were all big hits in Cali's salsotecas but were never once played on local radio. Other tunes have been made popular in the salsotecas and have subsequently been picked up by radio, such as Bobby Valentín's recording of "El muñeco de la ciudad."

Notably, as Cali's live scene grew and local bands such as Grupo Niche, Guayacán, and La Misma Gente scene began to establish an internationally recognized style of Colombian salsa, the salsotecas and tabernas maintained a virtual shutout of Colombian bands. Although local nightclubs and radio stations played the recordings of top local bands, Caleño salsa was almost never featured in the salsotecas. The only exceptions might be when a musician or bandleader was friends with a salsoteca owner willing to promote his or her music. Such was the case with Cheo Angulo, leader of the now-defunct Proyecto Omega, whose hard-driving style of salsa was modeled on the New York and Puerto Rican salsa dura stars featured by the salsotecas and whose records did get played in the salsotecas.[28] The refusal to support local salsa in the salsotecas was part of a class-based battle in which local bands were largely identified with commercial salsa romántica and the growing economic influence of the Cali cartel; below I discuss how gender ideologies further underlined this split. As grassroots commercial establishments set up by and for working- and middle-class melómanos, the salsotecas and tabernas provided an alternative space for Caleños who felt alienated by the social undercurrents of this new scene.

The Personalization of Technology
in the Age of Mechanical Sound

For any newcomer to Cali, the salsotecas and tabernas provide a unique cultural experience. For an ethnomusicologist, in particular, these establishments mark an unusual and exciting context in which to study musical reception. Like the karaoke bars that emerged during the 1980s, Cali's salsotecas clearly illustrate an unprecedented creative engagement with sound recordings. As Charles Keil notes for karaoke, such phenomena point to the "personalization of mechanical processes" (Keil and Feld 1994: 253). Indeed, it was in the salsotecas and tabernas that I observed some of the most humanizing instances of the Caleño adoption of salsa. These were far more immediate and accessible to me than performances by local bands, whose concerts on large stages, amplified by large sound systems, seemed remote and impersonal by comparison. In the following section I describe two of my favorite Caleño locales as two instances of the extraordinary creativity with which Caleño collector-entrepreneurs have personalized their encounter with sound technology. These two spaces, the Taberna Latina and Pablo y su Música, have become important nodes for listening to music and meeting with other melómanos.

The Taberna Latina

My principal haunt through my first year of fieldwork was the Taberna Latina, a cramped, intimate bar long revered among Cali's melómanos (see Ulloa 1992: 548). The Latina's engaging atmosphere clearly illustrates the imaginative workings borne through salsa's local adoption. Several photos and posters of New York salsa stars and old Cuban and Puerto Rican maestros adorn the walls, and the ceiling is covered with broadsides advertising past events held at the club (Figure 3.3). I saw similar décor in many other salsotecas and tabernas in Cali and throughout Colombia, but the Latina's rich and humorous bricolage of visual icons from the heydays of salsa and música antillana was the most sophisticated I ever observed.

A virtual hole in the wall only three meters wide and twelve meters long, the Latina is barely large enough for the fifteen small tables lining its perimeter to fit into. Two mammoth speakers are positioned at each end. On my first visit to the club, I was immediately taken by the trombone bell that juts impudently over the speaker by the entrance, seeming to blast along with the dynamic horn choruses. A DJ's booth by the right wall doubles as a bar that seats an extra five or six people. Behind this bar over a thousand classic, out-of-print salsa LPs are stashed alongside the console

Figure 3.3   Taberna Latina. Photo by Lise Waxer.

and playback equipment; nearly a hundred compact discs and cassette tapes are kept in a drawer beneath the turntables. The two waiters on duty were busy running up and down the stairway next to this bar, where the beer keg and liquor bottles are kept behind a small counter located near (but not too near) the basement john. Meanwhile, the owner, Gary Domínguez, in his trademark skullcap and T-shirt, kept records spinning from his booth (Figure 3.4). Domínguez, a bearded, reserved man born in the late 1950s, becomes extroverted and animated behind the turntables, flashing the house lights on and off to punctuate exciting percussion breaks and horn lines and interjecting frenetic commentary over a microphone as if doing a live radio show.

The salsa featured at the Latina and other tabernas and salsotecas is hard indeed, marked by driving percussion and piano, emphatic bass, catchy coros, aggressive horn lines, and dynamic musical arrangements. As fans

Figure 3.4   Gary Domínguez. Photo by Lise Waxer.

put it, this is music that makes you want to dance! Yet, owing in part to the modest economic means in which the Taberna Latina (like most salsote-cas) began, there is no dance floor to speak of. Those who feel inspired to dance must do so in the tiny spaces between tables. While hard-core aficionados often prefer to sit and focus on listening to the music, Caleños in general like to dance, and many tabernas and salsotecas have expanded in recent years, adding a dance floor in order to satisfy public demand. The Latina, however, remains small and cramped.

Despite space restrictions, however, people never sat complacently. On any typical evening during the mid-1990s there was plenty of movement, and it became more animated as the night wore on and quantities of beer, rum, and aguardiente were consumed. People swayed back and forth, and some enthusiasts, particularly young men, played along with the music by slapping out rhythms on the tabletops. The mood was always exuberant, and the crowd often sang along to the recordings, emphasizing the lyrics with spirited gestures. During the 1980s, clients used to bring cowbells and maracas to play, but the club banned this practice since it disturbed other customers. Once in a while, however, Domínguez let a friend take down one of the three *chékeres* (Afro-Cuban beaded calabash shakers) hanging on the left wall to play along with the music.

Twelve more tables line the outdoor patio at the club's entrance. An awning and potted palms frame this outdoor area, marking it off from the sidewalk on which people have parked their cars and providing marginal cover from the curious stares of those headed toward El Sandwich Cubano, a late-night fast-food joint next door. Those sitting outside can converse without having to yell above the music. My favorite place, however, especially when attending alone, was always at the bar. Because most people come here to enjoy the music, not to make sexual conquests, I was usually safe from the advances of strange men, and here, too, I also had a prime vantage point for viewing the slides and video clips that Domínguez featured at regular intervals throughout the night, projected on the screen and television monitor directly above the entrance. Domínguez's antics were entertaining, and he was always willing to let me look at album covers or answer my questions about the music being played. With the interesting musical selection, Domínguez's hospitality, the club's quality sound equipment, the photos and posters, the videos and slides, and the enthusiastic and participatory mood of the clientele, the Taberna Latina seemed like salsa heaven for a (relatively) novice fan from North America like me.

On most evenings I would arrive between 10:00 and 10:30 P.M., still early. People tended to show up after 11:00, with attendance peaking between midnight and 1:00 to stretch the Latina to its 80–100 person capacity—especially after *quincena,* or payday (the fifteenth or thirtieth of each month). If an *audición* or "listening" was featured, however, many clients would arrive earlier, in eager anticipation of the special musical tribute to the career of a particular artist or group. These audiciones became an institution at the Latina in the 1980s and early to mid-1990s and were usually featured twice a month. They provided more than just a nostalgic musical excursion for longtime salsa aficionados—they were also a rich opportunity for younger fans or newcomers to learn about salsa history and styles. Drawing from the more than eight thousand records in his collection, Domínguez would present a comprehensive and exclusive selection of musical items that spanned the career of the featured artist or group. Sometimes a retrospective of various artists was featured. A photocopied handout containing biographical information and additional background materials compiled from various sources was handed around, along with a playlist of the evening's selections. Embellished with musicians' photos and an engaging montage of visuals and graphics, these handouts are artisanal products in themselves, collected by patrons through the years (see Waxer 1998). Although Domínguez's audiciones of contemporary Cuban bands such as Los Van Van, Irakere, and NG La Banda always attracted large crowds, his tributes to 1960s and 1970s salsa stars such as Richie Ray and Bobby Cruz, Hector Lavoe, and Ismael Rivera seemed to be the most popular.

Among the large community of salsa fans and melómanos in Cali, Domínguez is a key figure, an organic intellectual who has long championed and disseminated knowledge about salsa and its Cuban and Puerto Rican roots. He has done this not only through events at the Taberna Latina, but also through regular radio programs, the organizing of "open-air salsoteca" *encuentros* or gatherings in city parks, and concert productions. Although melómanos and record collectors were already well established by the time Domínguez opened the Latina in 1982, it is certain that Cali owes much of its current musical memory to his remarkable efforts. One might even say that Domínguez has been a leader in creating and institutionalizing a unique local form of "edutainment" in Cali's salsa scene. Through audiciones and other special events, salsa artists have been showcased as serious subjects of aesthetic and intellectual contemplation within the rollicking, liquor-laced atmosphere of the rumba that frames Caleño popular culture as a whole.

Pablo y su Música

A unique offshoot of the salsotecas and tabernas is the informal enterprise run by Pablo Emilio Solano. Calling his outfit simply Pablo y su Música, Solano runs a small hangout from a room on the rooftop terrace of his house in Barrio Barranquilla, a working-class neighborhood in the city's north. A former army serviceman and then a worker in the Bavaria beer plant, for health reasons he took early retirement in the late 1980s. Capitalizing on the over ten thousand records he has been acquiring since the 1950s, Pablo built a new room on the roof of his house and opened the space to friends and acquaintances who wished to listen and sometimes even have tapes made from his diverse and extensive collection. People are free to drop by any afternoon or evening of the week. Most come on weekends, however, to listen to music, converse, and perhaps have a drink—

Figure 3.5   Pablo y su Música. Photo by Lise Waxer.

Doña Olimpa, his mother, sells beer from a fridge on the terrace, but people are also welcome to bring their own supply. Indeed, the family business
began with Solano's grandmother over five decades ago; the family is originally from Dagua, a small town on the road between Cali and Buenaventura, and the grocery store managed by his grandmother and then by Doña
Olimpa had a jukebox, which they kept stocked with 78 rpm recordings
purchased on the docks in Buenaventura. Pablo recalls making trips out to
the port with his mother to purchase supplies and new records. They
moved to Barrio Obrero in Cali when Pablo was an adolescent. My neighbors, old friends of his from Barrio Obero, introduced me to Pablo. After
a few visits, I discovered that melómanos I had met elsewhere in the scene
were also regulars at Pablo's, confirming my impression that his place is
an important meeting point for aficionados.

    The atmosphere at Pablo's is more relaxed and homey than at a taberna
or salsoteca. Smoking is not permitted inside the room, only on the terrace,
and the lights are not dimmed as in a taberna. The music is never too loud
to drown out conversation (or disturb the neighbors), which contributes to
the cozy and personable surroundings. Pablo sits at a desk in an enclosed
area where he keeps his records and stereo equipment, looking almost like a
DJ at a radio station (Figure 3.5). As do many collectors and taberna own-

ers, Pablo adorns his walls with a bricolage of cherished collectibles in his possession. Posters of Marilyn Monroe, Judy Garland, Bob Marley, and the Beatles line the walls alongside photographs of the Cuban soneros Benny Moré and Arsenio Rodriguez and sepia-toned images of Cali in the 1920s and 1930s. A row of beer bottles from countries around the world lines the shelf above his record collection. On the opposite wall hangs a large clock with the logo of Deportivo Cali—Solano's favorite soccer club.

Unlike many record collectors, who zealously hoard their collections and dislike copying the exclusive items in their collection, Pablo is more than happy to show off what he has. Although he will not lend his albums, he is happy to play requested cuts and dub things onto tape. Most of the recordings in his collection comprise salsa and música antillana, but he also owns rare 78s of Colombian música tropical and vallenato, as well as albums of jazz, Latin jazz, balada, contemporary Cuban timba, and even rock. The majority of tapes he makes are for salsa aficionados who request compilations of specific tunes and artists, most of them out of print and impossible to obtain elsewhere. Pablo proved to be a godsend to a foreign ethnomusicologist like me, who did not wish to impose on other collectors for tapes but who otherwise had no means of obtaining copies of rare, out-of-print recordings. Many of the tapes he prepared for me were made on vague specifications—for instance, "Please make me a tape of all the classic viejoteca tunes that Caleños listened to in the 1960s," or, "Could you oblige me with a selection of good salsa dura numbers?" Yet, like the best salsoteca DJs, Pablo had a shrewd musical ear and provided me with diverse and engaging mixes of songs and performers.

Pablo clearly enjoys sharing the music in his collection, as I witnessed in his interactions with myself and others. Given the fact that most music people request is impossible or very expensive to obtain by other means, Pablo provides an significant alternative for Caleño music consumers. His little room became my favorite hangout during the final stage of my sojourn in Cali, and not only for the music and cozy ambience. In a city characterized by small, home-operated businesses, Pablo y su Música is a clear example of how affective passion has been combined with grassroots enterprise in local salsero culture.

The DJ as Metamusician

Owing to the centrality of records in Caleño life since the 1950s, DJs have become key figures in local popular culture. Gary Domínguez told me that DJs have been more important than musicians themselves, especially since the salsotecas were established.[29] DJs already played an important role in selecting the music played at parties, agüelulos, and griles during the 1960s and 1970s. With the advent of salsotecas and tabernas in the 1980s, however, they became pivotal actors in the construction and maintenance of the city's musical memory. During my stay in the field, I was often struck by how critical a good DJ is to creating and sustaining a certain ambience and affective state through musical sound. Caleño fans often refer to this as *onda,* or wave—a natural force that can uplift your spirits or carry you away. People would often comment to me in private about the relative merits of different DJs at various tabernas and salsotecas, rating them in terms of their ability to select good music and maintain an interesting flow of sounds.

Recent scholarship on U.S. and British dance music points to the important role DJs have come to play in popular musical life during the second half of the twentieth century, equivalent to that of live club musicians in earlier years (Fikentscher 2000; Brewster and Broughton 2000). Although a DJ does not create the actual music, he or she (women DJs, while extremely rare, do exist in Cali as in other parts of the world) must have a musical ear and a sense of musical pacing, either maintaining a mood or contrasting it through the selection of recordings. These decisions are made via intuitive judgments about what will work to keep listeners interested, based on elements such as style, genre, tempo, lyric content, tonality (key), vocal timbre, horn arrangements, solo improvisation, delivery, song length, and other aspects of any given recording. As DJs become more experienced and acquire greater knowledge about different artists and recordings, this base serves as a repertoire to choose from in piecing together an evening of good music. This process is analogous to the way in which jazz players and musicians in other traditions draw on a stock of effective phrases and formulaic procedures in order to structure a good performance (Berliner 1994). My own experience as a radio DJ (jazz and Latin) entailed a similar process of musical judgment and ordering. From what I observed in Cali, those disc jockeys who are also collectors—such as Gary Domínguez, Kike Escobar, and Richard Yory, among others—are highly esteemed for their DJing skills, a talent that correlates directly with their knowledge about diverse artists, styles, and specific recordings.

Just like musicians, the best disc jockeys rely on a high degree of innate musical talent—the ability to know what will sound good. Many DJs I spoke with explained that they had become interested in this activity because it "felt natural" to do so. Gary Domínguez, who did his first DJing at the family parties organized by his older sister, said that one has to really be passionate about playing records to be a disc jockey:

It was a whole ritual. Right there at home and in other places. That is, it's like you're born with it, because the toughest thing at a family party is to put on the music, because the only one who doesn't dance is the disc jockey, all night long. So just imagine, you have to have, like, a passion for that, to be there for some eight hours, everyone having a great time and you putting on music in your own house. It's just crazy. And it gives pleasure, you feel good that, that the whole family would be dancing to the music that you put on all night. And there were dances from seven in the evening until seven in the morning. At the very end, I remember, when I would turn the last record over, it would scrape, *shwaw!*—and I'd be there sleeping at the table, imagine. Incredible.[30]

Kike Escobar outlined his conception of the role of a good disc jockey. The most basic principle is, Always satisfy the melómanos. Next is, Always be able to answer questions about artists, personnel on the recording, recording dates, the history of groups and musical stylistic developments, and so forth. He noted that one learns a lot this way, adding that "not everyone is capable of doing this." Furthermore, a DJ should never bore people by repeating the same songs too much over a given period. He said that DJs are expected to play an engaging musical mix, varying rhythms and styles, introducing new sounds, and balancing old and new recordings.[31] These considerations, especially the last, are ultimately ruled by economic terms—if people do not like the music or tire of your selection, they will not come back, the club will fail to attract new clientele, and the taberna or salsoteca will go out of business.

A DJ, according to Escobar, fills a Januslike position, looking back to the past and ahead to the future. One principal role of a taberna or salsoteca DJ is *recuperar y mantener viva la historia,* that is, to recuperate and keep alive Cali's musical history. Like Domínguez, Escobar does this by highlighting classic salsa recordings and also through special audiciones. The other principal objective is to develop and transcend the current scene, broadening the horizons of current tastes in salsa and música antillana. Escobar himself has done this by introducing a large amount of contemporary Cuban music at his clubs. He has also tried to promote what he calls *salsa positiva*—salsa songs with a positive and uplifting message that would override the negative, escapist aspect of the tabernas and salsotecas, that is, drinking and dancing to forget, rather than overcome, personal problems.[32] Escobar's comments articulate the didactic vision he and other Caleño DJs share. Through their musical selections and stylistic orientation,

DJs have been crucial brokers in defining local popular identity, central to Cali's record-centered scene.

From Dance to Discourse

On the other side of the turntables, melómanos have constituted an important counterpart to DJs in the construction and maintenance of Cali's musical memory. As an extension of the barrio context where working-class collectors became important culture brokers for the rest of the street, melómanos developed another important sphere of salsero activity during the 1980s. Although dancers consolidated the first important realm of cultural practice in Cali's salsa scene, melómanos formed its second, moving beyond dancing to records to actively listening to and engaging in verbal discussions about these albums. Notably, since salsoteca and taberna DJs play not for dancers but for listeners, being a DJ in Cali almost always means also being a good melómano.

Melómanos use their listening as the basis for lengthy verbal interactions focused upon aspects of musical style, lyric content, artists' biographies, and discographical details. A typical conversation, for example, might begin with discussion about the recording currently playing, with clarification of the year it was made, the lead vocalist and other personnel in the band, and the composer or arranger of the tune. Talk might then turn toward arguing what the most exciting moments in the piece are—a particular break, horn line, or solo, or an especially rousing coro or pregón. Just as easily, however, I heard many discussions turn to other pieces performed by the band—for instance, "Yeah, this is a good piece, but they never did one as good as [X], that one has a better [melody, coro, or arrangement]." Discussion might also veer toward other tunes by the composer or arranger of the song that initiated the discussion. Next might come reminiscences about the general career of the lead vocalist or other musicians in the band.

Although most melómanos do not have formal musical training, many have acquired a rudimentary technical vocabulary (adapted from formal conservatory terminology) that enables them to discuss aspects of rhythm, harmony, instrumentation, and arranging. Onomatapoeic imitations of melodic and rhythmic lines—that is, "musicking" about music (Seeger 1977)—are commonly used, often to more effect than technical terms. Verbal wit and rapid interchange are key traits of melómano discussions, and although conversations can become heated and argumentative, I never witnessed any that became antagonistic or led to physical aggression. Indeed, disagreement over personal opinions serves to heighten the mood of friendly and spirited debate, and whenever the discussion becomes too pitched, someone usually makes a funny quip to release the tension and bring the conversation back to the ground. Throughout these conversations, detours are frequently made to other topics, such as sports, daily life, or work. Combined with frequent pauses to listen and sing and/or clap along with the music, discussions can last for hours, especially (but not necessarily) when participants are lubricated by generous quantities of beer, aguardiente, or rum.

These kinds of discussions can be seen as an extension of the proclivity for conversation and verbal interaction that permeates social life in Colombia and other parts of Latin America and the Caribbean, strengthening interpersonal bonds and fostering social participation. Unlike other conversational practices, however, exchanges among melómanos are distinguished by a shift between different semiotic registers—reception of musical sound and speech communication about it. In this realm, listening consists not only of listening to each other, but also of listening to music. The rapid jumping between different levels in such conversations clearly resonates with Steven Feld's assertion that speech about music constitutes an important mode of musical reception, signifying an "awareness of the more fundamental metaphoric discourse that music communicates in its own right" (1984: 18).

Discussions among melómanos (speech about music) became a key metamusical activity in the salsotecas, replacing the more kinetic orientation toward dance (movement to music) in Cali's earlier scene. The kinds of dialectical "interpretive moves" that Feld describes in speech about music (locational, categorical, associational, reflective, and evaluative) helped to position salsa's meaning for Caleño fans, serving as a different channel for reacting to and understanding the music, beyond dance. I am not able to fully account for why this cultural practice emerged in Cali. It is possible that the reification of intellectual engagement with salsa arose in part as a result of Eurocentric attitudes—diffused at the national level through schools, universities, and other channels—that emphasize mind over body and the cultivation of intellectual rather than physical pursuits.

While the associations ascribed to different salsa tunes and artists represent, in part, an attempt to organize and make sense of musical sound, they also constitute an important locus of social interaction through which salsómanos have attempted to organize and negotiate other aspects of their daily lives. Even casual observance of such encounters suggests that the deployment of musical, historical, and discographical knowledge about salsa serves to at least some extent as cultural capital to compensate for whatever inadequacies or material limitations one might face in other spheres. José Limón analyzes a similar process in the ritual weekend barbecue among working-class Mexican men (1988). Just as prestige was accorded to better dancers in the earlier record-centered dance scene, so too do melómanos distinguish themselves in the salsotecas and tabernas. Similarly, just as dancers unwind and forget their long workweek through dance, so too do melómanos "discharge" through social activities of listening and discussion.

Salsa Dura, Salsa Romántica, and Gender Dynamics in Salsero Discourse

In Colombia, bars and cantinas have traditionally been the domain of men and of female prostitutes, off limits to "decent" women. Despite their similarity to bars, however, the salsotecas and tabernas became acceptable spaces for women to attend. The main focus in these establishments is the music, and the atmosphere of illicit sexuality pervading the bars and cantinas is absent. Medardo Arias claims that the transformation from bar to salsoteca or taberna also related to the disposition of the leftist intellectuals who became important patrons of the salsotecas and tabernas, and whose interests were different from those who conventionally patronized bars and cantinas: "The salsoteca gave a different dimension to the *rumba,* because it did away with, let's say, the connotation of being a bar or cantina, which had a darker meaning. The salsoteca had a message aimed more toward university people, toward the intellectuals, toward the people who were like a distinct crowd."[33] With this shift toward social "respectability," women began attending salsotecas, often with their husbands or boyfriends, but sometimes alone. Gary Domínguez notes that in the 1980s melómanas, or women aficionados, began to emerge, parallel to the development of salsotecas.

> There were "tough girls" that began to go alone, and they were respected because they also liked this music, that is, they were melómanas. So, melómanas started to appear, and they realized that in the salsotecas there was also a space for them, so now you saw, a girl went to a salsoteca alone, but they had to be women who knew a lot about music, or they couldn't stand it. They couldn't take this avalanche of music and rare salsa, so if you went looking for a man or a new boyfriend you weren't going to find one there, because everyone was into their own thing, listening to the song and listening to the breaks, and playing along with a bell and pounding on the table. The woman who entered was there because she liked that scene.[34]

Although Caleña women from all classes and racial backgrounds have participated in salsa's reception and consumption, especially as dancers but also, to a smaller extent, as melómanas, Cali's salsotecas have remained a male domain. When I spoke with male aficionados about this, most were quick to assert that many women are also involved, but they admitted that few women spend as much time and money purchasing recordings and attending salsotecas as do men. This development emerges from the fact that until recently men have had more economic resources with which to determine and indulge in the cultural practices that define superiority as a salsa fan. Male competition in this sphere further suggests that the acquisition of cultural capital through intellectual knowledge about salsa is a highly gendered set of practices, in which men seek both to identify with and distinguish themselves from other men.

From what I observed, interaction between male friends and acquaintances in the salsotecas and tabernas is often characterized by rituals of male bonding: drinking, arguing about who knows more about salsa and its Cuban roots, boasting about exclusive items in one's own record collection, and so forth. Like my research with all-woman bands, my frequent participation in melómano activities—in this case as a female outsider—provided me with a number of perspectives on gender roles and identities. Although women are welcome to attend the tabernas and salsotecas, they are expected not to interfere with the "serious" (i.e., men's) business of listening and demonstrating one's musical knowledge. When women attend these establishments, it is usually as the wives and girlfriends of male aficionados. Those few who actively assert themselves as melómanas usually abandon cultural codes that define sexual difference in other spheres and act like one of the boys. Nonetheless, in my own experience, melómanas are often treated ambiguously, both as honorary men and as objects of covert sexual scrutiny.

In this scene, debates about salsa dura and the newer salsa romántica style are inflected by a strongly gendered discourse. Melómanos exalt the percussive dynamism and (masculine) social consciousness of salsa dura while rejecting salsa romántica for its musical style and "trite" lyrics about love. Keith Negus characterizes such discourse (presented in Manuel 1991, 1995) as a "romanticized political aesthetic of male proletarian urban resistance," similar to the orientation of much writing about popular music and subcultures in the United States and Britain (Negus 1999: 137). Salsotecas and tabernas specialize in salsa dura, and it is no coincidence that this is generally considered men's turf. Women aficionados who become interested in salsa dura generally accept this qualification without questioning its sexist bias. One recalls Gary Domínguez's observation that women who go to salsotecas in search of a boyfriend or male company are out of luck. For most melómanos, salsa romántica is considered music that one listens to with one's girlfriend or wife, music by which to squeeze up together on the dance floor. Salsa dura, on the other hand, indexes a different social code, where patterns of heterosexual courtship and romance are eschewed in favor of male (or male–"gal pal") bonding and friendly competition.

The scorn that melómanos generally express for salsa romántica has a subtly sexist inflection. This disdain is most often expressed by claims that salsa romántica is bland and formulaic and lacks musical substance, but others speak with open contempt of its commercial orientation toward women and teenage girls. On the other hand, relatively few people complained about the blatant sexual objectification of women in early salsa romántica tunes, which formed a subgenre also known as salsa erótica or (in Colombia) *salsa cama* (bedroom salsa). When men did decry salsa erótica, it was usually just in general terms—for example, "That salsa is really bad"—without specific reference to its misogyny. Furthermore, I never heard melómanos complain about the misogyny in several popular 1970s salsa dura tunes, where women are portrayed as capricious *bandoleras* (tramps) and heart-breakers (Aparicio 1998). Implicit in this discourse is a masculinist bias that upholds salsa dura as the only legitimate style of salsa music. The dismissal of salsa romántica constitutes a sort of macho rejection of values conventionally associated with women (i.e., emotional intimacy and sentimental feeling) that threaten the supposed integrity of Latino male identity.

Yet, the economic and social inequalities depicted in earlier salsa dura tunes changed very little in the 1990s—inequalities that placed great strain on personal and family relationships. Furthermore, the increased financial independence of Latina and Latin American women as a result of their growing participation in the work force through the 1980s has challenged traditional gender roles and laid additional stress on romantic relationships. In a sense, salsa romántica musicians have not abandoned the issues that salsa dura musicians railed against—as most observers and writers claim. Rather, they are singing about the indirect effects that crowded barrios and underemployment have had on personal relationships. Marta Savigliano makes similar observations in her analysis of Argentine tango at the begin-ning of the century, pointing out how tango lyrics and dance symbolically transferred class and ethnic struggles to the "natural" space of gender dif-ference and romantic conflict (1995). This does not excuse the tendency to-ward sexist objectification of women and male-female relationships in the salsa romántica and salsa erótica. Salsa romántica's impact, however, requires a more objective consideration than it has conventionally received by melómanos; see Aparicio 2002 for an excellent analysis of salsa romántica's significance. Although the issue is highly complex and cannot be reduced to crude generalizations, the discursive boundaries between salsa romántica and salsa dura clearly grow out of tensions that have been defined not only in class-based but also in gendered terms of social difference and struggle.

Salsotecas on the Airwaves

Most melómanos I met in Cali were critical of the city's all-salsa radio stations, a by-product of the boom in the live scene during the 1980s and early 1990s. Prior to 1986 local FM radio stations—which allow for broadcasting in stereophonic sound—were limited. The few extant stations catered to the city's elites and featured primarily classical music. As more radio stations emerged in the 1980s, bids were made for FM licenses and suddenly popular sounds such as salsa and música antillana could be heard in stereo. The impact was staggering and served to revive salsa programming—in decline since the late 1970s—on local airwaves. By the early 1990s, six all-salsa FM radio stations had been established: Olímpica Stereo, Bienvenida Stereo, RCN Rumba Stereo, Fallarones Stereo, La Z (Todelar), and 99.1 Armony.[35] Parallel to this, local television stations also launched programs such as *El Solar* and *Soneros,* featuring local salsa orquestas and amateur vocalists. The commercial dictates of Cali's media, however, meant that salsa radio and television were dominated by contemporary salsa romántica. While salsa radio prevailed on the daily local soundscape—on public transport and spilling out of shops onto the street—it contrasted sharply with the music heard in the salsotecas and tabernas at night. Melómanos often told me that the so-called salsa stations actually played very little salsa—in other words, very little salsa dura.

These comments reveal new class-based antagonisms that had already divided Cali's salsa scene. As in the rest of Latin America, salsa romántica became identified as a slick, depoliticized style more attractive to non-leftist middle- and upper-class audiences than salsa dura. In Cali salsa romántica also came to be associated with the city's growing class of new rich, who patronized the luxury nightclubs, live local bands, and local radio stations that promoted this style. While many members of this group themselves came from working-class salsero barrios, there was a marked push to symbolize their new wealth and entry into upper-class lifestyles (if not into actual upper-class social circles) through conspicuous consumption and the adoption of salsa romántica. Class-based rifts between salsa dura and salsa romántica fans hence aggravated the tension between melómanos and local salsa media. Thus, when melómanos complained about the lack of salsa dura on local radio airwaves, they were really complaining about the lack of popular representation of working-class Caleño culture.

Most all-salsa stations in the 1990s actually did have slots for salsa dura shows. In early 1995 (before the viejoteca boom), I was able to account for at least forty-four hours a week of salsa dura radio shows—that is, almost ten hours more per week than the amount of *all* salsa programming in 1986 (according to Ulloa 1992: 478–79). Taberna owners Gary Domínguez and Kike Escobar played important roles in establishing salsoteca-style radio shows during the late 1980s and early 1990s with their programs *Raza Latina* and *Estrellas de la salsa*. Indeed, some salsa dura radio shows were sponsored by particular salsotecas, who provided music for the show in exchange for promotion. (Sometimes the show's host and salsoteca owner was the same person, as in the case of Domínguez and Escobar.) Other radio stations also incorporated salsa dura tunes into their regular daily programming through the mid-1990s. Most of these shows were pushed into weeknight slots, however, usually on Monday to Thursday from 8:00 to 10:00 P.M. or 10:00 P.M. to midnight. With the exception of Saturday afternoon programming on the two local university stations (Univalle and Javieriana), no local stations featured weekend programming of salsa dura, and Friday and Saturday nights—prime time for popular-music radio— were given over entirely to airplay of current commercial salsa romántica hits. Hence, although salsa dura was featured on local radio, most melómanos felt that its presence, in comparison to salsa romántica, was marginal. Despite the establishment of six all-salsa radio stations in Cali by the early 1990s, there was a strong perception that they had turned away from the city's working-class salsa fans—those responsible for establishing salsa as a local popular expression in the first place.

The struggle to establish salsa dura programming on local airwaves in the 1980s and early 1990s marks an important standoff in local popular culture, as DJs and melómanos battled the commercial interests largely responsible for and identified with the growth of the live scene. On two occasions—during the Feria of 1992 and again in 1994—Caleño DJs and melómanos sent a manifesto to local radio stations requesting that more salsa dura be played on the air, as befitted a city with claims to be the world salsa capital.[36] Such requests were met with a moderate response but did not succeed in establishing the presence for salsa dura that local aficionados intended. The perceived shut-out of salsa dura on local radio stations, however, fueled antagonism between those who felt they were the rightful guardians of Cali's musical and cultural heritage and those who bowed to the demands of the national and transnational music industry. One of the most dynamic bids to stake out a radio airspace for salsa dura during this period lies in the rise of a short-lived but extremely significant radio show that galvanized a popular movement among black and mulato working-class youth in Cali—the *movimiento guatequero*.

The Movimiento Guatequero

For young melómanos living in the Cali's northeast barrios and the eastern plains of Aguablanca District, a popular and important salsa dura radio show erupted on local airwaves: *El guateque de la salsa* (The Salsa Party), broadcast from 1989 to 1993. Hosted by the Afro-Colombian DJ Alberto "El Loco" Valencia, the program acquired a large following among working-class youths, not only in Cali but also in nearby Afro-Colombian towns such as Puerto Tejada. *Guateque* is a Cuban word that literally refers to a rural campesino party or fiesta, equivalent to the Dominican term *bachata*. In Cali, however, "guateque" came to be associated with a style of salsa dura that features slow, grinding son montunos with heavy bass and percussion. Son montuno is a genre that was created by the 1940s Cuban innovator Arsenio Rodríguez, whose music influenced many New York salsa musicians of the 1970s. This sound became associated with the term "guateque" as a result of Valencia's show. The music for the program, provided mainly by the Salsoteca Olafo, emphasized son montunos with a strong backbeat and a percussive base, often with trombone-heavy and slightly out of tune horn sections that accentuated the aggressive edge of this style. Several 1970s New York salsa bands featured this sound: Ernie Agosto, La Conspiración, La Dicupé, Tommy Olivencia, La Selecta, Impacto Crea, Salsa Fever, Angel Canales, Frankie Dante and La Flamboyán, Markolino Dimond, and the Lebron Brothers (Hermanos Lebrón). These groups, already familiar to Caleño audiences during the 1970s, were revived and made even more popular among the new generation of working-class salseros in the early 1990s. Among local barrio youth, this was referred to as *salsa de golpe*, hard-hitting salsa—a special subcategory within salsa dura—a term that soon became synonymous with "guateque." Although some have pointed out that this usage was a corruption of the original meaning of "guateque" (Domínguez n.d.), the term entered the local vernacular.

The records played on *El guateque de la salsa* contrasted with other local salsa dura radio programs, which featured more upbeat, punchy numbers by Celia Cruz, Johnny Pacheco, Eddie Palmieri, and the Fania All-Stars.

The distinction between these salsa dura substyles acquired racial and generational undertones, as guateque music began to be linked specifically to black and mulato working-class youth. Some salsa dura artists, to be sure, remained popular with a wide range of melómanos of all races, classes, and ages but the difference between guateque and other styles is striking. Indeed, the association of son montuno's laid-back groove with black Caleño working-class youth bears a striking parallel to the racialized division of Cuban audiences in the 1940s, where bands such as that of Arsenio Rodríguez were generally associated with black audiences. In contrast, groups performing lighter, more up-tempo tunes, such as the Sonora Matancera, were associated with lighter-skinned Cuban audiences (García 1999).

Broadcast live every evening on Bienvenida Stereo (initially, from 5:00 to 6:00 P.M.; it was later moved to a better evening slot, 10:00–11:00 P.M.), *El guateque de la salsa* became the most popular salsa dura radio program among working-class barrio youth during the late 1980s and early 1990s. Young working-class listeners, particularly (though not exclusively) Afro-Colombians, were attracted to the music on *El guateque* and also to Valencia's energetic and idiosyncratic announcing style, peppered with colloquial barrio expressions. Fans often called in to request numbers or chat briefly on air with Valencia, which heightened the popular base of the program. At a time when salsa radio began to be saturated by commercial salsa romántica, *El guateque de la salsa* offered a prominent media space for barrio-based salsa and working-class salsero identity.

Importantly, the show reinforced ideological links between salsa dura and working-class barrio identity for young listeners, who found great similarities between the images of 1970s New York ghetto life reflected in these songs and their own situation. In a 1992 newspaper interview, Kike Escobar observed: "On my rounds through the world of Cali's salsotecas, I've been able to understand the climate of violence that surrounds youngsters in the marginal barrios. These [kids] fully identify with 'heavy salsa,' which speaks to them about their problems, about the barrio, about their street corner, about their roots."[37] Having grown up in the working-class neighborhood of Chapineros, Escobar is in a good position to speak about barrio youth and their identification with salsa. In personal conversations, he repeated this viewpoint, noting that current working-class Caleño youths still face the same problems of crowded barrio life, limited economic resources, and racism that confronted earlier generations.[38] Although his comments indicate an internalization of populist discourses about salsa as "music of the people," he is correct in observing that the lyrics of salsa dura resonate with the deeply felt experiences of Cali's working-class youths. In conversations I had with other working-class salseros aged eighteen through early thirties, I heard similar opinions regarding salsa dura and its messages about barrio identity and experience.

By 1990 Valencia had consolidated his fan base into an official club called El Movimiento Guatequero (the Guateque Movement), with inscriptions and a special membership card. According to Kuky Preciado, who was a member, approximately three thousand people enrolled in the Movimiento Guatequero.[39] Funds were raised to bring Ralphy Leavitt and La Selecta from New York in May 1991, and plans were made (but never realized) to organize other presentations by artists associated with the guateque sound. In the meantime, Valencia organized special on-location shows from different working-class barrios, broadcast from the truck of the radio station's mobile unit. During these programs, Valencia would invite young salseros and guatequeros from the selected barrio to bring their favorite albums to the broadcast site. The best song, selected by a panel of judges chosen from local media and musical celebrities, would receive a prize. Needless to say, this kind of grassroots media exposure made the show even more popular among barrio youth, increasing the show's ratings. Kike Escobar says that Valencia's radio program had an extraordinary impact on young working-class salsa fans in Cali.[40] His show consolidated the sounds and social dynamic of the salsotecas and projected them citywide.

The Movimiento Guatequero came to an abrupt end in 1993, when Bienvenida Stereo began broadcasting commercials for a December concert appearance of the popular Dominican merengue singer Juan Luis Guerra. Valencia's listeners telephoned the station en masse to protest, complaining that Cali had nothing to do with merengue music and that three or four salsa dura bands could be hired for the fee that the Dominican superstar was allegedly charging.[41] The radio station, which had no involvement in the organization of the concert and was only airing paid advertising slots, decided that things had gotten out of hand and terminated Valencia's program. Valencia, who had already had conflicts with station management and with personnel at other radio stations, found doors in Cali closed to him and was obliged to relocate to Sogamusa, a small town four hours' drive northeast of Bogotá.

After Valencia left Cali, the Movimiento Guatequero dissipated, although in the barrios the preference for slow, grinding montunos persists. A distinct style of dance associated with this sound has also developed among working-class youth of certain barrios, especially among Afro-Colombian youngsters. This style involves the basic salsa step, but is danced almost a quarter of a beat behind the main pulse, with a stiff, strutting motion of the knees and hips. Despite having learned the subtle rhythmic inflections of Venezuelan, Puerto Rican, and Cuban dance styles, I was quite unable to get the hang of this step, which felt unnatural and out of sync to me. Nor was I successful in getting young dancers to explain the difference to me—"It just goes like this," they would say. This is a very local form of dancing salsa in Cali, although I have also observed young Afro-Colombians in Buenaventura and Puerto Tejada dancing this way, indicating the spread of this style to—or perhaps from—these towns.

In Cali, Buenaventura, and Puerto Tejada, the term "guateque" is still prominent in local usage, as I recently saw on a club placard advertising guateque music. Among some middle-class record collectors anxious to disassociate themselves from this movement, I sometimes heard the word used perjoratively, in the way "música de negros" was used a generation ago. Some melómanos claim aversion only to the term, not the music, taking issue with the incorrect usage of this Cuban word. In other contexts, however, the term "guateque" has even been accepted as a local commercial label—something I have never observed elsewhere in Colombia. For instance, I saw domestically produced pirate LPs of old salsa dura tunes being sold in downtown streets, with such titles as *Clásicos de guateque* (Guateque Classics). As of 1995–96, the record section of a major middle-class department store (Casa Grajales, in Unicentro) had even created a distinct guateque heading in their salsa section.

Though short-lived, the Movimiento Guatequero stands as a remarkable outgrowth of the salsoteca scene. The movement consolidated a racialized and generationally specific subgroup of the city's salsa dura fans. While light-skinned mestizo and mulato youth also participated in the Movimiento Guatequero, it was generally identified within the barrios as a black, working-class subcultural youth movement. This racial identification emerged in part from the program's strong fan base in Aguablanca district, the most impoverished sector of Cali and populated primarily by Afro-Colombian migrants from the Pacific coast. Notably, despite the Movimiento Guatequero's widespread impact in Cali's working-class barrios, many middle-class salseros remained untouched by the guatequero wave. I was surprised to discover, when I initiated a discussion of the phenomenon, that some middle-aged salsómanos from Cali's older bohemian-intellectual crowd were unaware of the history of the Movimiento Guatequero and its potent subcultural reverberations. Although they had heard the term "guateque," they had little idea of its origins or the impact of this subculture on black and mixed-race barrio youth. This neither negates nor reinforces the validity of the Movimiento Guatequero, but rather points to the extremely complex and variegated development of popular culture in Cali by the 1990s, in which salsa and its Cuban and Puerto Rican roots had branched into diverse racially and generationally based scenes.

Perhaps most significant is way in which the guatequeros forged a subculture through active and deliberate consumption of a transnational style from a former era.[42] While many of the guatequeros had grown up listening to salsa dura in their homes, there was no natural connection that predetermined their affinity for the guateque sound. Rather, through the aegis of El Loco Valencia, black and mixed-race barrio youth were exposed to a substyle of salsa dura and found that its messages could serve as a vehicle for their own race, class, and age-group identity. Rallying around music produced when their own parents were young, Caleño barrio youth of the late 1980s and early 1990s found messages that resonated with their own experience of continued struggle and social oppression.

Vinyl Museums, Tradition, and the Performance of Musical Memory

As self-appointed guardians of Cali's musical memory, record collectors and salsotecas DJs clearly see themselves as culture brokers in the preservation and maintenance of local popular tradition. Their discourses and self-representations are grounded in origin myths that situate the birth of Caleño popular culture in the arrival of música antillana recordings in the 1930s and 1940s. The tradition that collectors and DJs such as Gary Domínguez, Kike Escobar, Pablo Solano and countless others refer to has very little to do with the Sunday afternoon town band concerts in Parque Caicedo in the early years of the century or other musical activities that predate the appearance of Cuban and Puerto Rican sounds in Cali. Rather, to borrow Christopher Waterman's characterization of Nigerian jùjú (1990), Caleño tradition is a "very modern tradition." The local encounter with forces of modernity—economic expansion, industrialization, links to world markets, and rapid urbanization—produced the experiences and cultural practices that Caleños now understand to be part of what makes their city unique. These practices, centered around música antillana and salsa recordings, have not only been valorized as an authentic local tradition. As we have seen with the rise of record collecting and the salsotecas and tabernas, they have in turn provided the basis for the continued development of new cultural practices using these same material objects.

Kike Escobar's characterization of salsotecas and record collections as "vinyl museums" raises important issues concerning the cultural project of preservation and memory. Museums in the European and North American mold typically remove material objects from their original contexts and place them on display for aesthetic contemplation, often under glass, usually with labels that arbitrarily frame and guide viewer reception. As social theorists and museumologists have argued, this mode of isolation and display flows from ideologies of difference held by dominant groups in the maintenance and exercise of their own social distinction (Bourdieu 1984; Karp and Levine 1991). Cali has its own modest museums in this vein, such as the modern art gallery of the Museo de la Tertulia, and various minor colonial collections housed in historic sites such as La Merced, a downtown church. Although salsotecas and record collectors certainly isolate material objects—recordings—the practices of accumulation and display are far different from those of conventional museums. Here Joseph Roach's theory of surrogation and effigies, discussed in the introduction, provides a suggestive tool for understanding what goes on in Cali's vinyl museums.

Key to Roach's thesis about memory as an act of substitution is the element of performance (1996: 3, 36). That is, memory is not simply a virtual page in history that is held open by certain markers; rather, it is a deliberate and performed act that selectively draws upon past experiences in order to negotiate present circumstances (see also Bal 1999: vii). The cumulative and sedimented usage (Lipsitz 1990) of salsa and música antillana recordings as effigies in Caleño popular memory is clear. As we have seen, recordings have become potent symbolic objects that fill a "vacancy created by the absence of the original" (Roach 1996: 36). It is the constant use and reinsertion of recordings into new performative practices, however, that have maintained their surrogational potency. In the rise of the salsoteca scene in the 1980s—as with the resurgence of the viejotecas in the mid-1990s—we see a broad range of new cultural activities emerge in connection to salsa and música antillana recordings: collecting, interactive listening, avid study, and debate. These acts constitute a new range of cultural performances that have shaped and given meaning to Cali's vinyl museums.

In the rise of this scene, the discourse of "tradition" has emerged as a powerful ideological construct to anchor and stabilize Caleño subjectivity during a period of extreme historical disrupture. The city's rapid urbanization in the 1950s and 1960s, galvanized by economic expansion and the specter of La Violencia, was marked by daily struggles to consolidate dwellings and adequate water, electricity, paved roads, and transportation. Such patterns of migration and struggle continued through the 1980s and 1990s, particularly in the marginal barrios of Aguablanca district, built on swampland and plagued by floods, putrid gutters, malaria, and the worst urban poverty and crime in the city (Vanegas Muñoz 1998).[43] This process of flux was heightened by the rise of the Cali cartel and the escalated violence (particularly the increase in firearms) associated with their presence. Hence, the nostalgic reconstruction of Cali as a site of alegría and joyful dancing to records in homes and neighborhood griles has emerged as a powerful antidote to these more painful, residual memories and also to the continued growth of urban violence in the 1980s and 1990s. Examining his own experience as a Jewish child whose family fled to Bolivia to escape the Holocaust, Leo Spitzer observes that nostalgic memory is not merely reactionary or escapist. It can also be an important—indeed, critical—tool in selectively establishing positive images of the past as resources for reconstructing individual and group identities in the present (1999: 91–92). Cali's vinyl museums have thus become an important site for preserving and maintaining not only what is considered by many aficionados (including me) to be "good music," but also the ideals of alegría and peaceful good times associated with it.

This is the tradition that Caleño melómanos prefer to remember in their selective musical reconstitution not only of the city's past, but of its very future.

4

"Heaven's Outpost"

*The Rise
of Cali's
Live Scene*

In 1984 the Colombian salsa band Grupo Niche produced a tribute to Cali titled "Cali pachanguero." The song's title literally means "the partying city of Cali," and its lyrics celebrate salsa, soccer, local sights, and other icons of local popular culture. "Cali pachanguero" was immediately adopted as the city's new unofficial anthem and remains one of the most important Caleño salsa compositions ever produced. Its popularity extended throughout the rest of Colombia and even abroad, as North American salsa bands performed cover versions of the tune for audiences in New York, Toronto, and other cities.[1]

On the international scene, most salsa fans recognize Grupo Niche as Colombia's premier salsa orquesta. The fact that the band's home base was in Cali contributed substantially to the city's status as the center for live Colombian salsa during the 1980s and 1990s. Similarly, "Cali pachanguero," now Niche's signature tune, has served to enshrine an image of the city that endures in Caleño popular memory. With phrases such as "luz de un nuevo cielo" (light of a new sky) and "que todo el mundo te cante" (may the whole world sing to you), the lyrics of "Cali pachanguero" promote a positive and romantic vision of the city. The song also incorporates a local adage that had begun circulating the previous decade—that Cali is "el sucursal del cielo" (heaven's outpost). While this self-image of Cali dates from the 1970s, the notion of Cali as a glittering metropolis became strongly associated with the rapid urban growth of the 1980s. As local fortunes increased through the alleged influence of the Cali cartel, the sound of live salsa became a celebratory marker for the rise of economic prosperity and good times for all. Although deep rifts continued to separate working-class Caleños from the city's old elites and the growing class of new rich, the vibrant scene made Cali appear indeed to be heaven's base camp on Earth.

I arrived to do fieldwork in Cali when this image began showing considerable tarnish at the edges and found that the celebration of Cali as heaven's outpost was complicated by nostalgic yearnings for pre-cartel days and the resurgence of the viejotecas and salsotecas in local popular culture. In my numerous conversations with Caleño citizens, salsa fans, dancers, and musicians, some people seemed to imply that Cali was heaven's outpost *until* the Cali cartel emerged on the local scene. Others, however, spoke positively of the changes that occurred during the cartel's heyday, pointing to the exciting local live scene that flowered and succeeded in placing Cali on the international salsa map. In my own opinion, it is impossible to separate these contradictory positions. The meanings that currently surround Cali's salsa scene flow directly from the way historical developments over the last four decades have directly shaped subsequent moments in local popular life. Conversely, developments in the 1990s have in turn influenced the ways in which earlier periods in local popular culture are selectively remembered and commemorated. Cali's record-centered dance scene during the 1960s and 1970s established the conditions of possibility under which the city's self-representations as heaven's outpost took flight during the 1980s and 1990s—through the salsotecas, certainly, but especially through the flourishing of live salsa music. Most important, while the live scene appeared to break with the earlier record-centered salsero culture that preceded it, local salsa performance remained linked in very fundamental ways to recordings and their role in maintaining the city's musical memory.

In this chapter I focus on the roots of Cali's live scene, looking at the processes through which local live bands—a mere handful during the 1960s and 1970s—began to develop and exert their stamp not only on local music-making, but on the national scene as well. While dancing and listening to records continued to be important, live performance represented a significant new way of incorporating salsa in local cultural practice. I look at early Caleño salsa pioneers and their contributions, which laid the groundwork for the development of Cali's three principal salsa orquestas—Grupo Niche, Guayacán, and La Misma Gente. Their local, national and international success not only helped forge a distinctive Colombian salsa style but also put Cali on the world salsa stage in ways that the earlier record-centered dance scene—for all the city's prior claims to being a world salsa capital—did not. While melómanos attempted to stake a claim on Cali's future by cleaving to its past, local musicians were steadfastly interested in catching up to salsa's international present. By the end of the 1980s the images of "Cali pachanguero" and heaven's outpost had become indelibly entwined with the city's vibrant live scene.

Early Salsa Pioneers

Through the late 1950s and 1960s, youngsters in Cali's working-class neighborhoods listened primarily to música antillana, pachanga, and bugalú, and some of them aspired to perform these sounds. Radio and recordings both played a key role in this process. Since not everyone in the working-class barrios could afford playback equipment, however, radio became an especially important influence on young prospective musicians. By 1965 salsa could be heard on local airwaves, broadcast on daily afternoon and evening programs that multiplied through the early 1970s. Self-education was another key factor in the formation of early salsa musicians, since the only institute for formal training at this time was the city conservatory, which offered instruction in European classical music for the city elites.

Wilson "Saoco" Manyoma and his brother Hermes—two Afro-Colombian musicians who later became important figures on the national and local scenes, respectively—told me they learned how to play by imitating sounds heard on radio, substituting kitchen utensils and other household items for musical instruments.

Hermes Manyoma: We have to speak of a process that began more or less thirty years ago—we've lived here since 1962, we lived in this house. That part where you see the kitchen was a terrace. It was a terrace where we had a washtub, where we had some pots, and where we had things that we used to replace the instruments that we didn't even know about. Because at that time I didn't know what, more than having seen them on a record jacket, what timbale drums were. I didn't know what timbales were, but I wanted—

Wilson Manyoma: Nor a trumpet.

Hermes: Nor a trumpet, because—

Wilson: We used a hose! [*they laugh*]

Hermes: So, there we began to interpret music and try out, me as a timbales player because I didn't sing, and Wilson played his hose and sang the tunes from that time, of Cortijo y su Combo [*sings refrains of various tunes*]. And we spent every afternoon and night playing those tunes until [our mother] Señora Esneda said, "Please stop!" But in any case, when she went to work [washing laundry in the evenings] we kept going at night. That's where we started to make music, assimilating what we might have heard on the radio, or on the 78 rpm recordings that friends had picked up, that we never had.[2]

Other musicians in Cali similarly learned through an empirical process of listening and imitation. However, because most young Caleños were investing their creative talents in dance, not music making, the pool of budding musicians remained small.

Colombian bands that started to play salsa in the 1960s were not strict in their assimilation of the new styles emanating from New York and Puerto Rico. Earlier Colombian groups who performed in the style of 1950s Cuban ensembles such as the Sonora Matancera, in contrast, tended to follow their models fairly closely. Colombian salsa recordings from the 1960s and 1970s are characterized by an eclectic, experimental quality, as musicians adapted salsa to other popular currents of the time. During the 1960s and early 1970s, música tropical and its derivative, *raspa*, were still dominant styles in the national media and recording industry (see Wade 2000). British and U.S. rock bands also exerted an influence on Colombian youth, as did the *nueva ola* (new wave) of Spanish pop crooners such as Rafael and Julio Iglesias. Meanwhile, early New York salsa styles such as pachanga and bugalú were popular on both the Atlantic and Pacific coasts of Colombia, as was the salsa dura style developed by Eddie Palmieri, Willie Colón, Richie Ray, and other salsa pioneers. These diverse musical influences are evident in early Colombian groups, which fused salsa with elements of rock, música tropical, and other styles.

The earliest extant example of commercial Colombian salsa that I have been able to trace is the song "Pachanga del año nuevo" (New Year's Pachanga, on *Charangas con pachangas,* 1969), written by the Afro-Colombian guitarist-composer Julian Angulo and recorded by his band, Julian y su Combo. This group performed Cuban son, salsa, and Colombian música tropical, achieving prominence through their appearances on national television. Although based mainly in Bogotá and Medellín through the 1960s and 1970s, Julian y su Combo had special ties to Cali and the Pacific coast owing to his roots in the small coastal town of Guapi (approximately five hundred miles south of Buenaventura), a community with strong migratory links to Cali. Medardo Arias recalls that records of "Pachanga del año nuevo" sold widely in Buenaventura in the late 1960s and could frequently be heard at family and neighborhood parties. Pablo Solano similarly remembers that the recording was played in griles in Cali.[3] A home-grown salsa hit, this tune differed from the pachanga popularized by the early 1960s charanga ensembles of Joey Quijano, Johnny Pacheco, and other New York artists in that it adapted the conventional instrumentation to electric guitar instead of piano, and trumpet and saxophone in place of flute and violin. In other respects, however, the recording is a good assimilation of the New York pachanga style, with an upbeat tempo, brief opening verses, and sprightly call-and-response vocals in the montuno. The combination of trumpets and saxophones—probably an influence of Cortijo y su Combo—is played with a cheerful if unpolished enthusiasm (e.g., discrepancies of intonation and somewhat sloppy entries) characteristic of early Colombian salsa bands.

During the late 1960s a small handful of other Colombian salsa bands emerged. These include a group cofounded by Michi Sarmiento and a fledgling Joe Arroyo in Cartagena, La Protesta in Barranquilla (cofounded by Joe Arroyo and Johnny Arzusa), and Los Tremenditos in Quibdó, where Alexis Lozano, cofounder of Grupo Niche and later of Guayacán, got his start. To my knowledge, none of these groups ever recorded. One of the most important groups of the late 1960s, however, was Cali's own Los Supremos, led by the pioneer vocalist Edulfamit Molina Díaz—more commonly known as Piper Pimienta. An Afro-Colombian native of Puerto Tejada, Piper Pimienta was raised and spent most of his life in Cali's Barrio Obrero, a música antillana stronghold. Grounded strongly in the sound of Cuba's Sonora Matancera, Piper Pimienta and Los Supremos were also exposed to and absorbed the latest New York salsa styles while working as the house band in a Buenaventura cabaret called Monterrey in the late 1960s. Indeed, some of the band members were from the port; they later went on to become sidemen in Colombia's most important salsa orquestas, Niche and Guayacán.

In 1970 Los Supremos recorded the second album of Colombian salsa ever produced, prophetically titled *Atiza, ataja* (Push, Pull). Its rather unorthodox blend of New York salsa with elements of Colombian música tropical and rock seem to reflect the push-pull of different forces that were shaping Colombian popular tastes at the beginning of the 1970s.

"*Atiza, ataja*" (1970)
Piper Pimienta with Los Supremos

(in chorus:)

Hay un dicho sabroso que	There's a cool saying
se ha puesto de moda,	that's brand new,
Unos dicen "atiza"	Some people say "push"
Y otros contestan "ataja."	And the others reply "pull."
Cuando yo les diga "atiza"	When I tell you "push,"
ustedes contestan "Ataja!"	you all answer "Pull!"

The song is fast-paced for salsa, played at M.M. $\quarternote$ = 108, and emphasizes a frenetic *descarga* or jam-session feel that did not continue in later Colombian salsa. The ensemble used a format similar to that of New York salsa bands from that time: conga, timbal, bongo, piano, bass, saxophones, trumpets, and vocals. As with the album released by Julian y su Combo the year earlier, however, the most significant feature about this recording is the eclectic, experimental quality it displays, adapting salsa to other popular currents that permeated the Colombian musical landscape during this time. This experimental quality became a landmark of Colombian salsa through the 1970s and was crystallized in the unique sound produced by the Medellín artist Julio Ernesto Estrada, known as Fruko.

Fruko is widely recognized as Colombia's first major salsa star. While identified as white for his Antioquian background, he worked with many Afro-Colombian and mestizo musicians. His first vocalist was actually Piper Pimienta, who left Los Supremos to join Fruko's new band in 1971. When Pimienta went solo in 1973, he was replaced by the Caleño vocalist Wilson "Saoco" Manyoma—the same Afro-Colombian singer who as a child with his brother Hermes imitated música antillana bands using washtubs and hoses as musical instruments. The same year, Afro-Colombian Cartagena native Joe Arroyo also joined Fruko. Arroyo, now based in Barranquilla, would later go on to become one of Colombia's major salsa performers and the only Colombian artist outside of Cali to gain international fame. His fusions of salsa with Costeño and other Caribbean rhythms owes much to Fruko's innovative style.[4] Fruko, who is well known for mixing salsa with elements of música tropical and rock, did not refer to his unique sound as salsa at all, but as *salsíbiri*. He became extremely popular among small pockets of salsero youth in Cali and surrounding areas, providing especial inspiration to the group of young teenage musicians who later founded La Misma Gente, one of Cali's most important salsa bands of the 1980s. No doubt influenced by the bad-boy image of New York salseros such as Willie Colón and Hector Lavoe, album covers depicted Fruko in aggressive poses, fists raised or gun in hand, sometimes flanked by Saoco and Arroyo in similar henchman postures. Such images were previously unknown in Colombian popular culture.[5] The band's countercultural uniform of Afro hairstyles, Indian paisley prints, love beads, and leather vests, inspired by North American youth culture, further underscored Fruko's rebellious image. Indeed, their first appearance in Cali in 1973 almost did not materialize—they were nearly kicked out of the city because concert promoters thought they were shiftless hippies.[6]

Fruko's eclectic fusions are similar to the pop-oriented rock-bugalú-tropical tunes of two international artists very popular in Colombia during the early 1970s, Nelson y sus Estrellas (Venezuela) and Alfredito Linares (Peru)—artists who relocated to Cali in the late 1980s. A common feature in Fruko's arrangements is the tendency to use a piano-and-bass vamp in the montuno section, replacing the traditional tumbaos and the anticipated bass pattern normally played in this section. In addition, the rhythmic feel of Fruko's overall style is very much on top of the beat. This feel no doubt derives from the attack used in playing música tropical, and indeed, most of Fruko's band (including Fruko himself) had come up playing música tropical.[7]

Although he left Fruko's side in 1973, Piper Pimienta continued to produce recordings under Fruko's aegis, releasing landmark songs such as the 1975 classic "Las Caleñas son como las flores" (Caleña Women Are like Flowers), which became his signature tune.

"Las Caleñas son como las flores" (1975)
Piper Pimienta

Las Caleñas son como las flores	Caleñas are like flowers
Y vestidas van de mil colores	That go clothed in a thousand colors
Ellas nunca entregan sus amores	They never give love
Si no están correspondidas.	If it's not suitable.
Caminando van por las aceras	They go walking over the pavements
Contoneando llevan su cintura	swaying at the waist
Ellas mueven las caderas	they move their hips
como las cañaverales.	like the reeds.
A la la la la . . .	A la la la la . . .
(bis)	*(repeat)*
[Montuno]	[Call-and-response section]
Las Caleñas son	Caleñas are
Como las flores	*Like flowers*
Las sencillas son	The simple ones are
Como violetas	*Like violets*
Las bonitas son	The pretty ones are
Como gardenias	*Like gardenias*
Las hermosas son	The beauties are
Como las rosas	*Like the roses*
Las negritas son	The black ones are
Una ricura	*Smashing*
Las gorditas son	The plump ones are
Sabrosura	*Delicious*
Las flaquitas son	The skinny ones are
No hay cintura	*No waist*

| Las Caleñas son | Caleñas are |
| *Como las flores . . .* | *Like flowers . . .* |

"Las Caleñas son como las flores" was an instant hit in Cali, selling 180,000 copies within just one month of its release and winning accolades as the top song of that year's Feria.[8] As with Piper's other hits recorded under Fruko, this song mixes elements of salsa with música tropical and rock. The most striking feature of this arrangement is the use of rugged trombones, clearly derived from the New York salsa artists Eddie Palmieri and Willie Colón and further popularized during the early 1970s by Venezuela's Dimensión Latina. The verses are played over a quasi–música tropical rhythmic figure that emphasizes the piano chord on beat two and a modified anticipated bass that fuses Colombian and Cuban bass lines (Figure 4.1). The style changes to salsa at the montuno (call-and-response) section, but high-hat accents on beats two and four maintain the música tropical feeling. The song culminates in a bugalú-influenced vamp, characterized by handclaps on beats two and four, with a rising chord sequence in the bass and piano and a coro of "Con las mujeres de Cali me voy a gozar" (I'm going to have good time with the women of Cali). After the mid-1970s Piper Pimienta returned to a more traditional vein, releasing several albums in the música antillana vein and bending his growly, expressive voice to the type of sones and guarachas popularized by the Sonora Matancera in earlier decades.

In Cali other son conjuntos from earlier decades remained active through the 1970s, such as the Sonora Juventud (Youth Sonora), a successor to Tito Cortes's Cali Boys and the Sonora Cali. Los Hermanos Ospino also continued as a prominent fixture in the local scene. These groups performed the newer salsa sounds in addition to their stock of traditional música antillana tunes. Both Hermes and Wilson Manyoma performed with the Sonora Juventud. When Wilson left to join Fruko's nationally famous band in 1973, Hermes continued with the orquesta until they disbanded in 1979. Santiago Mejía, also a member of Sonora Juventud, remembers that the band consisted primarily of teenage boys (making it very popular with teenage girls) and was one of the bands that worked the most during the 1970s.[9]

In 1979–80 the Sonora Juventud disbanded and regrouped as the Octava Dimension (Eighth Dimension), an orquesta that performed cover versions of classic salsa dura in the style popularized by the Fania All-Stars and by El Gran Combo de Puerto Rico. The Octava Dimensión soon became one of the most popular local orquestas to hire for dances and as a warm-up act

Figure 4.1 *Música tropical* figure from "Las Caleñas son como las flores"

for international shows. Around this same time, Hermes Manyoma founded La Ley (The Law), the only local salsa band dedicated to the heavier, rough-edged barrio style of Willie Colón and the Lebron Brothers. Other local bands included Formula Ocho (Formula 8) and La Gran Banda Caleña (the Cali Big Band), música tropical ensembles that shifted toward salsa during the live boom in the 1980s. All of these bands are still active but in recent years have adapted to new currents and also perform salsa romántica.

With fewer than ten local bands active on the scene, there was plenty of work for everyone during the 1970s. According to both Santiago Mejía and Hermes Manyoma, a band performed as often as three, four, or even five times a week, playing at griles, salons, school dances, weddings, baptisms, *quinceaños* (girls' debutante parties) and other private parties, in addition to occasional performances for patron-saint fiestas in nearby towns. People would also often rent a salon and hire a local band for a party—a practice that disappeared by the late 1980s because of skyrocketing rates.[10] Wilson Manyoma recalls that the money from these performances wasn't a great deal, but needs were less in those days, and one's earnings always covered basic necessities.[11]

During this time other ensembles existed that specialized exclusively in música tropical or raspa—still the preferred music of Cali's middle and upper classes. Luis Carlos Ochoa told me said that when he founded La Gran Banda Caleña in 1975, he decided to specialize in música tropical because they wanted to work in the exclusive social clubs, which did not hire salsa bands.[12] Also active during this period were small guitar duos and trios available for hire to perform *serenatas* (street serenades). Centered in small business locales on Calle Quinta (opposite the Loma de la Cruz), these groups usually played boleros, Peruvian *valses* (waltzes), and Colombian and Ecuadorian pasillos.[13] Colombians performing Mexican mariachi in full *charro* regalia also began to appear during the 1960s, available for hire to perform serenatas and at parties. These groups flourished during the 1980s and are still active; their business locales are farther along Calle Quinta, past

Imbanaco on a strip called "Mexicali." On weekend nights one sees both the serenaders and the mariachi groups in these locations, fully dressed and instruments ready, waiting for clients to pull up and tell them where their services might be needed.

Most Caleño salsa bands in the 1970s performed a repertoire of salsa, música tropical, and pasodoble, no doubt finding that this mixed repertoire maximized performance opportunities. Middle- and upper-class patrons were the primary source of work for live bands, but given their preference for música tropical and Spanish pasodobles, they tended to hire bands that emphasized these repertoires. Salsa predominated in working-class parties, and occasionally live bands performed for these events, but financial constraints reinforced the predominance of recorded music at working-class festivities. Most salsa bands found work during the Feria, when they played an equal mix of salsa and música tropical.[14] This scene began to change substantially by the mid-1980s, however, when the increased wealth associated with the rise of the Cali cartel provided a large economic base for the live salsa bands.

The salsa tunes played by early bands in Cali were cover versions of tunes already popular in the record-centered scene: hits by Richie Ray and Bobby Cruz, Hector Lavoe, Ray Barretto, Cheo Feliciano, Adalberto Santiago, Roberto Roena, and Ismael Miranda. Since performances by international orquestas were rare, the bands did not face the competition from these more prestigious bands that they encountered later in the 1980s.[15] The slight increase in local bands during the 1970s suggests that the record-centered dance scene described in chapter 2 was beginning to expand to include dancing to live music. Significantly, however, the fact that these bands performed covers of hit recordings by international bands, rather than developing an original repertoire, suggests that recordings continued to exert an inordinate power over the local scene, determining musical tastes and shaping the very tunes people expected to hear.

Cali's Live Scene Expands

During the late 1970s and into the 1980s, Cali's live scene began to grow considerably. In my conversations with various people about this period, one name often arose—Larry Landa. Many point to this individual as the single most important influence on the rise of live salsa in Cali. Larry Landa was a mestizo fashion boutique owner who, according to legend, became involved in the cocaine trade during the mid-1970s. In contrast to the later barons of the Cali cartel, with whom Caleño citizens had an uneasy rela-

tionship, Landa is fondly remembered as a Robin Hood sort of figure—
a man who plowed most of his illicit profits into bringing famous New
York salsa orquestas to Cali and nearby Buenaventura. He was responsible
for the Colombian debut of the Fania All-Stars in a landmark concert tour
of the country's major cities in 1980. Featuring the major artists signed to
the Fania record label,[16] the Fania All-Stars was then considered to be the
most important and prestigious of all salsa orquestas. Their performance
in Cali on 9 August 1980 drew a record forty thousand people and stands in
most people's minds as the turning point in Cali's scene.

Before that event, however, Landa had already brought such groups as
the Orquesta Yambú (1975), the Orquesta Típica Novel (1976), Eddie
Palmieri (1976), Hector Lavoe (1977), Willie Colón and Rubén Blades
(1979), and Junior González (1980). While this who's who of salsa lumi-
naries regularly appeared in New York, Puerto Rico, and Caracas during
the 1970s,[17] Colombian entrepreneurs very rarely brought New York
orquestas—not even to Cali and Barranquilla, cities with large salsero populations. Before Larry Landa appeared on the scene, only a few salsa artists
had performed in Cali, brought for the December Feria—Richie Ray and
Bobby Cruz (1968), Ismael Miranda (1972), and El Gran Combo (1975).
Apart from these visits, the sole contact Caleño aficionados had with the
New York and Puerto Rico scenes was via recordings. Landa began bringing international salsa groups throughout the year, creating waves that
transformed Cali's local live scene.

Landa was a long-time salsero. Born in Buenaventura, he was raised in
the working-class Caleño barrio of Alameda, a traditional stronghold for
música antillana and salsa. As a teenager and young man he worked as a DJ,
renting out his own equipment, records and services for salsa dance parties.
Medardo Arias remembers him as a rather idealistic fan who had always
dreamed of bringing his favorite salsa bands to Cali.[18] These were bands
he had grown to know and love primarily through their recordings. Once
Landa had the economic resources to do so, he became a key player in
exposing local audiences—and, more important, musicians—to internationally acclaimed salsa orquestas. Most of these performances were
booked at a nightclub called Las Vallas, in the city's north, and also at the
Juan Pachanga Club in Juanchito. Built in 1978, the Juan Pachanga was
named after a popular 1970s salsa tune by Rubén Blades and Willie Colón.
The club's name not only refers to Cali's passion for pachanga in the 1960s,
but also invokes a character common to many local salsa scenes and certainly part of Cali's—the street hustler (Juan Pachanga) devoted to a life
of petty crime and rumba. Indeed, it is likely that Landa was projecting a

romanticized vision of himself with that name—the small-time barrio kid who makes it big.

Landa's contributions to Cali's salsa scene were critical. He established an unprecedentedly glamorous and exciting ambience for salsa. The appearance of internationally famous orquestas, known previously only through their recordings, provoked tremendous excitement in Cali, magnifying and reinforcing the cosmopolitan sensibilities forged in previous decades through consumption of salsa recordings. This, in turn, had an enormous effect on local music-making. With the opportunity to see New York bands in person, local musicians were exposed to new sounds and techniques, especially the members of Octava Dimensión and La Ley, whom Landa frequently contracted to open for or alternate sets with the New York orquestas. Santiago Mejía, leader of the Octava Dimensión, recalls that such gigs were a tremendous experience from which they learned a lot and at which they got the opportunity to converse with the visiting musicians, exchanging musical ideas and getting pointers.[19] Visiting international orquestas also inspired new musicians to take up salsa and helped spur the formation of more local bands. Although Landa's illustrious career was cut short in 1985, when he died (some say he was assassinated) in a New York prison while serving a drug trafficking sentence, his legacy lived on in the boom of Cali's local live scene.

The Cali Sound

Thanks to the changes wrought by Larry Landa's influence, by the early 1980s Cali was set to begin producing bands of international caliber. All through the decade Caleño bands acquired increasing prominence on the international stage.

Not only did this emerge from the media exposure surrounding events and festivals that featured international bands, but also the growing prominence of Cali as *the* center for salsa production and performance in Colombia. By the early 1990s Cali had become a principal site for South American salsa bands to record, produce, and launch new albums, and had also become a mandatory stop for all big-name artists on the international circuit. As a result, local salsa musicians were keenly motivated to develop their sound and compete in the international arena. At the heart of Cali's burgeoning live scene in the 1980s, hence, was the establishment of a distinctly Caleño style of playing salsa music—one that gained international recognition and cemented Cali's position on the world stage.

Three orquestas—Grupo Niche, Guayacán, and La Misma Gente—rapidly moved to the fore of the local scene and became Cali's most prominent musical ambassadors in international salsa. To this day they remain the most prominent of Colombian salsa bands. Grupo Niche, in particular, has garnered widespread recognition as a top international salsa band, ranking with the best orquestas from New York, Puerto Rico and Miami. In the following sections I outline the important contributions of each band.

Grupo Niche

Grupo Niche (Figure 4.2) was founded in Bogotá in 1978 and made its debut album in 1979–80. Its cofounders, the Afro-Colombian musicians Jairo Varela and Alexis Lozano, hailed from Quibdó, the capital of Chocó province. The town's recent musical history owes much to Father Isaac Rodríguez, a white Catholic priest who provided formal training for many of the Afro-Colombian musicians who became members of Niche and Guayacán—albeit against his intentions. Varela, a songwriter and lyricist, contacted the multi-instrumentalist and arranger Lozano with the idea of forming a salsa band, which they christened with the colloquial term *niche* (a term denoting someone of African descent, but among Afro-Colombians also used to mean "brother" or "pal"). Their first album, *Al pasito,* was released to little acclaim, but their second, *Querer es poder* (Working Is Doing, 1980), garnered many accolades and broke Fruko's monopoly on Colombian salsa.

The album in general represented a new face of Colombian salsa. Instead of Fruko's eclectic fusion of salsa with rock and músical tropical, Niche played salsa in the crisp, straight-ahead fashion of Puerto Rico's El Gran Combo, with a strong influence of 1950s Cuban son, especially the Sonora Matancera. Such influences are not surprising—according to Alexis Lozano, these groups have been particularly popular in Quibdó and have played a strong role in the sound of Quibdoceño salsa musicians.[20] Sometimes cited as Niche's best album, *Querer es poder* is generally lauded for its combination of salsa with musical and lyrical elements from Pacific Coast traditions. One example is "Mi mamá me ha dicho" (My Mother Has Told Me), which sets a traditional Chocoano song in a catchy salsa arrangement. The lyrics of another tune, "Digo yo," allude directly to Afro-Colombian religious practices.[21] The album's most successful tune, however, was "Buenaventura y Caney," which became a national hit. The song is dedicated to the Afro-Colombian population of Buenaventura—Caney was the name of a famous canteen in the port. With lyrics and melody by Jairo Varela and arrangement by Alexis Lozano, the song featured a structural coherence and polished execution not heard in previous Colombian bands.

Figure 4.2   Grupo Niche

"Buenaventura y Caney" (1981)
Grupo Niche

[Verse]
(Spoken)

Para Chava con cariño	To Chava with love
Que sepan en Puerto Rico,	So they know in Puerto Rico,
Que es la tierra del jibarito	The land of the little peasant,
A Nueva York hoy mi canto	To New York today, let them pardon
Perdonen que no les dedico,	that I don't dedicate my song to them,
A Panamá a Venezuela	To Panama and Venezuela
A todos todos hermanitos,	To all, all the little brothers,
El Grupo Niche disculpas pide	Grupo Niche begs pardon,
Pues no es nuestra culpa,	But it's not our fault,
Que en la costa del Pacífico	That on the Pacific Coast,
Hay un pueblo que lo llevamos	There's a town we carry
En al alma se nos pegaron.	In our souls, they really struck deep.

Y con otros lo comparamos,
Allá hay cariño, ternura,

And with others that we compare it
There's sweetness and tenderness there,

Ambiente de sabrosura,
Los cueros van en la sangre
Del pequeño hasta el más grande,
Son niches como nosotros
De alegría siempre en el rostro,
A tí mi Buenaventura
Con amor te lo dedicamos.

A delicious ambience,
The drums are in their blood
From the youngest to the oldest,
They're black like us
Smiles always on their faces
To you, my Buenaventura,
With love we dedicate this.

[Montuno]
(Coro)
Del Caney al Bulevard
Camino dos pasos
Ahí llegamos al piñal
Luego nos tapiamos.

(Chorus)
From Caney to the Boulevard
I walk two steps
There we arrive at the pineapple grove
Then we hole up.

Ahí tiene su monte
Ahí tiene su rey
Como el melao tiene el mamey
Y una negrita también.

There they have outback,
There they have their king
As molasses has its *mamey* [fruit]
And a black woman too.

(Coro)
Donde el negro solo solito se liberó
Rienda suelta al sabor y al tambor le dió.

(Chorus)
Where the black all alone freed himself
He gave free rein to the drum and *sabor.*

(Coro)
Lo mismo que por tus calles
Vi una morena pasar ¡ay! qué bella es.

(Chorus)
The same as in your streets
I saw a black woman pass by, hey, what a beauty.

(Coro)
Nos tapiamos, nos emborrachamos
Por Dios que por ti, todito lo brindamos

(Chorus)
We holed up, we got drunk
For God and for you, we offer a toast

(Coro)
Cuando lejos de ti me encuentro
Buenaventura siento ganas de llorar
Por tí.

(Chorus)
When I find myself far from you
Buenaventura I feel like crying
For you.

Figure 4.3 Melodic quote from "Mi Buenaventura" in "Buenaventura y Caney."

The tune became an instant hit in the port of Buenaventura, becoming the town's second anthem next to Petronio Álvarez's composition, "Mi Buenaventura." In both its lyrics and musical elements, "Buenaventura y Caney" pays direct homage to the port's Afro-Colombian people and their culture. The song's verse refers to the smiling friendliness, musicality, and "cariño, ternura [y] ambiente de sabrosura" (sweetness, tenderness, and delicious ambience) of port residents. The melody even quotes "Mi Buenaventura," originally composed as a currulao, the marimba-based Afro-Colombian and Afro-Ecuadorian tradition that predominates in the southwest Pacific littoral of Colombia and northwest coast of Ecuador. This quotation appears at the end of the first mambo section (Figure 4.2). The melody of "Mi Buenaventura" is transformed from the compound duple meter (6/8) of the original composition (Figure 4.3) to 4/4 time, in order to work over the salsa arrangement.

Notably, the explicit racial identifications of "Buenaventura y Caney"—in lines such as "black like us" and the musical reference to currulao—disappeared in Grupo Niche's later songs (until the albums *Etnia* and *Prueba de fuego* in the mid-1990s), and only the band's name remained as a direct reference to the band's roots. This early hit nonetheless features many basic elements that have continued to define Niche's sound. Despite stylistic shifts through the years, Niche's style retains the influence of classic, *típico* (typical, traditional) orquestas such as the Sonora Matancera, El Gran Combo de Puerto Rico, and Venezuela's Oscar D'León.[22] Varela confirmed this observation, noting that the influence was especially strong during Niche's early years.[23] As with earlier Colombian salsa bands, such influences were picked up primarily through recordings of these groups, rather than live exposure. The típico sound is quite evident not only on *Querer es poder* but also on Niche's other recordings through the mid-1980s. The arrangements are uncomplicated, with the bright, short horn phrases reminiscent of El Gran Combo's style and also strongly influenced by the horn writing characteristic of música tropical. Most songs are at mid-tempo (M.M. ♩ = 98), a good speed for dancing. By the early 1980s, Caleño dancers had abandoned the frenzied athletic

Figure 4.4 Incipit of "Mi Buenaventura" (original version)

style associated with pachanga and sped-up records, and had returned to the relatively relaxed short-short-long step that is standard throughout Latin America for dancing to salsa and Cuban son.

The overall texture of Niche's sound dating from this time is clean and uncluttered, reinforced by the crisp patter of the maracas and the steady pulse of the *campana* (cowbell). Percussion, bass, and piano provide a solid rhythmic foundation but are not played as aggressively as in New York and Puerto Rican salsa dura bands. Indeed, the bass is extremely relaxed in its placement behind the beat and does not "push" the music as does the bass in Puerto Rican and Cuban bands. The conga and timbal, on the other hand, are played squarely on top of the beat, as in Fruko's earlier style. This placement gives these instruments a lighter and more buoyant sound than that of Puerto Rican and New York players, who play slightly behind the beat, with a more "rooted" feel (see Washburne 1998). The maracas and campana, for their part, are placed behind the downbeat, as in the Cuban and Puerto Rican style, and it is these two instruments, ultimately, that lend the most propulsion to Niche's overall groove.[24] Even though some of the instruments in the rhythm section actually play behind the beat, the overall feel of all Colombian salsa is on top of the beat. The producer and arranger Jesus "Chucho" Ramírez, a white middle-class Caleño, observed that the rhythmic feel of Grupo Niche and, later, Guayacán relates to the influence of música tropical on Colombian players:

> Colombian salsa took on the style of Niche and Guayacán, which is a style that, since they're Chocoanos, they had some classic tunes. Even though Jairo Varela has made many changes, the percussion has always identified who we are. Why is the percussion different from that of Puerto Rico or New York? Because we've become—musicians from here haven't played salsa exclusively. They've played Colombian music, and that's why the attack is different from those from over there.[25]

In addition to the strong impact of the Sonora Matancera and other música antillana ensembles in Colombia, the influence of Colombian national styles has ultimately been a definitive factor in the Colombian sound, especially when compared to other transnational schools of salsa.

Niche relocated to Cali in 1982 and recorded two more albums before their landmark hit "Cali pachanguero" was released in 1984. The lyrics of the song pay tribute to Cali, evoking scenes from popular life with references to salsa and soccer and linking them to a romantic vision of Cali as "heaven's outpost."

"Cali pachanguero" (1984)
Grupo Niche

[Verse]

(Coro)	*(Chorus)*
Cali pachanguero,	*Cali pachanguero,*
Cali, luz de un nuevo cielo	*Cali, light of a new sky*
(bis)	*(repeat)*
De romántica luna,	From the romantic moon,
El lucero que es lelo	The star that is stunned,
De mirar en tu valle	To see in your valley
La mujer que yo quiero.	The woman I love.
Y el jilquero que canta	And the *jilquero* [bird] that sings
Calles que se levantan,	Streets that rise up,
Carnaval en Juanchito,	Carnival in Juanchito
Todo un pueblo que inspira!	A whole town that inspires!
Cali pachanguero,	*Cali pachanguero,*
Cali, luz de un nuevo cielo	*Cali, light of a new sky*
(bis)	*(repeat)*
Es por eso que espero	It's for this that I hope
Que los días que lejos	That the days when [I'm] afar,
No, no duren mi ausencia,	My absence is not prolonged,
Sabes bien que me muero,	You know well that I die,
Todos los caminos conducen a ti,	All roads lead to you,
Si supieras la pena	If you knew the pain
Que un día sentí,	That I felt one day,
Cuando enfrente de mí	When in front of me
Tus montañas no vi!	I did not see your mountains!
Que todo, que todo,	That every, every,
que todo qué!	every, what!
Que todo el mundo te cante,	That everyone sings to you,

Que todo el mundo te mime
Celoso estoy pa'que mires
No me voy más ni por miles.

[Montuno]
(Coro)
Que todo el mundo te cante,
Que todo el mundo te mime
Celoso estoy pa'que mires
No me voy más ni por miles.

Permite que me arrepienta
¡Oh! mi bella cenicienta
De rodillas mi presencia
Si mi ausencia fue tu afrenta

(Coro)
Qué noches, qué noches tan bonitas
Siloé en tus callecitas
Al fondo mi Valle en risa,
¡Ay! todito se divisa!

(Coro)
Un clásico en el Pascual

Adornado de mujeres sin par,
América, Cali, a ganar,
Aquí no se puede empatar!

(Coro)
Barranquilla puerta de oro,
París la ciudad de luz,
Nueva York, capital del mundo,
Del cielo, Cali la sucursal!

(Coro)
A millas siento tu aroma,

Cualquiera, justo razona,

Que Cali es Cali, señoras, señores,

Lo demás es loma!

That everyone indulges you,
I'm jealous that you'd look
I won't go one mile farther.

(Chorus)
That everyone sings to you,
That everyone indulges you
I'm jealous that you'd look
I won't go one mile farther

Let me repent
Oh, beautiful Cinderella
I'll bow down on my knees
If my absence was an outrage to you

(Chorus)
What nights, what pretty nights
Siloé with its alleyways
And beyond, my smiling Valle,
Ay! You can make out everything!

(Chorus)
A soccer game in the Pascual
  [stadium]

Adorned by women without equal
América, Cali, to victory,[26]
Here you can't have a tie!

(Chorus)
Barranquilla, golden gate,
Paris, city of light,
New York, capital of the world,
And of heaven, Cali is the outpost!

(Chorus)
From miles around I smell your
  aroma,
Whatever one, is just cause for
  reasoning
That Cali is Cali, ladies and
  gentlemen,
The rest is hillside! [i.e., "boondocks"]

[Mambo (horn chorus)]

(Spoken interjections)

¡Cómo, ah pues!	What, oh yeah!
Oye Cañandonga	Hey, Cañandonga
Sepárame la mesa!	Put a table aside for me
Ah, pues!	Oh yeah!
Manolo, escóndeme.	Manolo, hide me.[27]
¡Cali!	Cali!

Just as "Buenaventura y Caney" became an anthem of the port, "Cali pachanguero" became the popular hymn of Cali, underscoring the city's self-image as world salsa capital. The song become the official anthem of the 1984 December Feria, earning top honors as best song of the Festival de Orquestas, the marathon Feria salsa concert that became an important part of Cali's live scene after its inception in 1980. Notably, in contrast to the lyrics of "Buenaventura y Caney," "Cali pachanguero" makes virtually no reference to Caleños' racial background, which—despite the great ethnic heterogeneity of Caleño salsa fans—is still seen in the national and local eye as being strongly black and mulato. The musical arrangement of "Cali pachanguero" is basic, concentrating on the lyrics and the tune's catchy refrain. The horn phrases are short and simple, which emphasizes the vocals. The pinched, nasal coros of the tune recall 1940s and 1950s Cuban groups such as the Sonora Matancera, indexing sounds that were locally popular in earlier decades.[28]

Varela's ebullience in the wake of "Cali pachanguero" was clearly evident in the title of Niche's following album, *Triunfo* (Triumph; Figure 4.2). This recording featured another tribute to Caleño nightlife and salsa with "Del puente pa'llá" (Beyond the Bridge). The song refers to the bridge that spans the Cauca River between Puerto Mallarino and Juanchito, and its lyrics celebrate the jaunts of all-night partyers who cross over this viaduct on their way to Juanchito to continue dancing salsa until dawn. Needless to say, Caleños received this song with the same enthusiasm that accompanied "Cali pachanguero," consolidating Grupo Niche's literal triumph over the local scene.

Grupo Niche's rise to the fore of Cali's scene coincided with mounting fervor among local fans to demonstrate the legitimacy of Caleño orquestas alongside international ones. Despite the broad appeal of the group's first hits, however, critics belittled Varela for the "crossed clave" of these first hit tunes. In salsa and Cuban music, all the rhythmic accents of the words, horn lines and melodic phrases must coordinate with the accents of the

Figure 4.5   Crossed *clave* from introduction to "Cali pachanguero."

clave pattern, a two-bar ostinato that emphasizes either a three-two or a two-three feel, depending on where the line starts. If the flow of the clave clashes with the rhythmic accents of the phrase, musicians say the clave is *cruzado* (crossed). This usually happens when a line that should be played over a two-three clave is played over a three-two clave, or when a phrase with an uneven number of bars is repeated, hence "flipping over" the sense of where one is in the flow of the clave. In "Buenaventura y Caney," for example, a descending piano-bass vamp in the montuno section is five bars long, which results in the clave turning over from a two-three to a three-two feel every time the vamp is repeated. In "Cali pachanguero," uneven phrase lengths throughout the piece result in an even greater degree of crossed clave. During the instrumental fanfare that opens the song, the trombone plays a simple, syncopated rhythmic cell four times. The phrase bears an ambiguous relation to the clave. When the entire passage is repeated, however (doubled by the trumpets), the clave feel is turned around, but in this cruzado repetition, the accents of the phrase line up with the clave (Figure 4.5). For the listener who is sensitive to clave, the conjunction of cross-rhythmic accents with the erroneous crossing of the clave is almost too much to bear. Later in the piece, a vampy passage is repeated after a seven-bar mambo figure which turns the clave around and makes the entire recapitulation come out cruzado.

Varela defended himself by pointing out that well-known salsa orquestas have also recorded arrangements that cross the clave.[29] Notably, however, he invited famed the Afro-Venezuelan trombonist, composer, and arranger Cesar Monge to join Grupo Niche in 1987. One of Monge's first tasks was to write new arrangements of "Cali pachanguero" and other Niche songs, straightening out the clave and rewriting some of the horn parts and instrumental breaks.[30] The new arrangements were recorded as a commemorative double album titled *Historia musical* (Musical History). This is an unusual vinyl palimpsest in which Varela tried to set the record straight, as it were, by rereleasing the band's old hits in versions that sound essentially the same as the old ones, but with the bugs ironed out and the instrumental choruses given a new shine. The revised version of "Buenaventura y Caney," for example, simply removes the offending fifth bar of the vamp figure so that it lines up correctly with the clave every time. In "Cali pachanguero," new parts replace the problematic sections of the original. Even though the original cruzado recordings are the ones usually played in local nightclubs and at parties, the rectified versions are what Grupo Niche has since performed in its live shows. Varela's decision to release a recording of the new arrangements suggests that he wished to broadcast a new, improved image of Grupo Niche as a polished orquesta on a par with world-class bands from Puerto Rico and New York—and also indicates his belief in the power of recording as a medium in which to accomplish this.

Since its inception Niche has been under the tight artistic direction of Jairo Varela. Although not formally schooled in music, Varela has an innate ear and a definite concept of what he wants, and he demonstrates an uncanny instinct for what will go over well with an audience. José Agüirre, Niche's current musical director, explained that Varela often writes things that most composers and arrangers would never think of but that work despite their unusual or illogical twists.[31] Varela is meticulous about details, as I observed during the recording and mixing of *Etnia* in October 1995, and he works closely with his arrangers and musicians to obtain the results he is looking for. The band's lead singers during the 1980s were particularly good salsa vocalists, gifted with thick, colorful vocal timbres and the sense of inflection and phrasing typical of Cuban and Puerto Rican soneros.[32] In addition, Grupo Niche has also had a succession of strong pianists such as Nicolás "Macabí" Cristancho and Alvaro "Pelusa" Cabarcas, skilled instrumentalists whose rhythmic feel and elegant, jazzy solos clearly show the influence of the Puerto Rican maestro Papo Lucca (leader of the Sonora Ponceña).

Niche was the first orquesta to be identified with a distinctive new style in the Cali scene. Elsewhere I discuss their work at greater length (Waxer 2000). The band's popularity in the first half of the 1980s had a strong bearing on the rise of other local orquestas. Not only did Grupo Niche's success inspire other local players to take up salsa, but the band's sound also had a considerable impact on the stylistic orientation of many subsequent groups.

Their music, diffused in live performance and also via radio and recordings, played an important role in encouraging other musicians to strive for a polished, commercially viable sound. Despite internal rifts through the late 1980s, Niche continued to maintain its status as Colombia's premier salsa orquesta, both locally and internationally.

Guayacán

The multi-instrumentalist and arranger Alexis Lozano (Figure 4.5) founded Guayacán in 1983 after leaving Grupo Niche to pursue his own artistic vision.[33] At the time, Lozano was less interested in performing straight-ahead salsa than in fusing this style with elements of traditional Colombian elements, particularly Afro-Colombian genres from his native Chocó. Dubbing his style *salsa chocoana* and even *salsa folk,* Lozano experimented with rhythmic elements and horn lines from the Chocó chirimía ensembles of his native Quibdó.[34] The very choice of the band's name reflected the ethos of Lozano's interest in traditional expressions—the *guayacán* is a hardwood tree, prized for its strength and durability, that flourishes in Colombia's Pacific littoral. Although Guayacán succumbed to the commercial influence of salsa romántica in the early 1990s, Lozano is still credited for his earlier innovations, and the stylistic traits characterizing his earlier arrangements are still evident in his most recent tunes.

Like those of the Colombian pioneer Fruko, Lozano's salsa arrangements featured dramatic rhythmic and textural contrasts from one section to the next. In several Guayacán songs, for example, the arrangements alternate between salsa and a cumbia feel. This is quite evident in the band's first hit, "Vas a llorar" (You'll Cry), from *Llegó la hora de la verdad* (The Hour of Truth Has Arrived, 1985), where instrumental mambos are inserted between verses and coros, switching to a cumbia feel with accented eighth-note duplets on beats two and four, played by the cowbell.

Lozano's style represents one of the few concerted efforts, along with the salsa-Costeño fusions of Barranquilla-based Joe Arroyo, to develop a uniquely Colombian salsa. This is especially apparent in early recordings such as "Son cepillao con minuet" (1987), a salsa tune based on the *son cepillao* (a traditional Chocoano dance form) and also in "Cocorobé" (from *La más bella,* 1989). These tunes use the short, bright horn phrases and coros characteristic of Afro-Colombian music from the Atlantic and Pacific coasts, and which have become characteristic of Guayacán's sound. The lyrics refer to typical sayings from the Chocó region, and the arrangements are filled with melodic references to traditional genres of the Chocó and the Atlantic Coast region. "Cocorobé," for example, is based on the simple lyric structures and melodic patterns of traditional Chocoano songs. Much of the tune's appeal lies in the rather ingenuous quality of the lyrics, which emphasize rhyming wordplay and rhythmic flow more than they do thematic content.

"Cocorobé" (1989)

Guayacán

[Verse]

(Coro)	*(Chorus)*
Cocorobé, cocorobé,	*Cocorobé, cocorobé,*
Bailan los hijos de José,	*Dance the children of José*
Cocorobé suena otra vez	*Cocorobé plays one more time*
Mira no bailes al revés.	*Look don't you dance backward.*
(bis)	*(repeat)*
Es un ritmito	It's a little rhythm
Recordadito,	Remembered
Puedes gozarlo	You can enjoy it
Buen al pasito	Good for stepping
Si a ti te gusta	If you like it
Apretaíto	Squeezed up
Puedes bailarlo	You can dance it
Deslizíto.	Sliding around.
Da su paso para'lante	One step forward
Medio paso para atras	Half a step back
Contoneando la cadera	Swaying the hips
Taconeando con los pies,	Tapping with your feet
Los muchachos por la calle	The boys in the street
Van saltando bien los ve'	Go jumping, there we can see 'em
Cogiditos de la mano	All holding hands and
Cantando cocorobé.	Singing cocorobé.

[Montuno]

(Coro)	*(Chorus)*
Cocorobé, qué bueno es	*Cocorobé, how good it is*
Cocoroñanga, baile pachanga	*Cocoroñanga, dance the pachanga*
Cocororico, te beso el pico	*Cocororico, I'll kiss your beak*
Cocorobé, salta en-un pie!	*Cocorobé, jump on one foot!*

[Mambo]

(Spoken in chorus)

Figure 4.6
Alexis Lozano. Photo
by Lise Waxer.

Dos viejitas se agarraron	*Two women were grabbed*
Por una churumbela	*by a whatchamacallit*
La una era tu mama,	*One was your mamma,*
la otra era tu abuela!	*The other was your grandmother!*

The tune is set in a simple arrangement, with much internal repetition of verses and refrains. The mambo sections are based on the short phrase structure and arpeggiated melodic cells of Chocoano and Costeño genres. Indeed, the incipit of the famous cumbia "La pollera colorá'" is used as the basic theme in the mambo section and then as a horn background during the final coro (Figure 4.6). In addition, a well-known Chocoano children's rhyme is included in the middle of the tune, spoken as an a cappella interlude between the mambo sections. Finally, during the first mambo section, the lead vocalist names two gentlemen from the Magdalena region—probably friends or patrons of the band. The practice of naming people in songs is common in vallenato; wealthy patrons (often drug barons) give the band money and gifts in exchange for the prestige of being mentioned by the band.[35]

Figure 4.7 Opening measures of "La pollera colora," quoted in "Cocorobé"

In 1987 Guayacán moved to Cali, dissatisfied with the lack of opportunities in Bogotá and no doubt attracted by Cali's growing scene. Through the early 1990s their local popularity grew, along with their national and international fame. Their sound caught on widely with local fans, perhaps in part because it had a freshness and simplicity that Niche's increasingly sophisticated, international sound had abandoned. Guayacán's style from this period is well illustrated by "Oiga, mira, vea" (from *Sentimental de punta a punta)*, a very popular hit from 1992 and still a mainstay of the band's repertoire. This tune appeared during the height of Guayacán's local popularity, released as a contender for the best salsa song dedicated to Cali in the 1992 Feria. The title comes from the common local use of the imperatives *oiga* (listen), *mira* (look), and *vea* (see), usually to get someone's attention or emphasize a point. Just as "Cali pachanguero" did eight years earlier, the tune constructs and celebrates an image of Cali as a hub of festivity and salsa music, especially during the Feria. Specific salsa hot-spots are named, making the tune a self-congratulatory ode to the spirit of the rumba that rules Cali at the end of every year.

"Oiga, mira, vea" (1992)
Guayacán

[Verse]

Si huele a caña, tobaco y brea,	If you smell sugarcane, tobacco and tar,
Usted está en Cali, ay, mire, vea.	You're in Cali, hey, watch out.
Si las mujeres son lindas y hermosas,	If the women are lovely and beautiful,
Aquí no hay feas, para que vea!	Here there are no ugly ones, just look!
Mi Cali se está adornando	My Cali is getting dressed up
Para su fiesta más popular,	For its most popular fiesta
Con caña dulce el melao	With sweet cane and molasses
Hierve en la paila hasta amanecer,	Boiling in the pan until dawn,
Habrá corrida de toros	There'll be bullfighting
Y por la noche, fiesta y rumba!	And at night, fiesta and rumba!

En Cali mirá, se sabe gozá'	In Cali, look, they know how to enjoy
En Cali mirá, se sabe gozá'	In Cali, look, they know how to enjoy
De día su sol ardiente	By day its burning sun
hace que mi Cali se caliente,	Makes my Cali hot,
de noche sus callecitas	At night its little streets
con farolitos se ven bonitas,	Look pretty with their little lights,[36]
Afinen bien las orquestas	Let the bands tune up
Que esta año sí vamo' a reventá,	Because this year we're going to explode
La rumba empezó en la Sexta	The party began on 6th Avenue,
Vamo' a Juanchito es a rematá.	Let's go to Juanchito to wrap it up.
Con salsa de aquí, con mucho maní	With salsa from here, and lots of peanuts
Con salsa de aquí, con mucho maní	With salsa from here, and lots of peanuts

[Montuno]
(Coro) *(Chorus)*
Oiga, mira, vea, *Look, watch, listen*
Véngase a Cali para que vea, *Come to Cali to see,*
Oiga, mira, vea, *Look, watch, listen*
Goce la Feria para que vea! *Enjoy the Feria so you'll see!*

As in "Cocorobé," the arrangement is constructed from basic elements—simple phrase structures, bright, short horn phrases, and catchy coros. Horn lines are typically no longer than one or two measures and rely heavily on internal repetition. Coros are sung in doubled thirds. The exclamation "Qué que-que-que-que *qué!*" ("Wha-a-a-a-t!) that punctuates the final mambo derives from an expression typical of the Pacific Coast region.[37] This signature exclamation has been used by Guayacán since at least their debut recording in 1985. Also characteristic in "Oiga, mira, vea" is the use of a syncopated rhythmic break at the end of a section, heightening the shift to the next. Finally, the band has a distinctive and recognizable sound in the horns. Trumpets are placed near the top of their register, usually played in unison, and augmented with a bit of reverb and compression to give a particularly live and brilliant timbre. In contrast, trombones are placed in the middle to bottom of their range. Such writing, absent from "Cocorobé," became a hallmark of Guayacán's sound in the early 1990s.

Guayacán's overall sound is lighter than that of Niche. The rhythm section is characterized by a crisp, dry, almost clipped attack in the timbales and congas, with patterns placed squarely on top of the beat. Tempos are also a bit slower than that of Niche's tunes, ranging from about M.M. $\quartnote$ = 82 to M.M. $\quartnote$ = 104. The more relaxed pace of 1950s Cuban son probably has some bearing on this preference. Indeed, Lozano acknowledges that in Quibdó this influence has been stronger than later Puerto Rican and New York salsa styles.[38] The slightly slower tempo might also be related to the tempo of traditional Chocoano music as well, although I do not have good data to support this conjecture. Reinforcing Guayacán's lighter sound, the group's vocalists have all been tenors, with smooth but undistinctive voices.

More than Niche, Guayacán has maintained the hybrid eclecticism of earlier Colombian salsa. When I interviewed Lozano, he proudly emphasized this quality in his arrangements, pulling out several tunes to illustrate his point. One song, "Amor traicionero" (Treacherous Love; from *Con el corazón abierto,* 1993), combines elements of salsa, mariachi, bolero, and vallenato; Lozano told me that this was his most "daring" tune ever.[39] Lozano's writing is quite distinct from that of his predecessor, Fruko, but his heterogeneous approach also reflects the great diversity of styles that have influenced Colombian popular tastes for over half a century.

La Misma Gente

The most important Caleño orquesta to emerge in the mid-1980s was La Misma Gente (Figure 4.8). Founded in 1978, the group hails from the town of Palmira, twenty miles east of Cali. La Misma Gente (The Same People) is sometimes upheld as an exemplar of a salsa band that actually originated in Cali (or at least in Valle province)—unlike Niche and Guayacán, with their roots in the Chocó. The band grew out of a high school salsa-rock band modeled on Fruko y sus Tesos. In contrast to the predominantly Afro-Colombian membership of Niche and Guayacán (at least during their early years), La Misma Gente's members were primarily mestizo and white.

The group's first album, *La Misma Gente en su salsa,* was released to much popular acclaim in 1986. Two tunes in particular, "Juanita Aé" and "Titicó," caught on widely at both local and national levels. "Juanita Aé" won best song of the Festival de Orquestas of the 1986 Feria, establishing La Misma Gente as an important new Caleño orquesta. The group's co-founder and pianist, Jaime Henao, said he did not really know why the song became such a hit, but it is clear that the song's lyrics made a deep impression on the public.[40] "Juanita Aé" recounts the pathos of a father who is so poor he cannot afford to give his teenage daughter her *quinceaños,* an important event in Latin American culture, so he gives her this song of paternal love instead.

Figure 4.8   La Misma Gente

"*Juanita Aé*" (*1986*)
La Misma Gente

[Verse]

Allá muy cerca del Cauca	There near the Cauca River
En un humilde lugar,	In a humble place
Vive una niña muy linda	Lived a very pretty girl
Con su mamá y su papá.	With her mom and dad.
Si quieres saber su nombre,	If you want to know her name
Yo te lo voy a contar,	I'll tell you it,
Juaná Aé,	Juaná Aé,
Juaná Aé,	Juaná Aé,
Fue que la hicieron bautizar.	Is what they baptized her.
Sin mentira y sin engaños,	Without lies or tricks,
Había pasado los años,	The years passed,
Los quince iba a completar	She was going to turn fifteen,
Oíganme mamá y papá,	Hey, mom and dad,
Con una fiestica quiero celebrar.	I'd like to have a party to celebrate.

José María, su padre,
Trabajaba hasta bien tarde,
Su madre también cosía
Toda la noche y el día,
¿Y qué, y qué fue lo que pasó?
Que la plata no alcanzaba
Por más que ellos trabajaban.
Oye, Juanita, por Dios
Tu fiestica se daño,
Lo siento mijita,
Esa es la situación.
Ya no llores hija mía,
Le dijo José María,
Que aunque no tenga fortuna
Queda toda la vida,
No estés triste hija,
Por Dios te regalo esta canción.

José María, her father,
Worked until very late
Her mother also sewed
All day and night,
And what, what happened?
There wasn't enough money
No matter how hard they worked.
Hey, Juanita, for goodness' sake
Your party is canceled,
I'm sorry, daughter,
That's the situation.
Don't cry, daughter of mine,
Said José María to her,
Even though I don't have a fortune
We have the rest of our lives,
Don't be sad, daughter.
For goodness' sake I'll give you
    this song.

Juaná Aé, Juaná Aé,
Duerme que tienes mi corazón
(bis)

Juaná Aé, Juaná Aé,
Sleep, for you have my heart
(repeat)

[Montuno]
(Coro)
Juanita, duerme que te dí
La arrulladita,
¡aé!
(bis)
Ya no llores, hija mía,
Te lo pido por favor,
Vendrán otros días mejores
Te regalo esta canción,
¡aé!

(Chorus)
Juanita, go to sleep,
I sang you the lullaby,
aé!
(repeat)
Don't cry, daughter of mine,
I ask you please
Better days will come
I'll give you this song,
aé!

(Coro)
[Piano break/ mambo/ piano solo/ mambo]
Juanita
Juanita Nana, Juanita Nana
Juanita éa!
¡Aé!

(Chorus)
Juanita,
Juanita Nana, Juanita Nana
Juanita éa!
Aé!

Juanita	*Juanita*
Si tienes sueño	If you're sleepy
Bendita seas, bendita seas	Blessed are you, blessed are you
¡Aé!	*Aé!*

The final refrain of the song derives from a traditional Colombian Christmas carol that is very popular in Cali, "A la nanita nana." Since "Juanita Aé" was released during the December season, this parody further reinforced the song's enthusiastic reception. The melodramatic lyrics of "Juanita Aé" fit well with the popular taste for sad tunes, developed through years of listening to recordings of melancholy Cuban boleros and Argentine tangos. Working-class Caleños related strongly to the theme of economic misery and the shame a parent can feel over not being able to provide a child with things that those in the upper classes take for granted. According to Henao, the tune registered so strongly with the local populace that sentimental drunks could be heard singing its lyrics not only in salsa nightclubs, but also in local tango bars.

The song "Titicó" spoke to another key element of local popular culture—the audience member turned play-along musician, with his cowbell. Known as a *campanero,* or cowbell player, this grassroots audience musician coalesces with particular fervor during the Feria season. Since "Titicó" derives most of its local popularity and cultural meaning from this time, I discuss the tune in chapter 6.

Musically, both "Juanita Aé" and "Titicó" feature elements that became trademarks of La Misma Gente's style. Most notable is the pachangalike rhythmic feel, played on top of the beat as with earlier Colombian bands such as Fruko, but with a distinct "spring" to it. This feeling is achieved by having the güiro play a pattern consisting of a quarter note and two eighth notes, while both the campana and the smaller *cencerro* (timbales cowbell) play open accents on the first and third beats. Overall, this creates a rather vertical, bouncy effect, in contrast to the relaxed groove of Grupo Niche, which was closer to Cuban and Puerto Rican styles. The continued popularity of pachanga among older Caleño salsa fans, however, created a positive reception for this sound in La Misma Gente's style. Pinched, nasal coros are another prominent feature of the band's sound. Henao said these were originally inspired by Conjunto Clásico and Johnny Pacheco (important New York bands), who in turn derived this sound from classic Cuban groups of the 1940s and 1950s. The arrangements also feature Henao's elegant, jazzy soloing on the piano. Curiously, "Titicó" highlights its two saxophones during the mambo section, a sound that was discontinued not only in later recordings by La Misma Gente, but indeed in the local scene in general. (Niche's early recordings also feature saxophone, which was dropped in later years.) By the end of the 1980s, most Caleño salsa bands had begun to emphasize trumpets and trombones, in emulation of New York and Puerto Rican bands.

Besides the pachanga feel of these early hits, La Misma Gente's arrangements revealed the strong influence of Puerto Rican orquestas, which was gradually sublimated as they developed their own style. The strongest influence on the band during this early period was the Sonora Ponceña. Henao told me that hearing a Ponceña tune on the radio as a youth was a decisive experience in shaping his stylistic orientation. The horn parts in La Misma Gente's early songs are clearly modeled after those of the Sonora Ponceña, with dynamic trumpet lines written in closed voicings and placed high in the instrument's register, giving a tight, brilliant, compressed sound. (The Ponceña is typified by a horn section of four trumpets, and even though La Misma Gente also had two saxophones and a trombone, these instruments are clearly subordinate to the trumpets in nearly all the band's arrangements.) Henao also explained that his piano playing was very much influenced by Sonora Ponceña's bandleader and pianist, Papo Lucca. This is clear from the band's recordings, not only in the way Henao voiced and phrased his piano montunos, but also in his use of virtuosic fills and complex, jazz-oriented solos. The synthesizer effects in "Juanita Aé" are another borrowing from the Sonora Ponceña, which was experimenting with the Yamaha DX-7 and other new keyboard technologies of the day. When La Misma Gente released this tune, synthesizer sounds were considered quite innovative, especially the use of stereo separation and the bending of pitches that are heard in this tune. In addition, some of the band's early tunes use instrumental interludes that are played in Brazilian samba rhythm, following the innovative use of samba in well-known recordings by New York and Puerto Rican artists such as Willie Colón, the Sonora Ponceña, and Roberto Roena.[41]

In comparison to arrangements produced by Niche and Guayacán, La Misma Gente's were more elaborate, with longer horn lines and more complex, jazz-influenced voicings. In this respect the band is much closer to Puerto Rican and New York bands than Niche and Guayacán, which follow the less complicated style of classic Cuban son. Harmonic progressions and horn parts in La Misma Gente's tunes include half-diminished minor seventh chords, ninth chords, and even the dramatic $V^{7\#11}$ chord—voicings not used by Colombian arrangers before this time but prominent in New York and Puerto Rican salsa by the early 1980s. A good example is "Rosalia,"

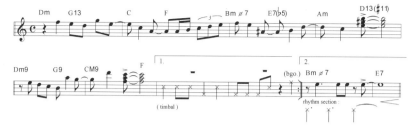

Figure 4.9   "Rosalia," instrumental break with jazz harmony.

from La Misma Gente's eponymous LP recording of 1987. Between the
verse and montuno of the song is an eight-bar passage played first by the
trumpets without any accompaniment and then repeated with the rhythm
section (Figure 4.7). Henao says the piercing $V^{13\#11}$ chord that caps the first
four bars of the phrase was an innovation in Colombian salsa. Although
such sounds have since become more characteristic of Caleño orquestas,
especially among younger arrangers influenced by the contemporary Puerto
Rican sound, at the time it was unusual for local bands to come out with
them.

As arrangers and codirectors of La Misma Gente, Jaime Henao and
Jorge Herrera have also paid close attention to the clave. Henao explained
to me that the band's music has always had "a lot of clave." Not only do
they avoid crossing the clave, but, as with the best New York and Puerto
Rican salsa bands, the vocals and horn lines really emphasize the clave pattern, so the music swings harder. He said this was accomplished through a
combination of good musical arrangements and diligent rehearsal but
noted that it also comes from years of careful listening to records of Puerto
Rican and New York salsa bands.

Other influences that La Misma Gente incorporated into their style during its early years included the use of funky electric bass slaps in tunes such
as "Titicó," which echo lines introduced by Willie Colón and the Fania All-
Stars in New York's scene during the 1970s. In late 1989 La Misma Gente
began to use a short break after the mambo sections, where the whole band
pauses before kicking into the following section with extra vigor. According to Henao, this was inspired by the Venezuelan artist Oscar D'León:
"Éso nos impacto tanto que allí quedó" (It made such an impact on us
that it stayed). This break first appears in "Chica de Chicago" (Girl from
Chicago; from *La Misma Gente en la jugada,* 1989) and was used in several
tunes thereafter. Other local orquestas have also picked up the use of this
break, possibly under the aegis of the band's leader, Jorge Herrera, who

does arrangements for a number of other Caleño bands in addition to La Misma Gente. The orquesta was also attentive to contemporary developments in other popular music styles and was the first Colombian band to incorporate rap into a salsa tune with their 1990 hit "Perfume de Paris." They recorded another salsa-rap tune, "El loco" (The Crazy Man), the following year but then seem to have tired of the gimmick.[42] Although still a steadfast orquesta in Cali, La Misma Gente has not sustained the popular impact of its peak years between 1986 and 1990.

Consolidating the Live Scene

Through the 1960s and 1970s salsa performance in Colombia was still largely relegated to the black and mixed-race working classes. As we have seen, most of the country's salsa pioneers were Afro-Colombian from the Pacific and Atlantic coasts and also Cali. The one exception to this pattern was Fruko, a white Colombian from Medellín. Through the 1980s, however, as salsa gained acceptance across class and race lines, the racial composition of Colombian salsa bands became more diverse. As I discuss in the following chapter, by the early 1990s salsa had shed its former plebian associations to become an acceptable and viable popular style that was widely taken up by young Caleño musicians—most of them working-class but some from the middle and even upper-middle classes. By this time Caleño salsa bands were also seen as important musical ambassadors to the world, offsetting negative images of Colombia as a nation ruled by corruption, terrorism, drugs, and violence (Ulloa 1992: 593).

The rise of Caleño salsa orquestas clearly illustrates the process of mutual influence between local and transnational processes that Steven Feld refers to as "schismogenesis" (1994: 265) and Thomas Turino calls the cycle of capitalist cosmopolitanism (2000: 334). In this process external ideas, technologies, and practices come into local culture and are internalized, but then the localized ways of doing and thinking feed back into larger national and international loops, which subsequently play back into the local, and so forth, in a mutually escalating cycle of interdependence in which single points of origin become meaningless. We have seen how salsa and its roots entered Cali via recordings and became incorporated into a wide range of local cultural practices that eventually gave birth to a fertile live scene. By the end of the 1980s Caleño orquestas had clearly made their mark on the international salsa scene. Grupo Niche toured regularly to New York, Puerto Rico, Mexico, Peru, and Ecuador. Guayacán and La Misma Gente, while not as famous, were also very popular abroad. Indeed, La Misma

Gente's 1986 local hit "Titicó" was quoted in the song "A Cali," written by Puerto Rico's beloved Sonora Ponceña. Such developments gave Caleño fans motive to feel that their city was now a bona-fide world salsa capital, truly an outpost of salsa heaven. In the wake of the local, national, and international successes of Grupo Niche, Guayacán, and La Misma Gente, Caleño bands mushroomed as if after a spring rain. Between 1980 and the early 1990s the number of local live bands grew from fewer than ten to over seventy. Most of them followed the stylistic parameters established by Niche, Guayacán, and La Misma Gente, and their national (and to some extent international) impact further reinforced the establishment of a distinct Colombian style of salsa.

By the early 1990s salsa orquestas were performing at almost any conceivable event that could be an occasion for live music. While local bands did not entirely succeed in penetrating the earlier barriers that kept them from being hired en masse in Cali's elite social clubs, I did observe some very lavish weddings and parties in the exclusive Hotel Intercontinental that featured Guayacán and other top salsa groups. More important, at the level of local popular culture, Caleños now had their own representative orquestas on the transnational scene after years of consuming salsa recordings from abroad. While salsa and música antillana recordings served to anchor the city's musical memory for musicians and aficionados alike, Caleño bands began fashioning a new voice from this heritage.

The enthusiastic response of Caleño fans to local orquestas—and vice versa—intensified and reaffirmed the city's salsero identity. Notably, the blossoming of local orquestas in the 1980s and early 1990s seems to have facilitated the recognition and acceptance of salsa among Cali's middle and upper-middle classes, beyond the nucleus of leftist intellectuals who had embraced salsa in the 1970s. Although this development is tied in part to the commercial rise of romantic salsa on the international scene, it is also closely pegged to the impact local salsa performers had on the city, especially through the mass media. In the next chapter, I further explore the dynamics that have shaped Cali's live scene, exploring factors that led to the boom of local orquestas and examining the sociocultural contexts for musical learning, creativity, and performance in Cali.

5

Taking
Center Stage

The Boom
of Local Bands

When I arrived in Cali, musicians and fans were gearing up for the onslaught of salsa performances that enliven the city's year-end festivities. Throughout November and December, I had the opportunity to observe several local orquestas in action—most average, some excellent, but all infused with the ebullient spirit that characterizes Cali's self-image as the world capital of salsa. What impressed me in particular was the extent to which Caleños had by the 1990s taken up salsa performance, mirroring the fervor with which earlier generations had taken up dancing to records. Live salsa was a frequent supplement to civic events and public gatherings. Orquestas could be seen performing not only in nightclubs and at parties, but also in shopping centers, at afternoon concerts in city parks, and in multi-event presentations held on weekend nights at sports arenas and playing fields. By the mid-1990s, over seventy local bands were active—quite a shift from earlier decades, when fewer than a dozen groups existed. In the following sections I examine the factors, contexts, and outcomes of the boom in Cali's live scene, situating it within other spheres of local salsa culture.

The Flowering of Local Orquestas

The growth of Caleño salsa bands through the 1980s and early 1990s is staggering. My enumeration of these groups is presented in Table 5.1. Compiled from listings in the Yellow Pages, newspaper articles, and personal communications, the table summarizes all orquestas and smaller bands active during the mid-1990s, shortly before the live scene collapsed with the arrest of the Cali cartel. The list also includes three bands that perform both salsa and música tropical, one group that performs traditional Afro-Colombian music with a salsa influence, and three Latin jazz combos. Notably, my findings suggest that from approximately 1988 through 1995 the number of

Caleño salsa bands doubled. In *La salsa in Cali,* Alejandro Ulloa accounts for only thirty-five orquestas by the end of the 1980s (1992: 556).

The table is divided into three main ranks, based on my own perception of a band's commercial status (as evidenced in radio play, record sales, media exposure, and concert billings) as well as on personal opinions culled from conversations with musicians, fans, and media people. The relative position of an orquesta was usually (though not always) related to their commercial status—an important factor when hiring them for a presentation. The average fee for a good band in 1994–95 was between US$700 and $800, although orquestas such as Niche and Guayacán often charged up to twice that amount. Generally, the lower down on the scale one went, the less money would have been offered.

In order not to imply an actual hierarchy within these rankings, I have chosen to list all the bands in alphabetical order. It should be noted, however, that Grupo Niche has remained the undisputed leader of the local scene, followed by Guayacán. Included with these orquestas are a small number of other internationally acclaimed bands that I have also designated as first tier, although their status is lower than that of Niche and Guayacán. Following this is a large pool of excellent but lesser-known bands, usually hired to perform at private parties, clubs, and public concerts. These second-tier groups usually had a relatively stable membership and played solidly, despite not having achieved the commercial breaks and success of the first rank. In the third and final category I have placed bands that were considered *regular* (mediocre, average), sometimes hired for private functions and often used as *relleno* (filler) at the Festival de Orquestas and other public concerts.[1] From what I observed in live performances, these third-tier bands were often plagued by problems such as poor intonation, inaccurate execution of parts, difficulty maintaining a steady tempo, and lack of cohesiveness as an ensemble.

Some of these orquestas did not perform salsa but rather related "tropical" genres (e.g., música antillana or *pop tropical*), which I indicate in parentheses after the band listing. These bands often appeared in the same venues as salsa orquestas, however, and performed alongside them at the Festival de Orquestas and regional ferias; hence, they constituted an important part of the local scene. I have also included a separate category of groups that were less interested in commercial success than in musical explorations in related styles such as Latin jazz or in fusing Cuban-based sounds with music of the Pacific littoral. Notable ensembles in this regard include Areito, a virtuoso Latin jazz group highly influenced by Cuban jazz bands such as Irakere, and Bahia, one of the few local groups dedicated to fusing Cali's

Table 5.1 Caleño orquestas (1995)

First Tier	Third Tier
Canela (❖)	Alma Latina (❖)
Grupo Niche	Anacaona (❖)
Guayacán	Ardillitas (❖, ⊛)
La Misma Gente	Boranda (❖)
Son de Azucar (❖)	Cali Sabor
	Chicas Madera (❖)
Second Tier	La Chiquibanda *(❖, ⊛)*
Alma del Barrio	La Conquista Mayor
Los Bronco	Dimensión Colombia
Los Bunker *(música tropical, salsa)*	Ecué
La Cali Charanga	Grupo Candelo
La Charanguita (⊛)	Grupo Cristal *(música romantica and*
Tito Cortés y Conjunto Calima	*música antillana)*
(música antillana)	La Fuga
Color *(pop tropical)*	Lucho Puerto Rico
D'Caché (❖)	Melao de Caña
Formula 8	El Minisón (⊛)
La Gran Banda Caleña *(música tropical)*	Orquesta La Fé
Grupo Bemtú	Orquesta Tropivalle *(música tropical)*
Grupo Mombassa (⊛)	Potencia Africana
La Identidad	Rafa y su Combo
Tito Gómez	La Rebelión
Kike Harvey	Renacer Antillano *(música antillana)*
La Ley	La Revelación
Marabá (❖, *música tropical, salsa)*	Rey Calderón
Matecaña	La Sociedad
La Máxima Identidad	Sol Naciente (⊛)
Nelson y sus Estrellas	Son de Euterpe *(música antillana)*
Los Nemus del Pacífico	Son de Trébol *(army salsa band)*
Los Niches Internacionales	Los Soneritos (⊛)
Octava Dimensión	Sonora Caleña
Piper Pimienta	Trapiche
Proyecto Omega	Yarabí
Orquesta Alfredito Linares	
Gustavo Rodríguez	**Related Ensembles (Latin jazz**
Sandunga	**and other fusions)**
Soneros 3 *(TV show house band)*	Almendra
Super Orquesta Café	Areito
La Suprema Corte	Bahia
Tumbadora (❖)	Doble Vía
Richie Valdés	Magenta (❖)
Yerbabuena (❖)	

(Key: ❖ = all-woman orquestas, ⊛ = all-youth orquestas)

salsa heritage with Afro-Colombian traditions. The short-lived group in which I performed, Magenta, is also among this set.

My inventory does not include earlier orquestas that had already disbanded by the time I arrived in Cali. Based on what I could gather from newspaper archives, personal comments, books, and articles, I estimate these disbanded groups to number between twenty and twenty-five. This figure is quite large relative to the total number of orquestas and suggests that economic circumstances or other factors curtailed the bands' longevity. Granted, some orquestas disbanded only to be reincarnated with virtually the same membership; this was the case in orquestas such as La Decisión, later reincorporated as Zona Caliente and currently known as Grupo Color.[2] Other bands were created after musicians splintered off from an established group, as was the case with Los Niches Internacionales, formed with several members of Grupo Niche who left Varela in 1988 over a pay dispute. In addition, musicians who have found themselves without work after an orquesta disbands are often picked up by other groups, especially newly formed ones. Despite the extraordinary number of local bands that appeared between 1985 and 1995 (over eighty), the pool of actual musicians probably increased at a smaller rate during this time, since many musicians migrated from one group to another.

I began compiling this list while still in the field, using it as an empirical exercise to determine just how many orquestas were active in the mid-1990s. Although the list is by no means definitive, the number of orquestas and ensembles I was able to trace totals seventy-three. Three of these orquestas (La Misma Gente, Matecaña, and Grupo Candelo) were based in nearby Palmira. The list does not include high-school salsa bands nor those formed within company enterprises from among contracted workers. Mention should also be made of other orquestas active in the region not noted on the list. These include Buenaventura-based orquestas such as La Integración Porteña, Puerto Tejada's La Sonora Porteña, and La Sabrosura, based in Cartago (about two hours' drive north of Cali). Although these are not Caleño bands, their existence relates to the enormous impact that salsa and música antillana have had in the region.

Calculating on the basis of an average of twelve members per group, the data suggest that by 1995 there were up to 875 or more musicians playing salsa or related styles in Cali. Even if we subtract, say, 50 or 60 musicians to account for people who performed with more than one orquesta, this still leaves over 800 salsa musicians in Cali! Of these, approximately 140 are women and girls (114 in the all-woman bands, plus women in mixed or predominantly male ensembles)—about 17 percent of the total scene. Based on my own empirical study of local orquestas for nearly two years, over half of these musicians were under thirty-five years of age, and the majority (regardless of age) are of black, mulato, or mestizo background from working-class and lower-middle-class neighborhoods; a controlled statistical survey, however, would be required to corroborate this. Per capita, the number of Caleño musicians involved in salsa and related styles is astounding. According to projections based on the national census, the population of Cali in 1995 was roughly 1.85 million.[3] Add to this the population of adjacent municipalities (Candelaria, Palmira, Jamundí, and Yumbo), where some members of Caleño orquestas live, for a figure of approximately 2.32 million people living in Cali and its immediate vicinity. Divide this number by seventy-three orquestas and ensembles, and you get a figure of one salsa band for about every 31,800 people. In short, by 1995 one in every 2,850 Caleños had chosen to become a salsa musician. I am unable to provide comparative figures for the diversity of ensembles that perform other musical traditions and styles in Cali, but even without them, the data here suggest an extraordinary burgeoning of musical activity in Cali in the past ten years. I do not have good information on the orquesta-to-population ratio in other centers such as New York, Miami, San Juan, and Caracas. From what I know of these other scenes, however, it seems that the per capita number of salsa and salsa-related orquestas and musicians in Cali during the late 1980s and early 1990s greatly exceeded that elsewhere.[4]

Of the orquestas that existed in the mid-1990s, not all were fully active during the whole year, but over 75 percent of them had a relatively stable membership (at least 80 percent of the band consolidated, without changes or substitute players) and rehearsed or performed at least once a month. In 1996, owing to the economic recession brought on by the fall of the Cali cartel, many groups were obliged to disband. I do not have data on the number of Caleño orquestas currently active, but I am aware from personal communications that the live scene has declined considerably. At the time of this writing, all the first-tier bands remain active. In addition, newspaper reports from the annual Feria suggest that new bands have continued to emerge since I left the field in mid-1996.[5]

The Cali Cartel

According to many observers, the expansion of Cali's scene was spurred both directly and indirectly by financial support from the burgeoning Cali cocaine cartel. The impact of "cocaine dollars" on the live scene was already evident in Larry Landa's sponsoring of international bands, but such support was minor in comparison to what followed. According to several observers, Cali's cocaine barons laundered significant amounts of money by becoming patrons of salsa orquestas. This included purchasing sound equipment, rehearsal space, and uniforms for bands; hiring them for private fiestas; and paying for record production and promotion costs. I was often regaled with fantastic anecdotes about lavish parties at private countryside estates. Some musicians told me about performing alongside famous New York and Puerto Rican salsa bands that had been brought to Cali on private jets exclusively for someone's wedding or birthday. Given the risk of getting closer to the cartel than I cared to, I did not investigate these stories further but accepted them as contemporary urban narratives surrounding Cali's salsa scene by the mid-1990s.

Importantly, the bonanza in the local economy gave Caleño citizens more spending power, which contributed to the growth of live musical entertainment in general. With the greatly increased economic base, many new groups formed, and the city became a mecca for salsa musicians. Not only did musicians from elsewhere in Colombia move to Cali for its favorable musical climate, so did individuals from Venezuela, Ecuador, and Peru. They included such famous Venezuelan bandleaders and composers as Nelson González (of Nelson y sus Estrellas), Dimensión Latina's cofounder Cesar Monge, Felix Shakaito of Los Bronco, and also the Peruvian bandleader Alfredito Linares. Even the Lebrón Brothers, an important New York salsa band, lived in Cali for a year in the late 1980s. In addition, Puerto Rican orquestas such as El Gran Combo and the Sonora Ponceña, as well as Venezuela's Oscar D'León, performed on a virtually annual basis at the annual Feria (see Appendix 3), making it seem as though they too had relocated to Cali.

Critics dismiss the economic boom, claiming that the rise of local bands and their impact on the international scene was based less on artistic merit than on backing from the cartel. In a scathing editorial, Rafael Quintero wrote:

> The salsa boom in Cali distorted many things. Among others, the musicians themselves, who glittered without having earned sufficient merit. From one moment to the next, those privileged conditions they were given by a self-enclosed market let them feel like respectable stars when they weren't even contenders. Moderate success and disproportionate earnings intoxicated them, and what should have been understood as a mere beginning, necessary to encourage them to keep working toward musical consolidation, was overrated to the point where they fell into mediocrity.[6]

Quintero's assessment, while accurate to a certain degree, denies the positive role that the cartel's financial support played in allowing new musical talent to flourish. Not all the music created during this period was mediocre. Excellent performers, arrangers, and orquestas emerged as a result of the intensified musical climate, and it is erroneous to reject them on the grounds that the live scene was artificially propped up by the cartel. Peter Wade notes that financial support of vallenato music in the 1970s by the Santa Marta marijuana cartel and, later, the Medellín cocaine cartel was not as decisive in the national rise of this music as some observers claim.[7] Rather, it just helped accelerate a process that was already under way (2000: 181). Similarly, in Cali live salsa would have probably expanded even without cartel support, although at a slower rate.

Company Salsa Bands

When the cartel began pouring money into the local economy, new local orquestas were already starting to emerge. While most bands, such as the Octava Dimensión, were formed from established networks of musicians, local *empresas* (businesses) also began forming orquestas from within its own ranks of employees, in much the same way North American firms put together amateur softball teams. These "company bands" would perform at parties and other social functions of the empresa, and although most are now defunct, a few still exist.[8] One of these ensembles, founded in 1981 by the employees of EMCALI (the municipal utilities company), went on to become La Identidad, an independent and commercially successful orquesta in its own right. According to the band's director, Edgar Díaz del Castillo, the EMCALI band was founded among musically inclined salsómano workers who decided to form a salsa dura band. During this time, many local orquestas (especially Formula 8 and La Gran Banda Caleña) mixed salsa with música tropical and were perceived as *flojo* (limp).[9] The founding of this band during the same period that Grupo Niche emerged on the national scene as an all-salsa orquesta suggests that the tide was beginning to turn for local salsa performance on a number of levels.

The live scene peaked during the late 1980s and remained strong through the early 1990s. While many orquestas prospered as a direct result of patronage by the cartel, not all the orquestas that emerged were connected to the cartel. Rather, the generally prosperous climate for live music seems to have generated a snowball effect. Even the local army base camp (the Third Brigade of the National Armed Forces) formed a salsa band, called El

Son del Trébol (the *trébol*, or cloverleaf, is the emblem of the Third Brigade). Established at Cali's Pichincha Battalion, this band was made up of young soldiers. Since its debut in the mid-1980s, El Son del Trébol has performed primarily during the December Feria, appearing at the *verbenas* (street parties) of Aguablanca District, one of the city's roughest and poorest zones. Recalls Medardo Arias:

> They sounded very good, but it was really funny to see that group play. All were dressed in army fatigues, with their khaki combat uniforms, that camouflage print, and their heavy boots. And they came out like that to play tunes like "La esencia del guaguancó" (The Essence of Guaguancó) and "Así se compone un son" (This Is How to Compose a Son) [famous New York salsa dura tunes], in the street parties of Aguablanca. It was seen as something to inspire "delinquent" youths so that they wouldn't follow a bad path. That's how they were presented by the commander of the Third Brigade.[10]

I had the opportunity to witness the current incarnation of this army salsa band at the 1995 Festival de Orquestas. Dressed in full army fatigues, they performed a mix of salsa dura and salsa romántica tunes and to my ears played very well. In other parts of the world, army musicians have been involved in non-army salsa bands (e.g., Puerto Ricans stationed at U.S. military bases in West Germany went on to become founding members of the internationally acclaimed Munich-based orquesta Conexión Latina). To my knowledge, however, no other army brigade in the world boasts a permanent salsa band—not even in Puerto Rico.[11] El Son del Trébol represents a unique phenomenon. This orquesta has never been connected to the cartel but can nonetheless be seen as a response to the rise of other local bands that flourished under its sponsorship.

"Cali Is Not Just Salsa"

Notably, as live salsa bands mushroomed on the local scene, journalists, writers, and cultural observers began insisting that Cali was not "just salsa." Criticism was directed primarily at local radio, whose saturation of local airwaves with commercial salsa sacrificed other musical styles and local expressions, including jazz, Colombian folk genres, and European classical music.[12] Some also commented that the emphasis on salsa ignored the wealth of artistic and literary expression that flourished in the city in the form of painting, film, theater, dance, poetry, and fiction.[13] Reading between the lines, one might also infer indirect criticism of the Cali cartel, which was seen not only as controlling local radio but also as having galvanized the local commercial boom for salsa in the first place.

Ironically, although música antillana and salsa took hold in Cali because of its transnational, cosmopolitan associations, by the 1980s some Caleños clearly felt that the salsa-capital myth was too parochial. Carlos Esteban Mejía, former director of culture in the mayor's office, viewed the Caleño passion for salsa as "cultural homogenization" —a sign of artistic poverty and regression in which the city became equated with only one genre.[14] Mejía and others clearly felt that a burgeoning cosmopolitan center such as Cali should recognize and nurture a diversity of artistic expressions that reflected the cultural heterogeneity of its inhabitants. These remarks express a highbrow disdain for salsa music that has persisted among the city's more conservative sectors, although in shifting terms, since the 1960s and 1970s. Behind anxious proclamations that "Cali doesn't live from salsa alone"— as a headline in the Sunday magazine of El País proclaimed—one detects the aspirations of Cali's bourgeoisie to reestablish a hold on the cultural tenor of the city. Most of the criticism, however, had little impact during this period and can be seen as disgruntled rumblings from a quarter that resented being pushed to the sidelines. Indeed, many of the artists, writers, and (non-salsa) musicians whose cause was promoted by anti-salsa critics were themselves avid salseros. Although it is certain that Caleños participated in activities other than salsa, no one could dispute that by the 1980s salsa dominated the local cultural landscape.

Music Education and the Second Generation of Caleño Salseros

A key factor in the flowering of local bands during the 1980s was increased access to musical training. Although only a small, elite sector could afford music lessons in previous generations, in the 1980s a number of institutions and private teachers began providing affordable musical instruction. These included the Instituto Popular de Cultura, the Universidad del Valle, the departmental Conservatorio de Bellas Artes (also known as the Conservatorio Antonio María Valencia), and small music schools such as the Academía Música Valdiri, Musikitos, and the Academy of Luis Carlos Ochoa. Valverde and Quintero attribute the rapid growth of Cali's all-woman orquestas to these institutions (1995: 46), but they have been equally as important for male musicians, and crucial to the development of the scene as a whole. In written surveys I conducted of twenty-five Caleño musicians (members of Proyecto Omega and Los Bronco) and informal oral surveys of about fifty-five other musicians, these institutions were mentioned repeatedly. The Instituto Popular de Cultura (IPC) and the Universidad del Valle (Univalle) figure the most prominently as a key source of musical training—unsurprisingly, given their orientation toward the working and lower-middle classes from which the majority of local salsa musicians hail.[15] The IPC has been particularly important in this regard, providing an attractive alternative to the elite Conservatorio for the study of music, art, and dance. Basic instruction on musical instruments and music rudiments is offered along with courses about música antillana, Afro-Colombian musical traditions from the Pacific and Atlantic coasts, and genres from other regions.

Among the musicians with whom I spoke, most had been playing their instruments or singing for an average of five or six years (instrumentalists' training ranged from two to eight years, while vocalists tended to have lengthier musical backgrounds). Older and more experienced musicians active before the 1980s had been playing for much longer, of course, averaging twenty years or more. In my estimate, the group of veterans constitutes about a fifth of the local scene. Yet, an unprecedented number of teenagers and young adults became salsa musicians between 1985 and 1995, and these made up the majority of Cali's salsa bands. This was evident at events such as the 1994 Festival de Orquestas, where over half the musicians in local orquestas appeared to be under thirty years of age. My observation of the rehearsals of several bands reinforced the impression that Caleño salsa bands had predominantly youthful memberships. It would appear that the current generation of Caleño youth has taken up salsa performance with the same fervor with which their parents took up dancing to salsa records in the 1960s and 1970s.

According to Sabina Borja, this trend is regional. In Bogotá and Medellín youngsters tend to form rock bands, while on the Atlantic coast they play in vallenato ensembles. In Cali, belonging to a salsa band seemed to guarantee a certain degree of prestige among one's peers.[16] Not only did playing salsa provide an opportunity to appear in public and perhaps even on television, it also offered a socially sanctioned avenue of recreation. I never met any young musicians whose parents disapproved of their being in a salsa band (unlike scenes in other parts of the world, e.g., punk rock in the United Kingdom). Indeed, most of the youngsters in Cali's salsa bands hail from families where salsa and música antillana were listened to, or they had close childhood friendships in circles where salsa prevailed. The establishment of all-child salsa orquestas in Cali has also had an influence on young Caleños, many of whom have taken up salsa less because of previous exposure to it than for the opportunity merely to play some sort of music.[17]

Given the adoption of salsa as the city's emblematic expression, it is no wonder that salsa performance became established as a viable pastime. Significantly, teenagers and young adults from both working-class *and* middle-class backgrounds took up salsa performance. This suggests that by the early 1990s salsa had shed many of the class-bound associations that continued to define social status in other areas of the popular scene—such as the salsotecas, which were still strongly linked with the working classes. This is probably due to the positive images of local bands promoted in local mass media and may also be related to the fact that in the late 1980s salsa romántica helped open doors for salsa into the middle and upper classes. Notably, during this same period several salsa dance academies and "salsa ballet" groups also flowered, including the Cali Rumba school, Liliana Salinas's Ballet de Azucar, Evelio Carabalí's Ballet Folclor Urbano, and Andrés Leudo's school. Modeled on 1970s troupes such as the Ballet de la Salsa, these groups represented a counterpart to the burgeoning of local musical ensembles.

Many young musicians explained to me that they approach their participation in salsa orquestas with discipline and pride. Despite exposure to the scurrilous behaviors traditionally associated with salsa musicians, they did not drink or smoke, nor did they indulge in drugs. Alvaro Granobles, a twenty-two-year-old vocalist with Octava Dimensión, commented on the distinction between older and younger musicians in Cali:

> The second generation of singers, or Caleño musicians, is very different from the previous one. I don't know if these differences are obvious in full daylight, but they are very strong. For example, in my case, I try to lead the new generation, trying to be a person who is very organized in my affairs. That is, I am very disciplined, as a singer I take great care of my voice, I don't drink cold things, I don't drink liquor, I don't smoke, and have nothing to do with drugs, nothing of that sort. Because for me, my voice is the most wonderful and greatest gift that God could have given me, so I have to take care of it and value it, and the best way to do that is taking care of myself. And that's how I'll last for many, many years, even into old age, with my voice intact. That's my main goal.[18]

As I discuss elsewhere (Waxer 2001a), young women are especially careful to maintain discipline, no doubt owing to their struggles to gain legitimacy as professional and responsible musicians.

Most of the younger musicians I spoke with were keenly interested in improving their musical skills, especially technical mastery of their instruments or voices. In the case of horn players, in particular, many of whom had been playing their instruments for less than two or three years, it was clear that much practice was needed before mastery would be attained.[19] While not all had the time or financial resources to engage in extensive formal training and practice, it was clear to me that many young musicians had taken up salsa performance with great earnestness, viewing it as an option for personal growth and not just mere diversion. Sarli Delgado, my seventeen-year-old colleague in Magenta Latin Jazz, shared her reflections on what playing music has meant for her:

> It seems to me that one of the nicest things in this field is the enjoyment with which one does things. People, at the moment when you get on a stage, when you let your hair down, as they say, express all the enjoyment you have in doing your thing—people feel it. And they help you to rise, or help you to fall as well. But sharing with people is really nice, to know many places, other countries, other cities, and different cultures.[20]

Notably, several young people from Cali's white and mestizo middle class have become involved in salsa performance, Sarli Delgado and Alvaro Granobles among them. In contrast to the associations that salsa held for middle-class youth during the early 1970s, salsa is no longer seen as plebeian or bohemian. The current generation of Caleño youth does not see salsa as a hotbed of leftist or countercultural ideals. Rather, it is viewed as an authentic local popular tradition, and performing salsa represents a viable resource for extending one's horizons. Young performers are aware that playing in an orquesta provides not only an avenue for earning a bit of money, but also an opportunity to travel to other parts of the country and even abroad. While older musicians with whom I spoke seemed jaded about the professional circuit, most of the young musicians I talked with seemed eager for the chance to do things that many of their contemporaries could not.

Women and Children in Local Salsa

One of the last and most remarkable waves in the mushrooming of local salsa bands was the emergence of all-woman and all-child ensembles during the late 1980s and early 1990s. Referred to respectively as *orquestas femeninas* and *orquestas juveniles,* these kinds of salsa bands mark the entry of two groups previously marginalized from active roles as salseros: women and children. Importantly, not only does the rise of the orquestas femeninas and juveniles underscore the fervor with which salsa performance had permeated local popular culture by the end of the 1980s, it also goes hand in hand with two significant developments that framed Caleño life at this time. The first relates to socioeconomic changes for Colombian women in general through the 1970s and 1980s, resulting in greater economic freedom for women and a loosening of patriarchal codes that had previously restricted women's participation in the public sphere. The second development is more local and concerns the way salsa, by the 1980s, had become legitimized as an authentic local tradition whose pedagogical potential for transmitting larger cultural values was channeled through the teaching and formation of salsa music ensembles. Both developments reinforced the Caleño self-image as the world salsa capital and a suitable outpost of heaven for world salsa fans.

Orquestas Femeninas: All-Woman Salsa Bands

Cali's orquestas femeninas can be divided into precommercial and commercial phases. The precommercial phase was undoubtedly pioneered by the Caleña vocalist and multi-instrumentalist María del Carmen Alvarado. Between 1983 and 1987, Alvarado was the leader and cofounder of three bands—Yemayá, Siguaraya, and Cañabrava—which were based between Cali and Bogotá and performed primarily in coffeehouses. Inspired by Euro–North American feminist ideals of solidarity, these groups emphasized musicianship and refuted commercial images of women as sexual objects. The names of these bands (referring, respectively, to the important Cuban and Yoruban deity of the seas and to two species of hemp and cane plants difficult to cut down) reinforced positive notions of female strength and perseverance. Another Bogotá-based all-woman band, Aché (the Yoruban word for "strength" or "essence"), similarly emphasized this concept. Owing to time constraints and other factors, however, these groups disbanded by the end of the decade.

The international success of the Dominican Republic's all-woman merengue band, Las Chicas del Can, indirectly spurred the growth of Cali's commercial orquestas femeninas. Woman musicians commented on having seen this group on television and being struck by their novelty appeal. Cali's first commercially successful orquesta femenina was Son de Azucar, originally called Gaviota (Spanish for "seagull"). The six friends who founded the group in 1987 were aware of the novelty of promoting an all-woman band within the burgeoning live scene and decided to capitalize on

Figure 5.1   Son de Azucar. Courtesy of Sony Music.

it. Says the bandleader, Olga Lucia Rivas: "The initial idea was, how do I tell you, was to do something as a hobby. . . . 'Let's put together something different, maybe we'll get to perform some place.' But we wanted it to be all women, because we wanted to have an impact, right? That is, not like your standard mixed orquesta, or the groups with men and maybe one women. No. The idea was to have an impact . . . and that everyone see that it was all women."[21]

By 1989 Gaviota had pooled together sufficient funds to record a single. It caught the ear of CBS Records (now Sony International), and a contract was offered. The company, however, insisted on changing the band's name and image in order to heighten the group's commercial appeal. First, CBS pressed for the name Son de Azucar, a play on words that not only hails salsa's Cuban roots—"*son* of sugar"—and references Cali's principal agroindustry, but also quips "they are [made] of sugar."[22] The company also insisted on tight jeans and miniskirts for the group, replacing the loose pants and jackets that had comprised their previous uniform (Figure 5.1). Rivas was strongly opposed to this demand and bowed to commercial dictates under protest (Valverde and Quintero 1995: 68). In spite of these constraints on their commercial image, however, Son de Azucar developed into a strong, musically solid orquesta. The band's local prominence was established when their tune "Caleño" received an award for best song of the 1992 Feria.

Son de Azucar's commercial success helped spur the formation of other orquestas femeninas. Following the pattern according to which the local live scene has grown in general, Cali's orquestas femeninas grew from individuals splitting off from one group to form bands of their own. Both Canela and D'Caché, the second most successful all-woman bands, formed in this way. Notably, unlike the orquestas femeninas of the precommercial phase, which projected images of feminine power or energy, Cali's commercial all-woman bands have sported names that convey more conventionally "feminine" qualities, such as sweetness or subtle eroticism. Given the heavy sugarcane cultivation in these two areas, it is not surprising that sweetness is a central theme, as suggested by the name Son de Azucar. Vera Kutzinski points out that in Latin America, however, "sugar" not only references feminine docility and good-natured cheerfulness, but also points to the fantasy of eroticism and potent sensuality stereotypically associated with the mulata of sugar-producing regions (1993). A variant on this theme, "sugar 'n' spice," is suggested by the name Canela (cinnamon). The term *canela* also suggests the golden-brown skin tone of the mulata and mestiza women that predominate in Cali and Cuba and, like the term "azucar," once again indexes the erotic qualities ascribed to these women. Notably, not many dark-skinned Afro-Colombian women perform in Cali's orquestas femeninas; the majority are indeed mulata and mestiza, reinforcing the eroticized imagery of the band names.

While these examples are the clearest instances of "feminine" band names, other orquestas femeninas also fall into this camp. D'Caché, for example, implies "classy" or chic sophistication. Yerbabuena, the name of another band, refers to the sweetness of peppermint. Record companies reinforced the eroticized image of Caleña musicians by putting only the first names of band members on album covers, similar to the way calendar girls and Playboy centerfolds are packaged. The relative youth of Caleña salsa musicians during the mid-1990s (their average age was nineteen) did not help offset this image. The infantilization of adult women as cute, childlike playmates was strong during the early 1990s but thankfully had died by the mid-1990s. None of the orquestas femeninas, however, has escaped the commercial insistence on their performing in high heels, miniskirts, and makeup.

The novelty of all-woman salsa bands in Cali undoubtedly contributed to the local demand for new orquestas femeninas. By 1995 eleven all-woman ensembles were active in the local music scene. Of these groups, Son de Azucar, Canela, and D'Caché found steady work throughout the year and toured internationally. Other groups also appeared regularly in local events, especially during the December festive season. During this same period, all-woman orquestas and ensembles emerged elsewhere in Colombia and Latin America. Along Colombia's Atlantic coast, all-woman vallenato ensembles modeled on Cali's all-woman salsa orquestas appeared after 1992.

Beyond Colombia, the Dominican Republic and Cuba have been important sites of activity for all-woman ensembles. In the Dominican Republic, several all-woman merengue orquestas and conjuntos have been established since the 1980s, although few of these groups have received exposure beyond national boundaries (Pacini Hernández 1995: 183; Austerlitz 1997: 116–18). Meanwhile, through the late 1980s and early 1990s there was a flowering of all-woman orquestas in Havana, Cuba, reminiscent of an earlier local trend of all-woman bands in the 1930s and early 1940s. (I conducted fieldwork on Cuban all-woman bands during brief trips there in 1995.) While the growth of these other all-woman scenes are not directly related to that in Cali (with the exception of the vallenato groups), their parallel rise is not fortuitous. Rather, both movements constitute part of a growing tide of women performers in the international Latin music world.

As I discuss at length elsewhere (Waxer 2001a), the rise of Cali's orquestas femeninas coincides with the greater participation of Colombian women in the labor force and other areas of public life.[23] Until recently Colombian women and their counterparts in the rest of Latin America, confined to traditional family roles (mothers, wives, sisters, and daughters) as caretakers in the domestic realm, depended strongly upon men for economic support. The hegemonic thrust of patriarchy has prevailed at nearly all levels of Colombian life. To rephrase Gramsci's well-known formulation on hegemony (1971: 12), women's consent to the dominant order has been won and maintained through various social practices and mechanisms in which women come to value their worth, their appearance, and their public and private roles in terms of men's needs and expectations. Colombian women did not even receive the right to vote until 1957, since a husband's or father's ballot was considered to represent the women in his family (Gutiérrez 1995). Since the 1950s, however, Colombian women, like those in other parts of Latin America, have nearly doubled their participation in the national workforce. In Colombia this has occurred at the same time as the percentage of economically active men has actually dropped. (Statistics indicate that between 1951 and 1990 the percentage of women in the Colombian workforce rose from 18.6 percent to 31.4 percent, while the percentage of men fell from 80.4 percent to 65.8 percent; Gutiérrez 1995: 304.) The growing economic power of women as both providers and consumers has contributed to their independence from men, in public and private life.

Although male decisions and male-oriented discourse continue to dominate the social order, small shifts or concessions in the prevailing attitudes
toward women have been necessary in order to retain women's consent to
what remains a strongly patriarchal system.

Studies of European "ladies' orchestras" in the nineteenth century and
of U.S. and British jazz bands in the 1930s and 1940s indicate that these
ensembles mirror women's increased presence in the labor force and public life. A common theme in all of these cases has been the virtual exclusion
of women from male-dominated ensembles (Myers 1993: 144; Placksin
1982: 87–90; Handy 1983: 69; O'Brien 1995: 72). Men have historically jus-
tified the bar against women musicians on the grounds of women's supposed artistic incompetence. Caleña musicians have certainly not been immune to such criticisms, and I often heard complaints that the orquestas
femeninas lacked the precision, force, and dynamism of a "real salsa band."
Yet, stereotypical dismissals of women musicians have often masked deeper
fears that women would become competitors for musical jobs, destabiliz-
ing men's control of the field. Indeed, while many second-rank orquestas
femeninas in Cali did suffer from problems of poor intonation, sloppy execution, and lack of polish, these factors can be directly attributed to the lack
of musical training among their members. The vogue for all-woman bands
created a sudden demand for which there was no pool of well-trained specialists, and many orquestas femeninas found themselves with fledgling
musicians with only a year or two of learning on their instruments. However, these bands sounded no worse than male orquestas with similarly in-
experienced musicians.

With the establishment of orquestas femeninas in Cali, women found a
new avenue through which to participate in a sphere previously inaccessible
to them. Although distinguished by gender in part for commercial reasons
—that is, because of the novelty all-woman bands presented—the very fact
that orquestas femeninas were established along these lines suggests that
gender is a significant category of social identity in Caleño culture. Men and
women have traditionally held very distinct social roles, which did not allow
for women to become public performers as men could. For most Caleña
musicians, it has been easier to band together and form all-woman salsa
groups than try to break into male orquestas. Elsewhere I analyze in detail
the challenges that Caleña musicians have faced in the struggle to establish
themselves as legitimate performers (Waxer 2001a).

The rise of all-woman salsa bands in Cali during the late 1980s and early
1990s resonates with the emergence of all-woman merengue bands in the
Dominican Republic and all-woman dance bands in Cuba during this same

period. The development of these orquestas femeninas can be seen as a response to larger historical processes in the late twentieth century, as women in Colombia and other parts of Latin America entered the labor force and became increasingly active in the public sphere as breadwinners and consumers. For Caleña musicians, the move into formerly exclusive male domains has been a slow process of negotiation over gender roles, and the adoption of a radical antipatriarchal position is not a viable choice. With the demands still made of Colombian women to comply with traditional roles as domestic caretakers and nurturing helpers, on the one hand, and as sexual objects, on the other, the orquestas femeninas have been granted conditional acceptance. Just as many local women have operated small cottage industries out of their homes in order to supplement (or in some cases supply) the family income, Caleña musicians and bandleaders have been permitted commercial success and recognition of artistic achievement only so as long as the masculine social order is not threatened.

The case of Cali's all-woman salsa bands enriches Ellen Koskoff's important formulation of the ways musical performance can reinforce, enact, protest, or challenge a society's gender structures (1987: 10–13). Where do we place the orquestas femeninas on Koskoff's scale? Although the bands reconfirm social and sexual norms in some ways (e.g., women as sex objects), they also challenge established gender roles by allowing women to move with more freedom than ever before in the realm of public entertainment. Although most women in the orquestas femeninas do not actively protest sexism, they do strive to be treated on the same ground as their male counterparts—that is, as musicians and professionals.

The emergence of all-woman salsa bands in Cali can be thought of as a "gender reversal" or transformation, similar to other cases in which women have moved into cultural domains dominated by men (Koskoff 1987: 11–12). Nonetheless, members of Cali's all-woman salsa bands tend to express their ideas about gender in terms of expanded opportunities for women, rather than in terms of denying their gender identity or adopting male behaviors. Other than learning instruments formerly played by men only, the behavior of most women salsa musicians reproduces conventional gender codes for Colombian women. These include the sometimes contradictory norms of presenting a sexually attractive appearance on stage (being a sex object for men) while conforming to "decent" behavior offstage (no drinking or drugs) so as to maintain an aspect of virtue. These standards do not apply to male salsa musicians, either locally or in the international scene, although this is starting to change with the new generation of Caleño performers. In short, while Cali's all-woman salsa bands can be seen as reinforcing and enacting certain gender roles, what is most significant about their emergence is the way Caleña musicians have worked within gender categories to negotiate and transform formerly negative cultural standards about women as public entertainers and musicians. Thus, following Koskoff's notion that musical performance can reinforce, enact, protest, or challenge a society's gender structures, one can also add that musical performance can serve to transform gender codes within the overall social and sexual order. This serves neither to reinforce nor to protest the existing gender structure, but to maximize the economic and prestige opportunities for the subordinate group in this system—women.

The title of Valverde and Quintero's book about Cali's orquestas femeninas, *Abran paso* (Make Way), is aptly chosen. Cali's all-woman bands have certainly broken new ground. The book's title, which is taken from a classic 1970s salsa tune popularized by Ismael Miranda, harks back to the era when salsa took a strong hold on Caleño life and affirms the impact all-woman bands made two decades later. Despite the sexually objectified image these bands have been obliged to adopt, the sheer fact of their existence and their unprecedented commercial success has broadcast a positive message to other women. The dozens of Caleña musicians with whom I talked are proud of their accomplishments and see themselves as playing an important role in helping to project an image of Caleña women as hard workers who are able to compete in a "man's world" without compromising their self-respect.

Salsa and Youth: All-Child Salsa Orquestas

Another important offshoot for local live music in the late 1980s and early 1990s was the rise of *orquestas infantiles* and *orquestas juveniles*—salsa bands composed of children and adolescents. Prior to this development, very few children and youths had participated in the local live scene. As with the orquestas femeninas, the appeal of the all-child orquestas lay partly in their novelty. However, they also represented a key nexus from the current generation of salsa performers to the next and underscored the way salsa and its roots had become part of local cultural tradition by the 1980s.

Some orquestas juveniles were established in local schools or private academies, such as Musikitos, run by the orquesta femenina pioneer María del Carmen Alvarado. The majority of Cali's all-child orquestas, however, have been associated with the music academy of Luis Carlos Ochoa. An Afro-Colombian saxophonist, clarinetist and community leader, Ochoa is a longtime veteran of the local scene, having founded such important orquestas as La Gran Banda Caleña and Los del Caney in addition to having performed with the Cali Charanga and served as musical director to D'Caché.[24] Although Ochoa hails from Guacarí (a town forty miles northeast of Cali), he was attracted to salsa when he moved to Cali in the early 1970s and became a prominent figure in the local salsa scene. In 1988, tired of his dual career as musician by night and schoolteacher by day, he took up the idea of forming a musical ensemble with his three children, who were studying at the central conservatory. The group was expanded to include some of their friends and became the basis of La Charanguita de Luis Carlos— "the little charanga," so named because flute and violin were among the instruments in the original orquesta. Even though the group later discarded this instrumentation in favor of trombones, the name persisted.

Officially launched in August 1989, La Charanguita garnered much attention for the promising talent in the band, particularly Ochoa's youngest son, Luis Carlos Jr., a piano prodigy who was only six when the band was formed. As La Charanguita's fame grew, other youngsters began to ask if they could attend rehearsals and learn how to play. To meet this demand, Ochoa began providing informal group classes in instrumental and vocal technique, music rudiments, and salsa performance. These classes were consolidated into an official music academy in 1993, and Ochoa hired other music teachers to take over teaching duties so that he could devote more time to its administration. In the early 1990s Ochoa formed seven orquestas infantiles and juveniles from his his best students, ranked by age and skill. These included two versions of La Charanguita (grouped by age, twelve to fifteen years and fourteen to seventeen years), Minisón (eight to twelve years) and Soneritos (five to ten years). There were two all-girl bands, corresponding to the city's orquestas femeninas: Ardillitas (eight to twelve years) and Chiquibanda (twelve to fifteen years). In addition, for youths too old to be in La Charanguita, Ochoa formed another orquesta called Mombassa (seventeen to twenty-two years).

Although most of the children came from working-class backgrounds, membership in these groups was racially diverse. As band members grew older, they graduated to the next successive band, while newer students came up through the ranks. The bands shared a core repertoire of songs, which facilitated the transition from one ensemble to another. All the bands performed at public and private functions, often for events connected in some way with children.

The orquestas juveniles served a didactic function not only in transmitting musical style, but also in teaching important lessons about responsibility, discipline, and teamwork. Ochoa explained to me that his primary pedagogical goal was to use popular music as a basis for teaching life skills. He tried to give his young musicians "una formación inte-gral, no solo como músico o artista, pero como persona, ser humano" (a complete development, not only as a musician or artist, but as a person, a human being).[25] Besides teaching basic musical skills, he instilled values of cooperation, accountability, and respect for others. In observing rehearsals of La Charanguita, I found Ochoa to be stern in his demand for discipline and order, reprimanding band members who had not learned their parts, who had arrived late, or who did not pay attention. His efforts paid off, however, since the youngsters who came up under his wing acquired a good reputation for being serious and responsible musicians. Ochoa told me that the child musicians in La Charanguita learned the norms of professional conduct that he learned only as an adult. Many of the adolescents and young adults who graduated from his orquestas went on to find immediate work with Cali's better orquestas.

One of the most notable features about La Charanguita was Ochoa's choice of repertoire. The ensemble's primary musical diet consisted of salsa tunes from the 1960s and 1970s, including songs by Richie Ray, Ismael Miranda, and other New York stars. Ochoa chose to emphasize this repertoire not only because of its demanding musical content, which provides good technical training, but also because he felt that the romantic and erotic lyrics of contemporary salsa were inappropriate for children and young adolescents. Significantly, the tunes performed by La Charanguita and Ochoa's other orquestas juveniles are longtime favorites in Cali and part of the local salsero tradition. Ochoa explained to me that La Charanguita fulfilled an important function in maintaining and preserving the old salsa dura classics, which few other local orquestas do.

> I chose songs by Richie Ray, Ismael Miranda, by the great salsa writers, no? . . . Because it was music that not all the bands played, and because it required a certain level of difficulty to put together, so this gave me a motive so that the children would have material to learn. And the other thing is that this music is always current, it's music for all times. We learned it then and we can also play it now. It doesn't go out of style easily. . . . [W]e wanted to preserve it, to tell other bands that we could play it, that it's a music that doesn't go out of style, that will always be liked, that it is a music that is, like, sacred for salseros, no?[26]

In addition to a pedagogical emphasis on the "classics," Ochoa also produced original compositions for La Charanguita, with lyrics directed to-

Figure 5.2   La Charanguita. Courtesy of Luis Carlos Ochoa.

ward other children. A good example of the band's original repertoire is "Compartir" (To Share), which appears on the recording *Podemos y debemos* (We Can and We Should), made by La Charanguita in 1994 (Figure 5.2). Unlike most recordings released by Caleño bands, this album did not use studio musicians (see below), but featured the young members of the band. The song's lyrics put forth a didactic message about the benefits of sharing and leading a good life. While unremarkable in terms of lyric content, the recording is notable for the rhythmic swing and tight delivery of the orquesta. The arrangement is in a straight-ahead salsa dura style, with a driving montuno section. Horn lines and vocals are cleanly executed and in tune (something I did not always hear in live performances by the band), and the harmonies on the coros add polish to the performance. When I began research on La Charanguita in 1995, the orquesta had abandoned some of the older repertoire and incorporated more contemporary songs by artists such as Gloria Estefan and Cuba's Los Van Van. The emphasis on interesting arrangements, "clean" lyrics, and technically challenging material, however, remained a constant.

Sarli Delgado, my colleague in Magenta Latin Jazz and a member of La Charanguita until 1994, explained to me that much of the group's success lay in the ability of its young musicians to perform demanding tunes at the level of an adult orquesta.[27] This earned them accolades on tours to Europe and Cuba—during their 1993 European tour there were even problems because some concert promoters did not believe that the youngsters were actually playing, so accomplished did they sound! I was much taken by the maturity of the musicians in La Charanguita, who demonstrated considerable stage presence and self-confidence in performance. When Oscar D'León saw La Charanguita perform at the Festival de Orquestas in 1992, he was so impressed that he formed Salserín, a well-known Venezuelan orquesta juvenil that is often erroneously credited as the first all-child salsa band on the international scene.

Ochoa's efforts constitute a significant link in transmitting the salsa tradition to a forthcoming generation of Caleño musicians. His characterization of salsa dura classics as "sacred" is striking and resembles Hernán González's remarks about the impact of música antillana in Cali in previous generations. Ochoa's reverential attitude toward old musical chestnuts, one shared by many Caleño fans, is rooted in the affective impact of these tunes on local popular culture during the height of the record-centered dance scene. The use of these old recordings as a basis for pedagogical material highlights their centrality in the local salsa tradition.

One of the standards in La Charanguita's repertoire is Richie Ray's "Sonido bestial," easily identifiable from its incorporation of the rousing piano arpeggios from Frédéric Chopin's "Revolutionary Etude," played over a salsa rhythm section. Among Caleño salsa fans the tune is a favorite, and for older ones its strains often evoke memories of Ray's landmark appearance at the 1968 Feria. I was told that during a visit to Cali in 1989, Richie Ray was invited to a performance by La Charanguita. Ray was astonished to hear six-year-old Luis Carlos Ochoa Jr. execute the virtuoso passages that Ray himself had popularized twenty years earlier.[28] For the audience it must have seemed as if history had come full circle, with the children of Cali's first salseros performing the same tune that had paved salsa's triumphant entry into popular life a generation previously.

Between Art and Commerce

In Cali being a salsa musician entails more than just learning music and finding like-minded people with whom to play. Owing to the strong commercial foundation of the live scene—both locally and internationally—being a salsa musician is closely tied to notions of professionalism (i.e., earning money for performance) and economic success. Several individuals shared with me their idealistic vision of playing salsa as a way to explore new musical sounds and "express themselves." In practice, however, these values were severely constrained by the dictates of the market—what would sell, what would enhance an orquesta's exposure, and what would enable one to survive professionally, not just artistically. Although few musicians actually worked full time, the goal of earning a living from music alone certainly prevailed and coheres with cosmopolitan notions about music professionalism that began circulating around the globe after the 1960s (Turino 2000: 272). Without this edge, musicians often disbanded for lack of focus. Some musicians criticized the drive for material gain, stating that getting together just to play music should be sufficient motivation and reward in itself. I often heard complaints that too many musicians respond to proposals to form a band or to play together with the question, "How much does it pay?" During my nearly two years in the field, however, I did not encounter a single group of musicians that was able to sustain activity without the incentive of an upcoming gig or recording project.

In keeping with the commercial orientation of the live scene, most Caleño bands had been organized as commercial enterprises by the early 1990s and were registered as actual businesses with the municipal Chamber of Commerce.[29] While membership in most bands is arranged informally and sealed by verbal agreement, orquestas such as Niche, Guayacán, and Canela required formal contracts from its members, stipulating wages, responsibilities, and fines for missed rehearsals and performances. Ironically, despite efforts to organize and run bands as efficient business enterprises, an almost complete lack of organization at the city-wide level has made it very difficult for musicians and orquestas to protect their interests within larger commercial contexts. No musicians' union has existed in Cali since the early 1960s (a small union lasted from 1948 to 1962), and musicians and bandleaders face chronic problems over payments, access to decent performance conditions, and fair contractual terms. During the peak years of the cartel bonanza, when there was regular work and the promise of handsome payments, not many complained—but when resources began drying up toward the mid-1990s, musicians were the first to feel the pinch. A formal association called PROMUSIVAL (Professional Musicians of El Valle province) was launched in early 1995 following the failure of the city-run Feria organization to pay several orquestas for their work in the 1994 fair —a sum amounting to several thousand dollars. Led by Jairo Varela of Grupo Niche and Luis Carlos Ochoa of La Charanguita, the organization attempted to exercise some form of collective bargaining with local businessmen in order to address the multiple grievances brought by local musicians and bandleaders. Faced with the increasingly disastrous national recession in the late 1990s, however, this organization has never managed to fulfill the promise of its vision. Throughout the 1980s and 90s, hence, Caleño musicians remained very much at the beck and call of local, national, and international economic forces beyond their control.

The tension between art and commerce has shaped local live music-making in very specific ways. Perhaps one of the most singular features of the local live scene is the way recordings dominate processes of learning, transmission, creation, and performance—much as recorded music has shaped other spheres of local popular culture. Unlike some popular-music scenes (e.g., rock), where a band will start with a basic idea or song and work up the final creation, in Cali new tunes are usually brought to an orquesta as a fully arranged piece, with parts notated by professional copyists. For economic reasons, most bands are now obliged to use studio musicians for their recording projects; only the vocalists from the group are heard on the album. From the master tapes of this recording, along with a written score, other band members learn their parts for the live performance. The first time that an orquesta performs a new tune together is therefore not before their recording is made, but rather afterward. This was not always the case; during the early and mid-1980s, Grupo Niche, La Misma Gente, and Guayacán all rehearsed and performed pieces before taking them to the studio. The high expense of studio time sharply curtailed this procedure, however, and nowadays it is common for most orquestas to learn in this reverse fashion. This development is a strange parody of early Caleño bands, which prepared cover versions of other artists' tunes—but now, orquestas perform songs based on their own recordings.

During the 1990s most bands were careful in live performance to remain faithful to the recorded version of a song; few strayed from the sound document. As some musicians explained, Caleño audiences were used to hearing a certain version of a tune from the recording or radio and generally wanted to hear the band perform that same version. Recordings are fixed texts, and given the primacy of recordings in popular life since the 1940s, it is not surprising that Caleños developed a propensity for established versions of pieces rather than variable renditions. Caleño orquestas hence are very precise in following the recorded version of a tune, and rehearsals are geared toward refining the band's ability to sound just like the recording. I observed that Niche's Jairo Varela was especially rigorous in this regard: he discourages spontaneous *descargas* (jam sessions) in live performance. Audiences in Cuba, New York, or Puerto Rico, on the other hand, are accustomed to and even expect such impromptu developments. In Cali I heard very few local orquestas indulge in a descarga, and then only in isolated circumstances. Experienced musicians familiar with the salsa tradition know where they can add small-scale variations that will make a performance interesting without altering the essential rendition—percussionists might add small fills, while bass players and pianists could vary their basic patterns using inversions or different voicings. Horn players, on the other hand, are more restricted in their ability to break from the arrangement, perhaps only doubling a note with a harmonic extension at a cadence.

Similarly, as I discovered while attending a shooting of the television program *El Solar,* orquestas featured on the show were videotaped while playing along to the prerecorded master tape of the song—a standard practice in music video. Although the musicians actually played their instruments, only the visual image was retained; the commercial recording was dubbed over it. Doubling is done primarily to prevent costly retakes; also, none of Cali's television studios are equipped with adequate acoustic facilities. Thus, despite the live music boom on Cali's scene, the recorded sound object has in many ways remained central, over and above what is considered "authentic" live performance in other contexts.

Caleño orquestas further underscore the impression of delivering a fixed "product" by paying considerable attention to the element of spectacle while onstage. Orquestas are always uniformed, and songs are performed with choreography developed and rehearsed beforehand. Indeed, most orquestas have two or three uniforms that they can choose from depending on the performance. The vocalists, similarly, work out dance routines for each song, sometimes with the hired help of professional dancers. Although orquestas play primarily for people to dance to, they are quite conscious of the fact that they are also putting on a show and take great pains to be good entertainers.

Local orquestas are also constrained by the need to regularly produce recordings in order to establish and maintain their professional image. While this is hardly remarkable in light of the fact that musical groups around the globe are producing compact discs and cassettes, it does reveal the increasing predominance in Cali of capitalist notions about musical creation as a commodified product. Recordings serve as sonic letters of presentation or business cards that represent the orquesta and open the possibility for public recognition, increased gigs, more record productions, and international concert tours. Proyecto Omega's leader Cheo Angulo explained:

> Our milieu is difficult, because there are many bands, so it's difficult to work and have people recognize you right away, right? So, if you have a tune to show, if you have something already recorded for people to listen to, it's easier to identify you. . . . People do it mostly for that, to have a letter of presentation. Because there are many bands, and because there are many bands and the majority of them haven't recorded, they all tend to get lost. They're more difficult to identify. But if you have a tune that's playing and you say, "Okay, that's that band that sings that tune," it's easier to identify.[30]

Several musicians and record producers told me that Cali is considered to be the strongest market for salsa records in Latin America, and many international salsa artists choose to launch new releases in Cali on the grounds that if a new album succeeds there, it will succeed anywhere (see also Ulloa 1992: 17). Since the music industry is based on capitalist expansion, however, coming up with new products is necessary in order to stimulate consumers to keep buying. Local artists face additional pressure to compete with international releases. As a result, Caleño orquestas must produce a new album every twelve to eighteen months or risk being completely forgotten.

According to the producer-arranger Chucho Ramírez, the average local salsa recording takes between four to six months to complete, from the initial planning stages to the final production run. To reduce studio time and cut down on expenses, most recordings are made with studio musicians who can execute their parts rapidly and without mistakes. The same nucleus of musicians works on all these productions in Cali, which is convenient for producers but less beneficial for audiences. Recordings by local bands tend to sound the same not only because of their adherence to stock musical ideas, but also because they literally use the same musicians. Ramírez told me that when he is producing an album he will sometimes look for different musicians in order to obtain different "color" and not have the recordings sound all alike.[31] There is still a degree of homogeneity, however, owing to the relatively small pool of musicians on whom producers can call.

In live performance, the choice of repertoire reveals important conceptual domains that are also entwined with commercial aspects and the predominant influence of recording, as musical practice, and records, as sound objects, on the local live scene. In public contexts such as nightclubs, parks,

civic events, and public concerts, most bands perform their own core repertoire. In contrast, for semiprivate dances and parties, most orquestas keep
an adjunct repertoire of tunes that can be pulled out as the event dictactes.
These are usually cover versions of old classics popularized in former years,
including música tropical numbers, classic 1960s and 1970s salsa dura tunes,
and—almost always—a version of Grupo Niche's "Cali pachanguero." Although top-ranking bands such as Niche and Guayacán never perform this
kind of adjunct repertoire, I was struck by how many other groups played
these tunes at dances, even when they had a respectable repertoire of their
own and did not need to fill out an evening's worth of music.

This pattern underscores significant boundaries between public and
semiprivate social domains. By playing the core repertoire (i.e., the tunes
with which the band is identified) in mass public contexts, a salsa band
affirms its distinctiveness—an important factor for commercial success. On
the other hand, by performing cover versions of old classics at semiprivate
dances, a band caters to audience tastes, promoting a popular canon and
not its own identity. In a sense, the public domain is relatively impersonal,
where people go not so much to be together and interact on a one-to-one
level as to hear a particular band play (although the former can and does
happen). Part of the social contract at such events depends on the fact that
listeners expect to hear a band's original songs. The performance of those
tunes ideally results in more record sales and concert appearances for the
orquesta. By contrast, in the semiprivate sphere the orquesta steps into a
different sort of contract, where the musicians do not stand opposite the
public but rather alongside it. At parties and dances, people gather for
the purpose of direct personal interactions with friends and family, and the
band is drawn into this context. Rather than selling themselves as Orquesta
X with the current hit "Y," the musicians are there to facilitate the participatory ambience of the event by playing tunes that get people moving together. Commercial factors are still present, since the band is paid for the
event, but the point is not to market a name or product so much as to provide a service, including playing sons by other bands that people will enjoy.
In particular, the performance of old hits from the record-centered dance
scene in these semiprivate contexts indicates the continued influence of classic recordings on the contemporary live scene.

Musical Style in the 1990s

When I asked local musicians, composers, and arrangers, "What makes
Colombian salsa sound 'Colombian'?" the unequivocal response from most

was "su sencillez" (its simplicity). While New York, Puerto Rican, and even Venezuelan orquestas are characterized by a driving percussive force and dynamic, punchy arrangements, Colombian salsa owes much of its appeal to catchy melodies, piquant lyrics, and short, uncomplicated horn lines— elements that derive from cumbia, currulao, and other Colombian genres. Following the parameters established by Niche, La Misma Gente, and Guayacán, as well as by Atlantic coast orquestas such as Joe Arroyo y La Verdad and Raíces, Colombian bands are characterized by a light texture, a crisp percussive attack, and an on-the-beat rhythmic feel. Interestingly, this manner of rhythmic phrasing is similar to the way Colombians dance the basic salsa four-step, in contrast to Puerto Rican and Cuban dancers, who tend to step just slightly behind the beat. The feeling of gravity or "heaviness" in the latter style, as opposed to the sprightliness of Colombian salsa, is a central distinction between these different schools. According to the Venezuelan pianist and arranger Felix Shakaito, leader of Los Bronco, Colombian percussionists tend to have a slower technique, which adds to this feel. For example, when a Colombian percussionist plays an *abañico* (short, sharp drum roll) on the timbales, the individual hits can be heard. Puerto Rican percussionists tend to be smoother and faster, so that this roll sounds like one line, instead of *dub-i-dub-i-dub*.[32]

During the late 1980s and 1990s, Caleño orquestas, attentive to shifts in the international salsa scene, began playing salsa romántica, also referred to locally as *salsa balada*. Maintaining its position at the vanguard of the local scene, Niche became the first Colombian salsa group to take up the new romántica style with their 1988 release *Tapando el hueco*. From that album, the song "Nuestro sueño" (Our Dream) became a popular hit, fusing pop-balada lyrics, melody, and harmony with a salsa rhythmic base. While they avoid the explicit sexuality of then-popular Puerto Rican singers such as Eddie Santiago and Lalo Rodríguez, the lyrics of "Nuestro sueño" are marked by an erotic romanticism, in keeping with contemporary commercial trends. The shift to romantic themes marks a strong break from earlier Caleño salsa songs, which were based more on scenes and images from daily life. Following Niche's lead, La Misma Gente and other bands began to incorporate salsa romántica tunes and the newer, muted style of performance. Niche's next album, *Sutil y contundente* (Subtle and Forceful, 1989) continued to break ground for local orquestas by incorporating lush synthesizer overlays. Through the early 1990s other Caleño bands also incorporated synthesizer tracks into their arrangements, primarily to create a thick wash of sound, in imitation of an orchestral string section. The one exception was La Misma Gente, which had used synthesizer effects since

1986, but only for rhythmic fills and breaks. Local audiences seemed dis-affected by the syrupy synth sound, however, and by 1992 or 1993 most bands had abandoned the effect.

Notably, salsa romántica tunes by Caleño orquestas have had to main-tain a somewhat danceable edge in order to gain acceptance among local audiences.[33] Caleño bands have been more successful with cleaner arrange-ments that do not obscure the rhythm section. In addition, although heavy synthesizer tracks lend themselves to slower tempos where pieces are geared more toward listening than dancing (as in some Puerto Rican salsa romántica between 1989 and 1991), they do not work for more upbeat tem-pos. Caleño salsa romántica tends to be mid-tempo, neither too slow nor too fast, in order to appease the local zeal for dancing.

Through the early 1980s and 1990s, other key traits distinguished Caleño orquestas from their counterparts abroad. One was the emphasis on vocals over and above instrumental arrangements or solo improvising. Part of this relates to the predilection of Colombian audiences for catchy lyrics and re-frains. Composers and arrangers know this and keep the listener's focus on the words. Most local lead vocalists during the 1990s had similar vocal tim-bres and ranges, however, which led to a homogeneous vocal style on the local scene and criticism from some local observers that the romantic, "crooning" tenors of Caleño vocalists were no match for the distinctive soneros of salsa's classic years.

Another trait of Caleño salsa bands has been the relatively simple horn parts. In most Colombian salsa arrangements, horn lines are less contra-puntal and harmonically complex than they are in Puerto Rican salsa ro-mántica tunes, creating a lighter texture that does not overwhelm the rhythm section. Some musicians and melómanos explained to me that Co-lombian salsa has less complicated horn lines owing to the dearth of players who can execute technically challenging parts, but it is probable that aes-thetic preferences for a lighter texture and basic harmonic progressions have also influenced this style. Grupo Niche, for example, has highly ac-complished horn players, but the band's arrangements have remained sim-ple. Chucho Ramírez pointed out to me that the tradition of town bands (*bandas del pueblo*) has been an important influence in Colombian music. It shaped not only the development of música tropical in the 1940s and 1950s, but also the style of horn parts in Colombian salsa during the 1980s and 1990s.[34]

Caleño arrangers and orquestas have also incorporated elements from the current transnational salsa sound, which is centered in Puerto Rico, in order to produce songs that are up to date and commercially viable on the international salsa market. An influence in this regard was Cesar Monge, who introduced basic principles now identified with the Puerto Rican sound, through arrangements that were more *cerrada,* or tight—that is, free of extra hits or fills, and pared down to the basic rhythmic flow for a cleaner, more polished sound.[35] During the early 1990s, with the advent of a few arrangers well attuned to the current Puerto Rican sound, the songs recorded and performed by local bands became more sophisticated and began employing a richer harmonic vocabulary influenced by jazz and pop ballads. This harmonic language features major, minor, and dominant ninth, eleventh, and thirteenth chords, modulation of keys by rising semitone, and stock harmonic progressions built upon secondary dominants and chord substitutions. Other aspects of the streamlined Caleño sound through the early 1990s include smooth, lyrical lead vocals, a polished delivery by the orquesta, compression and reverb in the horns, and tight execution. This sound owes much to technological improvements in the national recording industry and to the use of professional studio musicians in recording sessions.

Local musicians have become increasingly limited by the mechanisms of the international music industry and the star system it promotes. Caleño bands find that they must compete with recordings and appearances by current stars from Puerto Rico and New York. Although Colombia salsa can be characterized as simple, local salsa musicians and audiences do operate within larger globalized aesthetics that define what a good salsa tune is. Hence, a successful band cannot be too experimental or idiosyncratic, or it will fail to meet the expectations of salsa audiences and other musicians. Well aware of this condition, the national and international music industries manipulate public taste and often place considerable pressure on local musicians to conform to those tastes. Local musical style has therefore become more closely intertwined with larger national and international currents, constraining the choices of Caleño salsa musicians and composers at the same time they offer resources and ideas for musical creation.

Importantly, apart from Jairo Varela and Alexis Lozano, who produce their own bands (Niche and Guayacán), basically only five people are involved in arranging and producing all the salsa recordings made in Cali: Chucho Ramírez, José Aguirre, Andres Biáfara, Dorancé Lorza, and Jorge Herrera. Often these men will collaborate on the same album, completing the arrangements for different tunes. Lorza explained that, for example, salsa romántica tunes were often farmed out to Ramírez or Biáfara, while more dance-oriented or traditional Cuban-based arrangements were sent to him.[36] Herrera and Aguirre have arranged successful salsa dura and salsa romántica tunes for a number of local orquestas; Aguirre, who is a little younger than the others, has strongly absorbed the current Cuban and New York salsa-timba sound. These men, who hail from various racial and class backgrounds, have come to the fore on the basis of their talent, creativity, and musical expertise. Yet, the effect of having such a small nucleus of people in the critical creative processes of the local scene limits the potential for greater musical diversity. Although Cali boasted over seventy orquestas by 1995, this had not played out in richness and variegation of local styles.

∿∿

By the mid-1990s Caleño audiences had tired of salsa romántica. Local orquestas and radio alike had glutted the city with slick romantic tunes, and listeners clamored for a change. The viejoteca revival of the 1970s record-centered dance scene was one response to the monopoly of commercial salsa romántica. During this time, local orquestas and audiences also became receptive to sounds that were strong in other parts of Colombia, such as vallenato and Dominican merengue. Vallenato became an important national genre during the late 1970s. Merengue, which became hugely popular throughout Latin America during the 1980s (see Austerlitz 1997), became very popular on La Costa. Caleños, however, held firmly to their salsero self-image during this period, and vallenato and merengue were rarely heard on local airwaves (Ulloa 1992: 480). By 1996, however, popular tastes had shifted, and up to a third of radio programming on "tropical music" stations was vallenato and merengue. Reflecting this transition, local salsa orquestas worked merengue tunes into their repertoire and also experimented with pseudo-vallenato tunes, using synthesized accordion sounds to index this style. Rock music, particularly rock en español, also began making significant incursions on local airwaves during the mid-1990s. While the prime market for rock remained largely middle- and upper-class teenagers and young adults, as in previous generations, the strong national and international successes of the Colombian rock stars Shakira and Los Aterciopelados had a strong impact in Cali that cut across class lines.

Most significantly, however, in the mid-1990s Caleño salsa musicians began to pick up on the national *pop tropical* boom, incorporating Colombian genres such as cumbia and even currulao into their repertoire. Peter Wade analyzes the success of the 1990s pop tropical boom within the context of new paradigms following the official recognition of Colombia as a multicultural nation in the 1991 constitution (2000). Not since the 1970s had Colombian rhythms played such a strong role in national salsa. Although some groups such as La Misma Gente and Guayacán performed a handful of tunes that featured a contrasting section in cumbia rhythm, incorporation of national styles was relatively rare among Caleño salsa bands during the 1980s and early 1990s. Even in Colombia at large, only Joe Arroyo maintained a consistent fusion with Costeño sounds. In 1995, however, following the pop tropical boom, Caleño salsa orquestas began releasing albums that juxtaposed cumbia and currulao with salsa. Most notable among these were Niche's *Etnia,* Guayacán's *Como en un baile,* and Son de Azucar's *Con amor y dulzura.* In my conversations with various local bandleaders, composers, and arrangers about such hybridizations, most people reiterated the need to develop a more distinctive brand of Colombian salsa for the international market, one less imitative of Puerto Rican and other transnational norms. The strong nationalist bent of this argument resonates strongly with the discourses surrounding pop tropical during this time (Wade 2000: 223–25).

Paralleling the diversification of styles at the local level, the transnational salsa scene itself has opened up to new currents. Puerto Rican and New York arrangers, while retaining the lyric and melodic-harmonic aspects of salsa romántica, returned to the percussive roots of the salsa tradition, recuperating what Caleño musicians refer to as *golpe,* or "punch," in contemporary salsa. Spearheaded by the New York and Puerto Rican producer-arrangers Sergio George and Gunda Merced, the late 1990s salsa sound adopted many elements from contemporary Cuban timba, itself a fusion of funk, jazz, and rock elements over the traditional son base.[37] This development influenced Caleño musicians at the same time that a small group of local melómanos began taking timba to the salsoteca and taberna circuit— a trend reinforced by the growing local presence of recent immigrant Cuban musicians in the city. The most easily recognizable features of timba are the characteristic bass drum kicks on beats three and four of the bar

sometimes varied with

along with rapid reiteration of sixteenth notes in the horn parts. As in transnational contemporary salsa, these traits have become increasingly prominent in the Caleño sound since 1995.

At the local, national, and international levels, then, salsa began to open up from the commercial romántica mainstream to more diverse influences. The Caleño composer-arranger Dorancé Lorza pointed out to me that by 1996 salsa romántica was already over a decade old, and it was time to find a new sound.[38] Lorza and other musicians expressed to me their interest in developing a new Colombian style that would blend salsa with elements from traditional Colombian music. When I asked Chucho Ramírez his opinion about the current state of Colombian salsa, he simply replied, "Fusiones" (fusions).[39]

The shift toward a more heterogeneous repertoire in the mid-1990s marks a return to the spirit of eclecticism that characterized Colombian popular bands in earlier decades. Such diversification is not a rejection of salsa, but rather a widening of the salsa scene in order to recognize the diversity of other styles popular in Colombia. Geographically positioned at the gateway of South America, Colombia has been exposed to international influences since the early 1500s. The impact of numerous influences on national culture and identity was heightened during the twentieth century, enabling salsa and its Cuban predecessors to gain a strong foothold in Colombia in the first place. Some may be tempted to view the recent trend toward eclecticism as a sign that postmodern currents have finally swept the nation. Yet, the development of Colombian salsa reveals deeper historical patterns, born out of and continually shaped by the thirst of modern Colombians for diverse musical sounds, both national and international.

6

"Cali Is Feria"

Salsa and Festival
in Heaven's Outpost

My memories of the Feria center on its nights, when the city springs to life in a vivid wash of lights, people, music, and laughter. The opening night, in particular, seems to channel the excitement and energy of a town eager to launch itself into five days of nonstop merrymaking. Officially known as La Feria de la Caña de Azucar (Sugarcane Carnival), the Feria was inaugurated by the city's industrial and manufacturing leaders in 1957 and — like Carnival in Rio de Janeiro, and Port of Spain, or Mardi Gras in New Orleans — has become a centerpiece of Caleño popular culture and identity. For Caleño salsa fans, the Feria constitutes a resounding affirmation of salsa's central position in local popular culture. Indeed, many local salsa songs composed as a tribute to Cali center on the Feria, all of them proclaiming, in so many words, that Cali *is* the Feria and would be nothing without it.

The Feria, which begins on 25 December and lasts until 30 December, is officially launched in the afternoon, with a *cabalgata* or horse parade through the city in which local and regional gentry from as far north as Pereira and Armenia participate. The cabalgata strikes me as a curious inversion of colonial New World carnivals, when rich elites watched the plebeian masses parade through the streets — here the gaze is reversed. But to my mind, the Feria really kicks off with opening-night ceremonies, which highlight the music and dancing central to this annual jubilation. In a five-hour concert broadcast live from the amphitheater Teatro Los Cristales perched high on Cali's western flank, or from the Parque de la Caña de Azucar (Sugarcane Park) on the northeastern plain, local and international salsa bands perform for free to an audience of ten thousand. The crowd includes people of all socioeconomic strata, but especially those from the *barrios populares,* the working- and lower-middle-class neighborhoods. As aguardiente, beer, and snacks are passed from hand to hand, no one sits still; the dancing throng becomes an electric outpouring of joy and celebration. In the barrios outside the theater and the park, small neighborhood and street parties resonate with similar merriment. Crowds of revelers also pack local salsotecas, tabernas, and nightclubs, ready to carouse the night away. Calle Quinta bedazzles with its display of Christmas lights, a two-mile explosion of color and artistry extending from city hall to the Pan-American Park, next to the central soccer stadium.[1] This display is mirrored in the working-class barrios, where residents festoon their streets with colored paper, lights, ingeniously recycled plastic bottles, and painted road designs in the traditional local competition for the prettiest street in the neighborhood.

During the days to come, the Feria unfolds into multiple events. Live music at the Teatro Los Cristales, the Pascual Guerrero Stadium, and the Pan-American Stadium include free and ticketed concerts, highlighted by visiting international artists and a marathon Festival de Orquestas showcasing local and international bands. Salsa predominates, although música tropical, rock, and other popular Latin American styles are represented. Since the late 1990s Afro-Colombian chirimía and currulao from the Pacific coast have become increasingly strong contenders in local popular tastes. The middle- and upper-class patrons of the Feria's opening cabalgata have their own festivities, centered around daytime *corridas,* or Spanish bullfights, and exclusive evening parties at the elite Club Colombia and middle-class Club San Fernando. Photographs of elegantly dressed women at the bullring or at cocktail parties adorn the city newspapers' social columns during this time. Salsa fans can also go to listen and dance to local and international bands at the *casetas* or dance halls, ticketed venues now oriented primarily toward those who can afford the hefty cover charges. For Cali's majority working- and lower-middle classes, however, the Feria's revelry has long been associated with the *verbenas,* free street parties sponsored by the city, where local salsa bands perform on crude wooden stages erected in a closed-off central intersection in each barrio. Here the participatory ethos of Cali's Feria most clearly surfaces, in a populist fervor for music, dancing, and rumba that holds sway no matter the quality of the bands, the sound amplification system, the lack of seating and restroom facilities, or other factors.

Caleños have a reputation for partying throughout the year—a mythic image that masks the actual hard work and diligence of most Caleño citizens. National perceptions of Cali as a center of frivolous, year-round alegría do have their roots in the actual revelry that coalesces during the December festivities that culminate in the Feria. One might say that during this period, partying is raised to the status of a local industry, generating hundreds of thousands of pesos in revenue for entrepreneurs, club and restaurant owners, and local breweries and distillers. The popular image of a people engaged in a collective spiral of music, dancing, orquestas, liquor, sociability, and physical exuberance becomes actual, embodied practice during the Feria, projecting a subjectivity that sustains Caleño self-representations through the rest of the year. Guayacán's hit tune "Oiga, mira, vea," for instance, contains the line, "After the Feria, the party will keep going like this!" This image, close to the perception of happy-go-lucky Costeños from Colombia's Caribbean coast (Wade 2000: 187–95), contrasts sharply with other Colombian regional stereotypes, particularly the cold, serious reserve of Bogotanos and the industriousness of paisas from Medellín and other parts of the interior.

Like its counterparts elsewhere in the Americas, Cali's Feria draws together several important aspects of popular ritual and celebration. Music and dance propel the event, providing a context for bodies to participate in collective displays of friendship, mirth, sexuality, and exhilaration. Importantly, Cali's Feria not only helped push salsa music to the fore of local popular culture, but subsequently remained a key avenue for heightening and maintaining the presence of salsa in local popular tastes—particularly during the live music boom of the 1980s. In this chapter, I explore how the Feria has channeled several currents in Caleño popular culture to become the focal point for local salsero identity and the calendrical peak for all that characterizes Cali as heaven's outpost.

The Feria's First Two Decades

The Feria was inaugurated in 1957 during a decade of strong industrial growth in Cali and the surrounding Cauca River Valley. As Colombia was staggering under a grim political scene during the 1950s with the combined horrors of La Violencia and the dictatorship of General Gustavo Rojas Pinilla (1954–57), it was also undergoing strong industrial growth, in part owing to the protectionist policies of Rojas Pinilla. In Cali, the Corporación Hidroeléctrica Vallecaucana (CVC) was established in 1954 to provide and regulate hydroelectric power and irrigation for the region's burgeoning agroindustrial enterprises. The fertile plains surrounding Cali boomed as sugar refineries modernized their facilities and new paper, textile, cement, and agricultural processing plants were built. Despite the brutal images of La Violencia and displaced refugees streaming into the city during the 1950s, the era is also remembered as a time of positive growth and economic progress. One historian noted that Cali "exerted an enormous pull on people from diverse regions owing to its burgeoning progress; because people here believe that everyone can obtain a house, enjoy good public services, and have a better life" (Gómez 1986: 252).

Riding the wave of agroindustrial development, the city's economic leaders founded the Feria de la Caña de Azucar in 1957 in homage to the new patron saint of the city's advancement—sugar. Like patronal fiestas celebrated in towns throughout Valle province and the rest of the country (and indeed in all Latin America), the Feria was initially conceived as a time of official public celebration and holiday. Caleños have celebrated important national religious fiestas such as Corpus Christi since the nineteenth century, and the city's older barrios—San Antonio, San Cayetano, and San Nicolás (formerly El Vallano), among others—traditionally celebrate the feast days of the patron saints after whom their neighborhoods were named. Since at least the early twentieth century, local fiestas have been marked by parades and beauty pageants: a well-known historical photo gracing many Caleño history books and archives shows a beauty queen riding in one of the city's first automobiles in 1912 during the fiesta of Corpus Christi. For unclear reasons, however, Cali has never observed the fiesta associated with the patron saint of its founding, Santiago (Saint James). Instead, the Feria—with its strong ties to the concept of "progress" and its well-financed slate of diversions—quickly emerged as Cali's principal festival. I do not have good data on why the dates of 25–30 December were specifically chosen for the Feria. The placement of this festival squarely between Christmas and the New Year, however, certainly points to the organizers' desire to link the Feria to an already important season of religious and cultural celebration.

The first Ferias were marked by elements that have continued to this day—parades, bullfights, society balls and, most important, performances by local, national, and international dance orquestas. Among the famous orquestas to appear at the Feria between 1957 and 1965 were Lucho Bermúdez and Pacho Galán from Colombia's Atlantic coast;[2] Billo's Caracas Boys and Los Melódicos from Venezuela; Spain's Los Chavales de Madrid; and Machito and His Afro-Cubans from New York City (Ulloa 1992: 402). Through the second half of the 1960s, as the Caleño predisposition toward sports, partying, and dancing marked local cultural practice, the Feria came increasingly to be marked by spaces in which physical movement and joyful exuberance were concentrated. While bullfights and society balls remained the domain of Caleño high society, live music and orquestas moved to the fore of Feria festivities for the large working- and lower-middle-class population. During this time, música tropical still reigned supreme as the dominant national style, particularly in the simplified form known as raspa or chucu-chucu (Wade 2000), and most of the orquestas playing in Cali followed this trend. The growing influence of U.S. and British rock and roll in Colombia after the mid-1960s also spread to Cali, however, and rock-influenced raspa groups such as Los Teenagers and Los Graduados also performed before enthusiastic crowds at the Feria.

The unquestioned turning point for the Feria and its role in local popular culture, however, came in 1968, when the New York salsa pianist Richie Ray and vocalist Bobby Cruz were invited to perform with their band. This was the first-ever appearance by a famous salsa band in Cali (as distinct from earlier música antillana ensembles), and their visit electrified the city. Ray and Cruz performed at the huge Caseta Panamericana, located near the future site of the 1971 Pan-American Games. This caseta was a temporary structure built with wooden boards and a zinc roof and had a holding capacity of seven to eight thousand people. A full-page ad placed in the newspaper *El País* at the time indicates that the cover charge was ten pesos (approximately US$3), a bottle of aguardiente or rum cost 75 pesos (approximately $25), a bottle of gin was 100 pesos ($34), and hot dogs, sandwiches, hamburgers, *chuzos* (skewers of barbecued meat), and cigarettes cost two to three pesos ($1) each. Clearly, the caseta's owners planned on making most of their profits from liquor sales.

Billed alongside Richie Ray and Bobby Cruz were two raspa groups, El Supercombo de los Tropicales and Los 8 de Colombia, and the Colombian raspa-rock band Los Teenagers. Raspa (so named for the raspy sound of the *guacharaca* (scraper), which plays the basic quarter note–two eighth notes pattern that dominates the music, had by this time replaced the big-band porros of Lucho Bermúdez and Pacho Galán in national popularity. Raspa bands, most of them composed of middle-class white and mestizo musicians from Bogotá and Medellín, played a simplified variant of música tropical that by the late 1960s was becoming known by the commercial label cumbia (although it was quite distinct from the folkloric Afro-Colombian cumbia played on the Atlantic coast; for more details see Wade 2000: 144–86). Rock music had also gained a foothold among middle- and upper-middle-class youth in the interior, inspiring a rash of mop-topped youngsters to form groups with English-derived names such as Los Teenagers, Los Golden Boys, Los Flippers, Los Black Stars, and—in Cali—Los Bobby Soxers. Most of these groups played sugar-coated rock and raspa tunes (Wade 2000: 167). While related to the *nueva ola* (new wave) of Spanish and Argentine balada singers—crooners such as Julio Iglesias, Leo Dan, Rafael, and Sandro—Colombian rock groups were more strongly influenced by U.S. and British pop groups such as the Beatles and the Monkees. In Cali, both raspa and rock had a steady following among conservative members of the middle and upper-middle classes (locally identified as the bourgeoisie), which became increasingly polarized through the late 1960s and early 1970s from the burgeoning groundswell of working-class and bohemian middle-class salsa fans. Tension between these two camps came to a symbolic head during the appearance of Richie Ray and Bobby Cruz at the 1968 Feria and their return the following year.

So great was the furor over the Caseta Panamericana and Ray's visit in 1968 that the caseta's huge interiors resulted insufficient for the crowds, estimated to number over ten thousand:

> The Caseta Panamericana, one of the biggest attractions of the XI Feria, whose dimensions were considered enormous . . . has been incapable, in the past two nights, of containing the immense multitude that has moved over there, for the variety and order of the shows, their popularity, and the control over ticket sales [i.e., there was no scalping]. Designed for seven thousand or so people, during the last two nights the public has been estimated at more then ten thousand, and the caseta's gigantic dance floor has turned out to be inadequate for the thousands of couples dancing . . . in a unprecedented mood of fiesta. (*El País,* 29 December 1968)

The popularity of Richie Ray and Bobby Cruz among salsa fans in Cali, as in New York and Puerto Rico, emerged in part from Ray's virtuosity and brilliance as a pianist. A graduate of the prestigious Juilliard School of Music, Ray was classically trained and executed technically difficult passages into his solos and arrangements. One of his most famous compositions, "Sonido bestial" (Bestial Sound), includes a salsa version of Chopin's "Revolutionary Étude" for piano; another piece, "Juan Sebastian Fuga" (Johann Sebastian Fugue) incorporates J. S. Bach's Fugue no. 2 in C Minor (from Book I of *The Well-Tempered Clavier*) into a scintillating salsa arrangement.[3] For Caleño audiences, however, the band's crisp, high trumpets, dry maracas, sharp percussion, and nasal coros also clearly echoed the style of the Sonora Matancera—long the favorite música antillana ensemble in Cali and a group whose sound and style have unquestionably molded local popular taste.[4] Furthermore, Richie Ray and Bobby Cruz were among the more commercially popular New York bands that performed pachanga and bugalú, two genres that were extremely popular in Cali during the 1960s. This was also the era in which Caleño fans developed the custom of playing their 33 rpm bugalú records at 45 rpm, and Ray and Cruz, much to their surprise, were asked to speed up the tempo of their bugalú numbers in accordance with local fashion.

Richie Ray and Bobby Cruz walked away with top honors at the 1968 Feria, awarded the prize as best band of the event. The organizers of the Caseta Panamericana, hoping to repeat their success in the following year, brought Ray and Cruz back for the 1969 Feria, billing them opposite Gustavo Quintero y Los Graduados (the Graduates), an extremely popular Medellín-based raspa band of the time. This second appearance is documented in Andrés Caicedo's *¡Qué viva la música!* In this fictionalized account of three middle-class Caleño teenagers' awakening to salsa, Caicedo includes a vibrant description of Ray and Cruz's appearance at the Caseta Panamericana, emphasizing that the saccharine raspa-rock group Los Graduados just "couldn't compete" with Ray's performance (1977: 122–29). Although salsero fans greeted the return visit with enthusiasm, bourgeois Caleños, tired of the "din" (as one newspaper report put it)[5] of bugalú—and perhaps threatened by the orgiastic response of local salsa fans—tried to minimize Ray's impact. A newspaper article titled "The 'Mula Rucia' [Grey Mare] Kicks the Bugalú in the Butt" crudely elevated one of Los Graduados' hit tunes that year, "The Grey Mare," over Richie Ray and Bobby Cruz's performance. With an inaccurate spelling of the neologism *salsómano* (salsa fan), which at the time was just coming into use among Caleño fans (Ulloa 1992: 410), the reporter dismisses Ray and Cruz as a passing fad: "A part of the Caseta's audience danced to Richie and his orquesta, those who like that music and who have given to calling themselves *sansómanos* [*sic*]. There were considerable cries from the boisterous crowd who called out many times for this orquesta to get off the stage, we repeat the band is magnificent but doesn't please in totality" (*El Occidente,* 29 December 1969). Caicedo also captures this tension in his novel, through the scandalized voices of the organizers ("If we had known that we were going to bring a band of homosexuals and drug addicts, we'd have put records on") and their daughters ("Mom, what is this Bugalú, you can't dance to that, how vulgar . . . why don't Los Graduados come back on, how lovely") (1977: 128; also cited in Wade 2000: 170). This incident magnified the growing rift between working-class and bohemian Caleño salsa fans and the audience for raspa and música tropical, which was associated increasingly with the local bourgeoisie and paisas (Antioqueños) from the country's interior. Richie Ray and Bobby Cruz did not return to Cali for many years (and never appeared at another Feria), but their fans eagerly awaited a repeat visit. In 1971 posters appeared throughout the city:

THE PEOPLE OF CALI reject Los Graduados, Los Hispanos, and other cultivators of the "Paisa Sound," made to suit the bourgeoisie and their vulgarity—Because it's not a case of "Sufrir me tocó en la vida" [It's My Lot to Suffer in Life] but rather "Agúzate que te están velando" [Be Careful, They're Keeping Vigil for You]. Long live Afro-Cuban feeling! Long live a free Puerto Rico! WE MISS RICHIE RAY.[6]

The poster also appears in ¡Qué viva la música!, fictionalized as the act of one of the novel's fans, but the incident actually happened. In 1994 I saw this same slogan spray-painted as graffiti near the Hotel Intercontinental.

The tension between salseros and raspa fans highlighted in Caicedo's novel clearly points to some of the controversy caused by the artistic programming at the Caseta Panamericana. It also points, however, to a cultural dynamic in which different sounds competed for attention on the local cultural landscape. Although there is a tendency to pigeonhole the audiences for salsa and raspa into polarized class-based sectors, in reality this caseta opened the doors for a more fluid process wherein salsa music gained significant potential to attract more listeners from across social and class lines. The economic reasons for constructing casetas in middle-class neighborhoods are clear enough: profit-driven organizers, who were from Cali's middle class, set up shop where economically better off customers lived, but they also billed acts strong enough to draw working-class clientele from neighborhoods farther away. As a result, a key conjuncture was established for the penetration of salsa into Caleño popular culture at large. Although Caleños from the lower and upper strata of society had gathered together since the early 1900s to listen to music, this was the first time that working-, middle-, and upper-middle-class audiences danced together under one roof to music that catered to *all* sectors, not just the financially dominant one. No longer could salsa be dismissed out of hand as "música de negros." The appearance of Richie Ray and Bobby Cruz at the 1968 and 1969 Ferias represented, to a large extent, a middle-class legitimization of salsa on the local cultural scene. No wonder, then, that more conservative factions among the bourgeoisie tried to minimize the group's impact.

Through the early 1970s the Feria organizers—in clear deference to bourgeois sentiment—backed away from salsa and instead promoted raspa, pop rock, música antillana, and balada artists. A mainstay of these years was the Venezuelan rock-bugalú-raspa band of Nelson y sus Estrellas, who, like Fruko, combined elements of salsa with música tropical and North American rock and was enormously popular in Colombia's cities. (Nelson's style, however, was less oriented toward salsa dura than Fruko's was.) As can be seen in Appendix 3, a chart of major acts billed at the Feria between 1968 and 1995, representation by salsa bands is scarce in the first half of the decade. Only one international salsa artist, the New York star Ismael Miranda, appeared during this time, in 1972, although the local salsa pioneer Piper Pimienta began performing regularly after 1972, and Fruko appeared in 1973 and 1974. In contrast, however, several artists representing other genres were contracted. The música antillana star Daniel Santos was invited in 1971, possibly to appease working-class fans; however, his fame and presence in Cali were already well established by this time, and he represented no risk for Feria organizers.

Despite this clampdown, by the middle of the decade salsa had become a dominant force in local popular culture, with two "international" salsa dance championships having been organized to great local acclaim and week-long partying to salsa in griles and nightclubs. In 1975 Feria organizers invited not only Puerto Rico's most important salsa band, El Gran Combo, but also Venezuela's new contender on the international salsa stage, Dimensión Latina, making their debut appearance in Colombia. Both these groups had major salsa hits that year: El Gran Combo with "Un verano en Nueva York" (A Summer in New York) and Dimensión Latina with the vocalist Oscar D'León's now-classic "Llorarás" (You'll Cry). Not surprisingly, both of these tunes were enormously popular in Cali and remain classic favorites for local melómanos and salsa fans. After this point, salsa orquestas became a mainstay of Cali's Feria, with the presence of prominent New York, Puerto Rican, Venezuelan, and Cuban bands increasing through the late 1970s and into the 1980s.

From *Casetas* to *Verbenas*: The 1970s

In the 1960s casetas emerged as epicenters of the rumba in the Cali Feria. During the previous decade, in Cali and surrounding towns, casetas were originally small, semi-enclosed structures, with low walls and roofs built of palm fronds, where working-class people could go to snack on empanadas and beer while listening to recordings of música antillana.[7] Sometimes a drummer might accompany the music on a crude pair of timbales. Although these spaces were eventually replaced by the griles and nightclubs that began springing up in the 1960s, the concept of the caseta itself was retained and magnified into the large, wood-and-zinc dance halls erected during the Feria to house crowds of several thousand. The two principal casetas by the time of Richie Ray and Bobby Cruz's legendary visit to Cali were the Caseta Panamericana, on Calle 9, and the Caseta Matecaña, on Avenida

Roosevelt. Notably, both of these were located in the middle-class barrios of Templete and San Fernando, on what was then the city's southern flank. (Cali's vast southern zone was not built until after the 1971 Pan-American Games.) Other casetas of the period were also located in this same general area—for example, Los Chavales de Madrid (a famous band from Spain that performed pasodobles and fox-trots for more bourgeois audiences) had their own caseta in San Fernando. Caseta La Bomba was also located on the Avenida Roosevelt. What is striking about these casetas that they were clustered on one side of the city, in a middle-class area where salsa music was barely starting to make inroads among the bohemian and leftist sons and daughters of a sector that is (even to this day) perceived as being generally bourgeois. However, the casetas did open a new space through which salsa began entering the popular life of all classes of Caleños.

For Caleño high society, a more refined form of partying took place in the exclusive Club Colombia and in the ballrooms of the Hotel Intercontinental and Hotel Aristi downtown. Here big bands played música tropical, pasodobles, fox-trots, and Cuban sones and guarachas. Interestingly, newspaper ads indicate that vallenato groups from the Atlantic coast were also booked at the Hotel Intercontinental during the early 1970s for Fiestas Vallenatas. At the time vallenato was still viewed as very plebeian and rustic and had not yet replaced porro and raspa as the national sound (Wade 2000: 176–80). As Wade notes, however, around this period the accordionist Alfredo Gutiérrez started becoming enormously popular throughout Colombia, and it is no surprise that he was brought frequently to perform at the Cali Feria in the 1970s and 1980s (see Appendix 3).

In Cali's working-class neighborhoods, on the other hand, *verbenas* (street parties) emerged as the principal locus of Feria celebrations after the 1960s. Created as an outgrowth of the household champús bailables and bailes de cuota of the 1940s and 1950s, the verbenas initially were block parties where neighbors would close off their road to traffic, pull out a large sound system, and dance to salsa records in the street. Sofas and chairs were often brought out, and various households would share food and drink with neighbors. Alejandro Ulloa describes these verbenas in his memoir about growing up in Barrio San Carlos (1986). I have also attended similar street parties during the Feria season, although they are not as common as they once were.

By the late 1960s the municipal association in charge of organizing the Feria began sponsoring more-elaborate street parties. In these verbenas, major intersections in designated neighborhoods would be blocked off and crude wooden stages built on which local salsa, rock, and raspa bands performed for barrio residents. Unlike the casetas, social clubs, and hotels, the verbenas did not have a cover charge and were open-air events. Hence, they were much more accessible to the general working-class populace. Newspaper reports from 1968 through 1975 show the increasingly strong impact of these verbenas in working-class areas, which featured local bands with such quixotic names as Alfonso Haya y sus Caciques (Alfonso Haya and his Indian Chiefs), Los Alegres (The Happy Ones), Los Soles de Colombia (The Suns of Colombia), Los Bancarios (The Bankers), and El Zurdo Morales y sus Angeles Atómicos (Lefty Morales and his Atomic Angels).[8] Starting in 1975, large *verbenas populares* (people's verbenas) were also sponsored in the Paseo Bolivar, a pleasant, tree-lined park fronting the new city hall (CAM, or Centro Administrativo Municipal). Also that year, large open-air concerts were held for the first time in the newly built Teatro Los Cristales, described at the opening of this chapter; these too acquired the atmosphere of a verbena.

Despite the unsophisticated facilities, poor sound, and often mediocre performances that characterized the verbenas, these spaces became epicenters for participatory celebration. People came out to party no matter what—the important thing was to let loose and have a good time. Newspaper reports from the 1976 Feria capture some of the ambience of the verbenas held at this time. The first couple of observations are decidedly negative, indicating great disdain for the lack of resources available for the verbenas; the implication is that this lack somehow correlates to an inherent cultural and moral deficiency among the working class itself (cf. Fanon 1965).

> A working-class verbena is a show with a mediocre orquesta and sound equipment that reveals deficiencies at every instant. *(El País, 29 December 1976).*

> Although the orquestas that enliven the different acts are mediocre, the people have no other alternative for having a good time. They buy their four flasks of liquor at the corner store and then throw themselves into the street dances. *(El País, 28 December 1976)*

Other reports, however, emphasized the ebullience and spontaneous alegría of the verbenas, upholding these events and salsa music as a vehicle for genuine celebration and self-expression in the Feria. Notably, this set of reports focused on the huge open-air verbenas populares in the Paseo Bolivar, where international acts such as the beloved Sonora Matancera (in 1976) and Celia Cruz (in 1980) performed for free.

> It smelled of sweat, joy, marijuana, and spilled aguardiente. It smelled of Cali and when, from the trumpets and drums, from that invisible

pianist that every so often seemed to be submerged for all the tumult, the Sonora broke up the Feria . . . they showed the skeptics what popular fiestas should essentially be, if they want to survive. *(El País, 28 December 1976)*

It was a delirious spectacle, with fights, injuries, suffocation, fainting, aguardiente, marijuana and complete happiness among the Caleño people. *(El País, 28 December 1976)*

[Beneath a photo showing a Caleño dancer on his knees, arms flung wide, with the caption "Salsero Delirium"] Undoubtedly, in the very makeup of the verbena or popular fiesta during the most recent Ferias of Cali, salsa has been the vital center of diversion. *(El País, 28 December 1980)*

Through the late 1970s, as caseta prices climbed, working- and even middle-class Caleños began gravitating increasingly toward the verbenas. A 1980 newspaper headline announced: "Casetas Are No Longer Popular: People Prefer to Dance in the Verbenas." By this point the average caseta cover charge was 160 Colombian pesos (approximately US$8), a bottle of aguardiente cost 1,000 pesos ($50), and a bottle of whiskey ran as high as 3,000 pesos ($150).[9] While the casetas continued to book all the top international acts, their prices spiraled out of the range of most Caleño salsa fans. The Feria organizers attempted to redress this balance by booking cheaply ticketed concerts in the Evangelista Mora Gymnasium and in the Coliseo del Pueblo (Town Coliseum), but terrible acoustics marred these venues. The verbenas—particularly the large verbenas populares in the Paseo Bolívar—moved to the fore of popular Feria activities.

During the 1980s the ebullience of the verbenas populares was captured and transferred into the Festival de Orquestas, discussed below, which by the end of the decade had replaced the concerts in the Paseo Bolívar. Smaller verbenas continued in the barrios and became better organized, with sponsorship shifting from the municipality to Colombia's two major beverage conglomerates, Postobón soft drinks and Bavaria beer. Although the Feria organizers still paid for bands to go out and play at the verbenas, these companies provided good sound equipment and sturdy, prefabricated metal stages with canvas tents and stage skirts displaying their logos that could be transported to any neighborhood and erected in a few hours. Such stages are now the norm for verbenas and other live street performances throughout Colombia—I frequently saw them during my field research.

In the late 1980s, the casetas temporarily disappeared, priced out of existence, but they were reestablished with the building of the Caseta Carnival del Norte in 1990, a permanent concrete dance hall in the luxury nightclub zone of Avenida Sexta. This Caseta, still open today, was primarily geared toward the middle class and new rich. The verbenas, for their part, continued through the 1980s but were discontinued by Feria organizers in the early 1990s in an attempt to husband resources and centralize live performances in certain areas. Only Cali's most impoverished districts (Aguablanca, Siloé, and Terrón Colorado) continued to provide verbenas for its residents, as part of the special Feria programs run by local community leaders with financial help from the city. A decision in 1995 to decentralize the Feria and return festivities to all the barrios of Cali resulted in a comeback of the verbenas, and at the time of this writing they remain an important feature of the annual celebrations.

Feria Culture and the Participatory Ethos

Some of the newspaper reports quoted in the previous section indicate a clear disdain for the noise and mediocrity of the verbenas. Certainly, the quality of performers and sound was often substantially less than that provided, for a cover charge, by the casetas and nightclubs. How do we explain the popularity of the verbenas, then? If we follow the tone of some of the above reports, it would seem that the average working-class audience member simply did not have an alternative—or perhaps was too uncultured to care. In my own observations of Caleños audiences at live performances in the mid-1990s, however, I witnessed certain tendencies that suggest an emphasis on other important values, beyond concerns with artistic or aesthetic quality. Perhaps most notable is the participatory ethos that pervades virtually any live concert in Cali.

In the events I observed, the element of spectacle was secondary to moving the audience and the scene itself (Chernoff also describes this with respect to Dagbamba drumming in Ghana; 1979: 61–68). Although I certainly saw people just watching or listening to the performance, most of the audience would get up and dance to the music. It became clear to me that for Caleño audiences, the local live scene is really an extension of the record-centered dance scene of previous decades, during which dancing to salsa music was established as the primary expressive practice in local popular life. Musical sound, whether produced by a live band or a record player, cues the frame of social dancing, signaling people to engage in this gregarious physical activity.

Following Edward T. Hall's notions about collective body movement and culture (1977), Thomas Turino offers some important insights into the nature of music and dance that help explain what goes on with Caleño audiences. In his work on Aymara music in southeast Peru, Turino notes that moving together to music does not only reflect a spirit of community—it actually creates community, by getting people in "sync."

> Music and dance bring the state of being in sync—of being together—
> to a heightened level of explicitness. With each repetition of a piece in
> Conima, the possibility of "being in sync" is extended and the social
> union is intensified, contributing to an affective intensity. . . . Not
> unlike making love, music and dance open the possibility for deeper
> physical and spiritual connections between community members.
> During special moments, culturally specific rhythms and forms of
> movement are not merely semiotic expressions of community and
> identity; rather, *they become their actual realization.* (1993: 111)

Charles Keil and Steven Feld also speak about the power of repeated, sustained movement—"physical grooving"—to pull people together (1994: 23–24). Although Caleños interact and work together in a number of everyday contexts, the activity of salsa dancing explicitly delineates and heightens this state of being in sync. During my first months of fieldwork, I was constantly surprised at the enthusiastic response of Caleño audiences to performances by local bands, even if the group sounded out of tune, played sloppily, or had weak vocalists and players. Audiences were not completely undiscriminating—indeed, listeners did make negative comments about an orquesta that sounded bad, especially if they were aficionados or musicians themselves. However, people would still cheer the band, sing along, wave their arms in the air, sway in their seats, or get up and dance, alone or in couples. By and large Caleño audiences were loyal to their orquestas and seemed remarkably tolerant of mediocre playing. I came to recognize that live performances in Cali are not about "good music" so much as about having a good time. In other words, as long as there is a source of music to cue the frame of social dancing and interaction, Caleños are happy to enter the participatory, "pachanguero" mode of the rumba no matter how poorly a band plays.

In this context, dancing to music was paralleled by a proclivity for singing along with the lyrics of a tune. Caleño salsa fans like to join in the music through singing, and songs with catchy refrains are especially popular. Perhaps this is why local orquestas tend to emphasize the vocals during performance, over and above the instrumental arrangements and solo improvisations that are a hallmark of much New York and Puerto Rican salsa. Singing along with the music reinforces the sense of participation inherent in dancing together. These tendencies have significant implications when we consider the historical context of rapid expansion and social flux that has characterized city life since the 1940s. Dancing and singing to salsa forged a deeper cultural synchrony, both physically and emotionally, that served to anchor social bonds in Cali's highly unstable urban environment.

Indeed, the rise of local salsa musicians has not broken with the participatory, gregarious spirit that characterized the earlier record-centered dance scene. In some ways the rise of local performers intensified the affective impact of people coming together to dance salsa. The city's orquestas became a source of pride for local audiences, signifying the ability of Caleños to participate as actors, not just consumers, in the transnational scene. The apparent contradiction between valuing international sounds (especially via festishization of recordings), on the one hand, while demonstrating support and enthusiasm for even average-sounding local bands, on the other, does not simply underscore the uniqueness of Cali's local scene. It also explains the impact and importance of the verbenas as an important locus of festivities during the annual Feria. The atmosphere of participation established in the verbenas and (to a lesser extent) in the casetas in turn became the foundation of an important new space for salsa and celebration in the Feria with the Festival de Orquestas, and especially the rise of the amateur *campanero*.

The Campanero: The Audience Play-Along Musician

Probably the most vivid incarnation of the participatory ethos characterizing Caleño audiences is the figure of the play-along campanero (cowbell player), who appears at concerts, salsotecas, neighborhood parties, and particularly during the Feria to beat along with the music (Figure 6.1). Hopeful, enthusiastic amateurs in the true sense of the word, local campaneros became a common sight during the 1980s and early 1990s. In accordance with gender codes that restrict loud public behavior by women, this personage has always been male. Local campaneros took out their cowbells no matter how terribly or off the beat they played—indeed, some salsotecas such as the Taberna Latina eventually banned the presence of campaneros because the noise bothered other clients. Caleños, normally very tolerant and generous about sharing their acoustic space with loud cowbell players, do have their limits. I observed this one night at a concert by the Puerto Rican star Roberto Roena, where a hapless campanero who could not keep

Figure 6.1
Campanero
(cowbell player).
Photo by Lise
Waxer.

the beat so annoyed nearby listeners that he was finally asked to stop playing (Figure 6.2).

Such audience play-along musicians are atypical in most places where salsa is performed—indeed, in Puerto Rico it is considered downright disrespectful to play cowbell along with the band.[10] How, then, did this personage emerge in Cali, and with such force? Furthermore, why the predilection for the campana, a relatively minor, non-soloist percussion instrument in a salsa ensemble? As with many facets of Caleño salsero culture, the answer can be traced once again to the inordinate role of recordings in shaping local musical taste and practice.

In the early 1980s the New York percussionist and bandleader José Mangual Jr. recorded a song entitled "Campanero" in which he performed a virtuoso solo on campana—practically unheard of before that time.[11] While the cowbell plays an important functional role in salsa, marking the downbeat and also adding *hierro* ("iron") and dynamic force to the ensemble during the montuno section, it is never featured as a solo percussion instrument in the way that congas, timbales, or bongos are. Taking a cow-

Figure 6.2 Local *campanero* being asked to stop playing. Photo by Lise Waxer.

bell solo might be considered as atypical as having the percussionist in the back row of a symphony orchestra—who usually crashes the cymbals together only once every forty minutes—come forth and play a solo cadenza. Yet, Mangual succeeded in coaxing a variety of tone colors, hits, and rhythmic fills on this instrument, with exquisite taste.

For Caleño listeners, the impact of this recording was nothing short of electrifying. The tune was played widely on local radio stations and in salsotecas, and Mangual's virtuoso solo inspired a rash of amateur campaneros. Inexpensive to purchase and not requiring much skill to play, the campana became a key item for local salsa fans. As my friend Sabina Borja explained, "There's no self-respecting gang member who doesn't have his campana." (Cali's street gangs have traditionally been composed of die-hard salseros.) The high-quality but inexpensive campanas manufactured locally by the workshop of the percussion maker Hector "El Piernas" Rocha contributed to this mania, since they were readily available and affordable. Rocha's campanas have the low, resonant timbre preferred for salsa dura, similar to the Bronx-made

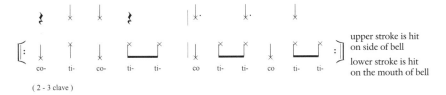

Figure 6.3   *Campana* bell pattern

JMV bells used by most New York salsa bands in the 1970s and 1980s. These bells use more iron than do the tinnier, brighter-sounding bells favored in salsa romántica and received immediate acceptance among salsa dura fans.

Reinforcing the campanero craze, Mangual performed in several New York salsa bands brought to Cali in the early 1980s by the promoter Larry Landa. On one of his first visits to the city, Mangual was invited to give a special percussion workshop—at the Bellas Artes music conservatory, no less—that attracted a large group of amateur campaneros seeking to learn more from him (he also demonstrated basic techniques on conga and bongo). At concerts there was always a large crew of his followers standing right at the foot of the stage where he was playing—perhaps as many as twenty or more campaneros banging along in a happy din to the music. According to Medardo Arias, who covered these events for the newspaper *El Occidente* and conversed on several occasions with Mangual, the percussionist seemed rather bewildered by his fame among Caleño fans—in New York and Puerto Rico, campaneros usually go unrecognized.[12]

By the mid-1980s the local cult of the campanero was so strong that the up-and-coming Caleño orquesta La Misma Gente decided to pay a special tribute to this figure in their 1986 song "Titicó." The title is from the onomatapoeic vocables that musicians often use when imitating the campana's characteristic rhythmic pattern (Figure 6.3). "Titicó" became a hit at the 1986 Feria, bolstering La Misma Gente's rising popularity and adding to the laurels they won that year with their song "Juanita Aé." Like "Cali pachanguero" two years earlier, "Titicó" celebrated Cali's salsa scene. Central places and people in Cali's rumba are named: Calle Quinta, Imbanaco (a corner where many nightclubs are clustered), the Taberna Latina, Gary Domínguez, and so forth. Even El Piernas, the famous local percussion maker and campana supplier, is named. Indeed, so enthusiastic was the local response to "Titicó" that the renowned Puerto Rican orquesta La Sonora Ponceña, which was also playing the Feria in 1986, quoted the song's refrain in their tribute to the city, "A Cali," two years later.[13]

"Titicó" (1986)
La Misma Gente

Campanero,	Campana player,
Oye.	Listen.
Mi canto va dedicado	My song is dedicated
A la gente como tú,	To people like you,
Que toca el hierro afinado.	Who play tuned iron.
Si hay una rumba en el barrio	If there's a party in the neighborhood
Festival en el Estadio	Festival in the Stadium
Concierto en el Coliseo	Concert in the Coliseum[14]
Tú siempre estás preparado	You're always ready
Para hacer sonar el hierro	To sound the bell
Y acompañar las orquestas	And accompany the bands
Que llegan del mundo entero.	That arrive from around the world.
Ella suena, titicó,	It sounds, *titicó,*
Y su cadencia emociona	And its cadence uplifts
Su ritmo nos apriciona,	Its rhythm imprisons us
Inconfundible titicó.	Unmistakable titicó.
Por la Calle Quinta andaban	Along Calle Quinta walked
Fernando y Carlitos	Fernando and little Carlos
Y en la Taberna Latina	And in the Taberna Latina
Oyeron el ritmo	They heard the rhythm
De una campana sonando	Of a cowbell sounding
El viejo Gary tocando	Old Gary playing,
Más arriba en Imbanaco	Further up in Imbanaco
Pillaron al Negro Paco	They saw Paco, the black man
Que alistaba su campana	Who readied his bell
Pa'gozar hasta mañana.	To get down until dawn.

[Mambo]

[Montuno]

(Coro)	*(Chorus)*
En Cali ya todos tienen	*In Cali everyone already has*
Todos tienen su campana	*Everyone has their cowbell,*
Titicó, ticó, titicó, cocó	*Titicó, ticó, titicó, cocó*
Pa'gozar hasta mañana!	*To get down until dawn!*
Primero fue "El campanero"	First there was "El campanero"
Y "La Mayoral" llegó	And "La Mayoral" arrived

Campaneros compañeros	Fellow cowbell players,
Llegó el ritmo titicó.	The rhythm titicó arrived.

En Cali ya todos tienen	*In Cali everyone already has*
Todos tienen su campana	*Everyone has their cowbell,*
Titicó, ticó, titicó, cocó	*Titicó, ticó, titicó, cocó*
Pa'gozar hasta mañana!	*To get down until dawn!*

Importantly, "Titicó" upheld a positive image of the amateur campanero, ready to accompany the famous international orquestas performing in town. Rather than portraying this person as ridiculous or annoying, the song idealized the local campanero as a local folk hero who represents the participatory ethos of Cali's salsa scene. At one level, this can be understood as simple gregariousness and a desire to get in on the fun. At a deeper level, however, the practice simultaneously expresses and structures a cosmopolitan sensibility. By playing along with visiting orquestas, the campanero quite literally articulates his concern with being in sync with musicians who represent the transnational salsa scene.

In Cali playing along with the band is not considered disrespectful, but rather serves as a way of symbolically placing oneself—by mimesis of the international orquesta—on the world salsa stage. By the 1980s Caleño musicians and fans held a firm conviction of their right to participate in the international salsa world—through small acts such as playing along at concerts, and also through the creation of large-scale marathon concerts at which local and international salsa bands performed together. Such was the philosophy behind the creation of the Festival de Orquestas.

Into the 1980s: The Festival de Orquestas

Since the 1980s a centerpiece of Cali's Feria has been the Festival de Orquestas, a marathon salsa concert initially held during the middle of the fair but pushed to the final night during the 1990s. Inspired by the marathon concert festival held for Barranquilla's Carnival, Cali's Festival de Orquestas was created in 1980 as a way to showcase local talent alongside visiting national and international orquestas. Since that time bands have competed for prizes awarded to the best band, song, and vocalist, as judged by a panel of local and international celebrities. The salsa legends Celia Cruz and Johnny Pacheco, for example, were guest judges in 1980, and Ismael Rivera and Hector Lavoe served in 1981. Although the first two years of the festival were embarrassing flops—several invited orquestas failed to appear for the event[15]—by the middle of the decade the Festival de Orquestas had emerged as one of the most exciting musical events of the year. The first festival was held in the Evangelista Mora Gymnasium, but later ones were in the Pascual Guerrero Stadium; it was moved to the Pan-American Stadium in 1993. Given the symbiotic relationship between soccer, salsa, and other sports among Cali's working and middle classes, these venues no doubt heightened the visibility of the festival and contributed to its increasing popularity. Not only is the Pascual Guerrero Stadium the site of all major soccer games played in Cali, but it also holds up to forty thousand people—certainly an asset for Feria organizers who aimed at making this a mass public event. In addition to salsa—the predominant genre performed during this eight-to-twelve-hour event—over the years vallenato and música tropical bands have also been featured. More recently, Afro-Colombian bands from the Pacific have performed modernized versions of currulao and chirimía.

Many fans and musicians reminisced to me about the glory days of the Festival de Orquestas in the second half of the 1980s. Crowds would usually begin to pour into the Pascoal Guerrero Stadium around 2:00 P.M. and continued carousing and dancing until 4:00 or 5:00 A.M. During this time over thirty orquestas performed in sets lasting approximately thirty to forty minutes each. It was during these years that local bands such as Grupo Niche and La Misma Gente won the honors of best orquesta and best tune (1984 and 1986, respectively), despite competition from such internationally acclaimed Puerto Rican bands such as El Gran Combo and the Sonora Ponceña. Given that Puerto Rican and New York orquestas won these prizes in other years, it seems that the judges were not predisposed to select Caleño bands only to pander to local interests. The accolades given to local groups served to reinforce Caleños' ebullience and pride in their self-image as world salsa capital and strengthened the popularity of the festival with each successive year.

Medardo Arias recalls that the festival always ended just before dawn with the Venezuelan star Oscar D'León, who would emerge from one end of the stadium wearing a sweatsuit. Hands in the air, D'León would run a "victory lap" around the track while his band played. Then, jogging up to the stage, he would grab the microphone and salute the euphoric public, still dancing after more than twelve hours of nonstop salsa.[16] The festivals I observed in the mid-1990s were shorter and less ebullient. They started around 5:00 P.M. and lasted only until 2:00 A.M., and crowds were considerably smaller than those of the 1980s—perhaps only a couple of thousand as opposed to the hordes of twenty thousand or more that thronged into the Pascual Guerrero Stadium during the 1980s. This has much to do, however, with the bad financing and lack of promotional support that plagued the Feria during the mid-1990s.

I spoke with Jairo Sánchez, creator of the Festival de Orquestas. Sánchez, a working-class mestizo entrepreneur, has been extremely active in Cali's musical scene since the 1980s and served as the Feria's musical director from 1980 to 1989. He founded the Festival de Orquestas as an exchange between international and local orquestas in an effort to promote the viability and status of local bands. Sánchez was able to procure the international orquestas by appealing to the empresarios who had contracted them for performances at the city's casetas—he asked for a free appearance at the Festival de Orquestas in return for not charging tax. Although initially ridiculed by his peers, who saw local bands as little more than filler for the international acts, Sánchez continued to uphold the festival as a prime opportunity for local orquestas to be exposed to and converse with world-class salsa musicians. The festival also spurred the formation of new orquestas.

Sánchez: I always thought that that interchange was what gave possibilities for local musicians to see other traits and other ways of working.
Waxer: So, can we say that it is really the Festival de Orquestas that was the first element in the emergence of the boom of all the bands here?
Sánchez: Yes! That's right. The Festival de Orquestas . . . was the vehicle that permitted the rise of all the bands.[17]

As with the international bands brought to Cali by Larry Landa, the Festival de Orquestas exposed local musicians to new musical ideas and performance values. Jairo Varela, for example, notes that Grupo Niche began to pay much greater attention to aspects of band uniforms and choreography in their presentations after performing opposite El Gran Combo and Oscar D'León during the 1984 Feria.[18]

Sánchez observed that the Festival de Orquestas had its strongest influence on the growth of the local scene in terms of providing musicians with a highly visible performance space each December. This became a strong motivation for bands to stay active and keep improving. Through the 1980s the ratio of local bands appearing in the festival to national and international orquestas steadily increased, earmarking the event as a showcase for local talent. Significantly, Caleño bands proved that they could put on as good a show as the international orquestas. No longer were they mere filler for international and national bands, as they had been in the 1960s and 1970s. While not as rigorously staged and media oriented as the Barranquilla Festival de Orquestas (when I attended the Barranquilla event in

1995, bands were limited to fifteen-minute sets, and pauses were rigidly timed to coordinate with sponsors' commercial breaks on the live television broadcast), Cali's Festival de Orquestas became an extremely important affair in the local live scene. At no other time in the year does the Caleño public turn out in such large numbers to listen to, dance to, and cheer its own orquestas. The opportunity for local bands to perform in the limelight hence further stimulated the growth of the Cali's live scene. As an extravagant "mega-verbena" that consolidated the best live music of the Feria, the Festival de Orquestas became a strong focal point for the annual year-end celebrations.

Encuentros de Salsotecas

The success of the Festival de Orquestas in boosting the local live scene galvanized a response from local melómanos and record collectors. If marathon salsa concerts could be organized on such a grand scale, why not a marathon salsoteca as well?

In 1991 Gary Domínguez organized a mass public event called the Encuentro de Salsotecas y Coleccionistas (Gathering of Salsotecas and Record Collectors) in a downtown park. The five-day *encuentro* was modeled on a smaller one-day event held at the Universidad del Valle in 1990, followed by another in the salsa-reggae taberna Nuestra Herencia in 1991.[19] Starting in the afternoon and lasting until dawn, DJs from several Cali's salsotecas alternated sets of recorded music with selections from the city's prominent record collectors to spin salsa dura and música antillana sides. The encuentro —still running strong—became the melómano equivalent of the Festival de Orquestas and the verbenas, except that people assembled to listen to records instead of live bands (Figure 6.4).

Special melómano programs had already been created earlier in the 1980s. For example, the First National Congress on Salsa was organized in 1982. It brought local and national intellectuals from as far away as Barranquilla to give special talks and hold round-table discussions on salsa's history and its social impact.[20] This was the only time such an event was formally realized—low attendance dissolved future attempts to organize such conferences. The Encuentro de Salsotecas, however, with its emphasis on the Caleño pastime of gathering to listen and dance to salsa records, became an instant success. The Encuentros de Salsotecas were initially held in the Parque de la Retreta near city hall, downtown, but they moved to various central locations through the 1990s before becoming consolidated in the Parque de la Música on Avenida Sexta (see Figures 7.5 and 7.6). In the Par-

Figure 6.4   First Encuentro de Salsotecas (1991). Courtesy of Gary
Domínguez.

que de la Música, Domínguez also established smaller monthly encuentros
beginning in 1993. (These monthly events were discontinued in 1994, revived again in 1996, and discontinued once again in 1998, but the association of the Parque de la Música with the encuentros has now been consolidated for the annual Feria.) Audiences at the smaller monthly gatherings
I attended in 1996 numbered around five hundred, but during the Feria
anywhere from two thousand to three thousand people might flock to the
park on a given evening.

For melómanos and salsa fans, the encuentros have represented a unique
opportunity to participate in a collective reaffirmation of Cali's musical
memory. The city's best DJs and collectors present an extraordinary range
of rare and exclusive recordings of salsa and música antillana from a small
elevated stage, announcing the artists, song title, and other brief data on the
piece to be heard. Enormous open-air speakers face the crowd, and the loud
music often attracts passers-by. No chairs or benches are provided for the
audience, so people stand, sit on the grass, or dance. Admission is free and
the ambience festive, with beer, aguardiente, and record vendors hawking
their wares from brightly lit tents. Several record vendors from Calle 15 and
other downtown spots are also there, selling used and rare salsa records.

Figure 6.5   Encuentro de Salsotecas in the Parque de la Música (1999). Photo by Lise Waxer.

The phenomenon of large crowds gathering to listen to records is unique in the international salsa scene. Although it is not uncommon to see people dancing to recorded music between live sets at major salsa concerts, I am not aware of any other place on earth where a mass public assembles with the express purpose of listening to recordings of salsa and música antillana. Perhaps one might draw parallels with the rave subculture among youths in Europe, North America, and Japan (Reynolds 1999; Silcott 1999; Courtney 2000; Milioto 2000), but the distinct uses and meanings of recorded music in the rave context diverge substantially from its signification in Cali. As an extension of the salsoteca and taberna scene, the encuentros represented an exciting new foothold for Caleño melómanos within the city's social spaces, especially for those who have assumed the mission of preserving and disseminating the city's musical memory with near-evangelical zeal. The positioning of this event within the celebratory, festive context of the annual Feria further heightens the impact of the encuentro. Owing to the large scale of this gathering, the symbolism of the salsa recording as a surrogate effigy and fetish (Roach 1996) of Cali's cultural roots is reinscribed in a mass public ritual. At the Encuentros de Sal-

Figure 6.6 Encuentro de Salsotecas in the Parque de la Música. Courtesy of *El Occidente.*

sotecas, memory, desire, joy, and yearning for the past are foregrounded as key elements of understanding and experiencing what in the 1990s became an increasingly confusing and disruptive present.

Even where rifts exist between different factions of collectors, fans, and aficionados, the encuentros have served as a site of temporary alliances. It is significant that although rival barrio gangs often attend these events, no fights have ever broken out between them (such gangs are divided less along lines of musical taste than by other tensions). A case in point is the last day of 1996 Feria encuentro, when several gangs showed up and began eyeing each other with hostility. Fearing a possible violent skirmish, Gary Domínguez, the organizer, took microphone in hand to announce, "We're all salsa fans and we're all here to listen to listen and enjoy, so please put aside your disputes, we don't want any trouble." Out of respect for Domínguez and for the spirit of the event, the gangs did indeed put aside differences to unite under salsa's banner.[21] I do not have data on whether or not similar tensions between gangs have threatened to surface at the Festival de Orquestas. While this anecdote certainly does not corroborate romanticized claims about salsa uniting people across social boundaries, the respect for a public space acoustically and ideologically defined by salsa recordings suggests their strong impact in molding Caleño cultural values and popular identity.

Salsa Street and Salsa Citadel: The Late 1980s and Early 1990s

In addition to the Festival de Orquestas and the Encuentro de Salsotecas, further attempts were made by Feria organizers to spotlight and centralize live salsa and other salsa-related events for the thousands of city residents and visitors who throng to the city for this festival. Following the success of the Festival de Orquestas in the mid-1980s, Feria organizers developed more elaborate contexts for live salsa performance. Their rationale was a desire to establish the Feria and its smorgasbord of live musical entertainment as a world-class festival. In 1988 a one-mile stretch of Calle Quinta was closed off between Santa Librada and the Parque Panamericano to create La Calle de la Feria—the Street of the Feria—with five verbenalike stages featuring live bands placed at regular intervals along this route. The festival's main stage was located at one end of this strip, in the Panamerican Park. The concept was borrowed from Miami's famous Calle Ocho, a major salsa festival held every March, where the central street of Miami's Cuban-American community is sealed off to traffic and sound stages are set up for live salsa bands to perform on. Calle Quinta was chosen since it was already a focal point for the Feria, owing not only to the month-long display of colored lights along its stretch, but also to the number of griles, nightclubs, and salsotecas located on this avenue. Cali's Calle de la Feria spotlighted Caleño salsa orquestas—including Grupo Niche, now an internationally recognized band—but also included música tropical and even local rock groups. Indeed, so great was its impact that it eclipsed the Festival de Orquestas.

The Calle de la Feria, as local newspapers proclaimed, converted Calle Quinta into a mile-long dance floor. An *El Occidente* journalist, Narciso de la Hoz, reported that the Calle de la Feria was "a true sociological phenomenon," with over 200,000 people of all classes and ages mixing to enjoy live, free salsa music in the streets.[22] Other responses to the Calle de la Feria were mixed. Residents of the middle-class San Fernando neighborhood through which most of the Calle de la Feria extended voiced complaints about the crowds, litter, and all-night noise. (Indeed, many packed their bags and left town to escape the tumult.) Caleños from the city's far-flung lower-class neighborhoods had to travel great distances to get to

Calle Quinta—as much as two hours by foot, since taxi fares were costly and buses did not run late at night. Although the novelty of the Calle de la Feria was sufficient to draw large crowds from outlying districts during its first couple of years, by 1990 the centralization of the Feria on one side of the city resulted in a significant bias against the majority of the Caleño working-class population. By this time Cali had grown far beyond the boundaries that existed in 1968, when the Caseta Panamericana—located in more or less the same area as the Calle de la Feria—also became the focal point for salsero celebration in the Feria. Back then, the working-class salsa fans who came out to hear Richie Ray lived in older neighborhoods such as Barrio Obrero, San Nicolás, San Cayetano, Alameda, Bretaña, and Cristóbal Colón—areas relatively close to the caseta site. By the late 1980s this had changed, yet major Feria events continued to be programmed in the same epicenter around Calle Quinta. Despite this, the Calle de la Feria might have continued, but intensive lobbying from conservative middle-class residents of San Fernando succeeded in finally shutting it down after 1991, its fourth and last year.

I spoke with some of the Feria organizers for those years, who lamented the disappearance of the Calle de la Feria. They felt that the consolidation of live, free sound stages along Calle Quinta really channeled the exuberance of the Feria, heightening its participatory and festive atmosphere.[23] When I arrived in Cali in late 1994, Feria organizers were putting the finishing touches on a similar attempt to centralize and harness annual festivities, with the planning of the Ciudadela de la Feria (Citadel of the Feria). Housed entirely in the Pan-American Stadium, the idea behind the citadel was to once again present a number of live sound stages and food booths, arranged in a circle around the perimeter of the area. As with the Calle de la Feria, the festival's main stage was located on one side. In contrast to its predecessor, however, at which only live acts were featured, the Citadel of the Feria also incorporated the annual Encuentro de Salsotecas. In order to monitor crowds and establish an additional profit-making source, a modest cover charge of a thousand pesos (US$1) was charged, although this increased to $6 and $12 for the special Super-Concert featuring that year's top international salsa bands.

On paper, the Citadel of the Feria looked like a great idea. Not only did it recuperate the collective, concentrated festival atmosphere of the Calle de la Feria, but it did so without blocking traffic or disturbing neighborhood residents (at least not as much as its precursor had). What festival organizers did not anticipate, however, was the resistance of Caleño crowds to paying (even if only a modest fee) for entertainment that only a few years before had been provided free of charge. Melómanos and record collectors, in particular, resented being charged admission to an event whose previous draw had been its character as a free public congregation devoted to listening to recordings of the city's most loved salsa and música antillana classics. Attendance at the Encuentro was especially low the night the Super-Concert boosted entry fees; it drew sharp criticism from loyal die-hard melómanos who felt that their event should not have been included. Finally, as in the previous Calle de la Feria, the citadel centralized over 80 percent of the Feria celebrations on one side of the city. During the following year, as I discussed the Feria with my working-class friends who lived in faraway barrios, they shared their feeling that the idea of making people travel all that distance and then charging them admission was *un abuso* (an abuse). They chose to stay home in 1994, listening to records at family and neighborhood parties and dropping in at local barrio salsotecas. Attendance at the citadel fell far below projected levels, and it was generally deemed a failure. As a result, the decision was made to decentralize the Feria the following year and return celebrations to their popular base in Cali's working-class barrios, with neighborhood-organized committees instated to run verbenas and other festivities in each barrio.

The launching of the Festival de Orquestas, the Calle de la Feria, and the Citadel of the Feria, followed by the decision to decentralize the Feria, indicates an increasingly strong desire on the part of Cali's civic leaders in the 1980s and 1990s to develop and establish a permanent model for this annual celebration. The back-and-forth deliberations over centralizing and decentralizing the Feria have been reinforced by competing ideologies about the city's cultural and social needs and about how best to serve local popular interest. The tension that surfaced between salsa and raspa supporters in the late 1960s and early 1970s, mirrored by criticism in the 1980s and 1990s that Cali was "not just salsa," continues to shape Feria programming to this day. Since about 1980, individual Feria organizers have tried to counterbalance salsa's strong hold with alternative events. Among these have been concerts of traditional Colombian and Latin American music, theater and literature recitals, and a "Street of Culture" with mimes, clowns, face painting, and acoustic folk music, held in Cali's exclusive residential neighborhood of El Peñon, near the Museo de la Tertulia. Many of the debates over how best to package the Feria have been tied to middle-class agendas of profit making, media exposure, creating cultural spaces, and developing a world-class festival with international tourist potential while retaining a populist orientation toward working-class Caleños. In contrast to the local industrial and economic elites who first established the Feria in the

1950s, however, the men and women involved in the Feria's organization in the 1980s and 1990s came from a broad spectrum of class and racial and ethnic backgrounds. These include members of the Caleño bourgoisie, the bohemian-intellectual middle and working classes, upwardly mobile individuals who have moved from working-class backgrounds into the middle and upper-middle classes, and community leaders from Cali's working-class barrios. Their diverse social objectives have driven the sometimes contradictory tendencies of Feria planning from year to year. The group's heterogeneity, however, has contributed substantially to the Feria's populist orientation and outlook.

The Feria: Space of Hope, Space of Memory

As Cali's major annual celebration, the Feria de la Caña de Azucar has become an important symbol of Caleño popular culture. Its festive orientation places it in the same cultural space as Carnival celebrations elsewhere in the Americas. To some, however, Cali's Feria may seem a relatively tame celebration in comparison to its counterparts. Although Cali's Feria has elements of masquerading, parades, floats, and costumes, they are not central to the event, as they are in Carnival in Rio de Janeiro and Port of Spain, Trinidad. Human stamina and imagination are certainly pushed to their limits during the Feria, but one could argue that this also occurs throughout the year in Cali—even though the week-long, nonstop round of partying in griles has declined. One might point to the fact that salsa—a style of the oppressed black and mixed-race working class—is upheld as the musical emblem of the Feria, just as samba is for Brazil's Carnival and calypso for Trinidad's. The valorization of salsa legitimizes not only Cali's racial past, rooted in the history of enslaved Africans brought to the region, but also its refashioning in the modern present, with increasingly cosmopolitan ties and sensibilities beyond national boundaries. Yet, the fundamental hierarchies that govern the city, in which people of color are relegated to the bottom of the social pyramid, are not really inverted by salsa's glorification during the Feria. Indeed, the main opening-day processional of the cabalgata and the round of bullfights and society balls that are dutifully covered by the city's newspapers seem to reaffirm the provisional control that Cali's elites maintain over city life during the Feria. (Roach 1996 observed a similar situation at the New Orleans Mardi Gras until the 1980s.) Finally, in a criticism similar to those raised about other carnival festivities (Manning 1983), some people see the Feria as pure escapism, a steam valve that lets overworked Caleños party hard and exhaust themselves in a five-day outpouring, without ever truly addressing the social problems that affect their daily lives.

What, then, is the fundamental significance of the Feria as a celebratory, carnivalesque space for Caleño popular culture and identity? Certainly, the liberal, populist bent of the Feria's musical and cultural offerings through the years reflects a strong ideological construct of Cali as socially and culturally diverse.[24] In turn, although the debates over highbrow versus lowbrow culture continue to mark the Feria's programming, the emphasis on salsa clearly underscores the role this style has played in the formation of local subjectivity and popular identity. Feria events concentrate and intensify the broad range of popular practices that take place all year long in Cali: dancing, listening and collecting salsa records in homes and at griles and salsotecas, and performing live salsa in local orquestas. Most important, however, the Feria embodies and intensifies various tensions that shaped urban life in Cali through the late twentieth century. Frank Manning notes that celebration "does not resolve or remove ambiguity and conflict, but rather embellishes them" (1983: 30). Similarly, in their study of carnivalesque transgression, Peter Stallybrass and Allon White point out that carnival celebrations do more than temporarily invert the relationship between highbrow and lowbrow culture. They reveal the dialectic between these poles and the ways in which concepts of high and low structure each other to shape social categories and identities (1986: 26). As a key public celebration, then, the Feria has become an important microcosm for all the diverse social, cultural, and economic processes that have shaped Caleño life and local identities.

If Cali is "the city of musical memory," then the Feria offers important keys for understanding the nexus between the city's recent history and the ways it fits into local collective memory. Cities are complex places where social interactions, spatial organization, modes of labor, economic infrastructures, information flows, and political action are all compressed and magnified. They are also sites where the transnational is encountered and absorbed into the national. Cities encompass both utopian dreams and dystopic fears. In *Spaces of Hope*, the sociologist David Harvey notes:

> The association between city life and personal freedoms, including
> the freedom to explore, invent, create, and define new ways of life, has
> a long and intricate history. Generations of migrants have sought the
> city as a haven from rural repressions. The "city" and "citizenship" tie
> neatly together within this formulation. But the city is equally the site
> of anxiety and anomie. It is the place of the anonymous alien, the un-

derclass . . . the site of an incomprehensible "otherness" (immigrants, gays, the mentally disturbed, the culturally different, the racially marked), the terrain of pollution (moral as well as physical), and of terrible corruptions, the place of the damned that needs to be enclosed and controlled, making "city" and "citizen" as politically opposed in the public imagination as they are etymologically linked. (2000: 158)

Cities hence become spaces of hope, as people work to collectively produce their urban environments and in so doing collectively produce themselves (Harvey 2000: 159). Cali has certainly become a strong space of hope for over three generations of residents and migrants who came to the city fleeing violence, seeking jobs, and wishing to create a better life for themselves. Indeed, as political violence threatens once again to tear up the country, Cali has become a haven for displaced refugees fleeing guerilla and paramilitary attacks.

The Feria stands as a microcosm of this larger hopeful space that Cali has become, a celebration of the collective effort to produce a new urban environment and new selves. Since Richie Ray appeared at the 1968 Feria, this annual fair has become increasingly tied to the creation and maintenance of the city's musical memory, understood as a metonym or trope for an entire social history of local popular culture and experience. This history is very recent and very modern. It is baptized in the origin myth that dates the birth of Caleño popular culture to the arrival of música antillana records in the 1930s and 1940s—precisely the moment at which Cali began to be inserted into an escalating series of global economic markets that transformed urban life. What emerged in the wake of the city's rapid expansion and urbanization was a racially and culturally heterogeneous society. National Colombian models of social order, still restrained by nineteenth-century Eurocentric ideals, did not provide adequate vehicles for understanding this diversity, nor the city's growing cosmopolitan ties. It was through the encounter with, and resignification of, música antillana and salsa that Caleños found resources for developing and reimagining their own emergent situation.

In Cali's case, salsa and música antillana have facilitated two things. On the one hand, they have shaped and given voice to Caleños' growing cosmopolitan—and indeed, actively cosmopolitical—sensibility, an orientation that developed to clarify local difference from the national as a result of Cali's historical insularity within Colombia. Even when Cali became a national clearinghouse for the coffee, sugar, and illicit cocaine economies, Caleño cosmopolitanism and a cultural sense of difference from the nation continued to be marked through salsa. On the other hand, salsa—with its Afro-Caribbean roots—has also provided a vehicle for negotiating issues of race and mestizaje within Cali's diverse racial landscape. Race mixture in Colombia does not mean a cultural blending into indistinction, but rather a preservation of differences invoked at specific moments to support competing ideologies about socioeconomic hierarchies and debates over cultural heterogeneity and unity (Wade 2000). In this sense the Caleño negotiation of complex race and class issues has been closely tied to national discourses about social hierarchy. What salsa has provided, nonetheless, is a means of defining local "unity within diversity" (Hall 1986) in a way that recognizes and to an extent legitimates Cali's racial history.

The citywide embrace of salsa is most clearly evident in the Feria, where even non-salseros provisionally put aside their differences to dance and celebrate to salsa's Afro-Antillean groove. Here the Afro-Colombian roots of Cali's majority working-class populace are acknowledged through the symbolic practice of music and dance. Blackness is not given pride of place in any way that fundamentally shifts or threatens white and mestizo control over the city's social hierarchy but is tacitly embodied through dance and listening. Peter Wade points out that in these expressive modes, mestizaje "resides in the body" not through blood (as conventional ideologies of race mixture emphasize), but rather through movement (2000: 211). In Cali, being salsero means learning how to move to salsa—a certain placement of the feet, a swing of the hips, a circular motion of the arms and shoulders, proximity to a dance partner of the opposite sex. Notably, however, learning to move in this way also carries connotations of "blackness" that can be positively embraced (in terms of spontaneity and healthy physical expression) or negatively rejected (through racist stereotypes). In Cali's case, however, these racialized elements have tended to become instruments not only for the transformation of personal subjectivity, but also for the creation of a collective identity in which social harmony and racial diversity—with all their ambiguity and unresolved conflict—are celebrated.

In a city racked by a sharp rise in urban violence since 1980 (see Vanegas Muñoz 1998), the Feria provides a symbolic reminder of the hope placed in Cali and its imagined landscape of peace and acceptance. One is reminded of Balzac's statement that hope is a combination of memory plus desire (Harvey 2000). As a projection of Caleño memory and desire, the Feria itself has become a key avenue for channeling this hope. In recent years the city has sustained a particularly harsh depression, a result not only of the boom-bust cycle following the collapse of the Cali cartel, but also of the severe national recession that has plunged Colombia into its worst economic situation ever. The situation was so drastic that by the year 2000 some city leaders considered canceling the Feria in order to husband scarce financial resources.[25] The low blow this would have dealt to an already depressed city seemed a fate worse than poverty, however, and Cali's annual Feria continues. Despite criticism of its expense and escapism, the Feria continues to function as a site of hope in which the uneasy process of producing urban space, memory, and popular identity is channeled through salsa music and other activities, reinforcing and sustaining Caleño identity and experience.

7
Epilogue
Del Puente
Pa'llá

A few months before completing my primary field research for this study, I performed with a salsa orquesta in the small Afro-Colombian town of Quinamayó, some forty miles due south of Cali, as part of the celebrations for the Adoración del Niño Dios, the most important religious fiesta of Afro-Colombian peasants living in the northern Cauca Valley. Our band, Los Nemus del Pacífico, had been invited to play as the principal salsa orquesta for the Saturday night festivities, alternating with a Caleño orquesta juvenil.[1] While we set up our equipment on a crude verbena erected at one end of a large field, I noticed a town band performing at the opposite end. The ensemble, comprising clarinets, euphonium, trumpet, bass drum, and hand cymbals, played for a small group of old and young townspeople, who danced in a circle in front of the band. A musician from our group explained that these were the traditional Afro-Colombian songs and dances of the region, the *jugas* of the northern Cauca Valley (Portes de Roux 1986a, 1986b).[2] I was fascinated by the image of these players and dancers and by the counterpoint they posed to the Caleño orquestas performing across the field. As a third strain in this sociomusical polyphony, guateque-style salsa recordings blared from a canteen off to another side of the field, alternating with recorded salsa romántica and vallenato music. In a concrete, spatial arrangement, thus, the scene mapped out the juxtaposition of distinct musical styles and tastes that prevail in this semirural zone, poised as different points around a field across which people could move at will. The multigenerational nature of this flow was personified through images such as an elderly black man wearing a traditional campesino straw hat, who caught my eye as he headed across the field toward the salsa stage, accompanied by two strapping fellows who were probably his sons or grandsons. To this day, memories of that night resonate strongly for me. Recalling the refrain of Grupo Niche's 1985 salsa hit

"Del puente pa'llá" (Beyond the Bridge), for me this scene embodies what lies beyond the viaduct linking Cali to Juanchito. It captures not only the history of salsa's influence and localization in Cali, but also its impact on outlying regions beyond the city. As a salsa capital and a city of musical memory, Cali's cultural reach extends far beyond its actual physical boundaries and imposes new memories and cultural traditions over more local microheritages such as the Quinamayó jugas.

From rural fiestas bearing Cali's salsero stamp to the image of geographic and cultural bridges, we come full circle to the questions posed at the outset of this book. In the introduction, I outlined my concern with exploring the nexus between music and memory as a significant affective site for understanding Latin American modernity. The signs of this modernizing process can clearly be seen not only within Cali but also beyond its immediate borders, as economic forces and urban culture have infiltrated the semirural zone around the city. In turn, however, Cali itself has been exposed to a number of economic and social forces over the past sixty years that have forced its residents to reassess or build new conceptual bridges to the world infiltrating the city's bounds. In roughly concentric circles, this includes the Cauca Valley and the Pacific coast, the nation, the Caribbean and North America (particularly New York City), and global points beyond —all locations to which Caleños have been tied in various ways, at various levels and historical moments. In this process, salsa and música antillana have emerged as a particularly potent resource for ideological and cultural bridge building. Not only did this music provide a stylistic vehicle for the growing cosmopolitan identity engendered by new economic and cultural links: the burgeoning cosmopolitics of "thinking and feeling beyond the nation" (Cheah and Robbins 1998) underscored by listening and dancing to salsa and música antillana was vital for negotiating tensions over Cali's difference from the rest of the nation and the city's history of social heterogeneity and race mixture.

My study has emerged from two interrelated stories. One is of salsa and its Cuban and Puerto Rican roots (specifically as they were adopted and resignified in Caleño popular experience and culture). The other concerns how this localized transnational style helped to anchor larger processes and historical ruptures affecting Caleños at several levels. In this book, we saw how the arrival of salsa and música antillana recordings were conceived as the virtual genesis of the modern city, and how these records generated a flourishing dance scene that was revived in symbolic victory after the fall of the Cali cartel. We saw a new set of performative practices enshrining local musical memory emerge with the rise of salsotecas and record collectors, in a nostalgic reconstitution of local cultural history that countered more violent realities. We saw how live salsa performance took flight as an extension of the city's musical memory—now consolidated as an authentic local tradition. Finally, we saw how all of the above processes have been magnified in the annual Feria, as a space of hope in the uneasy growth of this dynamic city.

In this narrative, Cali's bid for the title of "world salsa capital" has been matched by two equally potent slogans: that of Cali as "heaven's outpost" and, more significantly, that of being the "city of musical memory." All these slogans mask inherent contradictions and ambiguities surrounding Caleño popular culture. The "salsa capital" image does not cohere with the ways in which Caleño salsómanos still look to New York and Puerto Rico as salsa's creative wellspring. The fantasy of pleasure and alegría put forth in the "heaven's outpost" slogan conceals darker ruptures: struggling new migrants and land invasions, escalating urban violence, the illicit trade of the Cali cartel, and the specter of renewed political violence in the national sphere. Finally, despite being the "city of musical memory," Cali seems to have forgotten as much about its musical history as it remembers. In Caleños' selective reconstruction of the city's cultural past as an exclusively salsero one, nowhere do we see the other genres they have consumed and enjoyed during different historical periods and by different social sectors. However contradictory Cali's cherished self-representations may seem from outside, though, Caleños uphold these slogans as an integral part of their popular cultural image. Furthermore, the paradoxical effect of these claims is also part of the particular engagement with modernity that characterizes Latin American popular culture at large (García Canclini 1989; Rowe and Schelling 1991).

Recent developments are changing Cali's trajectory "beyond the bridge" in unexpected ways. In my return visits to Cali since 1996, I have witnessed several new dynamics on the local cultural landscape. One stems from the gutting of the local economy that followed the collapse of the cartel and the onset of national recession, which sharply curtailed resources for musical entertainment. Live salsa has suffered in particular, but nightclubs, griles, salsotecas, and even viejotecas limp along with a fraction of the business they generated during the mid-1990s. Although Grupo Niche and Cali's other top salsa bands persist, several others have disappeared, including the all-child band La Charanguita. As I was putting the finishing touches on this volume, I received the disheartening news that Gary Domínguez had just sold the Taberna Latina, marking the end of an era for Caleño salsotecas. Public spaces for maintaining the city's musical memory are drying up.

In surprising contrast to this trend, however, another force is emerging: the strong presence of Pacific coast Afro-Colombians, who are forging new cultural identities in Cali's urban environment. Since 1999, Calle Quinta has become the epicenter for black youths from the Pacific coast. New nightclubs with names such as El Bronx and Sandunga are packed every weekend with young Afro-Colombians, many from faraway Aguablanca district, who groove not only to salsa dura, but also to reggae, rap, techno, Cuban timba, and—most significantly—contemporary, salsa-inflected renditions of traditional chirimia and currulao music from the Pacific coast. In early 2001 a friend wrote me via e-mail to say that locally produced "techno chirimia" is now the latest craze.[3]

The groundswell of Pacific coast culture in Cali, in turn, emerges from political shifts in the early 1990s, with the official recognition of Afro-Colombian territorial rights on the Pacific (Law 70) and increased local government support for traditional Pacific coast arts and heritage. Since 1995, one individual—German Patiño—has been particularly influential in this regard. Through his position as director of culture for the mayor's office, he has provided substantial funding for the annual Festival Petronio Álvarez—drawing currulao and chirimía groups from the entire Pacific coast—and special projects such as Conuno 2000, a commissioned concert suite that fused currulao with jazz and salsa. Cali-based ensembles from Pacific coast migrant communities have taken the city by storm with salsa- and tropical pop–influenced arrangements of traditional Pacific coast genres. Some of these groups are starting to displace local salsa orquestas, at least for the moment: Saboreo (chirimía) and Bahía (currulao) earn top honors at the annual Feria and the Petronio Álvarez festivals. Since 1998 Guayacán's leader, Alexis Lozano, has returned to promoting the music of the Pacific coast, producing records by Saboreo, Markitos (Peregoyo's old vocalist), and other groups at his own studios in Cali. I examine these trends further in current research in progress (Waxer 2001b).

These cultural innovations mirror and also reinforce larger political and economic processes. As Peter Wade details in *Blackness and Race Mixture in Colombia* (1993), the Pacific coast's predominantly Afro-Colombian population and the difficulty of developing a region blanketed by rainforest have produced an image of backwardness and marginality. Accompanying the new constitutional recognition of Afro-Colombian political rights in the Pacific, however, has been a new national focus on exploiting the region's natural resources and finding ways to manage and control the land. Afro-Colombians have gained a significant new voice in the national context during the past decade. The selection of the first black Miss Colombia in 2001 within the traditionally conservative arena of the national beauty pageant is a telling marker of how much things have changed in Colombian mainstream culture—the winner was from Chocó province on the Pacific coast.

Since the mid-1990s Caleño industrial leaders have attempted to bolster the local and regional economy by focusing on Cali's geographic proximity to the entire Pacific Rim, encouraging trade links with Asian countries and setting up a free-trade zone close to the airport. Official recognition of Afro-Colombian rights and identity on the Pacific coast, combined with a progressive economic development agenda for this region, has introduced a radically different conceptualization of the Pacific coast as Colombia's new frontier—with Cali as its financial and industrial hub. Cali now occupies a much stronger position in the national context than it did a generation ago, and the city's long-rooted history of difference from the nation has become a trump card for pulling ahead in the race to lead Colombia's economy. While the escalation of kidnappings, bombings, peasant massacres, and armed clashes between guerilla and paramilitary forces in the region since 1999 (especially between Cali and Buenaventura) has substantially curtailed economic development, it is unlikely that political violence will succeed in halting this process altogether—even in the event of what some experts prognosticate will be a prolonged civil war. In Cali's case, it is clear from current shifts in the local cultural landscape that Caleños continue to negotiate their local and regional sense of difference from the rest of the Colombian nation—and the ways this is intimately tied to its heterogeneous racial history—through music.

During the 1980s and early 1990s, as Cali rode the crest of its economic boom and euphorically claimed its position as world salsa capital, critics and observers constantly reiterated that Cali was more than "just salsa." Since the fall of the cartel, Caleños have begun to relinquish their hold on the salsa capital myth—new social and economic forces are prompting Caleños to build other cultural bridges in addition to the salsero viaduct. Yet, as we saw with the emergence of the salsotecas and tabernas in the 1980s, the viejoteca revival of the mid-1990s, and even the rise of local live music, recordings of salsa and of its Cuban and Puerto Rican roots have consistently served as a basis for generating new popular practices in Cali. Despite the current shift toward more diverse musical styles, I suspect that salsa recordings will continue to sire new cultural responses in the future as Caleños continue to draw from the past in negotiating their current circumstances. The capacity of sound technology to create an "infinitely renewable present" (Lipsitz 1990: vii) reinforces the desire to construct a solid cultural foundation—a sense of tradition and cultural roots—that can anchor collective memory and identity during what is actually a time of great flux. As Cali's recent history demonstrates, this cultural foundation has flourished primarily—albeit not exclusively—as a result of salsa and música antillana records. While Cali's origin myth about the birth of local popular culture from the arrival of these sounds certainly conceals historical fact, it also reveals the potent impact of these particular sound recordings for the construction of collective popular memory.

The resignification of salsa in Caleño popular culture points to how physical movement, consumption, memory and musical performance are all braided into the core rhythm—the clave, if you will—of contemporary Caleño existence. Dancing and listening to records and live music are potent embodied pleasures that have inscribed a particular knowledge of what it means to be Caleño through a variety of subjective experiences. Not only have these activities formed the channels by which salsa has been incorporated into the grain of local popular expression, but they are also meaningful cultural practices through which Caleños have made explicit their own sense of being together. Just as the clave serves as a basic time line that governs and gives meaning to all the other interlocking rhythmic patterns and accents in salsa music, so too have salsa and música antillana provided the basis for the participatory activities that permeate everyday life in Cali. Over and above all other musical styles, salsa has served as the sonic cue for the participatory framework of the rumba that is the hub of Caleño collectivity, suturing the wounds of daily struggles and banishing the shadows of urban violence. Through dancing, listening, and performance, Caleños have forged activities that get them in sync and that reinforce and indeed structure the deeper synchrony of social life itself. In this sense, recreation is not mere pastime, but a constant re-creating of urban experience and selfhood.

For scholars of global popular culture, Cali illustrates the potent articulation of transnational capital flows (as manifested in the production and consumption of records and related media) to local cultural practice and everyday experience. Caleño popular culture has been a product of, and a response to, global forces of rapid technological development, urbanization, industrialization, and social change throughout the twentieth century and into the twenty-first. Through the diverse cultural practices shaping salsa's local adoption, we can detect, as Arjun Appadurai would say, "the workings of the imagination in a deterritorialized world" (1996: 63) via which Caleños have sought to reposition their sense of local identity during a particularly unstable period in recent history. Dancing, listening to, collecting records of, and performing salsa have emerged as quotidian but significant acts through which Caleños remember—in the literal sense of re-membering—how they first experienced and made sense of the city's transformation into a major urban and industrial center.

Appendices

Appendix 1   Map of Hubs of Salsa and *Música Antillana* in Cali

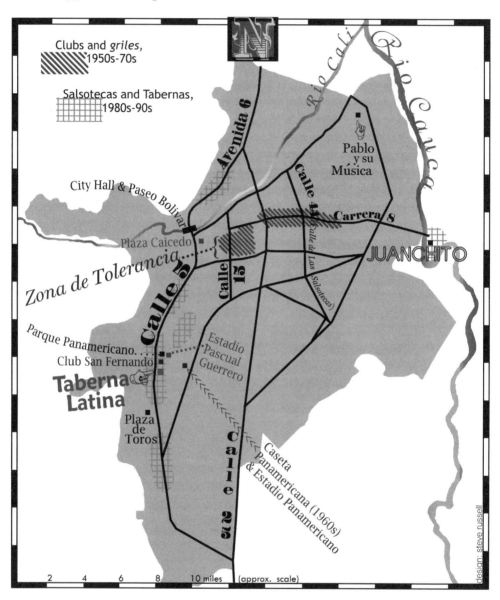

Clubs and *griles*, 1950s-70s

Salsotecas and Tabernas, 1980s-90s

Río Cali

Río Cali

Río Cauca

Avenida 6

Pablo y su Música

City Hall & Paseo Bolívar

Carrera 8

Plaza Caicedo

Calle 44 (Calle de Las Salsotecas)

JUANCHITO

Zona de Tolerancia

Calle 5

Calle 15

Parque Panamericano

Estadio Pascual Guerrero

Club San Fernando

Taberna Latina

Plaza de Toros

Calle 25

Caseta Panamericana (1960s) & Estadio Panamericano

design: steve russell

2   4   6   8   10 miles   (approx. scale)

264

Appendix 2   Map of Socioeconomic Zones in Cali

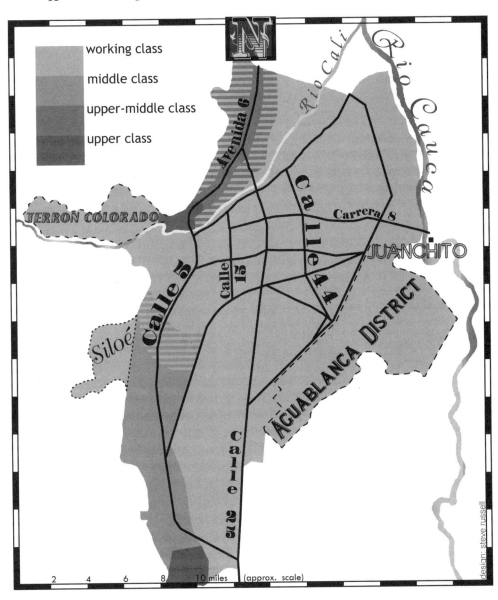

working class
middle class
upper-middle class
upper class

Appendix 3   Major International and National Orquestas Appearing at the Cali Feria, 1968–95

This list is compiled from newspaper ads and reports appearing in *El País* and *El Occidente* during the Feria dates for these years. Salsa and música antillana artists are highlighted in italics. The orquestas listed here are those who headlined in major concerts and at the *casetas* (dance halls). The list does not include several Caleño bands that also performed steadily during the Feria at downtown hotel

1968
- Los Corraleros de Majagual (Colombia)
- Los Melódicos (Venezuela)
- Los Ocho de Colombia (Colombia)
- *Richie Ray and Bobby Cruz (New York)*
- Los Teenagers (Colombia)
- Los Tropicales (Colombia)

1969
- Los Black Stars (Colombia)
- Los Graduados (Colombia)
- Los Hermanos Bernal (Colombia)
- Los Hermanos Martelo (Colombia)
- Los Hispanos (Colombia)
- Los Melódicos (Venezuela)
- Nelson y sus Estrellas (Venezuela)
- *Richie Ray and Bobby Cruz (New York)*

1970
- Billo's Caracas Boys (Venezuela)
- Combo Sabor (Colombia)
- Los Graduados (Colombia)
- Alfredo Gutiérrez (Colombia)
- Los Hispanos (Colombia)
- Lucho Macedo (Colombia)
- Los Melódicos (Venezuela)
- Nelson y sus Estrellas (Venezuela)
- Los Ocho de Colombia (Colombia)
- Los Reales de Colombia (Colombia)
- La Tropibomba (Colombia)

1971
- Fausto y Yolanda (Colombia)
- Ricardo Fuentes (Colombia)
- Los Hispanos (Colombia)
- Los Indios (Colombia)
- Los Melódicos (Venezuela)
- Orlando y su Combo (Colombia)
- Jimmy Salcedo y su Onda 3 (Colombia)
- Sandro (Argentina)
- *Daniel Santos (Puerto Rico)*

1972
- *Ismael Miranda (New York)*
- Nelson y sus Estrellas (Venezuela)
- *Piper Pimienta (Cali)*
- Los Soles de Colombia (Cali)
- Stone Luv and Trio Black Ivory (New York)

1973
- Chambers Brothers (U.S.)
- Los Flippers (Colombia)
- *Fruko y sus Tesos (Colombia)*
- Grupo Vallenato de Cesar (Colombia)
- Alfredo Gutiérrez (Colombia)
- Nelson y sus Estrellas (Venezuela)
- Los Soles de Colombia (Cali)
- Unidad 4 (Colombia)

ballrooms and in barrio verbenas but did not appear in larger shows. Numerous minor ensembles (e.g., trios, folkloric groups, and solo vocalists) are also left out. Countries or places of origin are indicated— I have tried to determine these as accurately as possible. Where "Colombia" is indicated, most of these bands were from Bogotá, Medellín, or the Atlantic coast. Also designated are artists specifically from Cali. Unfortunately, I am missing data on the year 1993. All errors in this chart are my own.

1974	1975	1976
Los Diferentes (Colombia)	Dimensión Latina (Venezuela)	Alfa 6 (Cali)
Formula 8 (Cali)	Leonor González Mina "La Negra Grande" (Colombia)	Los Caribes (Colombia)
Fruko y sus Tesos (Colombia)	El Gran Combo (Puerto Rico)	Chirivico Dávila (Puerto Rico)
Nelson y sus Estrellas (Venezuela)	Nelson y sus Estrellas (Venezuela)	Los Choqueros (Spain)
Piper Pimienta (Cali)	Piper Pimienta (Cali)	Claudia (Colombia)
José Luis Rodríguez "El Puma" (Ven.)	Rafael (Spain)	Formula 8 (Cali)
Tania (Colombia)	Los Soles de Colombia (Cali)	Los Graduados (Colombia)
		Los Latinos de Ritmo (Colombia)
		Piper Pimienta (Cali)
		Joey Quijano (New York)
		Sexteto Juventud (Venezuela)
		Sonora Matancera (Cuba)

1977	1978	1979
Los Bunker (Colombia)	Fruko y sus Tesos (Colombia)	Alfa 6 (Cali)
Los Caribes (Colombia)	La Gran Banda (Cali)	Folkloric troupes from Venezuela, Ecuador, Peru, Bolivia, Brazil, and Colombia
José Fajardo (Cuba/New York)	Octava Dimensión (Cali)	La Gran Banda (Cali)
Formula 8 (Cali)	Orquesta Fantasia (Colombia)	Octava Dimensión (Cali)
Fruko y sus Tesos (Colombia)	Orquesta Típica Novel (New York)	Orquesta Típica Novel (New York)
Los Graduados (Colombia)	Piper Pimienta (Cali)	Piper Pimienta (Cali)
Piper Pimienta (Cali)	Bobby Rodríguez (New York)	
Joey Quijano (New York)	Sexteto Miramar (Colombia)	
	Unidad 4 (Colombia)	

1980

Los Bunker (Colombia)
Los Caribes (Colombia)
Combo Palacios (Peru)
Conjunto Clásico (New York)
Constelación Vallenata (Colombia)
Celia Cruz (Cuba/New York)
Formula 8 (Cali)
Fruko y sus Tesos (Colombia)
Alfredo Gutiérrez (Colombia)
Lisandro Meza (Colombia)
Lucho Bermúdez (Colombia)
Mario Muñoz "Papaito" (New York)
Nelson y sus Estrellas (Venezuela)
Octava Dimensión (Cali)
Johnny Pacheco (New York)
Pastor López (Colombia)
La Revolución (Cali)
Unidad 4 (Colombia)
Helenita Vargas (Cali)

1981

Los Caribes (Colombia)
Dimensión Diez (Colombia)
Formula 8 (Cali)
Fruko y sus Tesos (Colombia)
Pacho Galán (Colombia)
Alfredo Gutiérrez (Colombia)
Integracion 2,000 (Cali)
Integración Porteña (Buenaventura)
Hector Lavoe (New York)
Alma Llanera (Colombia)
Octava Dimensión (Cali)
Piper Pimienta (Cali)
Juan Piña y La Revelación (Colombia)
Los Quillacingas (Colombia)
Raza Tropical (Cali)
Ismael Rivera (Puerto Rico)
Sonora Juventud (Cali)
Toto la Momposina (Colombia)
Los Tupumaros (Colombia)

1982

Bemtú (Cali)
Pablo Branda "Melcochita" (New York)
Los Bunker (Colombia)
Los Caribes (Colombia)
El Combo Cañaveral (Cali)
Conjunto Barroco (Colombia)
Constelación Vallenata (Colombia)
Diomedes Díaz (Colombia)
Los Empresarios del Ritmo (Cali)
Formula 8 (Cali)
La Gran Banda (Cali)
El Gran Combo (Puerto Rico)
Los Graduados (Colombia)
Grupo Niche (Cali)
Alfredo Gutiérrez (Colombia)
Hernán Gutiérrez (Colombia)
Integracion 2,000 (Cali)
Integración Porteña (Buenaventura)
Los Jordan (Cali)
Pastor López (Colombia)
José Mangual Jr. (New York)
Colacho Mendoza (Colombia)
La Misma Gente (Cali)
Octava Dimensión (Cali)
Orquesta Broadway (New York)
Piper Pimienta (Cali)
Los Soles de Colombia (Cali)
Los Tupumaros (Colombia)
Helenita Vargas (Cali)

1983

Bemtú (Cali)
María del Carmen (Cali)
Charanga América (New York)
Conjunto Clásico (New York)
Los Empresarios del Ritmo (Cali)
Formula 8 (Cali)
Integración Porteña (Buenaventura)
Integracion 2,000 (Cali)
Nueva Dimensión (Cali)
Octava Dimensión (Cali)
Juan Pachanga Charanga (Cali)
El Gran Combo (Puerto Rico)
Grupo Niche (Cali)
Alfredo Gutiérrez (Colombia)
Los Melódicos (Venezuela)
Lisandro Meza (Colombia)
La Misma Gente (Cali)
Piper Pimienta (Cali)
Sonora Dinamita (Colombia)
Sexteto Miramar (Colombia)
Los Soles de Colombia (Cali)

1984	1985	1986	1987*
Alfa 6 (Cali)	Bemtú (Cali)	Banda de San Pelayo (Colombia)	Bemtú (Cali)
Bemtú (Cali)	Lucho Bermúdez (Colombia)	Bemtú (Cali)	Los Bunker (Colombia)
Los Bunker (Colombia)	Billo's Caracas Boys (Venezuela)	Los Bunker (Colombia)	Alvaro del Castillo (Cali)
Los Caribes (Colombia)	Los Bunker (Colombia)	Cali Charanga (Cali)	Cali Charanga (Cali)
María del Carmen (Cali)	Cali Charanga (Cali)	Los del Caney (Cali)	Caña de Azucar (Cali)
Celina y Reutilio (Cuba)	Los del Caney (Cali)	María del Carmen (Cali)	Los del Caney (Cali)
Santiago Cerón (New York)	Alvaro Castillo y La Calentura (Colombia)	Alvaro del Castillo (Colombia)	María del Carmen (Cali)
Oscar D'León (Venezuela)	Combo Caribe (Cali)	Combo Caribe (Cali)	Celina y Reutilio (Cuba)
Los Empresarios del Ritmo (Cali)	Oscar D'León (Venezuela)	Oscar D'León (Venezuela)	Combo Caribe (Cali)
Formula 8 (Cali)	Henry Fiol (New York)	Fallarones (Cali)	Pedro Conga (Puerto Rico)
La Gran Banda (Cali)	Formula 8 (Cali)	Henry Fiol (New York)	Conjunto Caney (Cuba)
El Gran Combo (Puerto Rico)	La Gran Banda (Cali)	Formula 8 (Cali)	Alejo Durán (Colombia)
Grupo Niche (Cali)	El Gran Combo (Puerto Rico)	La Gran Banda (Cali)	Los Fallarones (Cali)
Hermanos Ospina (Cali)	Grupo Niche (Cali)	El Gran Combo (Puerto Rico)	Formula 8 (Cali)
Los Jordan (Cali)	Los Guaracheros de Oriente (Cuba)	Grupo Niche (Cali)	Grupo Clase (Cali)
Pastor López (Colombia)	Hermanos Ospino (Cali)	Hermanos Ospino (Cali)	Guayacán (Cali)
Lisandro Meza (Colombia)	Latin Brothers (Colombia)	La Identidad (Cali)	Hermanos Ospino (Cali)
Nelson y sus Estrellas (Venezuela)	Los Melódicos (Venezuela)	Integración Porteña (Buenaventura)	La Identidad (Cali)
Nueva Dimensión (Cali)	La Misma Gente (Cali)	Latin Brothers (Colombia)	Integración Porteña (Buenaventura)
Octava Dimensión (Cali)	Octava Dimensión (Cali)	La Misma Gente (Cali)	Los Jordan (Cali)
Piper Pimienta (Cali)	Los Soles (Cali)	Naty y su Orquesta (Venezuela)	Raphy Leavitt y La Selecta (Puerto Rico)
Sexteto Miramar (Colombia)	Son de Euterpe (Cali)	Nueva Dimensión (Cali)	La Ley (Cali)
Sonora Dinamita (Colombia)	Sonora Matancera (Cuba)	Octava Dimensión (Cali)	Manantial (Cali)
Los Tupumaros (Colombia)	Los Tropicales (Cali)	Piper Pimienta (Cali)	La Misma Gente (Cali)
		Siboney (Cali)	Octava Dimensión (Cali)
		Los Soles (Cali)	Piper Pimienta (Cali)
		Son de Euterpe (Cali)	Los Soles (Cali)
		Sonora Dinamita (Colombia)	Son de Euterpe (Cali)
		Sonora Ponceña (Puerto Rico)	Sonora Caleña (Cali)
		Super Orquesta Café (Cali)	Sonora Ponceña (Puerto Rico)
		Los Tropicales (Cali)	
		Los Tupumaros (Colombia)	

*Grupo Niche absent owing to breakup of group.

1988	1989	1990	1991
Adalberto Alvarez (Cuba)	Alvaro del Castillo (Cali)	Joe Arroyo (Colombia)	Jose Alberto "El Canario" (New York)
Joe Arroyo (Colombia)	Dimensión Latina (Venezuela)	Los Bronco (Venezuela/Cali)**	Joe Arroyo (Colombia)
Pablo Branda "Melcochita" (New York)	Los Hermanos Lebrón (New York)	J. C. Coronel (Colombia)	Costa Brava (Colombia)
Celina y Reutilio (Cuba)	Junior González (New York)	Los Corraleros de Majagual (Colombia)	Oscar D'León (Venezuela)
Cheo Feliciano (New York)	Grupo Clase (Cali)	Oscar D'León (Venezuela)	Rafael Escalona y su Combo (Colombia)
Henry Fiol (New York)	Grupo Niche (Cali)	Grupo Gale (Colombia)	El Gran Combo (Puerto Rico)
Grupo Niche (Cali)	Guayacán (Cali)	Grupo Niche (Cali)	Grupo Niche (Cali)
Guayacán (Cali)	Joe Arroyo (Colombia)	Guayacán (Cali)	Guayacán (Cali)
La Misma Gente (Cali)	La Misma Gente (Cali)	Juan Luis Guerra (Dominican Republic)	La Misma Gente (Cali)
NG La Banda (Cuba)	Los Niches (Cali)	Hermanos Rosario (Dominican Republic)	New York Band (New York)
Orquesta Aragón (Cuba)	Piper Pimienta (Cali)	Latin Brothers (Colombia)	Son de Azucar (Cali)
Orquesta Riverside (Cuba)	(plus numerous other local Caleño orquestas)	La Misma Gente (Cali)	Mariana la Sonera (Venezuela)
Toto La Momposina (Colombia)		Naty y su Charanga (Venezuela)	Bobby Valentín (Puerto Rico)
(plus numerous other local Caleño orquestas)		Nelson y sus Estrellas (Venezuela/Cali)**	(plus numerous other local Caleño orquestas)
		Los Originales de Manzanillo (Cuba)	
		Sonora Dinamita (Colombia)	
		Sergio Vargas (Colombia)	
		(plus numerous other local Caleño orquestas)	
		**Both Nelson and Felix Shakaito, leader of Los Bronco, moved from Caracas to Cali in this year and reformed their bands with local musicians.	

1992	1993	1994	1995
Nicola Di Bari (Italy)	Data unavailable	Joe Arroyo (Colombia)	Billo's Caracas Boys (Venezuela)
Billo's Caracas Boys (Venezuela)		Billo's Caracas Boys (Venezuela)	Oscar D'León (Venezuela)
Santiago Ceron (New York)		Henry Fiol (New York)	Rey Ruiz (Miami)
Leo Dan (Spain)		Hermanos Rosario (Dominican Republic)	Salserín (Venezuela)
Oscar D'León (Venezuela)		Tito Gómez (Puerto Rico)	Conjunto Caney (Cuba)
Grupo Niche (Cali)		Grupo Niche (Cali)	Los Generales (Buenaventura)
Guayacán (Cali)		Guayacán (Cali)	La Grande de Madrid (Spain)
Hermanos Rosario (Dominican Republic)		Lisandro Meza (Colombia)	Grupo Niche (Cali)
Ray Pérez y Los Kenya (Puerto Rico)		Nelson y sus Estrellas (Venezuela/Cali)	Guayacán (Cali)
Los Tupumaros (Colombia)		Puerto Rican Power (Puerto Rico)	Nelson y sus Estrellas (Venezuela/Cali)
(plus numerous other Caleño orquestas)		Rey Ruiz (Miami)	Orquesta Aragón (Cuba)
		Jerry Rivera (Puerto Rico)	Los Tupumaros (Colombia)
		Sonora Ponceña (Puerto Rico)	Carlos Vives (Colombia)
		Los Terry (Cuba)	(plus numerous other Caleño orquestas)
		Los Tupumaros (Colombia)	
		(plus numerous other Caleño orquestas)	

Notes

Recorded interviews are documented in the notes according to the date and tape catalog number in my research archive.

Notes to Introduction

1. Ulloa outlines five interrelated factors to explain salsa's popularity in Cali: (1) the presence of a large Afro-Colombian population with a colonial history of slavery and exploitation similar to that of Afro-Caribbeans; (2) industrial growth, leading to the formation of new social classes and a large working class receptive to new musical sounds; (3) the rapid urbanization of Cali and migration from other regions, contributing to the cultural heterogeneity of Cali's working classes; (4) the perceived lack of a local musical tradition, allowing for international styles such as música antillana and salsa to enter with strong impact; and (5) the strong influence of mass-media technologies in transmitting música antillana to Cali during the 1940s and 1950s, establishing these sounds in local popular life and paving the way for salsa's adoption later.
2. A similar process occurred in Caracas, Venezuela (see Waxer 2002).
3. Kike Escobar, personal communication, 11 April 1996 (interview Col96-59).
4. With the exception of some Cuban big bands of the 1940s and 1950s such as La Gigante de Benny Moré, the Orquesta Casino de la Playa, and the Orquesta Riverside. These big bands paralleled the New York mambo orchestras of Machito, Tito Puente, and Tito Rodríguez that directly preceded salsa in the New York scene.
5. There is a surprising dearth of research on the Puerto Rican *cuatro,* owing in large part to the sensitivity of its nature as an icon of Puerto Rican culture — and hence nationalism — within the current colonial regime. Attempts to showcase cuatro history by local cultural organizations and even by the Instituto de Cultura de Popular have been repeatedly squelched by the government. In this regard, recent work by the Cuatro Project, an independent research consortium, has been especially valuable. See their Web site, www.cuatro-pr.org, and their recently completed documentary film, *Nuestro Cuatro: Los puertorriqueños y sus instrumentos de cuerda, vol. 1,* available in Spanish and English.

6. To a lesser extent, salsa also spread to countries such as Ecuador, Peru, and the Dominican Republic.

7. Timba is an outgrowth of the *songo,* a mix of Cuban son, rumba, funk and rock that was created in the late 1960s and has been Cuba's most significant post-revolution dance style. Modernized Cuban son bands from the 1980s, such as Son 14, have also been referred to as "Cuban salsa," but their sound did not incorporate the elements that became a hallmark of Cuban dance music by the early 1990s.

8. In Cali these writers are Medardo Arias Satizábal, Umberto Valverde, Rafael Quintero, Gary Domínguéz, and Orlando Montenegro. In Bogotá, Cesar Pagano and Jose Arteaga are among the most prolific writers. Sergio Santana is Medellín's most prolific commentator on salsa (and also renowned as a national expert of reggae).

9. I would argue that this holds even for a large degree of communications and cultural studies research, which has led the field in studies of music and mass media.

10. These volumes contain papers presented at congresses of the Latin American branch of the International Association for the Study of Popular Music (IASPM).

11. See Waxer 2002 for a collection of essays by some leading salsa scholars, discussing salsa's global spread and localization in several different parts of the world.

12. Salsa-related Web sites include Latin Music On-line, OasisSalsero, the Willie Colón Web-site and Forum, Descarga Records, San Francisco/Bay Area Salsa and Latin Jazz, Salsa Web, Picadillo, Latin Dance, Der Salsaholic, Hot Salsa (Le Guide de la Salsa), Musica Salsa Forum, Salsa Jam, Salsa Brasil, SalsaJazz, Jazz con Clave, Salsa con Cache, Noti-Salsa, Salsatecas, Bamboleo, Sonero, SalsaNet, Latino, Cadena SalSoul, Dimensíon Latina, Salsa in Finland, Samurai Latino, NYC Salsa, Salsa em Brasil, Master Timbaleros, Timba Website, Richie Blondet's Montuno Papers, and Nestor Louis's Web page. Most commercial salsa artists also have their own Web sites, as do Fania and RMM Records.

13. Robertson notes that the terms "glocal" and "glocalization" actually emerged as jargon in the multinational business world during the 1980s, to refer to global or near-global promotion of goods and services to increasingly distinct local or sublocal markets. The major locus of origin of these terms, according to Robertson, was Japan, modeled on the concept of *dochakuka,* adapting to local conditions. In Japan, long-standing attention to that country's spatio-cultural relationship to the rest of the world has been cultivated, and this country has been a leader in adapting global business strategies to local situations (i.e., "micro-marketing") in the late twentieth century (Robertson 1995: 28).

14. I am indebted to Alejandro Lugo for drawing my attention to this important theoretical distinction.

15. This was a notion suggested to me by Gustavo de Roux (personal communication, 7 November 1994), a prominent Colombian sociologist who has worked extensively with Afro-Colombian communities.

16. In colonial Latin America and the Caribbean, a complex caste system ranked people by terms that designating their racial mixture, naturalizing "blood" as an inalienable essential force that determined social identity (see Mörner 1967). Terminology in this system included classificaitons such as *negro* (black), *mulato* (half white), *tercerón* (three parts white) *cuarterón* (four parts white), *quinterón* (five parts white), and so forth, with further subdivisions made according to whether one was a recently arrived slave from Africa *(bozal)* or from Spain *(ladino)*, or born in the colony *(negro criollo)*, or was a free black *(negro libre* or *pardo)*. Minute subdivisions designated the offspring of those with varying "degrees" of African blood, e.g. the child of a quinterón and a cuarterón was called *tentenelaire* (held in the air), while the child of a quinterón and a mulato was referred to as *salatrás,* or "step backward" (de Friedemann 1993: 64). After 1783 the Spanish Crown ordained a decree allowing rich mestizos to purchase a "certificate of whiteness" called the *cédula de gracias al sacar*—literally, a certificate of "gratitude for taking out," i.e., of racial opprobrium. This "royal cleansing," as Peter Wade puts it, usually cost twice the value of a prime slave (1993: 9).

17. Evidence shows that this is not unique to the case of Colombia (Whitten and Torres 1998). *No Longer Invisible: Afro-Latin Americans Today* (Minority Rights Group 1995) offers recent scholarship about how this situation is changing for black people in the Americas.

18. By "whitening" I refer to the Latin American notion of *blanquemiento*—virtually a "bleaching out" the so-called dark spots of one's origins—rather than the growing body of North American literature about "white" ethnicity (Delgado and Stefancic 1997; Ignatiev and Garvey 1997; Fine 1997; Alba 1990).

19. Cartagena was the principal port for the South American colonial economy, serving as the nexus for importing African slave labor and for exporting gold back to Spain.

20. This breaks down into 14 percent *mulato,* 4 percent black, and 3 percent mixed black and indigenous. Source: *Statesman's Yearbook 1998–99,* 409.

21. See Wade 1993 for an excellent ethnographic study of this dynamic.

22. Spearheaded by scholars such as Nina S. de Friedemann, Jaime Arocha, and Gustavo de Roux.

23. The program in question is *Sábados Felices,* which was condemned by the United Nations Human Rights Commission in early 1997 (see "Solicitan sospender Sábados Felices," *El Pais,* 18 March 1997). Jokes and anecdotes that belittled blacks comprised up to 80 percent of the show's "entertainment," until Afro-Colombian activists succeeded in having such "humor" removed.

24. See Edgardo Díaz-Díaz (1998) for an analysis of how ethnic, class, and gender identities are enacted and negotiated in Latin dancing.

25. A rich cross-section of studies in various cultures is presented in Koskoff 1987. For an excellent book-length investigation of how music operates in engendering subjectivities, see Sugarman 1997.

26. *Recuerdos de mi Barrio* (*Recuerdos* 1986) was produced as a commemoration of the 450th anniversary of Cali's founding in 1534. A citywide competition for the best written memoir generated 192 responses—some of them the length of a short book—of which the best were published by the mayor's office in

limited editions, e.g., Ulloa 1986. The entire collection is housed in an archive at the library of the Universidad del Valle.

Notes to Chapter 1

1. Personal communication, 11 January 1997. Medardo Arias wrote a feature on González that refers to this video collection; "Mascaras de Carnaval en la Loma de la Cruz," *El País*, 12 January 1997.
2. In his analysis of Colombian música tropical, Peter Wade gives an excellent discussion of the origin myths of Atlantic Coast musical genres (2000). His treatment has indirectly influenced my own analysis here.
3. According to anthropologists and historians, most of these groups were anthropophagic and existed in uneasy warfare with other. They include the Timba, Jamundí, and Lilí, due south and southwest of where Cali now stands, as well as the Calacoto and Aguale by the Cauca River, the Gorrón and Calima to the northwest, the Quimbaya to the north, and the Atunceta near the Pacific coast (Gómez 1986: 33–34).
4. Gold mining extended from the area now covered by the Chocó province down through the highland regions south of Popayán .
5. The Pacific Railway from Buenaventura to Cali was completed in 1915; by 1917 it extended to Palmira, a former hacienda and important agricultural town on the other side of the Cauca River (Escobar Navia 1986).
6. In the Valle del Cauca, sugarcane is planted and harvested continually, throughout the year—there is no specific season for either activity. Rather, planting and harvesting is done on a rotation basis, so that the different fields produce sugarcane constantly (personal communication, Alvaro Burgos, 5 January 2000).
7. La Violencia (The Violence) is one of the most brutal and violent episodes in recent Colombian history, emerging from pitched tensions between followers of the country's two political parties, the Liberals and Conservatives (see Guzmán Campos 1962). Although technically it lasted from 1948 through 1958, violent outbreaks and repercussive waves continued through the mid-1960s.
8. Source: *Anuario Estadístico del Valle de Cauca, 1972–74*. According to the 1973 census, Cali had a population of 991,549.
9. Source: *Anuario Estadístico del Valle de Cauca 1994*. These figures are derived from the official national census, and probably do not account for a large margin of recent migrants and land squatters, who also make up an important part of the city's population and mobilize much of its informal economy.
10. In Colombia, "Atlantic coast" refers not only to the littoral per se (e.g., the coastal cities of Cartagena, Barranquilla, and Santa Marta), but all the lowland areas that slope down along the Magdalena Basin toward the Caribbean Sea. This includes the inland *departamento* (province) of Cesar—home of the vallenato—and the inland areas of Bolivar, Sucre, and Cordoba provinces. I even heard one person refer to the area around Bucaramanga and Barrancabermeja (in northern Santander province) as "the Atlantic," although geographically speaking this is high into the mountainous interior.
11. As Heliana Portes de Roux observes in her excellent study of this tradition (1986a), the actual date of the fiesta varies each year, depending on economic

resources, but it is usually held in January or February. A fiesta I attended 1996 in Quinamayó, for example, was held during the weekend of 17–18 February (see epilogue). Very little recorded documentation of this music exists. See *Música religiosa de negros nortecaucanos, en las voces de las cantoras de Mingo*, recorded and produced by Portes de Roux (1986b).

12. Carlos Ramos, personal communication, 6 June 1997.

13. Although the African influences are predominantly sub-Saharan, since slaves brought to the Americas were from this region, North African musical traits also passed into much Iberian music and hence have also been indirectly transmitted.

14. This style was even adopted by sectors of the urban middle class in some African countries, especially during the 1950s. West African bands such as L'Orchestre Nacional de Mali or the Orchestre Baobab can be seen as part of this cosmopolitan development.

15. Afro-Cuban rumba and the son-based "rhumba" are distinct musical expressions. See Moore 1997 for a detailed analysis of the relation between Afro-Cuban *rumba* and its whitened *son*-based salon counterpart. The Afro-Cuban rumba is characterized by a modified clave pattern and a complex polyrhythmic structure, performed on a set of three conga drums of different sizes. The rumba complex is divided into three subgenres, with distinct tempos: *yambú* (slow couple dance associated with older people), *guaguancó* (medium couple dance with symbolic sexual interplay), and *columbia* (fast male solo dance in 6/8 meter,). See Crook 1982 and Daniel 1995 for more details.

16. See Mauleón 1993 for a complete outline of the different rhythmic patterns used in Cuban *son* and salsa.

17. I have also heard the claim this slower rhythm is related to a *montuno* or "country-style" way of playing but have not been able to find much substantiation of this explanation.

18. See the PBS documentary *Roots of Rhythm* (New Video 9435) for excellent archival film footage and analysis of this period.

19. The Cuban sound influenced several African urban styles of the 1950s, e.g., Ghanaian highlife and contemporary Malian and Senegal styles. Most important, it formed the basis for *rumba congolaise,* which later developed into Zairean *soukous.*

20. Carlos Ramos, personal communication, 6 May 1997.

21. When Arsenio Rodríguez and other members of his band moved to New York City in 1952, the remaining group was reconstituted by Arsenio's lead trumpet, Félix Chappotín, who together with the pianist Lilí Martínez and Miguelito Cuní established what many consider to be the best Cuban conjunto of the 1950s. The New York collector and musicologist René López, for example, considers "Lilí" to have been "the architect" of Cuban son (personal communication, 6 April 1992). In my own conversations with musicians and musicologists in Havana, it is clear that the Arsenio-Chappotín school has also continued to hold great importance on the island.

22. Helio Orovio, personal communication, 30 November 1995 (interview Cub95-8). Orovio, who used to hang out stageside at Sonora Matancera performances as a young boy (personal communication, 31 May 1996), is gener-

ally considered to be an expert on the Matancera. I am indebted to him for his insights and comments about the stylistic contributions of this group.

23. Cruz joined the Matancera on 1 August 1950, replacing their former female vocalist, Myrta Silva, who had decided to return to her native Puerto Rico.

24. Valverde himself hails from Barrio Obrero, a working-class neighborhood considered to have been the hotbed of Sonora Matancera fans and one where Celia Cruz is especially revered.

25. Personal communication, 12 August 1998.

26. Rondón erroneously notes that before the Venezuelan band Dimensión Latina performed in New York City in 1975, New York salsa audiences had only seen local bands that whose "attraction was limited to the simple execution of the music, without filling out the presentation with dance and color" (1980: 232). This remark ignores the importance of El Gran Combo for Puerto Ricans on the island and mainland and the occasional appearances of El Gran Combo in New York City itself during this time.

27. Moré, a contemporary of Rivera, is himself considered to be Cuba's greatest *sonero,* a legend who died prematurely in 1962. Pagano reports Moré's attribution of the title *sonero mayor* to Rivera in Pagano 1993: 3.

28. This comment was made to me by the Havana-based musicologist Adriana Orejuela during a conversation we had about contemporary Cuban dance bands. Personal communication, 8 December 1995.

29. I am indebted to Carlos Ramos for this observation (personal communication, 17 April 1996).

30. Cesar Machado, personal communication, 20 February 1996. From what I understand, the highly mountainous terrain separating Cali from the Atlantic coast would have made it difficult for most shortwave sets to pick up radio waves. By the time Machado was involved in shortwave radio, however, in the mid- to late 1950s, more powerful equipment existed that he might have owned, thus enabling him to tune in to Havana stations without interference.

31. Peter Wade, personal communication, 12 January 1995.

32. The musicologist Cristóbal Díaz Ayala, for instance, purchased several thousand 78s in 1994 from a radio station in Barranquilla that had been lying in a vault, forgotten and unused for decades. In 2001 he donated these, along with the thousands of other recordings in his collection, to Florida International University.

33. Jaime Camargo Franco, personal communication, 19 May 1996.

34. Later appropriated by Desi Arnaz and introduced to U.S. audiences through the *I Love Lucy* television series.

35. Personal communication, 20 February 1996 (interview Col96-50).

36. As noted above, the Cuban "rhumba" popularized in North America and Europe during the 1930s was a watered-down version of son performed by urban dance bands. It is not to be confused with the Afro-Cuban rumba tradition, which uses only conga drums, small percussion, and vocals.

37. Medardo Arias, personal communication, 8 May 1996.

38. The archbishop of Lima, Peru, also condemned the mambo (ibid.).

39. Isaacs mentions the *bambuco* in the context of a fiesta celebrated by enslaved Africans working on the Paraiso hacienda, an actual site that lies about ten

miles from Cali. In currulao, *bambuco viejo* is a central genre, and there has been considerable debate as to whether the name "bambuco" is actually of African origin, subsequently adopted during the era of slavery as the name for a completely distinct genre associated with música andina.

40. Personal communication, 30 January 1996 (interview Col96-42). Before signing with Seeco, the Matancera recorded with Panart Records.

41. Personal communication, 23 January 1997. Revered as an old maestro, Tito Cortés continued to perform música antillana until his death in 1998, fronting a group called Tito Cortés y su Conjunto Calima.

Notes to Chapter 2

1. The title of this section is adopted from a 1990 documentary produced for Imágenes TV by Medardo Arias (itself named after a well-known 1972 salsa recording by Ismael Rivera) about the entry of recordings of música antillana and salsa into southwest Colombia.

2. Personal communication, 13 February 1996, (interview Col96-48).

3. Medardo Arias describes this setting in his novel *Jazz para difuntos* (1993).

4. According to Arias, onshore dress was usually a tropical version of a Harlem zoot suit, complete with Panama hat, two-toned shoes, watch fob and chain, and walking stick, all swathed in a thin cloud of vetivert cologne (personal communication, 6 May 1996, interview Col96-61).

5. Interviewed in the television documentary *Memorias de Buenaventura* (1989, Imágenes TV, produced by Medardo Arias).

6. Personal communication, 20 February 1996 (interview Col96-50).

7. Personal communication, 6 May 1996 (interview Col96-61).

8. These included Peregoyo y su Combo Vacaná, La Gigante del Pacífico, and the Orquesta Tumbacasas (literally, "make the house fall down," so named because when they played, people danced so hard that they fell right through the rickety wooden floors typical of houses at the time).

9. Ivan Forbes is an Afro-Colombian philosopher from Buenaventura. He was interviewed in the television documentary *Memorias de Buenaventura* (1989, Imágenes TV, produced by Medardo Arias).

10. Personal communication, 19 February 1996. The following details about the record trade are based on the taped interview conducted with Lisímaco Paz on this date (interview Col96-49).

11. The same year, incidentally, that Cali was appointed the capital of the newly created province of El Valle.

12. Personal communication, 20 February 1996. This and the following anecdotes about the Zona are taken from our taped interview on this date (interview Col96-50).

13. Medardo Arias, personal communication, 6 May 1997 (interview Col96-61).

14. Personal communication, 19 February 1996 (interview Col96-49).

15. Hernán González, personal communication, 11 January 1997. This speech is similar to the *jeringonza* still used by older people on the Pacific Coast, with the vocable "po-" inserted between each syllable of a word.

16. Indeed, movies influenced the Zona's "community" in multiple ways. The transvestites who converged along Carrera 12, for example, all had nicknames

adopted from Mexican film actresses, e.g., Tongolele (Cesar Machado, personal communication, 20 February 1996).

17. This step involves alternating the left and right feet on each beat of a 4/4 bar, but stepping back on the same foot for beats 4 and 1 (or beats 2 and 3, if the move is inverted to start on the second half of the bar). Hence, the step is: left–right–left–left / right–left–right–right / left–right–left–left, etc. Some dance instructors conceptualize this as a series of two "short" (lasting one beat) steps and one "long" (lasting two beats) step, alternating left and right feet: short (L)–short (R)–long (L) / short (R)–short (L)–long (R), etc.

18. Personal communication, 8 May 1997 (interview Col96-63).

19. Personal communication, 13 February 1996 (interview Col96-48).

20. Personal communication, 8 May 1996 (interview Col96-63).

21. Dancers from the first period (1940s–50s) included Alberto Insuasto, Antonio Silva, El Negro Johnson, Manuel "Natilla," Félix Blanata, Juan Salazar, Benigno Holguín, "El Tuerto" Vinasco, Fanor Escobar, Manuel Rosero, Dimas Gómez, José Domingo, El Negro Conde, Pedro Nel Colonia, and "Chango." In the second period (1950s–early 60s) were "Cayayo" (Pedro Ramos), "Lovaina" (Ghandi Hazzi), "El Chato" (Miguel Angel Barrios), Pedro Castro, Carlos Valencia Parra, Alberto Barritos "El Papero," and Jaime López "Chocolatina" (these last three formed a show group called Trío de los Pachucos), Carlos Ríos (dubbed the Colombian Tin Tán), "Romil" (Jaime Vidal), and Armando "El Profesor" Bernal. The last period (late 1960s–1970s) included Evelio Carabalí and Esmeralda, Jimmy "Boogaloo," Amparo "Arrebato" Ramos and Telembí King, Watussi and María, Félix "Veintemillas," "Catacolí," "La Leona," Ada Umaña, Diego Dusán, Cheché, Horacio Henao, and "Lápiz" (Marcos Torres).

22. Hernán González, personal communication, 11 January 1997.

23. Personal communication, 25 August 1995 (interview Col95-28).

24. Gary Domínguez, personal communication, 20 November 1995 (interview Col95-34).

25. This observation was made to me by Pedro Ariza, a university student from Bogotá who often visits friends in Cali and attends the viejotecas regularly (personal communication, 24 August 2000). I myself did not notice this during my study of the viejotecas, but this may simply be the fault of my untrained eye, since I am not really a soccer fan and could easily have overlooked it.

26. Personal communication, 30 July 1995 (interview Col95-18).

27. During a visit with Hernán González, he pulled out a video with clips from old Mexican movie musicals to show me. One of these clips featured a family party in which everyone was learning how to dance mambo, and Don Hernán enthusiastically explained that Cali's champús bailables looked just like that (11 January 1997).

28. See Guzmán Campos, Fals Borda, and Umaña Luna 1962–64; Pearce 1990; Bushnell 1993; and Bergquist, Peñaranda and Sánchez 1992, 1999, for greater historical analysis of violence in Colombia. A recent issue of the *NACLA Report on the Americas,* "Colombia: Old Wars, New Guns" (vol. 34, no. 2 [Sept.–Oct. 2000]), analyzes the current situation in Colombia and the so-called war on drugs.

29. Indeed, after the 1999 earthquake that devastated the region around Armenia and Pereira, the Caleño government, faced with hundreds of displaced quake victims, threatened to seal city borders and remove all land invasions.

30. Esneda de Caicedo, personal communication, 30 July 1995 (interview Col95-19).

31. This list is taken from "La juventud caleña: Castiga la baldosa" (Caleño Youth Punish the Floor Tiles), in *El Occidente,* 6 July 1974, page 13.

32. This refers to dancing so close to one's partner and so rapidly that one's belt buckle gets polished. According to Carlos Ramos, this expression was also used among Puerto Rican youth of the 1970s (personal communication, 2 June 1997).

33. Personal communication, 31 May 1996.

34. Lisímaco Paz, personal communication, 19 February 1996 (interview Col96-49).

35. Watussi's influence on Caleño dancing has also been corroborated for me on many occasions by Medardo Arias, who was a boy in Buenaventura when Watussi emerged as a prominent local dancer.

36. Medardo Arias, personal communication 6 May 1996 (interview Col96-61); Arias also recounts this in 1991: 247.

37. The Panamian reggae–dance hall artist El General notes that when he was growing up in the town of Rio Abajo during the 1970s, he and his friends would similarly speed up recordings of Jamaican reggae music for a faster dance-hall feel (*Latin Music On-line, 27* May 1997).

38. Gerardo Rosales, personal communication, July 1992.

39. Gary Domínguez, personal communication, 20 November 1995 (interview Col95-34).

40. Henry Manyoma, personal communication, 24 January 1997 (interview Col97-70).

41. Personal communication, 28 May 1995.

42. Personal communication, 24 January 1997 (interview Col97-70).

43. Ulloa's conceptualization of Caleña bodies as objects and not vehicles of pleasure, however, is problematic. Caleña women are relatively "independent" from patriarchal stereotypes of the virtuous, modest and subservient woman, but they are hardly free from male dominance. In the sphere of salsa dancing, for instance, men are still generally expected to make the "first move," be it simply asking for a dance or (where appropriate) moving the language of dance toward a more intimate sexual or romantic encounter. Aparicio suggests an alternate model for understanding Latina sensuality as a re-appropriated "aesthetics of the body," in which high heels, makeup, short skirts and tight clothes are seen as ways of asserting sexual agency and freedom from the confines of patriarchy and the Church, which impose norms of chaste behavior for "decent" women (1998: 151).

44. Reported in *El Occidente,* 29 December 1968.

45. The list presented here, although no doubt incomplete, is compiled from various personal accounts, newspaper ads, and Ulloa 1992: 411.

46. Amparo "Arrebato" Ramos recalls winning as much as 500 pesos at one contest, a significant amount back in the late 1960s (personal communication, 25 August 1995, interview Col95-28).

47. Amparo Ramos, personal communication 25 August 1995 (interview Col95-28).

48. Carabalí explained that he actually had been involved with the Ballet de la Salsa during its initial stages but left after a dispute over leadership roles (personal communication, 8 May 1996, interview Col96-63).

49. *El Occidente,* 16 August 1975.

50. Personal communication, 19 February 1996 (interview Col96-49).

51. Personal communication, 16 April 1996 (interview Col96-54).

52. Medardo Arias, personal communication, 10 April 1998.

53. Based on my own archival research of these newspapers during and immediately following Holy Week that year—it may have been reported at some other point.

54. Gary Domínguez, personal communication, 20 November 1995 (interview Col95-34).

55. The Cali cartel was much less incendiary than its rivals in Medellín, using bribery and political influence on government and court officials, rather than outright attacks (Bushnell 1993: 264). Occasional attacks between the two cartels sometimes contributed to Cali's urban violence but were not significant. Most of the fighting in clubs and restaurants occurred between hit men hired by the cartel and its local enemies. The influx of wealth into Cali during the 1980s and 1990s also prompted crimes attributed to "marginals" from the city's poorer sectors, as nighttime revelers became targets for muggings and homes were subject to break-ins.

56. Amparo Ramos, personal communication, 25 August 1995 (interview Col95-28).

57. The professional Caleño salsa dancer Andres Leudo explained to me that different styles of 1970s salsa dancing, associated with different barrios and even with specific clubs, have survived into the mid-1990s. Unfortunately, we were never able to coordinate our schedules so that I could go observe these spots (personal communication, 16 May 1996).

58. María Teresa Vélez, personal communication, 28 January 1999.

59. Changó, whose name invokes the Yoruba deity of thunder and force, is a luxury nightclub in Juanchito. It was the first place to adopt the viejoteca idea after the demise of the Cali cartel.

Notes to Chapter 3

1. The Asociación Puertorriqueña de Coleccionistas de Música Popular, spearheaded by Pedro Malavet Vega, Cristóbal Díaz Ayalá, and others.

2. Fernando Taisechi, personal communication, 24 August 1995 (interview Col95–27).

3. Located on Calle 19 between Carrera 1 and Carrera 2, in the working-class neighborhood of San Nicolás, El Bar de Wiliam was the unofficial headquarters of the leftist intellectual set (Ulloa 1992: 412). Alberto Borja recalls that the atmosphere was always incredibly raucous, with people drinking, laughing, and dancing on tables. A local shoemaker from Barrio Obrero used to hang out next to the DJ and in the silence after each song ended would declaim "Mamacita ¿porqué me hiciste tan rumbero? hijo 'e puta!" (roughly, "Baby, why did you make me such a partier, dammit!"), a cue for everyone to

fall into spasms of laughter (personal communication, 24 August 1997, interview Col95-26).

4. Personal communication, 24 August 1995 (interview Col95-27)

5. This observation is again Taisechi's. I should note, however, that Taisechi belongs to an important circle of Caleño intellectuals who embraced salsa during the 1970s, and I take his commentary to be representative of a large group of local salsa aficionados.

6. After armistice negotations following the bombing, M-19 laid down arms and became a legitimate political party in 1990. The data about M-19 and salsa meetings was given to me by various informants in Cali, whose identities I prefer to keep anonymous.

7. Personal communication, 24 August 1995 (interview Col95-27).

8. By the 1980s exploits such as car bombings and kidnappings had become conventional acts of urban terrorism in Colombia; but in the 1970s, less harmful deeds were also done, such as robbing milk trucks and distributing the bottles free to a poor barrio of Cali. (Understandably, I choose to keep my sources anonymous.)

9. Personal communication, 9 November 1995 (interview Col95-31).

10. This calculation is based on figures cited to me by Cesar Machado (interview Col96-50) and Victor Caicedo (interview Col95-18).

11. To me this seems to be one of the key "symbolic values" that Ulloa alludes to in his assessment of salsa's impact in Cali, but he does not fully analyze it in his appraisal of recordings and their significance in Caleño popular life (1992: 443–45).

12. Personal communication, 20 November 1995 (interview Col95-34).

13. Personal communication, 29 December 1995 (interview Col96-40).

14. According to Gary Domínguez, Cali is the largest market for recordings in all Colombia (ibid., Col95-35). Although Medellín is the center of the national recording industry, more records (both domestic and import) are actually sold in Cali. According to Henry and Wilson Manyoma, since the 1970s vendors have come from as far afield as Tumaco and even Quito, Ecuador, to buy large stocks of records wholesale in Cali (personal communication, 24 January 1997, Col97-71).

15. Kuky Preciado, 29 December 1995 (interview Col96-40).

16. Personal communication, 10 March 1995.

17. Although the Domínguez family is middle class, according to Gary's mother, Doña Stella (a woman of paisa background), Mallarino's close friendships with teammates from América (one of Cali's top soccer clubs) often brought them to Barrio Obrero, hence the family's strong orientation toward música antillana and salsa. Personal communication, August 1995.

18. Desi Arnaz's "Babalu" routine, introduced to U.S. audiences on the *I Love Lucy* series, was modeled directly on Miguelito Valdés's performances.

19. After living in Cali since the 1970s, Camargo returned to his native Cartagena in early 1997, taking his collection with him.

20. Personal communication, 25 March 1996 (interview Col96-55).

21. Personal communication, 20 November 1995 (interview Col96-34).

22. These include Gary Domínguez (Taberna Latina) and others such as Kike Escobar (Congo Bongó, Bachata) and Richard Yory (Tiempo Libre, Convergencia).

23. Personal communication, 20 November 1995 (interview Col95-34).

24. Personal communication, 11 January 1996 (interview Col96-39).

25. Personal communication, 1 June 1996 (interview Col96-64b).

26. Personal communication, 1 June 1996 (interview Col96-64b). The Puerto Rican term *salsateca*, referring to a discotheque for dancing salsa, might also have had an influence. I am unable to explain why Caleños use an "o" instead of the grammatically correct "a," but this might relate to cognate local terms such as *salsómano* (salsa fanatic).

27. Personal communication, 11 April 1996 (interview Col96-59)

28. This was also prompted as a show of solidarity for the fact that Proyecto Omega received no support from city radio stations—Angulo refused to pay bribe money for his records to be aired.

29. Personal communication, 20 November 1995 (interview Col95-34).

30. Personal communication, 20 November 1995 (interview Col95-34).

31. Personal communication, 11 April 1996 (interview Col96-59).

32. Personal communication, 16 March 1995. See also note 37.

33. Personal communication, 1 June 1996 (interview Col96-64b).

34. Personal communication, 20 November 1995 (interview Col95-34).

35. RCN, Caracol and Todelar are connected to large national radio networks (see Múnera 1992).

36. See "El tambor exige su respeto: melómanos cuestionan línea del FM," *El Pais,* 29 December 1992. I personally witnessed the formation of the 1994 manifesto.

37. "La terapia de la 'salsa positiva': Kike Escobar, un melómano que trabaja por la juventud," *El Pais,* 27 December 1992.

38. Personal communication, 3 November 1995 and 10 April 1996 (interview Col96-58).

39. Personal communication, 11 January 1996 (interview Col96-38).

40. Personal communication, 10 April 1996 (interview Col 96-58).

41. Kuky Preciado, personal communication, 11 January 1996 (interview Col96-38).

42. Brewster and Broughton describe a similar phenomenon with the rise of northern soul in Manchester and other working-class industrial towns of northern England in the late 1970s, where a huge youth club scene—predating the later raves—was formed around rare 1960s Motown records (2000, Chapter 4).

43. Vanegas Muñoz details, through interviews and ethnographic study, the pernicious culture of youth gangs, robberies, drug use, and murders that residents of Aguablanca district live through every day.

Notes to Chapter 4

1. Christopher Washburne notes that he played this tune at several dances in the New York City area during the mid to late 1980s (personal communication, 30 October 1996). The song is also enshrined in the forgettable Hollywood movie *Salsa* (1988).

2. Personal communication, 24 January 1997 (interview Col97-70).

3. Personal communications, 31 December 1996 and 23 January 1997, respectively.

4. See Arteaga 1990: 119–25 for further details on Fruko's early years and Joe Arroyo's subsequent development.
5. Medardo Arias, personal communication, 3 August 1997.
6. Felipe Jaramillo, Discosfuentes publicist, personal communication, 6 March 1995. This observation was later confirmed for me by Wilson Saoco, Fruko's lead vocalist at the time (personal communication, 24 January 1997, interview Col97-70).
7. Fruko performed in Los Corralejos de Majagual, one of the most popular música tropical bands in Colombia of the 1960s, before embarking on a career as a salsa musician.
8. "El disco de la Feria: 'Las calcñas son como las flores,'" *El Occidente,* 26 December 1975. According to Peter Wade, figures for successful record sales in Colombia are relatively low: an album that sells only 20,000 is considered gold, and one that sells over 120,000 is considered triple platinum (personal communication, 10 January 1995).
9. Personal communication, 20 March 1996 (interview Col96-53).
10. Santiago Mejía, personal communication, 20 March 1996 (interview Col96-53).
11. Personal communication, 24 January 1997 (interview Col97-70).
12. Personal communication, 15 November 1995 (interview Col95-33a).
13. Medardo Arias, personal communication, 24 March 2001.
14. Medardo Arias, personal communication, 29 September 2001.
15. Hermes Manyoma, personal communication, 24 January 1997 (interview Col97-70).
16. The artists on this tour included Celia Cruz, Johnny Pacheco, Papo Lucca, Rubén Blades, Cheo Feliciano, Pete "Conde" Rodríguez, Roberto Roena, Adalberto Santiago, Pupi Legaretta, Ismael Quintana, Luigi Texidor, and Yomo Toro (*El Pais,* 2 August 1980). Also appearing opposite the Fania All-Stars was Conjunto Clásico with Tito Nieves, a popular new New York salsa band that is said to have been founded, in part, with Landa's backing.
17. A quick perusal of salsa magazines from the period, such as *Latin New York* (published in New York City) and *Swing Latino* (published in Caracas, Venezuela), confirms that this circuit was the principal route for international live salsa during the time.
18. Most of my information about Larry Landa's life history has been provided through various conversations with Medardo Arias. Arias was never an employee of Landa's but often covered events that Landa sponsored.
19. Personal communication, 20 March 1996 (interview Col96-53).
20. Personal communication, 6 February 1995 (interview Col95-22).
21. Medardo Arias, personal communication, 17 October 1997.
22. José Agüirre, personal communication, 4 February 1996 (interview Col96-45).
23. Personal communication, 9 April 1996 (interview Col96-57).
24. Charles Keil's suggestive commentaries about "on-the-beat" and "behind-the-beat" grooves (1966) are particularly helpful in conceiving the differences between Colombian salsa and other styles. These rhythmic subtleties, of course, comprise minute distinctions that are extremely difficult to convey through written description but are immediately perceived upon hearing.

25. Personal communication, 22 February 1996 (interview Col96-51).
26. A reference to Cali's two main soccer teams, América and Deportivo Cali. Both teams have an enormous popular base in Cali's working and middle classes, and this scene is closely tied to salsa.
27. During the last section of the tune, allusion is made to two very popular nightclubs in the 1980s scene: Cañandonga and El Escondite (owned by a fellow named Manolo).
28. At the time that "Cali pachanguero" became a hit, Varela acknowledged the influence of the Sonora Matancera and other Cuban groups (*El Occidente*, 24 December 1984).
29. Interview with Umberto Valverde, "Jairo Varela: La moda pasa, la salsa queda," *La Palabra* 34 (November 1994): 8–9.
30. Cesar Monge, personal communcation, 14 August 1995 (interview Col95-22).
31. Personal communication, 4 February 1996 (interview Col96-45).
32. The singers during this period were Alvaro del Castillo (1980–84) and Moncho Santana (1984–1987). When Santana left to form his own salsa band, Varela contacted the Puerto Rican vocalist Tito Gómez (former vocalist with the Sonora Ponceña), and Gómez fronted Niche from 1987 to 1990.
33. Alexis Lozano, personal communication, 6 February 1995 (interview Col95-4).
34. Lozano's involvement with chirimía dates back to his childhood. Since the late 1980s he has produced record albums and also a television documentary featuring old chirimía maestros from Quibdó. In the late 1990s, he began recording and producing the contemporary chirimía band Saboreo, which gained widespread popularity in Cali.
35. This practice is also common in West African popular styles such as Yoruban *jùjú* (Waterman 1990).
36. Every 7 December (Feast of the Virgin of Mercy) colored lights are strung up throughout the streets of Cali, and they remain there until after the Feast of the Three Kings, or Epiphany (6 January).
37. In rhythmic transcription the figure reads:

38. Personal communication, 6 February 1995 (interview Col95-4).
39. Personal communication, 6 February 1995 (interview Col95-4).
40. Personal communication, 12 May 1995 (interview Col94–1b). All other comments by Jaime Henao in this section are taken from this interview.
41. These include "Plástico" (Willie Colón and Ruben Blades), "Bomba carambomba" (Sonora Ponceña), and "Mi desengaño" (Roberto Roena). These tunes are from the late 1970s and early 1980s and were very popular among Caleño salsa fans.
42. From, respectively, *Perfume de Paris* (1990) and *La Misma Gente: Ah! Tú sabes* (1991).

Notes to Chapter 5

1. This term, although common, is often used pejoratively. Carrying with it the implication of "mediocre" and "insignificant," the term obscures the actual

merit of many lesser-known bands, e.g., Proyecto, Omega. It also places long-standing and musically excellent local bands such as Octava Dimensión, La Ley, and La Gran Banda on a second tier because they have not gained the same international exposure and commercial success as top-ranking bands.

2. Rafael Restrepo, presentation at the Universidad del Valle, 6 December 1994.

3. Source: *Anuario Estadístico del Valle de Cauca 1994,* p. 90.

4. Peter Manuel, for example notes that about fifteen top-name salsa orquestas and an undetermined number of lesser bands (often assembled at the last moment for a gig) are active in New York (1994: 84). Even if up to sixty salsa bands can be accounted for in New York, however, this is distributed over a municipal population roughly three to four times larger than that of Cali's.

5. For instance, I did not recognize a quarter of the names of local bands listed in the 31 December 1997 online edition of *El País.*

6. Rafael Quintero, "Crisis y esplendor de la salsa caleña," *La Palabra* 47 (1 March 1996): 5.

7. See, for example, Jeremy Marre's 1983 film *Shotguns and Accordions: Music from the Marijuana-Growing Regions of Colombia* (Shanachie 1205).

8. Richard Sandoval, a melómano acquaintance of mine whom I often ran into at Don Pablo Solano's and at the Taberna Latina, explained to me that he played congas in his company's orquesta (personal communication, 24 February 1996).

9. Personal communication, 29 February 1996. La Identidad broke off from EMCALI in 1987, recording its debut album. By this point the live scene in Cali was starting to peak, and no doubt the band saw that more commercial opportunities lay in being an independent orquesta than in staying with the company.

10. Personal communication, 20 November 1997.

11. According to Luis Figueroa, the band that most closely approximates El Son del Trébol in Puerto Rico is the Police Band of San Juan, which is well known for its big-band performances of danzas, plenas, and bombas—but they do not perform salsa (personal communication, 22 March 1998).

12. Guido Hoyos, "De salsa hasta la coronilla," *La gaceta dominical, El País,* 16 July 1995, 14–17.

13. Alvaro Bejarano, "No solo salsa," *Cali Cultural,* July 1989, 47–50.

14. Guido Hoyos, "El caminante de la cultura," *La gaceta dominical, El País,* 20 August 1995, 19.

15. The Instituto Popular de Cultura was actually established in 1947 as a small institution dedicated to the study, preservation, and transmission of Colombian folkloric genres. It did not start to have an impact on local musical life, however, until the 1980s, when programs were expanded to include basic musical training. Similarly, the music department of the Universidad del Valle was established in 1961, but it did not begin to have an impact on local musical life until the 1980s—a result not only of greater numbers of students attending the public university, but also of increased interest in musical performance.

16. Personal communication, 27 December 1995.

17. Sarli Delgado, personal communication, 12 May 1996 (interview Col96-64a).

18. Personal communication, 20 March 1995 (interview Col95-53).

19. The salsa world's standards for mastery of brass and wind instruments are similar to those established for European classical music—i.e., accurate intonation, breath control, ability to play rapidly and fluidly, facility with double-tonguing techniques, volume, and strength in the high register.

20. Personal communication, 12 May 1996 (interview Col96-64a). As a vocalist and bass player, Sarli Delgado has been performing salsa since she was nine, when she joined the orquesta juvenil La Charanguita.

21. Personal communication, 9 August 1995 (interview Col95-20).

22. Vera Kutzinksi explores the discursive synthesis of sugar, race, and sexuality in nineteenth-century Cuba in the figure of the "hot-blooded plantation mulata" (1993). Similar stereotypes have spread to other Latin American countries, including Colombia, and seem to have informed the image that CBS Records executives wished to impose on these Caleña musicians.

23. As several feminist scholars have pointed out, the dichotomy between "public" and "private" (or "domestic") domains naturalizes different spheres of social life in gendered terms, assigning masculine attributes to the former and feminine ones to the latter. This dichotomy, often taken for granted even in academic discourse, erases the historical process whereby the public/private distinction was engendered in the first place to legitimize and reproduce certain systems of access to economic, political, and cultural resources (Yanagisako and Collier, 1987).

24. Personal communication, 15 November 1995 (interview Col95-33a). The following data come from this same interview.

25. Ibid.

26. Ibid.

27. Personal communication, 12 May 1996 (interview Col96-64a).

28. Patricia, Ochoa's niece and administrative assistant, personal communication, 16 December 1994.

29. The 1995 listings indicated fifty-two officially registered dance orquestas. Although not all of these are strictly salsa bands, these figures represent the great majority of local orquestas.

30. Personal communication, 10 November 1995 (interview Col95-32).

31. Personal communication, 22 February 1996 (interview Col96-51).

32. Personal communication, 23 November 1995.

33. Chucho Ramírez, personal communication, 20 February 1995.

34. Personal communication, 22 February 1996 (interview Col96-51).

35. Chucho Ramírez, personal communication, 22 February 1996 (interview Col96-51).

36. Dorancé Lorza, personal communication 18 February 1996.

37. The hallmarks of timba include a dynamic polyrhythmic base, virtuoso horn lines, jazz-influenced solos, and emphatic bass and drum kicks. The most representative exponent of timba is NG La Banda.

38. Personal communication, 23 February 1996 (interview Col96-52). The first salsa romántica production ever was *Noches calientes,* produced by the New York musician and composer Louie Ramírez in 1982.

39. Personal communication, 22 February 1996 (interview Col96-51).

Notes to Chapter 6

1. The display of lights, located on Cali's main commercial road, is mounted from 7 December (Feast of the Virgin of Mercy)—a national holiday celebrated in honor of the Virgin Mary's trip to Bethlehem—and stays up until 6 January, the Feast of the Three Kings (Epiphany).
2. During the late 1950s, Bermúdez was contracted to bring his orquesta as the resident band of the Club San Fernando, a social club for the Caleño middle class. His famous porro "San Fernando" dates from this period.
3. Richie Ray and Bobby Cruz, "Sonido bestial," *El bestial sonido* (Vaya 1, 1971); "Juan Sebastian Fuga," *1975* (Vaya 33, 1974).
4. Umberto Valverde, personal communication, 6 November 1995 (interview Col95-30).
5. *El País,* 30 December 1969, p. 9.
6. Medardo Arias, "Y Richie no volvió: sus seguidores lo esperan cada año en Cali," *El País,* 29 December 1977. The two song titles refer to a popular raspa number and one of Richie Ray's signature tunes.
7. Medardo Arias, personal communication, 5 March 2001.
8. Compiled from Feria reports in *El País* and *El Occidente* for these years.
9. "Casetas no son populares: Las gentes [sic] prefieren bailar en verbenas," *El País,* 28 December 1980.
10. Ricky Rodríguez (Puerto Rican salsa arranger and pianist of Orquesta Mulenze), personal communication, 18 June 1995.
11. Rereleased on José Mangual Jr., *Tribute to Chano Pozo* (True Ventures 1001, 1989), and also on *Mis mejores exitos* (Campanero 514, 1994).
12. Personal communication, 3 June 1996. The other anecdotes about Mangual's percussion workshop and his following are also from this date.
13. See Sonora Ponceña, *On the Right Track* (Inca I 1084). The quote comes during the montuno, when the Ponceña names various Caleño salsa bands, and sings "La Misma Gente, con su 'Co, titico, titico, co, co'."
14. The Coliseo del Pueblo (Coliseum of the People) was another popular concert venue through the 1980s. This is where the Fania All-Stars performed in 1980.
15. *El País,* 27 December 1980; *El País,* 27 December 1981.
16. Personal communication, 20 November 1997. D'León performed at the Feria during three successive years, 1984–86. During the 1990s he has continued to appear, but only every two or three years, and without this ritual closing act.
17. Personal communication, 5 February 1996 (interview Col96-46).
18. Personal communication, 9 April 1995 (interview Col96-57).
19. Kike Escobar, personal communication, 11 April 1996 (interview Col96-59). The very first event at the Universidad del Valle was organized in order to raise funds to send the water polo team to an international tournament.
20. Reported in "Homenaje a la Rumba," *El Occidente,* 31 December 1982. The event was organized by Rafael Quintero, and invited speakers were Reynaldo Ceballos (Cali); Cesar Pagano (Bogotá); and Rafael Bassi, Jairo Solano, and Gilberto Marrenco (Barranquilla).
21. Stella Domínguez personal communication, 6 January 1997. Vanegas Muñoz 1998 confirms the importance of salsa music for Caleño gang members.

22. Front-page report in *El Occidente*, 28 December 1988.
23. Alvaro Béjarano and Umberto Valverde, personal communications, 22 December 1995 (interview Col95-36) and 4 May 1995 (interview Col95-6).
24. Bauman and Sawin (1991) observe similar tendencies in U.S. folk-life festivals.
25. These debates were reported in *El Pais* (online) through the month of October 2000.

Notes to Chapter 7

1. Los Nemus is led by the Quibdo-born vocalist Alexis Murillo, who resettled in Cali during the early 1990s. The band has recorded a number of albums with Discosfuentes and is well known in Europe, owing to a 1992 concert tour and distribution arrangements with World Circuit Records in London. Ironically, the band is relatively unknown in Cali or the rest Colombia—Murillo's principal followers are Afro-Colombians from the Pacific coast and the northern Cauca Valley, who love the son montuno style that forms the backbone of his repertoire and his ability to improvise earthy, picaresque soneros. I was invited as a substitute to play piano for this gig, since he did not have a regular pianist at that moment.
2. *Juga* is a genre of strophic songs associated with the Adoraciones del Niño Dios. What I heard was similar to the recording made by Portes de Roux (1986b), featuring singers and musicians from another town (Mingo).
3. Ana María Arango, personal communication, 3 March 2001.

Glossary

agüelulo: In Cali, a popular afternoon dance context for teenagers in the late 1960s, with no alcohol served. These were usually held on weekends. Athletic prowess was emphasized, and dances would last from 3:00 to 8:00 P.M. The *agüelulos* died out by the mid-1970s.

alegría: Happiness, delight.

audición: Literally, "listening." In Cali, this term refers to special discographical tributes to individual salsa artists and ensembles, usually featuring a retrospective of their musical careers. These were initiated on a weekly or bimonthly basis by Gary Domínguez at the Taberna Latina, but other *salsotecas* and *tabernas* adopted the *audición* format in order to generate special interest among their clientele.

balada: Spanish-language sentimental pop ballad.

bolero: Cuban lyrical song form developed during the late nineteenth century and popularized throughout Latin America during the 1920s, 1930s, and 1940s, especially by Mexican and Argentine singers. It features a slow tempo and poetic lyrics, usually of lost love and heartbreak.

bomba: Afro-Puerto Rican genre dating back to colonial days, developed by slaves on the sugar plantations of eastern Puerto Rico. Performed on three barrel-shaped drums called *barriles* and accompanied by vocals and small percussion. *Bomba* features a very volatile and kinetic dance style characterized by much interplay between the lead solo drum and dancers.

bugalú: Popular early salsa form of the mid- to late 1960s, fusing rhythm and blues elements with Cuban-based sounds. It is characterized by slow to midtempo performance, I–IV–V–I progressions, and hand claps and/or percussion on beats 2 and 4.

Caleño (fem. *Caleña*): A person or thing from Cali.

campana: Large cowbell, usually played by the bongo player, used during the *montuno* section of a *son* or salsa tune to play downbeat accents.

campanero: Cowbell player. In Cali, this also refers to the audience play-along musician who brings this instrument to concerts to accompany the music.

caseta: Dance hall.

chachachá: Variant of the danzón that uses a medium-slow tempo and is marked by a strong downbeat accent. Dancers' feet emphasize "cha-cha-*chá*."

champús bailable: Prototype of the *agüelulo* dance context.

charanga: Typical ensemble of Cuban music, associated with *danzón* and *cha-chachá* and characterized by flute, violins, and timbales.

chirimía: Typical Afro-Colombian town-band music from Chocó province, featuring raucous brass and clarinet playing, double-headed bass drum, cymbals, and a small drum kit. Not to be confused with the fife-and-drum ensembles of indigenous culture that extend from Mexico down through the South American Andes.

chombo: Local Buenaventura slang for black U.S. and Caribbean sailors who docked in the port.

chucu-chucu: See *raspa.*

clave: Central time line of salsa and Cuban music. Can be phrased as 3-2 or 2-3:

conga: Large, conical single-headed hand drum of Cuban origin, also known as *tumbadora,* featured in all salsa bands.

conjunto: Literally, "combo." Small six- or seven-piece ensemble for Cuban *son* that emerged during the 1920s with the format of *tres* (Cuban guitar), bongo, claves, maracas, bass, voices, and sometimes trumpet. During the 1930s this was enlarged with the addition of piano, more percussion, and more trumpets.

conjunto de gaita: Small flute-and-drum ensemble that plays traditional *cumbia* on Colombia's Atlantic coast.

coro: Literally, "chorus." Refers to the backup chorus that alternates with the lead singer in salsa and Cuban music. The term also refers to the refrains sung by the backup chorus, in alternation with the *pregones* (calls) of the lead vocalist, or a solo instrumentalist.

Costeño: Literally, "from the coast." In Colombia this term almost always refers to the Atlantic coast.

cumbia: Principal musical style of the Atlantic coast. It features a strong pulse on 2 and 4, also characterized by a ♩ ♫ ♩ ♫ rhythm. Traditionally played by the *conjunto de gaita* ensemble. The term also refers to a simplified variant of this music (referred to as *raspa* in Colombia) that spread internationally to Mexico, Central America, Ecuador, Peru, and Bolivia.

currulao: Afro-Colombian music from the Pacific coast, traditionally performed on marimba with drum and percussive accompaniment. Strongly African in its polyrhythmic features and vocal style, it is usually performed for social dances but can also be used to accompany religious hymns (*arrullos*).

danzón: Elegant salon dance of Cuban origin. It is traditionally performed by the flute-and-violin *charanga* ensemble.

gaita: This term refers to the double-reed flutes that are used in traditional *cumbia* ensembles (known as *conjunto de gaita*), but most Colombians use it to mean a popular mid-tempo instrumental dance form in *música tropical,* characterized by lilting second and fourth beats.

grile (pl. *griles*)*:* In Cali, a discotheque or nightclub that plays a variety of commercial dance music for clients, mainly *salsa romántica* but also merengue and techno-pop. Decor in such establishments typically includes colored lights, mirrored disco balls, plush upholstered seats, reflective chrome and mirrored surfaces, and, of course, a central dance floor.

guache: Large round shakers used in Costeño music and *música tropical* bands.

guaracha: Light, uptempo Cuban form, emphasizing witty lyrics and a sprightly arrangement. It is very popular among Caleño listeners.

guateque: Literally, a small peasant house or shack, typical in rural Cuba. In Cuba a *fiesta de guateque,* refers to a rollicking, down-home party (cf. *bachata* in the Dominican Republic). *Guateque* has come refer to a certain brand of *salsa dura,* particularly the slow, grinding *son montunos.*

joropo: Harp-based style of the interior plains of Colombia and Venezuela.

mambo: Popular 1940s and 1950s dance craze emphasizing dynamic brass and energetic dancing.

melómano (fem. *melómana*): In Colombia, *melómanos* are more than mere fans; they are aficionados who considers themselves cultivated listeners and knowledgeable connoisseurs. Melómanos tend to be fanatic record collectors, spending huge sums on record purchases and stereo equipment. They share a concern with "authenticity" and tend to favor styles and genres that are musically more complex than typical commercial sounds.

merengue: Principal popular dance genre of the Dominican Republic characterized by a fast duple rhythm, sprightly horn choruses, and catchy refrains.

montuno: Second half of *son* and other Cuban forms. It features call-and-response and heightened rhythmic intensity; instrumental solos might also be played. The term can also refer to the specific syncopated pattern played by the piano.

música andina: In Colombia, the string-based genres performed in the mountainous interior of the country. These are not to be confused with Andean music from Ecuador, Peru, or Bolivia.

música antillana: Literally, "Antillean" music, i.e., music from the (Spanish) Caribbean. In Colombia, this term refers specifically to Cuban-based styles of the 1930s, 1940s, and 1950s.

música tropical: Literally, "tropical music." In Colombia, *música tropical* denotes the cosmopolitan dance band style that emerged in the 1940s and 1950s and features big-band arrangements of traditional Costeño forms, especially *porro* and *gaita* (subgenres of *cumbia*).

orquesta: Literally, "orchestra." The term refers to a dance band with brass and/or wind instruments, piano, bass, and percussion. The *orquesta* can perform various styles, but in Cali the term usually denotes a salsa band.

orquesta femenina: All-woman band.

orquesta infantil: All-child band.

orquesta juvenil: All-youth band.

pachanga: Early salsa form extremely popular in Cali and characterized by an up-tempo, "on-the-beat" feel, with a [♩ ♪ ♩ ♪] pattern emphasized.

papayera: Town band tradition of the Atlantic coast, usually characterized by brass instruments, including trumpets and euphonium, plus mixed European and African-derived percussion.

pasodoble: Marchlike dance of Spanish origin; traditionally popular in Caleño fiestas, particularly of the middle and upper classes.

pelayera: Same as *papayera,* but specifically refers to the bands of San Pelayo, where many innovations were made in adapting traditional Costeño genres to town-band instrumentation.

picó: Large, mobile sound systems developed for street block parties in Cartagena and Barranquilla during the 1960s. Originally associated with salsa dances in working-class Afro-Colombian neighborhoods, the *picós* were instrumental in the local adoption and popularization of African and Afro-Caribbean styles such as *soukous,* Afropop, *mbqanga, soca,* and *zouk* among Afro-Colombians in these cities during the 1980s and early 1990s. These sounds are collectively referred to as *champeta* or *terápia* music and are still strongly associated with *picó* culture.

plena: A Puerto Rican style mixing African and European elements, developed in the working-class neighborhoods of Ponce during the early twentieth century. Played on small round frame drums called *panderetas, plena* is characterized by topical and satirical lyrics and is sometimes referred to as the "singing newspaper."

popular: Refers not only to mass appeal, i.e., popularity, but also to a grassroots sense of "the people." Often used to denote "working class," as in *barrio popular* (working-class neighborhood).

porro: A variant of *cumbia,* developed by town bands (*papayeras*) of the Atlantic coast and further taken up by 1940s and 1950s Costeño dance bands. *Porro* became the main form of *música tropical* and features a vocalist and backup chorus.

pregón: The "call" of a call-and-response form.

raspa: Simplified style of *música tropical* associated with *paisa* (Antioquian) audiences and musicians of Colombia's interior. In *raspa,* the rhythmic swing and syncopated percussion fills of *cumbia* and other Costeño styles are reduced to a more on-the-beat feel. *Raspa* bands of the 1960s were characterized by their use of electric bass, drum kit, and gimmicky Wurlitzer organ sounds. Also known as *chucu-chucu,* this sound spread to Mexico, Central America, Ecuador, Bolivia, and Chile in the 1960s, where it formed the basis for local *cumbia* traditions.

rhumba: A watered-down North Americanized version of Cuban *son,* for ballroom audiences. Not to be confused with Afro-Cuban *rumba.*

rumba: In Colombia, a party or festive outing. Among musicians, references to *rumba* as a musical form follow specialized Cuban usage of the term, which denotes an Afro-Cuban folkloric style performed on *conga* drums. Afro-Cuban *rumba* is subdivided into three main subgenres: *yambú* (slow), *guaguancó* (mid-tempo), and *columbia* (fast).

salsa dura: Literally, "hard" or "heavy" salsa. The term refers to the rougher-edged sound of the 1970s, with a driving rhythm section, punchy brass, and usually some kind of social message in the lyrics.

salsa romántica: Fusion of pop *balada* with salsa rhythm. Less rhythmically intense, but with more sophisticated harmonies and passionately romantic or even erotic lyrics. Main commercial style on the international scene since the late 1980s.

salsoteca: Strictly speaking, a *taberna* that specializes only in salsa, particularly *salsa dura.* Recognizing that salsa is primarily dance music, some of these establishments have modified the "for-listeners-only" philosophy and expanded the premises to include a dance floor. The term *salsoteca* is a cognate derivative of *discoteca,* or discotheque, but diverges sharply from the commercial orientation of these nightclubs (see *grile*).

son: Predominant form of Cuban music, characterized by a two-part verse-*montuno* structure. Traditionally played by small *conjuntos,* it has become the main basis for salsa

sonero: Typical singer of *son,* characterized by a thick, expressive voice and the ability to improvise words and melody.

son montuno: Slow-paced *son,* lacking a verse section, with a very compelling feel.

sonorazo: Caleño slang for a 78 rpm recording of the Sonora Matancera, commonly used during the 1950s and 1960s.

taberna: Literally, "tavern." In Cali a *taberna* commonly refers to a bar that caters to *melómanos,* where clients come not so much to dance as to listen to music. *Tabernas* specialize in a variety of Antillean and South American genres, although the tendency is to play Cuban styles, salsa, and Latin jazz. One of the prime draws in attracting clientele is being able to offer rare or exclusive musical selections. Most *taberna* owners invest a lot of money in top-of-the-line stereo equipment and also have large television screens on which video clips of performers are interspersed with audio selections.

tango: Important Argentine dance style from the late nineteenth and early twentieth centuries. The *canción*-tango (song-tango) emerged during the 1930s and became popular throughout Latin America. Tango was played in the cantinas of Cali's red-light district during the 1940s and 1950s, for listening to more than for dancing.

timbal(es): Set of two tom-toms, mounted on a stand and played with thin sticks. Used traditionally for the *charanga* ensemble, it was then adopted into the *mambo* bands and, later, salsa groups.

tumbao: Rhythmic pattern played by the *conga* drum; also refers to the line played by the double bass or bass guitar in salsa music.

vallenato: Variant of the *cumbia* performed by a small accordion-based ensemble.

verbena: Outdoor temporary stage erected in a street or park for live concerts.

viejoteca: A recent revivalist phenomenon in Cali, *viejotecas* specialize in the variety of dance styles that were popular in Cali during the 1960s, hence the term *viejo* (old). These include proto-salsa forms such as *pachanga* and *bugalú,* as well as Cuban *son* and *guaracha,* Argentine tango, Spanish *pasodoble,* North American fox-trot and charleston, and the *porros, cumbias,* and *gaitas* of Colombian *música tropical.* Unlike the *tabernas* and *salsotecas,* which cater to listeners, the key philosophy of *viejotecas* is to dance.

Bibliography

Abadía Morales, Guillermo. 1973. *La música folklórica colombiana.* Bogotá: Universidad Nacional.

Alba, Richard. 1990. *Ethnic Identity: The Transformation of White America.* New Haven: Yale University Press.

Alén, Olavo. 1984. *De lo afrocubano a la salsa: géneros musicales de Cuba.* San Juan: Cubanacán. [Reprinted in English as *From Afro-Cuban Music to Salsa,* with accompanying CD. Berlin: Piranha Records BCD-PIR 1258, 1998.]

Anuario Estadístico del Valle de Cauca, 1972–74. 1976. Cali: Gobernación del Valle de Cauca.

Anuario Estadístico del Valle de Cauca 1994. 1995. Cali: Gobernación del Valle de Cauca.

Aparicio, Frances R. 1998. *Listening to Salsa: Gender, Latin Popular Music, and Puerto Rican Cultures.* Hanover, N.H.: Wesleyan University Press.

Appadurai, Arjun. 1996. *Modernity at Large: Cultural Dimensions of Globalization.* Minneapolis: University of Minnesota Press.

Aretz, Isabel. 1991. *Historia de la etnomusicología en América Latina: desde la época precolombina hasta nuestros días.* Caracas: Ediciones FUNDEF-CONAC-OEA.

Arias Satizábal, Medardo. 1981. "Esta es la verdadera historia de la salsa." Printed as an eleven-part series in *El Occidente.*

———. 1993. *Jazz para difuntos.* Bogotá: Xajamaya Editores.

Arocha, Jaime. 1992. "Afro-Colombia Denied." *NACLA Report on the Americas* 25 (4): 28–31.

Arteaga, José. 1990. *La Salsa.* 2d rev. ed. Bogotá: Intermedio Editores.

Austerlitz, Paul. 1997. *Merengue: Dominican Music and Dominican Identity.* Philadelphia: Temple University Press.

Averill, Gage. 1997. *A Day for the Hunter, a Day for the Prey: Popular Music and Power in Haiti.* Chicago: University of Chicago Press.

Baéz, Juan Carlos. 1989. *El vínculo es la salsa.* Caracas: Fondo Editorial Tropykos.

Bal, Mieke. 1999. Introduction to *Acts of Memory: Cultural Recall in the Present,* ed. Mieke Bal, Jonathan Crewe, and Leo Spitzer. Hanover, N.H.: Dartmouth University Press.

Barber, Benjamin. 1992. "Jihad versus McWorld." *Atlantic Monthly,* March, 53–63.

Bauman, Richard, and Patricia Sawin. 1991. "The Politics of Participation in Folk-life Festivals." In *Exhibiting Cultures: The Poetics and Politics of Museum Display,* ed. Ivan Karp and Stephen Levine. Washington, D.C.: Smithsonian Institution Press.

Benjamin, Walter. 1968 [1936]. "The Work of Art in the Age of Mechanical Reproduction." In *Illuminations,* edited by Hannah Arendt, translated by Harry Zohn. London: Fantana.

Bergquist, Charles, Ricardo Peñaranda, and Gonzalo Sánchez, eds. 1992. *Violence in Colombia: The Contemporary Crisis in Historial Perspective.* Wilmington, Del.: Scholarly Resources.

———. 1999. *Violence in Colombia, 1990–2000: Waging War and Negotiating Peace.* Wilmington, Del.: Scholarly Resources.

Berliner, Paul. 1994. *Thinking in Jazz: The Infinite Art of Improvisation.* Chicago: University of Chicago Press.

Berríos-Miranda, Marisol. 1990. "Salsa—Whose Music Is It?" Paper presented at the 35th Annual Meeting of the Society for Ethnomusicology, Berkeley, Calif.

———. 1999. "The Significance of Salsa Music for National and Pan-Latino Identity." Ph.D. diss., University of California, Berkeley.

Betancur Alvarez, Fabio. 1993. *Sin clave y bongó no hay son: música afrocubana y confluencias musicales de Colombia y Cuba.* Medellín: Editorial Universidad de Antioquia.

Blum, Joseph. 1978. "Problems of *Salsa* Research," *Ethnomusicology* 22 (1): 137–49.

Boggs, Vernon W., ed. 1992. *Salsiology: Afro-Cuban Music and the Evolution of Salsa in New York City.* Westport, Conn.: Greenwood Press.

Bourdieu, Pierre. 1984. *Distinction: A Social Critique of the Judgement of Taste.* Trans. by Richard Nice. Cambridge, Mass.: Harvard University Press.

———. 1990 [1980]. *The Logic of Practice.* Stanford: Stanford University Press.

Brewster, Bill, and Frank Broughton. 2000. *Last Night a DJ Saved My Life: The History of the Disc Jockey.* New York: Grove.

Burgos Palacios, Alvaro, ed. *Cali: 450 Años.* Cali: Grupo Amigos 80.

Bushnell, David. 1993. *The Making of Modern Colombia: A Nation in Spite of Itself.* Berkeley and Los Angeles: University of California Press.

Caicedo, Andrés. 1977. *¡Que viva la música!* Cali: Editorial Victor Hugo.

Calhoun, Craig. 1995. *Critical Social Theory.* Cambridge: Blackwell Press.

Camargo Franco, Jaime E. 1994. *¡Caribe Soy! Raices musicales afroantillanas.* Medellín: Ediciones Salsa y Cultura.

Cepeda, María Elena. 2001. *"Florecitas rockeras:* Gender and Transnationalism in Colombian Rock." Paper presented at the 2001 Annual Meeting of the American Studies Association, Washington, D.C.

Cheah, Pheng, and Bruce Robbins, eds. 1998. *Cosmopolitics: Thinking and Feeling beyond the Nation.* Minneapolis: University of Minnesota Press.

Chernoff, John Miller. 1979. *African Rhythm and African Sensibility.* Chicago: University of Chicago Press.

Citron, Marcia J. 1993. *Gender and the Musical Canon.* Cambridge: Cambridge University Press.

Crook, Larry. 1982. "A Musical Analysis of the Cuban *Rumba.*" *Latin American Music Review* 3 (1): 93–123.

Courtney, Dave. 2000. *Raving Lunacy: Clubbed to Death; Adventures on the Rave Scene.* London: Virgin.

Cuervo, Germán, ed. 1989. *Historias de amor, salsa, y dolor.* Cali: Cuervo Editores.

Daniel, Yvonne. 1995. *Rumba: Dance and Social Change in Contemporary Cuba.* Bloomington: Indiana University Press.

de Friedemann, Nina S. 1984. "Estudios de negros en la antropología colombiana." In *Un siglo de investigación social: antropología en Colombia,* ed. Nina S. de Friedemann and Jaime Arocha. Bogotá: Etno.

——. 1993. *La Saga del Negro: presencia africana en Colombia.* Bogotá: Instituto de Genética Humana, Pontificia Uniersidad Javeriana.

Delgado, Richard, and Jean Stefancic, eds. 1997. *Critical White Studies: Looking Behind the Mirror.* Philadelphia: Temple University Press.

Derrida, Jacques. 1967. *Of Grammatology.* Baltimore: John Hopkins University Press.

——. 1978. *Writing and Difference.* Chicago: University of Chicago Press.

Díaz-Díaz, Edgardo. 1998. "Salsa, género y etnicidad: el baile como arena social." *Revista de ciencias sociales* (Universidad de Puerto Rico) 4: 80–104.

Domínguez, Gary. n.d. "Salsoteca abierta: ¿Qué es el guateque?" *El Occidente.*

Douglas, Mary, and Baron Isherwood. 1979. *The World of Goods: Towards an Anthropology of Consumption,* 2d ed. New York: Routledge.

Duany, Jorge. 1984. "Popular Music in Puerto Rico: Toward an Anthropology of Salsa." *Latin American Music Review* 5 (2): 186–216.

Dufrasne-González, Emanuel. 1994. *Puerto Rico también tiene ¡tambó! Recopilación de artículos sobre la plena y la bomba.* Río Grande: Paracumbé.

Echevarría Alvarado, Félix. 1984. *La plena: Orígen, sentido, y desarollo en el folklore puertorriqueño.* Santurce: Express.

Escobar Navia, Rodrigo. 1986. "450 años de solidaridad." In *Cali: 450 años,* ed. Alvaro Burgos Palacios. Cali: Grupo Amigos 80.

Fanon, Frantz. 1965. *The Wretched of the Earth.* Translated by Constance Farrington. New York: Grove.

Featherstone, Mike. ed. 1990. *Global Culture: Nationalism, Globalization, and Modernity.* London: Sage.

Feld, Steven. 1984. "Communication, Music, and Speech About Music." *Yearbook for Traditional Music* 16: 1–18. Revised and reprinted in Charles Keil and Steven Feld, *Music Grooves,* Chicago: University of Chicago Press, 1994.

Fikenstscher, Kai. 2000. *"You Better Work!" Underground Dance Music in New York City.* Hanover, N.H.: Wesleyan University Press.

Fine, Michelle, ed. 1997. *Off White: Readings on Race, Power, and Society.* New York: Routledge.

Flores, Juan. 2000. *From Bomba to Hip-Hop: Puerto Rican Culture and Latino Identity.* New York: Columbia University Press.

Foucault, Michel. 1977. *Discipline and Punish.* New York: Pantheon.

——. 1978–88. *The History of Sexuality.* 4 vols. New York: Pantheon.

Frank, André Gunder. 1967. *Capitalism and Underdevelopment in Latin America: Historical Studies of Chile and Brazil.* New York: Monthly Review Press.

Fraser Delgado, Celeste, and José Esteban Muñoz, eds. 1997. *Everynight Life: Culture and Dance in Latin/o America.* Durham, N.C.: Duke University Press.

Friedman, Thomas. 1995. "Global System, Globalization, and the Parameters of

Modernity." In *Global Modernities*, ed. Mike Featherstone, Scott Lash, and Roland Robertson. London: Sage.

García, David. 1999. "Music, Race, and Cuban *Conjuntos* in Havana, 1940s and 1950s: An Historical Perspective on the Típico Conjunto Movement and Salsa Aesthetics." Paper presented at the 44th Annual Meeting of the Society for Ethnomusicology, Bloomington, Ind.

García Canclini, Nestor. 1989. *Culturas híbridas: estrategías para entrar y salir de la modernidad*. Mexico City: Grijalbo.

Gerard, Charley. 1989. *Salsa! The Rhythm of Latin Music*. Crown Point, Ind.: White Cliffs.

Gilroy, Paul. 1993. *The Black Atlantic: Modernity and Double Consciousness*. Cambridge, Mass.: Harvard University Press.

Glasser, Ruth. 1995. *My Music Is My Flag: Puerto Rican Musicians and Their New York Communities, 1917–1940*. Berkeley and Los Angeles: University of California Press.

Gómez, Alvaro, et al. 1986. *La historia de Cali, 1536–1986*. Cali: Ediciones Andinas.

González Henríquez, Adolfo. 1989. "La influencia de la música cubana en el Caribe colombiano." *Huellas* 25: 34–42.

Gramsci, Antonio. 1971. *Selections from the Prison Notebooks*. Edited and translated by Quintin Hoare and G. N. Smith. New York: International.

Gregory, Derek. 1994. *Geographical Imaginations*. Cambridge, Mass.: Blackwell.

Guilbault, Jocelyne. 1993. *Zouk: World Music in the West Indies*. Chicago: University of Chicago Press.

Guzmán Campos, Germán, Orlando Fals Borda, and Eduardo Umaña Luna. 1962–64. *La Violencia en Colombia*. 2d ed. 2 vols. Bogotá: Tercer Mundo.

Gutiérrez, Myriam. 1995. "Mujeres y vinculación laboral en Colombia." In *Las mujeres en la historia de Colombia*, ed. Magdala Velásquez Toro. Vol. 2. Bogotá: Editorial Norma.

Habermas, Jürgen. 1987. *The Philosophical Discourse of Modernity*. Cambridge, Mass.: MIT Press.

Hall, Edward T. 1977. *Beyond Culture*. New York: Anchor.

Hall, Stuart. 1981. "Notes on Deconstructing 'the Popular.'" In *People's History and Socialist Theory*, ed. R. Samuel. London: Routledge.

———. 1986. "Gramsci's Relevance for the Study of Race and Ethnicity." *Journal of Communication Inquiry* 10 (2): 5–27.

Hall, Stuart, and Paddy Whannel. 1964. "The Young Audience." In *On Record: Rock, Pop, and the Written Word*, ed. Simon Frith and Andrew Goodwin. New York: Pantheon.

Handy, D. Antoinette. 1983. *The International Sweethearts of Rhythm*. Metuchen, N.J.: Scarecrow Press.

Hannerz, Ulf. 1990. "Cosmopolitans and Locals in World Culture." In *Global Culture: Nationalism, Globalization, and Modernity*, ed. Mike Featherstone. London: Sage.

Harvey, David. 2000. *Spaces of Hope*. Berkeley and Los Angeles: University of California Press.

Held, David. 2000. "Regulating Globalization?" In *The Global Transformations*

Reader: An Introduction to the Globalization Debate, ed. David Held and Anthony McGrew. Cambridge: Polity Press.

Hernández Vidal, Fernando. 1992. "Bailadores." *Revista gaceta* 13: 35–39.

Ignatiev, Noel, and John Garvey, eds. 1996. *Race Traitor.* New York: Routledge.

Isaacs, Jorge. 1867. *María.* Medellín: Editorial Bedout [1968].

Jameson, Fredric. 1991. *Postmodernism, or, the Cultural Logic of Late Capitalism.* Durham, N.C.: Duke University Press.

Jaramillo, Luis Felipe, ed. 1992. *Música tropical y salsa en Colombia.* Medellín: Ediciones Fuentes.

Karp, Ivan, and Stephen Levine. 1991. *Exhibiting Cultures: The Poetics and Politics of Museum Display.* Washington, D.C.: Smithsonian Institution Press.

Keil, Charles. 1966. "Motion and Feeling through Music." *Journal of Aesthetics and Art Criticism* 24 (3): 337–50. Reprinted in Charles Keil and Stephen Feld, *Music Grooves.* Chicago: University of Chicago Press, 1994.

——. 1984. "Music Mediated and Live in Japan," *Ethnomusicology* 28 (1): 91–96. Revised and reprinted in Charles Keil and Stephen Feld, *Music Grooves.* Chicago: University of Chicago Press, 1994.

Keil, Charles, and Steven Feld. 1994. *Music Grooves.* Chicago: University of Chicago Press.

Kenney, William Howland. 1999. *Recorded Music in American Popular Life: The Phonograph and Popular Memory, 1890–1945.* New York: Oxford University Press.

Koskoff, Ellen, ed. 1987. *Women and Music in Cross-Cultural Perspective.* Urbana: University of Illinois Press.

Kutzinski, Vera. 1993. *Sugar's Secrets: Race and the Erotics of Cuban Nationalism.* Charlottesville: University of Virginia Press.

Limón, José E. 1988. "*Carne, Carnales,* and the Carnivalesque": Bakhtinian *Batos,* Disorder, and Narrative Discourses." *American Ethnologist* 16 (3): 471–86.

——. 1994. *Dancing with the Devil: Society and Cultural Poetics in Mexican-American South Texas.* Madison: University of Wisconsin Press.

Lipsitz, George. 1990. *Time Passages: Collective Memory and American Popular Culture.* Minneapolis: University of Minnesota Press.

——. 1994. *Dangerous Crossroads: Popular Music, Postmodernism, and the Politics of Place.* London: Verso.

Livingston, Tamara. 1999. "Music Revivals: Towards a General Theory." *Ethnomusicology* 43 (1): 66–85.

López, Oscar Luis. 1981. *La radio en Cuba.* La Habana: Editorial Letras Cubanas.

Loza, Steven. 1999. *Tito Puente and the Making of Latin Music.* Urbana: University of Illinois Press.

MacGuigan, Jim. 1992. *Cultural Populism.* New York: Routledge.

Manning, Frank. 1983. "Cosmos and Chaos: Celebration in the Modern World." In *The Celebration of Society: Perspectives on Contemporary Cultural Performance,* ed. Frank Manning. Bowling Green, Ky.: Bowling Green University Popular Press.

Manuel, Peter. 1985. "The Anticipated Bass in Cuban Popular Music." *Latin American Music Review* 6 (2): 249–61.

——. 1991. "Salsa and the Music Industry: Corporate Control or Grassroots Expression?" In *Essays on Cuban Music: North American and Cuban Perspectives,* ed. Peter Manuel. Lanham, Md.: University Press of America.

―――. 1993. *Cassette Culture: Popular Music and Technology in North India.* Chicago: University of Chicago Press.

―――. 1994. "Puerto Rican Music and Cultural Identity: Creative Appropriation of Cuban Sources from *Danza* to *Salsa.*" *Ethnomusicology* 38 (2): 249–80.

―――. 1995. *Caribbean Currents: Caribbean Music from Rumba to Reggae.* Philadelphia: Temple University Press.

Martínez Fernández, Luis. 1994. *Torn between Empires: Economy, Society, and Patterns of Political Thought in the Hispanic Caribbean, 1840–1878.* Athens: University of Georgia Press.

Mauleón, Rebeca. 1993. *Salsa Guidebook for Piano and Ensemble.* Petaluma, Calif.: Sher Music.

―――. 1999. *101 Montunos.* Petaluma, Calif.: Sher Music.

Mauss, Marcel. 1973. "Techniques of the Body." *Economy and Society* 2 (1): 70–85.

McClary, Susan. 1991. *Feminine Endings: Music, Gender, and Sexuality.* Minneapolis: University of Minnesota Press.

Middleton, Richard. 1990. *Studying Popular Music.* Milton Keynes: Open University Press.

Mignolo, Walter. 1998. "Globalization, Civilization Processes, and the Relocation of Languages and Cultures." In *The Cultures of Globalization,* ed Fredric Jameson and Masao Miyoshi. Durham, N.C.: Duke University Press.

Milioto, Jennifer. 2000. "Trance Dance: The Tokyo Rave Scene." Paper presented at the 45th Annual Meeting of the Society for Ethnomusicology, Toronto, Canada.

Minority Rights Group. 1995. *No Longer Invisible: Afro-Lain Americans Today.* London: Minority Rights Publications.

Mitsui, Toru, and Shuhei Hosokawa. 1998. *Karaoke around the World: Global Technology, Local Singing.* New York: Routledge.

Moore, Robin. 1997. *Nationalizing Blackness: Afrocubanismo and Artistic Revolution in Havana, 1920–1940.* Pittsburgh: University of Pittsburgh Press.

Mörner, Magnus. 1967. *Race Mixture in the History of Latin America.* New York: Little, Brown.

Múnera G., Luis Fernando. 1992. *La radio y la televisión en Colombia: 63 Años de historia.* Bogotá: Apra Ediciones.

Myers, Margaret. 1993. *Blowing Her Own Trumpet: European Ladies' Orchestras and Other Women Musicians, 1870–1950, in Sweden.* Göteborg: Göteborg University.

Negus, Keith. 1999. *Music Genres and Corporate Cultures.* London: Routledge.

NACLA Report on the Americas—Colombia: Old War, New Guns. 2000. Vol. 34 (2), September–October.

O'Brien, Lucy. 1995. *She Bop: The Definitive History of Women in Rock, Pop, and Soul.* London: Penguin.

Ochoa, Ana María. 2001. *Actas del III congreso latinoamericano IASPM.* Bogotá: Ministerio de Cultura.

Pacini Hernández, Deborah. 1993. "The *Picó* Phenomenon in Cartagena, Colombia." *América negra* 6: 69–115.

——. 1995. *Bachata: A Social History of a Dominican Popular Music.* Philadelphia: Temple University Press.

Padilla, Felix. 1989. "Salsa Music as a Cultural Expression of Latino Consciousness and Unity." *Journal of Behavioral Sciences* 2 (1): 28–45.

——. 1990. "Salsa: Puerto Rican and Latino Music." *Journal of Popular Culture* 24 (1): 87–104.

Pagano, César. 1993. *Ismael Rivera: el sonero mayor.* Bogotá: Ediciones Antropos.

Pearce, Jenny. 1990. *Colombia: Inside the Labyrinth.* London: Latin American Bureau.

Pérez Firmat, Gustavo. 1994. *Life on the Hyphen: The Cuban-American Way.* Austin: University of Texas Press.

Placksin, Sally. 1982. *Jazzwomen: 1900 to the Present.* London: Pluto Press.

Posada-Carbó, Eduardo. 1996. *The Colombian Caribbean: A Regional History, 1750–1870.* Oxford: Oxford University Press.

Portes de Roux, Heliana. 1986a. "Las Adoraciones Nortecaucanas del Niño Dios, un estudio etnomusicológico." Ph.D. diss., Universidad del Valle.

——. 1986b. Liner notes for *Música religiosa de negros nortecaucanos* (noncommercial LP recorded and produced by Portes, issued by Sonolux Records).

Quintero Rivera, Angel. 1998. *¡Salsa, sabor, y control! Sociología de la música "tropical."* Mexico City: Siglo Ventiuno Editores.

Ramírez Bedoya, Hector. 1996. *Historia de la Sonora Matancera y sus estrellas.* Medellín: Impresos Begón.

Ramón y Rivera, Manuel. 1977. *La música folklórica de Venezuela.* Caracas: Monte Avila Editores.

Recuerdos de mi barrio: historia de los barrios de Cali. 1986. [Archival collection of nearly two hundred personal memoirs, written on the occasion of the 450th anniversary of Cali's founding.]

Reynolds, Simon. 1999. *Generation Ecstasy: Into the World of Techno and Rave Culture.* New York: Routledge.

Roach, Joseph. 1996. *Cities of the Dead: Circum-Atlantic Performance.* New York: Columbia University Press.

Roberts, John Storm. 1979. *The Latin Tinge: The Impact of Latin American Music on the United States.* New York: Tivoli.

Robertson, Roland. 1995. "Glocalization: Time-Space and Homogeneity-Heterogeneity." In *Global Modernities,* ed. Mike Featherstone, Scott Lash, and Roland Robertson. London: Sage.

Rondón, Cesar Miguel. 1980. *El libro de la salsa: crónica de la música del Caribe urbano.* Caracas: Editorial Arte.

Rose, Tricia. 1994. *Black Noise: Rap Music and Black Culture in Contemporary America.* Hanover, N.H.: Wesleyan University Press.

Rowe, William, and Vivian Schelling. 1991. *Memory and Modernity: Popular Culture in Latin America.* London: Verso.

Santana, Sergio. 1992. *¿Qué es la salsa? Buscando la melodía.* Medellín: Ediciones Salsa y Cultura.

Santos Febres, Mayra. 1997. "Salsa as Translocation." In *Everynight Life: Culture and Dance in Latin/o America,* ed. Celeste Fraser Delgado and José Esteban Muñoz. Durham, N.C.: Duke University Press.

Savigliano, Marta.1995. *Tango and the Political Economy of Passion.* Boulder, Colo.: Westview Press.

Schaeffer, R. Murray. 1977. *The Tuning of the World.* New York: Knopf.

Seeger, Charles. 1977. *Studies in Musicology, 1935–1975.* Berkeley and Los Angeles: University of California Press.

Silcott, Mireille. 1999. *Rave America: New School Dancescapes.* Toronto: ECW Press.

Singer, Jefferson A., and Peter Salovey. 1993. *The Remembered Self: Emotion and Memory in Personality.* New York: Free Press.

Singer, Roberta. 1982. "'My Music Is Who I Am and What I Do': Latin Popular Music and Identity in New York City." Ph.D. diss., Indiana University.

———. 1983. "Tradition and Innovation in Contemporary Latin Popular Music in New York City." *Latin American Music Review* 4 (2): 183–202.

Sinisterra de Carvajal, Amparo. 1986. "Rasgos de una identidad." In *Cali: 450 Años,* ed. Alvaro Burgos Palacios. Cali: Grupo Amigos 80.

Spitzer, Leo. 1999. "Back through the Future: Nostalgic Memory and Critical Memory in a Refuge from Nazism." In *Acts of Memory: Cultural Recall in the Present,* ed. Mieke Bal, Jonathan Crewe, and Leo Spitzer. Hanover, N.H.: Dartmouth University Press.

Spottswood, Richard. 1990. *Ethnic Music on Records: A Discography of Ethnic Recordings Produced in the United States, 1893–1942.* 7 vols. Urbana: University of Illinois Press.

Stallybrass, Peter, and Allon White. 1986. *The Poetics and Politics of Transgression.* Ithaca, N.Y.: Cornell University Press.

Stewart, Gary. 2000. *Rumba on the River: A History of the Popular Music of the Two Congos.* London: Verso.

Straw, Will. 1991. "Systems of Articulation, Logics of Change: Communities and Scenes in Popular Music." *Cultural Studies* 5 (3): 368–88.

Sugerman, Jane. 1997. *Engendering Song: Singing and Subjectivity at Prespa Albanian Weddings.* Chicago: University of Chicago Press.

Taussig, Michael. 1980. *The Devil and Commodity Fetishism in South America.* Chapel Hill: University of North Carolina Press.

Taylor, Timothy D. 1997. *Global Pop: World Music, World Markets.* New York: Routledge.

Torres, Rodrigo, ed. 1998. *Música popular en América Latina: actas del II congreso Latinoaméricano IASPM.* Santiago de Chile: Fondart.

Turino, Thomas. 1993. *Moving Away from Silence: Music of the Peruvian Altiplano and the Experience of Urban Migration.* Chicago: University of Chicago Press.

———. 2000. *Nationalists, Cosmopolitans, and Popular Music in Zimbabwe.* Chicago: University of Chicago Press.

Ulloa, Alejandro. 1986. *San Carlos, te acordás hermano: historia del Barrio San Carlos.* Cali: Editorial Feriva.

———. 1992. *La salsa en Cali.* Cali: Ediciones Universidad del Valle.

Valverde, Umberto. 1972. *Bomba camará.* Bogotá: Editorial La Oveja Negra.

———. 1981. *Celia Cruz: reina rumba.* Bogotá: Editorial La Oveja Negra.

———. 1997. *Memoria de la Sonora Matancera.* Cali: Caimán.

Valverde, Umberto, and Raphael Quintero. 1995. *Abran paso: historia de las orquestas femeninas de Cali.* Cali: Ediciones Universidad del Valle.

Vanegas Muñoz, Gildardo. 1998. *Cali tras el rostro oculto de las violencias.* Cali: Instituto Cisalva, Universidad del Valle.

Velásquez Toro, Magdala, ed. 1995. *Las mujeres en la historia de Colombia.* 3 vols. Bogotá: Editorial Norma..

Wade, Peter. 1993. *Blackness and Race Mixture: The Dynamics of Racial Identity in Colombia.* Baltimore: John Hopkins University Press.

———. 1998. "Music, Blackness, and Identity: Three Moments in Colombian History." *Popular Music* 17 (1): 1–20.

———. 2000. *Music, Race, and Nation: Música Tropical in Colombia.* Chicago: University of Chicago Press.

Wallach, Jeremy. 1997. "Beyond Performance: Music Recordings and the Materiality of Sound." Paper presented at the 42d Annual Meeting of the Society for Ethnomusicology, Pittsburgh.

Wallerstein, Immanuel. 1974. *The Modern World System.* 3 vols. New York: Academic Press.

Washburne, Christopher. 1998. "*Con Filin:* The Expression and Swing of Salsa." *Latin American Music Review* 19 (2): 160–85.

———. 1999. "Salsa in New York: A Musical Ethnography." Ph.D. diss.. Columbia University.

Waterman, Christopher A. 1990. "Our Tradition Is a Very Modern Tradition": Popular Music and the Construction of Pan-Yoruba Identity." *Ethnomusicology* 34 (3): 367–79.

Waxer, Lise. 1991. "Latin Popular Musicians in Toronto: Issues of Ethnicity and Cross-Cultural Integration." Master's thesis, York University.

———. 1994. "Of Mambo Kings and Songs of Love: Dance Music in Havana and New York from the 1930s to the 1950s." *Latin American Music Review* 15 (2): 139–76.

———. 1997. "Salsa, Champeta, and Rap: Black Sounds and Black Identities in Afro-Colombia." Paper presented at the 42d Annual Meeting of the Society for Ethnomusicology, Pittsburgh.

———. 1998. "*Cali pachanguero:* A Social History of Salsa in a Colombian City." Ph.D. diss., University of Illinois at Urbana-Champaign.

———. 2000. "*En Conga, Bongó, y Campana:* The Rise of Colombian Salsa." *Latin American Music Review* 21 (2): 118–68.

———. 2001a. "Las Caleñas Son Como Las Flores: All-Women Salsa Bands in Cali, Colombia" *Ethnomusicology* 45 (2): 228–59.

———. 2001b. "*Golpe de currulao:* Black Music and Resistance on Colombia's Pacific Coast." Paper presented at the 36th World Conference of the International Council for Traditional Music, Rio de Janeiro, Brazil.

———. 2001c. "Record Grooves and Salsa Dance Moves: The *Viejoteca* Phenomenon in Cali, Colombia." *Popular Music* 20 (1): 61–81.

———. 2002. "*Llegó la Salsa:* The Rise of Salsa in Venezuela and Colombia." In *Situating Salsa: Global Markets and Local Meanings in Latin Popular Music,* ed. Lise Waxer. New York: Routledge.

Waxer, Lise, ed. 2002. *Situating Salsa: Global Markets and Local Meanings in Latin Popular Music.* New York: Routledge.

Whitten, Norman E. 1974. *Black Frontiersmen: Afro-Hispanic culture of Ecuador and Colombia.* Prospect Heights, Ill.: Waveland Press.

Whitten, Norman E., ed. 1981. *Cultural Transformations and Ethnicity in Modern Ecuador.* Urbana: University of Illinois Press.

Whitten, Norman E., and Arlene Torres, eds. 1998. *Blackness in Latin America and the Caribbean.* 2 vols. Bloomington: Indiana University Press.

Wright, Winthrop R. 1990. *Café con Leche: Race, Class, and National Image in Venezuela.* Austin: University of Texas Press.

Yanagisako, Sylvia Junko, and Jane Fishburne Collier. 1987. "Towards a Unified Analysis of Gender and Kinship." In *Gender and Kinship: Essays toward a Unified Analysis,* ed. Jane Fishburne Collier and Sylvia Junko Yanagisako. Stanford: Stanford University Press.

Selected Discography

La Charanguita de Luis Carlos. 1992. *Podemos y debemos.* Fonocaribe 16.0010.
Diaz, "Piper Pimienta." 1970. *Atiza, ataja.* Discosfuentes.
———. 1998. *Homenaje a Piper "Pimienta" Díaz* (re-release). DiscosFuentes 10701.
Grupo Niche. 1981. *Querer es poder.* Codiscos 22200347.
———. 1984. *No hay quinto malo.* Codiscos 22200462.
———. 1985. *Triunfo.* Codiscos 22200490.
———. 1987. *Historia musical.* Codiscos 69821167.
———. 1988. *Tapando el hueco.* Codiscos 29821260.
———. 1989. *Sutil y contundente.* Codiscos 22200654.
———. 1995. *Etnia.* Sony 81719.
———. 1997. *Prueba de fuego.* Sony 82375.
Guayacán. 1985. *Llegó la hora de la verdad.* Sonolux 01031301418.
———. 1989. *La más bella.* FM Discos LP (11) 2435.
———. 1992. *Sentimental de punta a punta.* FM Discos.
———. 1993. *Con el corazón abierto.* FM Discos. 0110002547.
———. 1995. *Como en un baile.* Fonovisa 44013.
Julian y su Combo. 1969. *Charangas con pachangas.* Sello Vergara 206.
Mangual, José, Jr. *Tribute to Chano Pozo.* True Ventures 1001, 1989.
La Misma Gente. 1986. *La Misma Gente en su salsa.* Sonolux.
———. 1987. *La Misma Gente.* Sonolux 07(0131)00009.
———. 1989. *La Misma Gente en la jugada.* Sonolux 07(0131)00030.
———. 1990. *Perfume de Paris.* Combo 2074.
———. 1991. *LMG: Ah! Tú sabes.* Sonolux 01(0131)01762.
Richie Ray and Bobby Cruz. 1970. *Agúzate.* Alegre 8800.
———. 1971. *El bestial sonido.* Vaya 1.
———. 1974. *1975.* Vaya 33.
Son de Azucar. 1992. *Con sabor a caña.* Sony 54 473103.
———. *Con amor y dulzura.* Sony Tropical 81497.
Sonora Ponceña. *On the Right Track.* Inca 1084.
Vives, Carlos. 1993. *Clásicos de la provincia.* Sonolux 0103101937.

Index

Numbers in *italics* indicate a table or photographic illustration.

Keil, Charles, 13, 130, 235, 285 n. 24
King, Telembí, 98
Koskoff, Ellen, 205–6

La Barola, 126, *126*
La Charanguita, 207–10, *209*, 258
La Conspiración, 146
La Dicupé, 146
La Gran Banda Caleña, 161, 194, 206,
    287 n. 1
La Identidad, 194
La Ley, 161, 163, 287 n. 1
La Misma Gente, 129, 158, 180–87, *181*,
    191, 212, 216, 220, 239–42
Landa, Larry, 162–64, 192, 239, 243
La Protesta, 157
"Las Caleñas son como las flores," 26,
    159–60
Las Chicas del Can, 200
LaSerie, Rolando, 99
Latin jazz, 111, 136, 188–89,
La Violencia, 34, 60, 67, 88, 151, 224,
    276 n. 7, 280 n. 28
Lavoe, Hector, 54, 134, 158, 162, 241
Leavitt, Ralphy, y La Selecta, 146, 148
Lebrón Brothers, 114, 146, 161, 192
Linares, Alfredito, 158, 192
Lipsitz, George, 10
Listening to Salsa (Frances Aparicio),
    25–26
Lorza, Dorancé, 218, 221
Los Aterciopelados, 39, 210
Los Bronco, 193, 197
Los Cali Boys, 52, 65
Los Chavales de Madrid, 225, 231
Los Graduados, 61, 62, 226–29
Los Melódicos, 225
Los Nemus del Pacífico, 256, 290 n. 1
Los Supremos, 157
Los Teenagers, 226
Los Tremenditos, 157
Los Van Van, 134, 210
Lozano, Alexis, 157, 165, 175, *177*, 180,
    218, 259, 285 n. 34
Lucca, Papo, 174, 184

M-19, 116, 283 n. 6
Machado, Cesar, 58, 72–73, 77–79
Machito, 54, 225, 273 n. 1
Magenta Latin Jazz, 191, 199, 210
mambo, 5, 46, 58, 69, 77, 79, 81–82, 87,
    91, 94

Mangual, José, Jr., 237–39
Manizales, 39
Manyoma, Henry, 96
Manyoma, Hermes, 155, 160–61
Manyoma, Wilson, 96, 155, 158, 160–61
Marini, Leo, 52
Markitos, 259
Marley, Bob, 136
Marrenco, Gilberto, 123
Martínez, Alberto. *See* Resortes
Medellín, 35, 39, 55, 58, 60, 111, 156, 186,
    194, 197, 226, 282 n. 55, 283 n. 14
Mejía, Carlos Esteban, 196
Mejía, Santiago, 160–61, 164. *See also*
    Octava Dimensión
melómanos (music aficionados), 29, 111,
    120, 126, 129–36, 138, 145, 244–47,
    250
memory, 3–4
    and movement, 70
    and recordings, 6–13, 112, 150–52
    effigy, 11–12, 246. *See also* recordings,
        as commodity fetishes
    in discourse about salsa, 139–44
    popular memory, 9–13, 69–70,
        108–10, 150–52, 252
    surrogation, 11–12, 28, 151, 246
Merced, Gunda, 220
merengue, 40, 41, 148, 200, 202, 219
"Mi Buenaventura," 65, 165
"Micaela," 94, 98
Miltinho, xi
Miranda, Ismael, 162, 163, 206, 208, 230
modernity, 3, 24, 150–52, 257
Molina Díaz, Edulfamit. *See* Pimienta,
    Piper
Monge, Cesar, 173–74, 192, 218
Monkees, The, 227
Monroe, Marilyn, 136
Morales, Noro, 5
Moré, Benny, 48, 54, 58, 136, 273 n. 4,
    278 n. 27
Movimiento Guatequero (Guateque
    Movement), 146–50
musicals, movie
    Hollywood, 49, 80–82
    influence on Caleño dancers, 57,
        80–82
    Mexican, 57, 80–81, 94
música andina (Andean music)
    Colombian, 37, 62–63, 80, 87
    Peruvian–Ecuadorian, 38